Donated by
The Public Interest Institute
to The Heartland Institute
2016

Y0-AWH-415

THE HEARTLAND INSTITUTE
www.heartland.org

ECONOMIC FREEDOM

OF THE WORLD

1997 Annual Report

PROPERTY OF
PUBLIC INTEREST
INSTITUTE

NOV 17 1997

PROPERTY OF
PUBLIC INTEREST
INSTITUTE

ECONOMIC FREEDOM

OF THE WORLD

1997 Annual Report

James D. Gwartney,
Florida State University

Robert A. Lawson,
Capital University

Copyright © 1997 by The Fraser Institute. All rights reserved. No part of this book may be reproduced in any manner whatsoever without written permission except in the case of brief quotations embodied in critcal articles and reviews.

The authors of this book have worked independently and opinions expressed by them are, therefore, their own, and do not necessarily reflect the opinions of the members or the trustees of The Fraser Institute.

Printed and bound in Great Britain by
Redwood Books, Trowbridge, Wiltshire

Canadian Cataloguing in Publication Data

Gwartney, James D.

Economic Freedom of the World: 1997 Annual Report

ISBN 0-88975-175-7

1. Free enterprise.   2. Economic history—1990-   3. Economic development.
I. Lawson, Robert, 1967-   II. Fraser Institute (Vancouver, B.C.)   III. Title.
HB95.G93 1997   330.9'049   C97-910304-5

TABLE OF CONTENTS

ACKNOWLEDGMENTS

Given the nature and history of this project, we owe an enormous debt to many people. Without the assistance and guidance of both Mike Walker and Milton Friedman, this project would never have gotten off of the ground. Mike organized the Fraser Institute/Liberty Fund conference series that provided the foundation for our measure of economic freedom. He also edited several of the conference volumes and provided both input and encouragement throughout. Milton Friedman's criticisms and suggested modifications shaped the research design of the project.

We also are indebted to several of the participants and contributors to the Fraser/Liberty Fund Series. Alvin Rabushka's paper presented in July 1988 at the second symposium sharpened the concept of economic freedom and provided direction with regard to how it might be measured. A theoretical paper by Ronald Jones and Alan Stockman presented at the fourth symposium held in Sea Ranch, California moved the process forward and influenced our thought process. Walter Block edited one of the volumes summarizing conference proceedings and he was also a co-author with us of *Economic Freedom of the World: 1975-1995*. At various stages of this project, the comments and suggestions of Stephen Easton, Zane Spindler, Douglass North, and Gary Becker have been particularly helpful.

The institutes of the Economic Freedom Network provided invaluable support for this report. They helped verify information, supplied us with missing data, and assisted with the text of the county profile chapter. As we move to the next phase—the design and development of a still more comprehensive index—we look forward to a continuing working relationship with them.

Finally, we would like to thank the following individuals—some of whom are not associated with co-publishing institutes—who provided us with particularly valuable assistance in the preparation of this report: Erwin Bendl (Austria), Ralph Massey (Bahamas), Jose Carvalho (Brazil), Krassen Stanchev (Bulgaria), Eugenio Guzman (Chile), Priscilla P. K. Lau and Sung Yun-wing (China), Dora Ampuero (Ecuador), Juan Bendfeldt (Guatemala), Alan Siu and Richard Wong (Hong Kong), Laszlo Urban (Hungary), Haukur Benediktsson (Iceland), Paul MacDonnell (Ireland), Robert Loewenberg and Alvin Rabushka (Israel), Giuseppe Russo (Italy), Samson Kimenyi (Kenya), Roberto Salinas Leon (Mexico), Krystyna Bobinska (Poland), Daniel Stancu (Romania), Andrei Illarionov (Russia), Linda Low (Singapore), Jan Oravec (Slovakia), Eustace Davie (South Africa), Sung-No Choi (South Korea), Mattias Bengtsson (Sweden), Guneri Akalin and Gozde Ergozen (Turkey), Colin Robinson (United Kingdom), and Hugo Faria (Venezuela). Of course, we bear the full responsibility for any errors in the text, including that of the country profiles.

We would also like to express our appreciation to the Policy Sciences Center of Florida State University for providing the research and computer support that made the project feasible. Barbara Morgan and Frank Keuchel assisted with data gathering and calculations. Amy Gwartney, Jennifer Platania and Ed Bierhanzl checked and re-checked the figures in the manuscript through its many phases. Kristin McCahon, Director of Publications at the Fraser Institute, did an excellent job of coordinating the design and publication of the book. Finally, no one will be happier to see this project completed than Valerie N. Colvin, Senior Art/Production Specialist. She maintained her patience during numerous occasions when data were updated, a variable or a country added, or an exhibit redesigned. It was a challenging task and she handled it well.

James Gwartney
Robert Lawson

ABOUT THE AUTHORS

James Gwartney is a Professor of Economics and Policy Sciences at Florida State University. He has a doctoral degree in economics from the University of Washington. Along with Richard Stroup of Montana State University, he is the author of *Economics: Private and Public Choice* (Harcourt Brace). This text, now in its 8th edition, has been used by more than 1 million students during the last two decades. A member of the Mont Pelerin Society, during 1993-94, Professor Gwartney taught at the Central European University in Prague, Czech Republic. He has published in the leading journals of professional economics, including the *American Economic Review, Journal of Political Economy, Industrial and Labor Relations Review, Cato Journal,* and *Southern Economic Journal.*

Robert Lawson is an Assistant Professor of Economics at Capital University in Columbus, Ohio; he taught previously at Shawnee State University. He earned his B.S. from the Honors Tutorial College at Ohio University in 1988 and his M.S. and Ph.D. from Florida State University in 1991 and 1992, respectively. He has published articles in several journals, including *Public Choice,* the *Journal of Labor Research,* and the *Journal of Public Finance and Public Choice.* Professor Lawson has written extensively on public policy issues such as welfare reform, Medicaid, tax policy, and prevailing wage regulations. He has recently been named the Director of Fiscal Policy Studies for the Dayton-based Buckeye Institute for Public Policy Solutions.

ABOUT THE PARTICIPATING INSTITUTES,
Co-publishers of *Economic Freedom of the World:
1997 Annual Report*

ACER, Albania   The Albanian Center for Economic Research is
a public policy institute that focuses on research and advocacy activities. In addition to providing policymakers and academics with
applied economic research, it works to build public understanding
of economic development issues.
(E-mail: ZEFI@QSKE.TIRANA.AL)

**African Research Center for Public Policy and Market Pro-
cess, Kenya**   The African Research Center for Public Policy and
Market Process, Kenya, is the first research center founded in Africa by the African Educational Foundation for Public Policy and
Market Process, an independent educational oragnization registered in the United States. The primary mission of the Center and
the Foundation is to promote ideas about free markets and voluntary associations in Africa. The Center seeks to conduct research
on all aspects of free markets, voluntary association, individual
liberty, and dissiminate the results to as wide an audience as possible. The Center also organizes seminars and conferences to examine issues related to liberty and enterprise in Africa.

**Association pour la Liberté Economique et le Progrès Social
(ALEPS), France**   The ALEPS objective is to promote the idea
of free market, generating social progress. It connects French liberal intellectuals with the world scientific community. Thanks to
its permanent contacts with various prestigious foreign institutes,
in 1990 ALEPS published "Manifeste de l'Europe pour les Eu-
ropéens," signed by 600 faculties from 28 countries.

The economic collapse of central planning and the disappearance
of totalitarian regimes in Eastern Europe has not solved all social
problems. The post-socialist society remains to be set up. This re-
quirement in Eastern Europe is also needed in Western countries,
such as France, where 40 years of the welfare state have led to
mass unemployment, fiscal oppression, a social security explo-
sion, an increase in poverty and inequality, and a loss of moral virtues and spiritual values. ALEPS provides the political and
intellectual push for this necessary revival.

Association for Liberal Thinking, Turkey The objectives of the Association for Liberal Thinking as a non-profit, non-governmental organization are to introduce the liberal democratic tradition to the Turkish public; to engage in activities that promte understanding and acceptance of ideas like liberty, justice, peace, human rights, equality, tolerance; to help the development of academic writing on liberal themes that will improve the ability of the Turkish people to assess contemporary domestic and international changes; and to attempt to find effective solutions to Turkey's problems within liberal thought. The Association for Liberal Thinking is not involved in day-to-day politics and has no direct links to any political party or movement. Instead, as an independent intellectual group, it aims to set and influence broader political agendas so as to contribute to the liberalization of Turkey in economics and politics.

Cato Institute, United States of America Founded in 1977, the Cato Institute is a public policy research foundation dedicated to broadening the parameters of policy debate to allow consideration of more options that are consistent with the traditional American principles of limited government, individual liberty, free markets, and peace. To that end, the Institute strives to achieve greater involvement of the intelligent, concerned lay public in questions of policy and the proper role of government through an extensive program of publications and seminars.

The Center for the Dissemination of Economic Knowledge (CEDICE), Venezuela CEDICE is a non-partisan, non-profit, private association dedicated to the dissemination, research, and promotion of philosophical, economic, political, and social thinking that focuses on individual initiative and activities conducive to better understanding of the free market system and free and responsible societies. CEDICE carries out a variety of activities and programs to meet its objectives, including operating a library and bookstore, researching and writing the *Venezuela Today* series and other studies, conducting economic training for journalists, and offering special events and community programs.

Center for Policy Research, Sri Lanka The Center for Policy Research (CPR) is a non-partisan advocacy and policy research institute dedicated to fostering demoncracy and promoting free enterprise. As part of its philosophy, CPR actively takes positions on critical policy reform issues and aggressively lobbies key decision-makers in the country.

The Center for Research and Communication, Philippines

The Center for Research and Communication (CRC), which started operations in 1967, conducts research and publishes works on domestic and international economic and political issues, focusing on the Asia-Pacific region. It provides fora for discussion and debate among academicians, businessmen, civil officials, and representatives of other sectors that help shape public opinion and chart the course of policies. CRC, which is the main research arm of the University of Asia and the Pacific in Metro Manila, Philippines, also currently serves as the Secretariat of the Asia Pacific Economic Cooperation (APEC) Business Advisory Council.

Center for the New Europe, Belgium

The Center for the New Europe is a European research institute based in Brussels. It aims to promote the advancement of a market-oriented economy, personal liberty, and creativity and responsibility in an ordered society. CNE is founded on the belief that European integration can work only in a society led by a spirit of democratic capitalism. The Center focuses on developing policy alternatives encouraging economic growth and deregulation; seeking new market-based solutions for social and environmental concerns; and promoting individual freedom, choice and responsibility.

Centro de Investigaciones Académicas (CIVILIZAR), Colombia

The Centro de Investigaciones Académicas is a private, non-profit economic and social research organization. Established in 1996, the Centro is affiliated with the Sergio Arboleda University of Bogata. It is dedicated to the scientific study of economic and social topics. It defends individual liberty and recongnizes it as a basic principle to guide programs of research and eduction. The Centro supports research and publishes studies on economic, social, and legal issues in order to promote Colombian economic growth and human development.

Centro de Investigaciones Económicas Nacionales, Guatemala

The Center for Research on the National Economy (CIEN) was established in Guatemala in 1982. It is a private, non-partisan, not for profit public policy institute, funded by the sale of its books and periodical publications, income from conferences and seminars, and the support it receives from its members and the public. The Center's program is devoted to the technical study of economic and social problems that need to be resolved to promote the stable development of the nation. Its members, staff, research associates, and its supporters share the principles of a social order of free and responsible individuals interacting through a market economy functioning within the rule of law.

Centro de Investigaciones Sobre la Libre Empresa, A.C., Mexico The Centro de Investigaciones Sobre la Libre Empresa (CISLE) is a nonprofit educational and public policy organization founded in 1984. Its aim is to defend and promote the ideals of free trade and free enterprise in all areas of society. CISLE maintains that the fundamental source of well being and the wealth of nations is a sound institutional order which guarantees competition, private ownership, and open markets. CISLE's activities are financed by a select group of generous donors.

Centrum im. Adama Smitha, Poland The Adam Smith Research Center is the first private, non-profit, non-partisan institution in Poland and in Eastern Europe whose statutory goals are strongly associated with the ideals of the free market economy. The Adam Smith Research Center realizes its mission of supporting the development of a free market economy and a democratic society through research, education, and publishing. Its current programs include reform of the pension system, the influence of corruption on economic processes in Poland, effectiveness of the institutional order and the constitutional system, changes to the tax system, and the decentralization of power and the function of local government.
(E-mail: adam.smith@pol.pl; Internet: www.adam-smith.pol.pl)

Centro de Investigacion y Estudios Legales (CITEL), Peru CITEL was organized in 1989. Its principal field is the economic analysis of law. To that end, it conducts research on different legal institutions, publishes books, and organizes seminars and colloquia.

Edmund Burke Institute, Ireland The Edmund Burke Institute is a non-profit and non-political organization that believes that Ireland's political, academic, and cultural leaders have failed to draw the natural conclusions from the collapse of state socialism and the growth of free-market ideas across the industrialized and developing world. It believes that these ideas are directly relevant to Ireland, and that hostility towards free markets and individual freedom needs to be challenged by an institution which promotes debate and discussion about the role of the state in our lives.
(Internet: http://www.his.com/~chyden/ebi/)

The Estonian Institute for Open Society Research The Estonian Institute for Open Society Research was established in 1993 as an independent non-profit public policy research institute. EIOSR's research and public communication programs focus on the key issues of Estonian social and political development: building a free market economy and open civil society; enhancing social stability and integration of minority groups; promoting Estonia's integration into European and world structures. EIOSR's first effort was the Estonian translation of Milton Friedman's book *Capitalism and Freedom* in early 1994. Current EIOSR projects include promoting the idea of philanthropy to local businesses and elaborating future scenarios concerning the integration of the Russian minority into Estonian society.

The F.A. Hayek Foundation, Slovak Republic   The F.A. Hayek Foundation is an independent, non-profit organization that brings together social scientists, business people, and policy-makers to exchange their ideas on economic, social, political, and other issues. It provides practical reform proposals for the transition of economics, health, education, social welfare, retirement and legislative systems. The F.A. Hayek Foundation established a tradition that was virtually absent in Slovakia until 1989—the tradition of liberal thinking and its further cultivation in order to demonstrate the advantages of market economy solutions as better alternatives to collectivist policies. The Foundation promotes the following liberal ideals: limited government; and a free market economy and an open society based on the concept of individual choice and personal responsibilities.

The Fraser Institute, Canada   The Fraser Institute is an independent Canadian economic and social research and educational organization. It has as its objective the redirection of public attention to the role of competitive markets in providing for the well-being of Canadians. Where markets work, the Institute's interest lies in trying to discover prospects for improvement. Where markets do not work, its interest lies in finding the reasons. Where competitive markets have been replaced by government control, the interest of the Institute lies in documenting objectively the nature of the improvement or deterioration resulting from government intervention. The work of the Institute is assisted by an Editorial Advisory Board of internationally renowned economists. The Fraser Institute is a national, federally chartered, non-profit organization financed by the sale of its publications and the tax-deductible contributions of its members (Email: info@fraserinstitute.ca).

The Free Enterprise Commission, Panama   The Free Enterprise Commission is a working group within the Panamanian Association of Executives (APEDE). APEDE is a non-partisan, non-profit association dedicated to the improvement of enterpreneurship, management, and the development of the individual in a free society. As such, APEDE invests a good part of its efforts in education and individual liberties.

The Free Market Foundation of Southern Africa   The Free Market Foundation of Southern Africa was established in 1975 to promote economic freedom. The FMF sponsors and conducts research, publications, conferences, lectures, training programs and lobbying efforts in support of the free market. Its funding comes from membership subscriptions, project sponsorships, and income from sales and fees.

Fundación Economía y Desarrollo, Inc., Dominican Republic
The Fundación Economía y Desarrollo, Inc. (FEyD) is a private non-profit organization dedicated to fostering the principles, mechanisms, and advantages of the economy of competitive markets and private enterprise as well as the economic policies which back this strategy of economic development. To meet its objectives, FEyD has several regular publications in the most important newpapers in the country. It also produces a weekly television program called "Triálogo," a one-hour program that is broadcast three times week, and elaborates numerous studies related to the performance of the Dominican economy and its sectors.

Fundacion Libertad, Democracia y Desarrollo, Bolivia   The Fundacion Libertad, Democracia y Desarrollo (FULIDED), is a non-profit organization created by a group of citizens interested in promoting democracy and freedom. The Foundation has the purpose of investigating, analyzing, and spreading issues of national priority, keeping in mind that economic, political, and social topics are of great importance to strenghten the free market and private initiative, within the ideal of an open, pluralist, and honest society. Through seminars, debates and publications, FULIDED seeks to create a current of opinion according to Bolivia's reality and in the framework of a global economy.

Gruppo Giovani Imprenditori and Centro Luigi Einaudi, Italy
The Turin Group of Young Entrepreneurs was founded in 1959. It is composed of 300 entrepreneurs and managers under the age of 40. A member of the Confederation of Italian Industry, it has always been on the forefront of the liberalization of the Italian economy.

Established in 1963, the Centro di ricerca e documentazione "Luigi Einaudi" is one of Italy's most influential independent think tanks. Its aim is to further free market policies and personal freedom, promote leaner government, and enhance political pluralism.

The Hong Kong Center for Economic Research   The Hong Kong Center for Economic Research is an independent free market policy research institute. The Center was established in 1987 as a charitable trust. Until 1992 it was affiliated with the Chinese University of Hong Kong, and since then it has been affiliated with the University of Hong Kong. The Center recognizes that the economic success of Hong Kong is the result of policies that protected private property rights, free enterprise, and limited the role of the government. It also recognizes that the political foundation of these policies is always vulnerable, and that the case for preserving these policies and expanding its scope has to be continuously articulated. The main activities of the Center are to influence public opinion and policy outcomes through a program of research and education.

יהוי האמרים לדע שב ולשב רעי ישעיה הב

Institute for Advanced Strategic and Political Studies, Jerusalem   The mission of the Institute for Advanced Strategic and Political Studies is the development of policies in economics, strategic studies, and politics, directed toward the understanding and realization of limited government in domestic affairs and the balance of power in strategic planning. The Institute's Division for Economic Policy Research (DEPR) produces *Policy Studies* in both English and Hebrew, while the Division for Research in Strategy and Politics produces one series of documents in strategic studies, and another series in politics.

The Institute for Economic Freedom

The Institute for Economic Freedom, Bahamas   The Institute for Economic Freedom is an independent non-political, non-profit Bahamian institute that promotes economic growth, employment and entrepreneurial activity. It believes that this can best be achieved with a free market economy and a decent society . . . one that embraces the rule of law, the right of private property, the free exchange of property and services, and the individual virtues of self-control, commitment, and good will.

Institut für Wirtschaft und Politik

Institute for Economy and Politics (IWIP), Austria   IWIP is an affiliate institute of the Federation of Austrian Industry. Its duty is to give objective information to the general public about the economy, politics, and culture. It supports a social free market economy and protection of the environment. IWIP organizes meetings, workshops, symposiums, and lectures, and is editor of *Conturen*, a quarterly magazine aimed at the liberal and critical reader who is interested in diverse discussions about the economy, politics, and culture.

Institute For Market Economics, Bulgaria   Established in 1993, IME is the first independent economic think tank in Bulgaria. It is a private, registered, non-profit corporation with a mission to elaborate and advocate market approaches to the problems

xvi

Bulgaria is facing in its transition to a market economy, thus supporting market reforms. IME's objectives are to provide the following: independent assessment and analysis of the government's economic policies; a focal point for an exchange of views on market economics and relevant policy issues; and an internationally supported Bulgarian think thank which is widely respected for its expertise. (E-mail: IME@SF.CIT.BG or G=Krassen; S=Stanchev; O=IME; A=BG 400; C=BG)

The Institute of Economic Affairs, England   The IEA's mission is to improve public understanding of the foundations of a free and harmonious society by expounding and analyzing the role of markets in solving economic and social problems, and bringing the results of that work to the attention of those who influence thinking. The IEA achieves its mission by a high quality publishing program; conferences, seminars and lectures on a range of subjects; outreach to school and college students; brokering media introductions and appearances; and other related activities. Incorporated in 1955 by the late Sir Anthony Fisher, the IEA is an educational charity, limited by guarantee. It is independent of any political party or group, and is financed by sales of publications, conference fees, and voluntary donations.

The Institute of Economic Affairs, Ghana   The Institute of Economic Affairs (IEA) Ghana is an independent, non-governmental institution dedicated to the establishment and strengthening of a market economy and a democratic, free and open society. The IEA was founded in October 1989. It considers improvements in the legal, social and political institutions as necessary conditions for sustained economic growth and human development. The IEA supports research, and promotes and publishes studies on important economic socio-political and legal issues in order to enhance understanding of public policy.

Institute of Economic Analysis, Russia   The Institute of Economic Analysis is a macroeconomic research institute designed to: analyze the current economic situation and policies; provide expert analysis of acts, programs, and current economic policy; consult Russian government bodies, enterprises, and organizations; prepare and publish scientific, research and methodological economic literature; and conduct seminars, conferences, and symposia on economic topics. The Institute is an independent, non-governmental, non-political, non-profit research center that works closely with leading Russian and international research centers. Its research focuses on macroeconomic, budget, and social policy.

Institute of Economic Studies, Iceland The Institute of Economic Studies was founded in 1989. It operates within the Department of Economics in the Faculty of Economics and Business Administration at the University of Iceland. From the outset, the Institute has been active in carrying out applied research projects commissioned by a great variety of private and public clients ranging from small Icelandic interest groups, to the Nordic Investment Bank, to the governments of Iceland, Denmark, and the Faroe Islands. More recently, funded by research grants, the Institute has put greater emphasis on large scale applied research projects with substantial analytical content and economic research.

Institute of Public Affairs, Australia Established in 1943, the IPA is Australia's oldest and largest private-sector "think tank." Its aim is to advance the interests of the Australian people. Those interests include prosperity and full employment, the rule of law, democratic freedoms, security from crime and invasion, high standards in education and family life. To identify and promote the best means of securing these values, the IPA undertakes research, organizes seminars, and publishes widely.

Instituto Ecuatoriano de Economia Politica, Ecuador The Instituto Ecuatoriano de Economia Politica (IEEP) is a private, independent, non-profit institution. Its mission is to defend and promote the classical liberal ideals of individual liberty, free markets, limited government, property rights, and the rule of law. The IEEP achieves its mission through publications, seminars, and workshops that debate socio-economic and political issues. The IEEP's funding comes from voluntary donations, membership subscriptions and income from sales of its publications. (E-mail: dampuero@ecua.net.ec)

Instituto Liberal do Rio de Janiero, Brazil Instituto Liberal is a non-profit insitution supported by donations and the sponsorship of private individuals and corporations. Its by-laws provide for a Board of Trustees as its supreme body, and forbid any political or sectarian affiliations. Its principal objective is to *persuade Brazilian society of the advantages of a liberal order*. To attain this goal, the institute publishes books, organizes seminars, and elaborates policy papers on subjects related to public policy.

The Korea Center for Free Enterprise The Korea Center for Free Enterprise is devoted to ensuring national progress under a free market economy and through the healthy growth of business. The Center has focused its efforts on formulating practical policy recommendations on the basis of its research on the short and long-term trends of the Korean economy and the nation's enterprises.

Libertad y Desarrollo, Chile Libertad y Desarrollo is a private "think tank" committed to free market ideas and devoted to research, study, and anlysis of public policy issues inspired by political and economic freedom. Libertad y Desarrollo is wholly independent of any religious, political, financial, or governmental groups.

Liberales Institut, Germany The Liberales Institut (Liberty Institute) is the think tank of the Friedrich-Naumann-Foundation. The Bonn-based institute devotes itself to spreading classical liberal/free market ideas through the publication of classical liberal literature, the analysis of current political trends and the promotion of research. By organizing conferences and workshops, the institute tries to stimulate an intellectual exchange among liberals around the world.

Liberales Institut, Switzerland The Liberal Institute provides a platform where the basic values and concepts of a free society can be discussed and questioned. The Institute offers a meeting place for practitioners and theoreticians from different walks of life and professions. The aim is to examine issues in an open atmosphere, to inquire and experiment. The Liberal Institute is not associated with any political party. It wants to foster the development and dissemination of liberal ideas in the classical European sense, ideas about personal freedom, limited government, and free markets.

Liberální institut, Czech Republic The Liberal Institute is an independent, non-profit organization for the development and application of liberal ideas and programs based on the principles of classical liberalism. The Liberal Institute's activities are based on the recognition of the following: each individual has inalienable rights, and the individual's life is valuable; the principle of voluntary action applies in all human activity; the institutions of private property, contract, and the rule of law are essential in the protection of human rights; self-regulating markets, free trade, and a clearly defined government sphere are crucial factors for the development of any society. The Liberal Institute is financed by funds realized from its various activities and by donations from individuals and private corporations.

The Lithuanian Institute of International Political and Economic Relations The Lithuanian Institute of International Political and Economic Relations is a non-profit organization that propagates the rightist ideas both in politics and economics. It collaborates with municipalities, leading democratic parties, and public movements in the areas of self-government development and municipal economy managment, and in the preparation of small-business support and job creation programs based on Western standards. The institute also provides economic consulting to private Lithuanian enterprises and foreign investors; it prepares business plans, conducts market research, and assists in establishing and maintaining business contacts. It also conducts reasearch on the Lithuanian market and Lithuania's import-export activities.

Making Our Economy Right (MOER), Bangladesh MOER champions free market concepts and the freedom of the individual. Bangladesh is a fully statist society where politicians promise jobs and economic development, but are unaware that the function of the state and the government is merely to protect individual freedom, liberty, life, property, and the national geographic boundary. MOER solicits international support and cooperation in its efforts to fully liberalize Bangladesh's economy and thereby democratize Bangladesh society.

The New Zealand Business Roundtable The New Zealand Business Roundtable is an organization of chief executives of about 60 of New Zealand's largest business organizations. Its aim is to contribute to the development of sound public policies that reflect overall New Zealand interests. It has been a prominent supporter of the country's economic liberalization reforms.

SZAZADVEG: Budapest School of Politics, Hungary The Budapest School of Politics is a non-partisan, non-profit organization financed by the contributions of its supporters and the sale of its publications and services. It is independent from any state organization and any political party. The BSP was founded in 1990 to provide professional training for those entering politics as members of Parliament or members of local governments, as well as for those in NGOs, trade unions, etc. Over the years, the BSP has entered the field of pubic policy research and advising. The BSP carries out its research and publication activities in areas such as public administration, labour markets, taxation, agro-economic restructuring, welfare reform, and education.

Timbro, Sweden Timbro is a Swedish free enterprise think tank. Its goal is to mold public opinion favourably toward free enterprise, a free economy, and a free society. Timbro publishes books, papers, reports and the magazine *Smedjan*. It also arranges seminars and builds human networks. Founded in 1978, Timbro is owned by the Swedish Free Enterprise Foundation, which has as its principals a large number of Swedish companies and organizations.

The Ukrainian Center for Independent Political Research

The Ukrainian Center for Independent Political Research was established in early 1991 as a non-profit, non-partisan, and non-governmental research institution. Its purpose is to enhance the awareness of the Ukrainian people of democracy and to further the analytic research of Ukrainian domestic and international politics and security. The UCIPR is politically independent; it does not accept any funding from either the state or any political party. The UCIPR publishes books and research papers on Ukraine's domestic and foreign policy issues, economy in transition, security doctrine, relations with neighbouring states, the Crimean dilemma, inter-ethnic relations, and media freedom, etc. The Center has hosted a number of national and international conferences and workshops on the above issues.

CHAPTER 1

Introduction and Overview of the Index

This report is a continuation of an ongoing process designed to develop a comprehensive and accurate measure of economic freedom across countries. The roots of the project go back more than a decade. Motivated by a stimulating discussion concerning the differences between political freedom and economic freedom, Michael Walker, the Executive Director of the Fraser Institute, organized a series of symposia focusing on the measurement of economic freedom. Milton and Rose D. Friedman agreed to co-host the series with Michael Walker, and the Liberty Fund of Indianapolis, Indiana provided the necessary financial support. The series attracted some of the world's most talented economists and challenged them to help develop a reliable measure of economic freedom. The participants included Nobel Prize winners, Milton Friedman, Gary Becker, and Douglass North; development economist Peter Bauer; Sweden's Assar Lindbeck; and Sir Alan Walters. Alvin Rabushka of Stanford, Ronald Jones and Alan Stockman of the University of Rochester, Governor Ramon Diaz of the Central Bank of Uruguay, Steven Easton of Simon Fraser University, and Gerald Scully of the University of Texas at Dallas were among those presenting symposium papers that moved the process forward.[1]

As the result of our participation in several of the conferences, we co-authored (with Walter Block), *Economic Freedom of the World: 1975-1995*.[2] Published in early 1996 by a consortium of 11 institutes from around the world, this book presented an index designed to identify the consistency of a nation's institutions and policies with economic freedom. Following the publication of this book, Milton Friedman and Michael Walker hosted a conference in San Francisco that led to the formalization of the Economic Freedom Network, which had grown to a group of 47 institutes interested in the development of a quality index of economic freedom. The institutes that consituted the Network agreed to assist us in the updating of the index (with minor modifications) through 1995 and publish the results in our 1997 Annual Report. The Economic Freedom Network also plans to broaden the index and seeks to provide more detailed information on factors that influence economic freedom in subsequent annual reports.

THE CONCEPT OF ECONOMIC FREEDOM

Development of a sound measure of economic freedom requires one to clearly define the concept. The central elements of economic freedom are personal choice, freedom of exchange, and protection of private property. When economic freedom is present, individuals are free to make economic choices such as how to use their time and other resources, what goods to consume, and what business and investment alternatives to pursue. Of course, they will often find it advantageous to cooperate with others and markets will coordinate their choices and bring them into harmony.

The use of government—whether directed by a monarch or a democratic process —to decide what (and how) goods will be produced and who will consume them violates personal economic freedom.

The use of government—whether directed by a monarch or a democratic process—to decide what (and how) goods will be produced and who will consume them violates personal economic freedom. Other things constant, freer economies will rely more on markets and less on government to answer these basic economic questions. This is not to say that government has no role. Protection of property acquired without the use of force, fraud, or theft from physical invasions by others is also an integral element of economic freedom.[3] This protection generally involves a legal structure and other institutional arrangements (for example, monetary arrangements consistent with price stability) that enhance the operation of markets. Governments promote economic freedom when they provide these structures.

In an economically free society, the fundamental function of government is the protection of private property and the provision a stable infrastructure for a voluntary exchange system. When a government fails to protect private property, takes property itself without full compensation, or establishes restrictions (and follows policies) that limit voluntary exchange, it violates the economic freedom of its citizens.[4]

CONSTRUCTION OF THE INDEX

A sound measure of economic freedom will identify the extent to which individuals are free to choose for themselves and engage in voluntary transactions with others, and have their rightly acquired property protected from invasions by others. Like a compass, these criteria guided us as we developed the Index of Economic Freedom. When constructing the index, we tried to design components that were both (a) good indicators of economic freedom across a large number of countries and (b) based on objective information that could be updated regularly. To the extent possible, we sought to minimize the significance of "judgment calls" and subjective evaluations.

As Exhibit 1-1 illustrates, the index contains 17 components that are divided into four major areas: (1) money and inflation, (2) government operations and economic structure, (3) takings, and (4) international trade. These components provide an indication of the degree to which a nation's institutional arrangements and policies are consistent with sound money, reliance on markets, avoidance of plunder and discriminatory taxes, and freedom of international exchange. While they may not be as comprehensive as we would like, nonetheless, they comprise central elements of economic freedom.

Since a detailed description of the components and procedures used to construct the summary rating was provided in *Economic Freedom of the World: 1975-1995*, we will present only a brief overview here. The four components in the Money and Inflation area reflect the availability of *sound money*. Expansionary monetary policy (rapid growth in the money supply) "waters down" the outstanding monetary units and thereby erodes their value. This is wrongful seizure of property. Monetary institutions and policies that lead to substantial variations in the general level of prices create uncertainty and undermine the efficacy of money. Therefore, countries with high rates of monetary growth (relative to potential real GDP) and large variations in the inflation rate are given low ratings. The highest ratings go to the countries with less money growth and more stable (and therefore more predictable) rates of inflation.

The four components in the Money and Inflation area reflect the availability of sound money.

Exhibit 1-1: Components of the Index of Economic Freedom

I. MONEY AND INFLATION (Protection of money as a store of value and medium of exchange)

(4.7) A. Average Annual Growth Rate of the Money Supply During the Last Five Years Minus the Potential Growth Rate of Real GDP

(5.3) B. Standard Deviation of the Annual Inflation Rate During the Last Five Years

(3.0) C. Freedom of Citizens to Own a Foreign Currency Bank Account Domestically

(2.7) D. Freedom of Citizens to Maintain a Bank Account Abroad

II. GOVERNMENT OPERATIONS AND REGULATIONS (Freedom to decide what is produced and consumed)

(6.2) A. General Government Consumption Expenditures As a Percent of Total Consumption (Private + Government)

(6.5) B. The Role and Presence of Government-Operated Enterprises

(7.1) C. Price Controls—the Extent that Businesses are Free to Set Their Own Prices (This variable is included in only the 1990 and 1995 Indexes.)

(6.7) D. Freedom of Private Businesses and Cooperatives to Compete in Markets (This variable is included only in the 1995 Index.)

(4.7) E. Equality of Citizens Under The Law and Access of Citizens to a Nondiscriminatory Judiciary (This variable is included only in the 1995 Index.)

(3.4) F. Freedom from Government Regulations and Policies that Cause Negative Real Interest Rates

III. TAKINGS AND DISCRIMINATORY TAXATION (Freedom to keep what you earn)

(10.9) A. Transfers and Subsidies as a Percent of GDP

(12.7) B. Top Marginal Tax Rate (and income threshold at which it applies)

(3.6) C. The Use of Conscripts to Obtain Military Personnel

IV. RESTRAINTS ON INTERNATIONAL EXCHANGE (Freedom of exchange with foreigners)

(6.7) A. Taxes on International Trade as a Percent of Exports Plus Imports

(6.2) B. Difference Between the Official Exchange Rate and the Black Market Rate

(3.7) C. Actual Size of Trade Sector Compared to the Expected Size

(5.9) D. Restrictions on the Freedom of Citizens to Engage in Capital Transactions with Foreigners

(Note: The numbers in parentheses indicate the weight attached to each component when the summary rating is derived.)

Money offered by other monetary authorities is a substitute for money issued by the government of a given country. When residents are allowed to maintain bank accounts in foreign currencies, it is easier for them to avoid the uncertainties accompanying an unstable domestic monetary regime. Thus, countries that permit their citizens freely to maintain bank accounts in other currencies—both domestically and abroad—are given higher ratings.

The six components in the Government Operations and Regulations area are designed to identify the extent that resources are directed by *personal choice and markets* rather than political planning and coercion. Consumption is the ultimate objective of all economic activity. As more and more of total consumption expenditures are undertaken by the government, consumers exert less and less impact on what is produced and consumed. Government consumption reduces the ability of consumers to decide for themselves. Thus, countries are given a lower rating as government consumption increases as a share of the total (government + private consumption).

No private business firm, regardless of its size, can force potential consumers to purchase its products. Private firms must provide consumers with sufficient value to induce them to pay a price that will cover unit production costs. Government is fundamentally different. Governments can levy taxes and thereby force citizens to pay for goods regardless of the value received. Similarly, government-operated firms can be used to produce goods even when consumers are unwilling to cover the production cost. Thus, countries are given a lower rating as state-operated enterprises comprise a larger portion of the economy.

Governments can levy taxes and thereby force citizens to pay for goods regardless of the value received.

Since price controls both constrain exchange and take property from owners, they are inconsistent with economic freedom. Freedom to compete in the marketplace; a legal structure that clearly defines property rights, enforces contracts, and provides a mutually agreeable mechanism for the settlement of contractual and property-right disputes; and a competitive and stable credit market are also important foundations for the operation of a market economy. Countries providing this infrastructure are given higher ratings.

Taken together the six components in the Government Operations area indicate a great deal about the structure of the economy. Who determines what will be consumed: the private choices of individual consumers or the central planning of the government? Are goods produced by private firms directed by markets or by state-operated enterprises? Do the prices and interest rates reflect market forces or are they controlled by the government? Is entry into markets open? Does the legal structure protect private property, enforce contracts, and are individuals treated equally under the law? High ratings in each of these areas reflects reliance on personal choice and market allocation; low ratings indicates political choices and centralized planning are used to allocate goods and resources.

The three components in the Takings and Discriminatory Taxation area indicate the degree to which governments honor and protect property rights rather than engage in plunder activities. When governments tax income from one person in order to transfer it to another, they are denying individuals the fruits of their labor. The larger transfers and subsidies as a share of GDP the lower the rating for this component. High marginal tax rates discriminate against productive citizens and seize wealth from taxpayers without providing them any equivalent increase in service. Thus, countries are given lower ratings as they impose higher marginal tax rates that take affect at lower income thresholds. Conscription denies draftees the property right to their labor services. It is also an in- kind tax that is not registered through the budgetary process. As a result, the budget figures for both taxes and expenditures are understated in the case of those countries that utilize conscription to obtain military personal. A lower rating for this component is necessary to adjust for this bias.

Finally, the four components in the International Exchange area indicate the consistency of policies with free trade.

Finally, the four components in the International Exchange area indicate the consistency of policies with *free trade*. Taxes on international trade limit the freedom of domestic residents to trade with foreigners. Thus, the larger the taxes on trade relative to the volume of international trade, the lower the rating. Exchange rate controls often make it difficult for individuals and businesses to obtain the foreign exchange (other currencies) required to trade with foreigners. The black market exchange rate provides an indicator of the degree to which exchange rate controls limit trade with foreigners. Thus, the larger the black market premium, the lower the rating for this component. Many nations restrain trade through the use of quotas, monopoly grants, "buy local" schemes, and various other types of discriminatory regulations. Such restrictions reduce the volume of international trade. A model was developed and used to derive an "expected size of the trade sector" for each country which was then compared with the actual size of the country's trade sector. A smaller trade sector relative to the expected size (given the geographic size, population, and location of the country) suggests that the country imposes move non-tariff trade barriers.

6

Thus, countries with the smallest trade sectors (relative to the expected size) are given the lowest ratings for this component.[5]

Many countries require foreigners to get permission from the government in order to make an investment or remit their earnings. The freedom of their citizens to make investments abroad may also be limited. The greater the restrictions on the mobility of capital, the lower the rating for this component.

Data for each of these 17 components were compiled for 115 countries and statistical procedures used to determine the component rating for each.[6] Since we want the ratings to be easily comparable across countries and time periods, a zero to ten rating scale was used for each component in the index. Countries were given higher component ratings when their institutions and policies were more consistent with economic freedom. A ten represented the highest possible rating and a zero the lowest.[7]

How should each component in the index be weighted? In the previous edition, we presented three summary indices based on alternative component weights. In most cases, the variation in the weights exerted only a small impact on the summary rating. Given their similarity, presentation of the three alternative ratings was unnecessarily confusing. Therefore, in this edition we will present only one summary index, the one with weights based on a survey of the participants in the Fraser-Liberty Fund Symposia Series. (Note: This index was referred to as the Is1 summary index in *Economic Freedom of the World: 1975-1995*.) We constructed a survey instrument which described the 17 components in our index and asked the participants of these conferences to provide us with their views concerning the weights that should be attached to each of the components. Since all of these people attended at least one of the conferences, we were reasonably sure of their familiarity with the concept of economic freedom and the factors that influence it. The average weight suggested by the respondents was then used to weight the components and derive the summary index for each of the years. These weights are indicated by the number in parenthesis at the left of each component in Exhibit 1-1.

WHAT'S NEW IN THIS REPORT?

While the methodology employed in the construction of this index is identical to that of *Economic Freedom of the World*, the 1997 Report contains several additions and adjustments that improve both index and the accompanying material. We would like to highlight five of these factors.

1. More Countries Are Rated. In this report, we were able to obtain the required data for 115 countries compared to 102 for the prior index. The following countries were added: Albania, Bahamas, Bahrain, Barbados, China, Croatia, Estonia, Latvia, Lithuania, Oman, Russia, Slovenia, and Ukraine. Given their size, additions of Russia and China are particularly important.

2. The Assistance of Economic Freedom Network Institutes. Since the last edition was published, the number of co-publishing institutes of the Economic Freedom Network has increased from 11 to 47. Even more important, we were able to work closely with these institutes, use their expertise to verify information, supply missing data, and provide useful background material. Thus, the underlying data for this edition is more complete and the accompanying text of the country profile chapter is more comprehensive than in the prior edition.

3. Final 1995 Index. When the prior index was published, data for several components were only available through 1993. Thus, the mid-1990s index was preliminary. The 1995 data are now available (although not necessarily for every country). Thus, we were able to update the information and finalize the 1995 index. This provides us with economic freedom ratings covering a 20-year time period.

4. Expansion in Country Profile Chapter. The country profile chapter of this report contains detailed information for 81 countries, 23 more than in the prior edition. We have also included more supplemental data than in the prior edition. In this regard, inclusion of a graphic on total government expenditures as a share of GDP during 1975-1995 is particularly important. Trends in the size of government expenditures as a share of GDP will help us better interpret changes in our index of economic freedom. They also provide an indication of what would happen if the components related to government expenditures (government consumption and transfers and subsidies) were weighed more heavily in the index.

5. Marginal Improvements in the Index. Even though the underlying methodology is unchanged, some minor revisions were made in the index. First, discussions with other researchers convinced us that the government consumption component should be divided by total consumption (government plus private) rather than by GDP as was done in the last edition. We believe this revision provides a more accurate measure of the proportion of consumption that is directed by government rather than markets. Second, in a few cases, information supplied by recent publications and the cooperating institutes convinced us to revise a few component ratings for years prior to 1995.[8] These changes almost always involved only a one unit change in the rating for a component. Finally, the money, GDP deflator, consumer price index, and national account data used in this edition are from the International Monetary Fund rather than the World Bank. For most countries, these two data sets are identical, but this was not always the case. When there was a disparity, the IMF data, which are available more readily (from *Monthly International Financial Statistics*), were used in this edition. Taken together, these revisions exerted only a minor impact—changes of a few tenths of a point—on summary ratings prior to 1995.

DIFFERENCES FROM OTHER INDEXES

During the last several years, two other organizations—the Heritage Foundation and the Freedom House—have published measures of economic freedom.[9] It is encouraging to see others developing an interest in this topic. At our invitation, Richard Messick the editor and coordinator of the Freedom House Index and Kim Holmes and Bryan Johnson, the lead authors of the Heritage project, met with us at a San Francisco meeting of the Economic Freedom Network. Presentations on the background and nature of these two indexes, as well as our own, were made. While there are some similarities between the three indexes, there are also major differences.

First, our index is the only one of the three that starts with a clear presentation of what economic freedom is and then uses that as the foundation for the development of a measuring rod. Given the meaning of economic freedom, what variables should be used for its measurement? What weight should be given to each? What set of components would provide a sound measure for a specific category? We wrestled with these questions and related issues for several years. They were the focal point of the Fraser Institute/Liberty Fund symposia series. Input was obtained from numerous sources, including some of the world's leading economists. We sought—and are continuing to seek—to develop objective indicators of economic freedom for all major areas. The variables in our index work together—for example, it is important to measure not only monetary and price stability, but it is also important to identify whether it is possible to shift to another currency if monetary instability is present. Since some factors that affect economic freedom are more important than others, accurate measurement requires that the more important factors be weighted more heavily. Neither Heritage nor Freedom House attempt to deal with any of the these issues. They simply average their components, which in effect weights them all equally.

Second, we developed ratings for five different years over two decades. This makes is possible to track the economic freedom of various countries over time. In contrast, both the Heritage and Freedom House Indexes cover only a few years in the mid-1990s.

Third, both the Heritage and Freedom House indexes are highly subjective. Neither presents an underlying set of data which is then used in a systematic manner in the rating process. While both list factors considered in their ratings, it is often unclear precisely how these factors influence their category ratings. Furthermore, evaluation of countries on the basis of the factors listed requires the authors to make numerous subjective judgments.[10] This results in ambiguities regarding why a rating for a country is high, middle or low in a specific area. In contrast, we did not inject our subjective views into the component ratings. Most of the components of our index are objective variables (for example, standard deviation of the inflation rate or government consumption as a share of the total) designed to measure important elements of economic freedom. In cases where subjective judgments would influence the relative standing of countries, we use survey data or evaluations by others rather than injecting our own views.[11] We also present the underlying data set used to rate countries and carefully explain how it was used to derive the component ratings. We wanted our index to be transparent in order to enhance its credibility.

Perhaps none of this would matter very much if it did not lead to some unusual outcomes. Consider the case of Bahrain, a country which the 1997 Heritage Index ranks as the third freest economy in the world. Bahrain is characterized by monetary stability and liberal financial markets. It deserves high marks in these areas. But it is also an economy dominated by government. In fact, 45% of all consumption expenditures are determined by the government rather than by the personal choices of its citizens. This is the largest share—more than Sweden, more than Russia, more than any former Soviet bloc country—among the 115 countries in our study. Can a country that uses central planning and political power to allocate almost half of total consumption be classified as one of the freest in the world? In essence, Bahrain is a big government welfare state financed with oil revenues. Since the Heritage Index gives very little weight to size of government, Bahrain earns an exceptionally high rating.[12]

The Freedom House Index also has serious internal deficiencies that lead to unusual outcomes. One of the six categories in the Freedom House Index is "Freedom to Earn a Living." This is certainly a basic element of economic freedom. Inspection, however, reveals that this rating is primarily based on the freedom to organize labor unions. High taxation does not affect the rating received in the "freedom to earn a living" category. Apparently persons living in countries imposing 50%, 60% or even 100% tax rates would be "free to earn a living" as long as they could organize labor unions. The Freedom House Index ignores the size of government altogether. The use of government to channel 50% or 60% of GDP does not reduce a country's economic freedom rating in the Freedom House survey. For example, in 1995 the total government expenditures of Sweden and Denmark summed to 68% and 61% of GDP, respectively. Thus, taxation, government expenditures, and political decision-making control more than three-fifths of the Swedish and Danish economies. Nonetheless, these two economies (tied with four others) are rated as the freest in the world by the Freedom House.

Our index differs from that of Heritage and Freedom House because our initial objectives were fundamentally different. The participants in the Fraser Institute/Liberty Fund series were mostly academic economists. The focus on the series was the development of an accurate measure of economic freedom—one that would be useful to scholars investigating the relationship between economic freedom and other factors such as political freedom, economic growth, income inequality, and economic mobility. If an index of this type was going to have credibility, it needed to be based on a sound theoretical foundation, the components needed to be objective, and the relationship between the components and the summary index needed to be transparent. Again and again, conference participants reminded us of these points. The structure of our own index was revised and broadened several times as we sought to improve its accuracy.

The focus of the Fraser/Liberty Fund series was the development of an accurate measure of economic freedom— one that would be useful to scholars investigating the relationship between economic freedom and other factors.

The development of the Freedom House and Heritage indexes was based on a different set of objectives, including public relations and political considerations. At the October meeting in San Francisco, Freedom House made it clear that they sought to improve the image of economic freedom in circles—particularly among proponents of labor unions and activist government—where it has traditionally had a bad name. Perhaps, this explains why the Freedom House index does not consider high taxes and large government expenditures as an infringement on economic freedom. The Heritage Foundaton has made it clear that their index was designed to influence Congress, particularly the allocation of the foreign aid budget of the United States. As a result, the Heritage spolesmen explained, it was necessary to keep the index simple.[13] Given these factors, the absence of a clear statement in either the Freedom House or Heritage publications concerning the meaning of economic freedom and the relationship between the concept and their index is not surprising.

The bottom line is this: the indexes of both the Heritage Foundation and Freedom House are ambiguous and poorly structured, and they often generate inaccurate and misleading outcomes. Measures of this type will leave many with the impression that economic freedom is nebulous and highly subjective, and therefore largely a meaningless concept. We reject this view; we believe that economic freedom is highly meaningful and that it is possible to measure it objectively. This is why we feel compelled to point out that our index is fundamentally different from those of Freedom House and the Heritage Foundation. We have one objective—to develop the best possible measure of economic freedom. In that regard, we realize that much more needs to be done.

IMPROVING THE MEASURE OF ECONOMIC FREEDOM

We recognize that economic freedom is multi-dimensional and that our index fails to incorporate all of its many facets. As we look to the future, we want to develop a more comprehensive index. In particular, we need to more fully incorporate regulatory restrictions into our index. Many countries use discriminatory tax concessions and other indirect subsidies to modify market outcomes. Regulations such as mandated benefits (for example, mandated severance pay, health care and other fringe benefits) and laws that impose a centralized wage setting structure exert a major impact on the labor market and the degree of economic freedom present in that market. In addition, there are sectors of the economy, such as housing and education, where arrangements more (and less) consistent with economic freedom can be identified. This is an ongoing project. Plans are already underway to develop a more comprehensive index that will provide a better measure of economic freedom in the future.

Additional analysis is also needed concerning the proper weighing of components. The importance of various components may differ across countries. For example, trade restraints may exert a lesser impact on economic freedom when applied to a large country than would be the case for a small nation. Correspondingly, restrictions in one area (for example, stable money) may be less important if economic freedom in other areas (such as freedom to use other currencies) provides individuals with an alternative means of reaching their goals. Highly imprudent policies—hyper-inflationary monetary policies or insecure property rights, for example—may effectively undermine both the market process and significance of economic freedom in other areas. All of these issues are related to how one combines the components into an index that provides the most meaningful measure of economic freedom. Additional research is needed in each of these areas.

The current index supplies valuable information on the consistency of institutional arrangements with sound money, reliance on markets, protection of private property, and free trade. While these are not the sum total of economic freedom, they are important elements. Thus, the current index provides researchers with a tool to undertake more serious analysis of the relationship between economic freedom and other important variables such as economic growth, democratic political institutions, civil liberties, and economic inequality. As this research moves forward, it will enhance our knowledge of economic freedom and provide information that will assist with the development of a still more accurate measure in the future.

Developing a better measure of economic freedom and enhancing our knowledge of how it impacts our lives is an exciting research agenda. This will be the focal point of the 1998 Annual Report of the Economic Freedom Network. We encourage other researchers to join with us as we pursue these topics.

ENDNOTES

1. For those interested in the papers and a summary of the discussion from the Fraser Institute/Liberty Fund series, see Michael A. Walker, ed., *Freedom, Democracy, and Economic Welfare*, (Vancouver: Fraser Institute, 1988); Walter Block, ed., *Economic Freedom: Toward a Theory of Measurement*, (Vancouver: Fraser Institute, 1991); and Stephen T. Easton and Michael A. Walker, eds., *Rating Global Economic Freedom*, (Vancouver: Fraser Institute, 1992). For additional details on the historical background of the index, see Michael Walker "Introduction: Historical Development of the Economic Freedom Index" in *Economic Freedom of the World: 1975-1995* (Vancouver: Fraser Institute, 1996).

2. James Gwartney, Robert Lawson, and Walter Block, *Economic Freedom of the World: 1975-1995* (co-published by the Fraser Institute in Canada, Cato Institute in the United States, the Institute of Economic Affairs in England, and institutes in eight other countries, 1996).

3. Of course, the most basic property right of individuals is the property right to their person. This protection of individuals from "invasions" by others is the central element of criminal law.

4. See Ronald W. Jones and Alan C. Stockman. "On the Concept of Economic Freedom" in Stephen T. Easton and Michael A. Walker (ed.), *Rating Global Economic Freedom*, (Vancouver: The Fraser Institute, 1992) and Alvin Rabushka, "Preliminary Definition of Economic Freedom," in *Economic Freedom: Toward a Theory of Measurement*, ed. Walter Block, (Vancouver: The Fraser Institute, 1991), pp. 87-108. for additional background on the meaning of economic freedom and an analysis of how it might be measured.

5. Factors such as geographic size, population, and location will also influence the size of the trade sector. In order to adjust for these factors, we regressed country size (in terms of area), population, whether it was land-locked, and the proportion of the population living within 150 miles of a potential trading partner on the size of the trade sector for the countries in our study. The characteristics of each country were then plugged into the equation and used to derive an expected size of the trade sector. A large trade sector would imply that few regulatory constraints were imposed on trade. Thus, when the actual size of the trade sector as a share of GDP was large relative to the expected size, the country was given a high rating. See *Economic Freedom of the World: 1975- 1995* (Chapter 1, footnote 28) for additional details.

6. The data series used for the price controls component (I-C) was available for only 1990 and 1995. The data for the freedom of entry into business (I-D) and equality under the law (I-E) components were only available for 1995. Thus, the index has only 15 components in 1990 and only 14 components for the years 1975, 1980, and 1995.

7. In the case of continuous variables like standard deviation of the inflation rate or government consumption as a percent of total consumption, the data for 1985—our base year—were arrayed from highest to lowest and divided into 11 groups of equal size. The 1/11th of the countries that achieved the outcomes most consistent with economic freedom (for example, those with the most stable level of prices) were assigned a rating of ten. The next 1/11th were assigned a nine, and so on. For example, if there were 110 countries (for which the required data were available), then the ten countries that rated best in this category in 1985 would receive a rating of ten, the next nine would receive a rating of nine, and so on. The cutoff points between groups in the 1985 data were then used to rate each country in the other years (1975, 1980, 1990 and 1995). To determine the interval cutoff points between, for example, a ten and a nine rating, we calculated the midpoint in the 1985 data between the country with the lowest ten rating and the country with the highest nine rating. This same procedure was used to determine the interval for each of other ratings classes.

The advantage of using only the base year 1985 to derive the conversion table is that this approach allows the ratings of countries to either improve or worsen in the other years. Thus, while the rating system judges countries relative to one another during the 1985 base year, if most countries improve (or regress) relative to the base year, this system allows their ratings to reflect this improvement.

8. Data provided by the World Bank Research Report, *Bureaucrats in Business: The Economics and Politics of Government Ownership* (Oxford: Oxford University Press, 1995) were called to our attention after the prior edition was published.

This report provided information on the size of government enterprises as a share of the economy over a lengthy time period. A number of the country ratings for this component were revised in light of the information derived from this source.

9. Richard E. Messick, *World Survey of Economic Freedom: 1995-1996*,(New Brunswick: Transaction Publishers, 1996) and Kim R. Holmes, Bryan T. Johnson and Melanie Kirkpatrick, *1997 Index of Economic Freedom*, (Washington, D. C.: The Heritage Foundation and The Wall Street Journal, 1997). The Heritage Foundation also published a similar index for 1995 and 1996.

10. The following is a list of actual variables used by the authors of the Heritage Index to rate different countries:

"Are there any significant non-tariff barriers?"

"Is there corruption in the customs service?"

"Does the government set prices for any products? If so, to what extent?"

"Is the legal system free from government influence?"

"Is it easy to obtain a business license?"

"Is there corruption within the bureaucracy?"

"Does the existence of regulations impose a burden on business? If so, to what extent?"

These are interesting questions but what criteria was used to decide that Country A would receive a rating of one, while Country B is given a three or a five. No underlying information was supplied or methodology explained that would provide a basis for ratings given to different countries. This is simply a beauty-contest approach where the ratings reflect the subjective views of the authors. It is not indicative of serious research.

11. There are three variables in our index—price controls, freedom to compete in markets, and equality of citizens under the law—that involve some judgment. We used the survey data from the *World Competitiveness Report* published by the World Economic Forum as the primary source for the price controls component. Freedom to compete and equality under the law are two elements of the Freedom House political and civil liberties survey. We used their ratings for these two components in order to avoid injecting our subjective views into the country ratings. In the future, we hope that we will be able to develop objective variables for each of these components.

12. Consider the following: two of the variables in the Heritage Index are (a) government consumption as a share of GDP and (b) Can foreign companies receive local financing? While both of these variables influence economic freedom, their relative importance varies widely. However, this is not reflected in the index. A country where government consumption takes 50% of GDP, but denies local financing to foreign firms gets the same rating (for the aggregate of these two components) as another country with government consumption equal to 10% of GDP and a prohibition against the local financing. We expect that the authors of the Heritage Index would agree that government taking half of the income of citizens is a more significant violation of economic freedom than denial of financing to foreign investors. Their index, however, treats the two as equals.

13. As one of the authors of the Heritage Index put it at the San Francisco conference, "Our index reflects what the Heritage Foundation is and where it is located." On the opening page of Heritage's initial report, the authors stated that their index "represents an excellent tool for deciding how best to allocate development aid." The first three chapters of that report focus on the foreign aid program. See Bryon T. Johnson and Thomas P. Sheehy, *The Index of Economic Freedom,* (Washington, D. C., Heritage Foundation, 1995)

CHAPTER 2

Ratings, Rankings, and Highlights

This chapter focuses on the presentation of the updated ratings and highlights some of the interesting changes that have taken place during the last two decades. Section 1 presents the 1995 component ratings and explains how they were used to derive the summary ratings. Section 2 focuses on the 1995 rankings. Section 3 indicates the countries that have experienced the largest changes in economic freedom during various time periods. Finally, the concluding section illustrates the basic relationship between economic freedom on the one hand and per capita GDP and growth of income on the other. Graphics are used freely in the chapter in order to help the reader quickly grasp the major points.

1995 COUNTRY RATINGS

Exhibit 2-1 presents the 1995 ratings for each of the 17 components in our index, as well as area ratings, and the summary index. The underlying data and the country ratings for each of the 17 components are presented in the tables of Appendix II. We also derived both component and summary ratings for 1975, 1980, 1985, and 1990. Appendix I contains this information—similar to that of Exhibit 2-1—for the earlier years. The roman numeral and letter labels of the tables in Appendix II match the component labels of Exhibits 1-1 and 2-1. The note following each of the tables in Appendix II indicates both the source of the data used to derive the rating for the component and precisely how the underlying data are converted to the zero to ten rating scale used for all components. Readers interested in the details of the relationship between the underlying data and the component ratings will want to review Appendix II carefully. Throughout, a component rating of "10" indicates that for this dimension of economic freedom the nation is among the freest in the world. On the other hand, a rating of zero indicates that the country is among the least free in the category measured by the component.

17

Exhibit 2-1: Component, Area, and Summary Index Ratings: 1995

Part 1: Component Ratings: 1995

INDUSTRIAL COUNTRIES	I: Money and Inflation				II: Government Operations						III: Takings			IV: International Sector			
	A	B	C	D	A	B	C	D	E	F	A	B	C	A	B	C	D
United States	10	10	10	10	5	8	9	10.0	7.5	10	3	7	10	9	10	3	10
Canada	9	10	10	10	2	6	7	7.5	7.5	10	2	4	10	9	10	10	8
Australia	7	10	10	10	4	6	7	10.0	7.5	10	3	4	10	8	10	6	8
Japan	10	10	10	10	8	8	5	7.5	7.5	10	3	2	10	8	10	0	8
New Zealand	9	10	10	10	5	8	10	10.0	10.0	10	3	7	10	9	10	3	10
Austria	8	10	10	10	2	2	8	7.5	7.5	8	1	4	0	9	10	6	8
Belgium	10	10	10	10	5	6	5	7.5	10.0	10	0	1	0	10	10	10	10
Denmark	10	10	10	10	0	4	9	10.0	10.0	10	0	1	0	10	10	2	8
Finland	8	10	10	10	1	6	9	7.5	10.0	10	1	2	0	9	10	4	8
France	10	10	10	10	2	6	8	7.5	7.5	10	0	4	0	10	10	5	5
Germany	9	10	10	10	2	6	9	7.5	7.5	10	1	3	0	10	10	5	10
Iceland	8	9	10	10	2	4	6	10.0	10.0	8	4	4	10	9	10	2	5
Ireland	9	10	10	10	3	4	8	7.5	7.5	10	0	3	10	8	10	10	8
Italy	10	9	10	10	4	2	5	7.5	7.5	10	0	1	0	10	10	5	8
Netherlands	10	9	10	10	5	6	7	7.5	10.0	10	0	2	0	10	10	8	10
Norway	9	9	10	10	1	2	7	7.5	10.0	10	1	5	0	9	10	5	8
Spain	10	10	10	10	4	4	5	7.5	5.0	10	2	2	0	10	10	4	8
Sweden	10	8	10	10	0	4	8	10.0	10.0	10	0	1	0	9	10	6	10
Switzerland	10	9	10	10	5	8	6	10.0	10.0	10	2	8	0	8	10	4	10
United Kingdom	9	9	10	10	2	6	9	10.0	7.5	10	2	5	10	10	10	5	10
CENTRAL/-SOUTH AMERICA																	
Argentina	0	0	10	10	-	8	8	10.0	2.5	10	4	9	0	6	10	0	10
Bahamas	10	8	0	0	6	6	4	5.0	5.0	10	9	10	10	1	7	2	2
Barbados	9	7	0	0	2	4	6	5.0	7.5	10	10	5	10	7	6	0	2
Belize	10	10	0	0	5	8	6	7.5	7.5	10	10	5	10	1	6	2	5
Bolivia	1	1	10	10	7	4	8	7.5	0.0	8	8	10	0	8	8	5	5
Brazil	0	0	0	0	5	4	6	7.5	0.0	0	3	8	0	7	6	1	0
Chile	2	6	10	10	9	8	10	10.0	5.0	10	5	4	0	7	7	4	5
Colombia	1	7	10	10	1	6	5	7.5	0.0	8	7	8	0	6	5	3	5
Costa Rica	5	4	10	10	3	8	6	10.0	7.5	8	5	9	10	6	10	4	8
Dominican Rep	3	5	0	0	10	6	6	5.0	0.0	8	9	9	10	1	7	2	2
Ecuador	1	2	10	10	7	4	0	7.5	2.5	6	9	9	0	7	4	3	5
El Salvador	6	9	10	10	10	8	6	5.0	2.5	10	8	8	0	7	8	1	5
Guatemala	3	2	10	10	10	8	6	5.0	0.0	8	9	8	0	6	10	1	8
Haiti	1	1	10	10	-	4	0	5.0	0.0	0	-	-	10	-	2	0	2
Honduras	3	2	10	10	9	6	4	7.5	2.5	4	7	7	0	-	8	6	5
Jamaica	0	1	10	10	6	4	4	7.5	2.5	6	7	8	10	-	5	5	8
Mexico	1	2	10	10	8	6	5	7.5	0.0	8	7	7	0	8	10	7	5
Nicaragua	0	0	0	0	8	2	2	7.5	2.5	6	5	8	10	5	5	5	5
Panama	7	10	10	10	4	4	4	7.5	2.5	10	5	9	10	9	10	3	8
Paraguay	1	5	10	10	10	6	6	7.5	2.5	8	8	10	0	8	4	9	5
Peru	0	0	10	10	10	8	6	7.5	2.5	6	7	8	0	6	10	1	8
Trinidad/Tobago	3	5	10	10	4	2	4	7.5	7.5	6	4	5	10	-	6	1	8

18

Exhibit 2-1 (con't)

Money and Inflation	Govern-ment Operations	Takings	Inter-national Sector	Summary Rating	Grade	INDUSTRIAL COUNTRIES
10.0	8.2	5.8	8.6	7.9	(B)	United States
9.7	6.4	4.0	9.2	6.9	(C)	Canada
9.1	7.2	4.4	8.2	7.0	(B)	Australia
10.0	7.4	3.5	7.2	6.7	(C)	Japan
9.7	8.7	5.8	8.6	8.0	(A)	New Zealand
9.4	5.6	2.3	8.5	6.0	(C)	Austria
10.0	6.8	0.5	10.0	6.3	(C)	Belgium
10.0	6.9	0.5	8.2	5.9	(D)	Denmark
9.4	6.9	1.3	8.2	6.1	(C)	Finland
10.0	6.6	1.9	7.9	6.1	(C)	France
9.7	6.8	1.8	9.2	6.4	(C)	Germany
9.1	6.4	4.8	7.1	6.5	(C)	Iceland
9.7	6.4	2.7	8.9	6.5	(C)	Ireland
9.7	5.6	0.5	8.7	5.5	(D)	Italy
9.7	7.3	0.9	9.7	6.5	(C)	Netherlands
9.4	5.8	2.7	8.4	6.1	(C)	Norway
10.0	5.6	1.7	8.5	5.9	(D)	Spain
9.3	6.7	0.5	9.0	5.9	(D)	Sweden
9.7	7.9	4.5	8.4	7.4	(B)	Switzerland
9.4	7.3	4.5	9.2	7.3	(B)	United Kingdom
						CENTRAL/-SOUTH AMERICA
3.6	7.8	5.8	7.2	6.4	(C)	Argentina
5.7	5.7	9.6	3.1	6.2	(C)	Bahamas
5.1	5.3	7.7	4.3	5.7	(D)	Barbados
6.4	7.1	7.7	3.6	6.3	(C)	Belize
4.3	5.9	7.9	6.7	6.4	(C)	Bolivia
0.0	4.3	4.9	3.9	3.7	(F-)	Brazil
6.3	8.8	3.9	6.0	6.4	(C)	Chile
6.3	4.6	6.5	5.0	5.5	(D)	Colombia
6.5	7.0	7.5	7.3	7.1	(B)	Costa Rica
2.6	5.9	9.1	3.1	5.6	(D)	Dominican Rep
4.6	4.4	7.8	5.0	5.5	(D)	Ecuador
8.5	6.8	6.9	5.8	6.9	(C)	El Salvador
5.2	6.3	7.3	6.8	6.5	(C)	Guatemala
4.3	2.1	10.0	1.5 *	2.9	(F-)	Haiti
5.2	5.7	6.1	6.4	5.9	(D)	Honduras
4.0	5.0	7.9	6.1	5.9	(D)	Jamaica
4.6	5.8	6.1	7.6	6.1	(C)	Mexico
0.0	4.6	7.1	5.0	4.6	(F)	Nicaragua
9.1	5.1	7.5	8.0	7.0	(B)	Panama
5.6	6.7	7.9	6.3	6.8	(C)	Paraguay
3.6	6.9	6.5	6.8	6.3	(C)	Peru
6.2	5.0	5.3	5.6	5.4	(D)	Trinidad/Tobago

19

Exhibit 2-1: (Continued)

Part 1: Component Ratings: 1995

CENTRAL/- S. AMERICA (con't)	I: Money and Inflation				II: Government Operations						III: Takings			IV: International Sector			
	A	B	C	D	A	B	C	D	E	F	A	B	C	A	B	C	D
Uruguay	0	1	10	10	7	6	6	7.5	5.0	6	2	10	10	7	10	0	10
Venezuela	1	1	0	0	10	2	0	7.5	0.0	0	6	7	0	7	2	4	5

EUROPE/MIDDLE EAST

	A	B	C	D	A	B	C	D	E	F	A	B	C	A	B	C	D
Albania	0	0	10	0	5	0	4	5.0	2.5	6	3	-	0	-	10	3	2
Bahrain	10	8	10	10	0	2	4	5.0	0.0	8	10	10	10	9	10	5	2
Bulgaria	0	0	10	10	5	0	4	7.5	5.0	2	3	3	0	8	6	6	5
Croatia	0	0	10	0	0	0	2	5.0	5.0	4	-	-	0	-	5	-	2
Cyprus	10	10	0	0	4	6	2	10.0	7.5	10	4	4	0	7	6	2	0
Czech Republic	2	1	10	10	2	4	6	10.0	5.0	6	0	5	0	9	10	10	5
Egypt	8	4	10	10	8	0	2	2.5	0.0	10	4	3	0	5	6	5	0
Estonia	0	0	10	10	1	2	6	10.0	7.5	0	3	8	0	9	10	10	8
Greece	4	7	10	0	7	2	5	7.5	5.0	8	0	5	0	10	10	1	5
Hungary	3	6	10	0	7	2	7	10.0	7.5	6	0	4	0	-	10	7	5
Iran	1	2	0	0	6	2	2	2.5	0.0	0	8	4	0	6	1	3	0
Israel	5	6	10	0	0	2	5	7.5	5.0	8	2	4	0	10	10	3	2
Jordan	10	10	0	0	1	6	2	5.0	2.5	6	8	-	10	4	8	9	2
Latvia	0	0	10	10	1	0	6	7.5	5.0	2	2	7	0	9	7	7	8
Lithuania	0	0	10	10	7	0	4	7.5	7.5	0	4	7	0	9	10	9	8
Malta	10	10	10	0	2	4	2	7.5	10.0	10	3	7	10	6	6	5	2
Oman	10	4	10	10	0	2	4	2.5	2.5	10	8	10	10	9	10	5	2
Poland	1	2	10	10	3	2	6	7.5	5.0	6	1	4	0	4	10	3	5
Portugal	7	5	10	10	3	2	5	7.5	7.5	10	3	5	0	10	10	3	8
Romania	0	0	10	0	5	0	6	5.0	5.0	10	3	1	0	7	6	2	5
Russia	0	0	10	10	0	0	2	5.0	2.5	8	1	8	0	2	7	1	5
Slovakia	5	2	10	10	1	4	4	7.5	5.0	6	-	4	0	-	10	10	2
Slovenia	0	0	10	0	1	2	6	5.0	7.5	8	-	-	0	-	10	5	0
Syria	3	6	10	0	6	2	0	2.5	0.0	0	-	-	0	6	0	6	0
Turkey	0	1	10	10	7	4	5	7.5	0.0	0	5	4	0	9	7	3	2
Ukraine	0	0	10	0	8	0	2	5.0	5.0	0	-	-	0	-	6	10	2

ASIA

	A	B	C	D	A	B	C	D	E	F	A	B	C	A	B	C	D
Bangladesh	6	7	0	0	7	6	0	5.0	5.0	8	-	-	10	-	3	2	0
China	3	3	10	0	3	0	3	5.0	0.0	4	-	6	0	9	5	10	5
Fiji	8	7	0	0	3	6	6	7.5	5.0	8	8	7	10	6	8	6	2
Hong Kong	9	5	10	10	8	10	9	10.0	7.5	10	10	10	10	9	10	10	10
India	6	9	0	0	7	2	4	5.0	2.5	8	5	5	10	0	5	4	2
Indonesia	5	10	10	10	8	2	2	2.5	0.0	10	10	8	0	8	10	9	2
Malaysia	4	10	10	10	4	6	4	7.5	2.5	10	7	7	10	8	10	10	5
Nepal	3	5	0	0	9	2	2	5.0	0.0	-	-	-	10	6	4	6	0
Pakistan	7	8	10	0	8	4	4	5.0	0.0	6	-	4	10	0	6	4	2
Philippines	5	6	10	10	8	6	4	5.0	2.5	10	10	7	10	5	10	10	5
Singapore	10	10	10	10	6	8	8	7.5	0.0	10	9	9	0	10	10	10	10
South Korea	6	9	10	10	6	6	3	7.5	7.5	10	8	5	0	8	10	6	5
Sri Lanka	7	10	0	0	9	4	4	5.0	0.0	10	5	7	10	6	7	7	2
Taiwan	10	10	10	10	4	6	6	7.5	5.0	10	5	7	0	8	10	5	5
Thailand	9	10	10	10	7	6	4	5.0	2.5	10	10	7	0	7	10	10	5

20

Exhibit 2-1 (continued)

Part 2: Area Ratings				Part 3: Summary Index		
Money and Inflation	Govern-ment Operations	Takings	Inter-national Sector	Summary Rating	Grade	CENTRAL/- S. AMERICA (con't)
4.0	6.3	6.8	7.5	6.3	(C)	Uruguay
0.6	3.6	5.7	4.6	3.9	(F-)	Venezuela
						EUROPE/MIDDLE
1.9	3.6	2.3	5.4	3.4	(F-)	Albania
9.3	3.0	10.0	6.8	6.7	(C)	Bahrain
3.6	4.0	2.6	6.3	4.1	(F)	Bulgaria
1.9	2.5	0.0	3.5	2.4	(F-)	Croatia
6.4	6.2	3.5	4.1	5.0	(D)	Cyprus
4.6	5.5	2.3	8.4	5.2	(D)	Czech Rep
7.4	3.3	3.0	4.0	4.0	(F)	Egypt
3.6	4.7	4.9	9.2	5.6	(D)	Estonia
5.5	5.6	2.3	7.2	5.0	(D)	Greece
4.8	6.6	1.9	7.4	5.1	(D)	Hungary
1.0	2.3	5.1	2.6	2.9	(F-)	Iran
5.4	4.3	2.7	6.8	4.6	(F)	Israel
6.4	3.6	8.5	5.4	5.4	(D)	Jordan
3.6	3.7	4.1	7.9	4.7	(F)	Latvia
3.6	4.5	4.9	9.0	5.5	(D)	Lithuania
8.3	5.3	5.8	4.8	5.8	(D)	Malta
8.0	3.0	9.2	6.8	6.3	(C)	Oman
4.6	4.9	2.3	5.8	4.3	(F)	Poland
7.4	5.4	3.5	8.3	5.9	(D)	Portugal
1.9	4.8	1.7	5.4	3.6	(F-)	Romania
3.6	2.5	4.1	4.0	3.5	(F-)	Russia
5.8	4.5	3.1	7.0	4.9	(F)	Slovakia
1.9	4.6	0.0	5.1	3.8	(F-)	Slovenia
4.8	1.9	0.0	2.8	2.7	(F-)	Syria
4.0	4.5	3.9	5.6	4.5	(F)	Turkey
1.9	3.5	0.0	5.4	3.4	(F-)	Ukraine
						ASIA
4.2	4.8	10.0	1.6	4.2	(F)	Bangladesh
3.8	2.5	4.7	7.0	4.3	(F)	China
4.8	5.8	7.8	5.5	6.1	(C)	Fiji
8.0	9.1	10.0	9.7	9.3	(A+)	Hong Kong
4.8	4.5	5.7	2.6	4.4	(F)	India
8.5	3.7	7.7	7.1	6.3	(C)	Indonesia
8.2	5.4	7.4	8.1	7.0	(B)	Malaysia
2.6	3.7	10.0	3.9	3.8	(F-)	Nepal
6.7	4.6	5.3	2.8	4.6	(F)	Pakistan
7.2	5.7	8.6	7.2	7.0	(B)	Philippines
10.0	6.7	7.8	10.0	8.2	(A)	Singapore
8.5	6.3	5.5	7.4	6.7	(C)	South Korea
5.5	5.1	6.6	5.4	5.6	(D)	Sri Lanka
10.0	6.2	5.3	7.3	6.8	(C)	Taiwan
9.7	5.5	7.3	7.8	7.2	(B)	Thailand

Exhibit 2-1: (Continued)

Part 1: Component Ratings: 1995

	I: Money and Inflation				II: Government Operations						III: Takings			IV: International Sector			
	A	B	C	D	A	B	C	D	E	F	A	B	C	A	B	C	D
AFRICA																	
Algeria	6	2	0	0	2	0	2	5.0	0.0	0	-	-	0	-	1	5	2
Benin	9	2	0	0	8	4	2	7.5	5.0	2	-	-	0	-	8	3	0
Botswana	10	5	10	0	0	6	6	7.5	7.5	6	5	7	10	1	7	9	5
Burundi	6	3	0	0	6	2	2	2.5	0.0	4	-	-	10	-	2	0	0
Cameroon	9	1	0	0	7	4	2	5.0	0.0	4	9	0	10	3	8	1	0
C African Rep	4	2	0	0	6	6	2	5.0	5.0	6	-	-	0	-	8	1	0
Chad	10	1	0	0	7	4	2	5.0	0.0	4	10	-	0	8	8	4	0
Congo	10	10	0	0	1	0	0	5.0	2.5	2	-	3	10	-	8	6	0
Cote d' Ivoire	5	2	0	0	7	4	4	5.0	0.0	4	-	3	0	-	8	7	0
Gabon	10	1	0	0	1	6	4	7.5	2.5	4	10	1	10	4	8	3	0
Ghana	1	1	0	0	8	2	6	5.0	2.5	4	7	7	10	2	7	3	0
Kenya	3	3	10	0	6	4	4	5.0	0.0	4	9	3	10	6	7	8	8
Madagascar	1	1	0	0	10	6	4	5.0	2.5	-	10	-	0	2	7	6	0
Malawi	1	2	0	0	4	4	2	7.5	5.0	4	-	7	10	-	8	4	2
Mali	6	2	0	0	7	4	4	5.0	2.5	6	-	-	0	-	8	8	2
Mauritius	9	9	10	10	7	6	4	10.0	7.5	10	7	8	10	4	10	5	8
Morocco	10	10	0	0	4	2	4	5.0	0.0	8	8	3	0	1	8	5	5
Niger	9	1	0	0	6	6	2	5.0	2.5	6	-	-	0	-	8	2	0
Nigeria	1	1	0	0	10	2	0	2.5	0.0	0	-	7	10	-	0	5	0
Rwanda	2	4	10	0	5	6	-	2.5	0.0	0	8	-	10	0	6	0	0
Senegal	9	2	0	0	10	6	4	5.0	2.5	4	-	0	0	-	8	5	0
Sierra Leone	1	0	10	0	9	6	2	5.0	0.0	2	7	-	10	3	7	1	0
Somalia	-	-	0	0	-	4	-	2.5	0.0	0	-	-	0	-	-	-	0
South Africa	3	9	0	0	2	4	6	7.5	7.5	10	6	4	10	9	10	6	2
Tanzania	1	3	10	0	10	0	4	2.5	5.0	4	-	8	0	-	8	10	0
Togo	6	9	0	0	8	4	2	5.0	0.0	8	-	-	0	-	8	3	0
Tunisia	10	10	0	0	4	2	6	5.0	0.0	8	5	-	0	1	8	8	5
Uganda	1	1	0	0	10	2	4	5.0	2.5	4	-	8	10	-	6	1	0
Zaire	0	0	0	0	6	2	2	2.5	0.0	0	10	1	10	5	6	1	2
Zambia	0	0	0	0	6	0	2	5.0	2.5	0	8	7	10	6	6	2	2
Zimbabwe	1	3	0	0	3	4	4	5.0	2.5	8	-	4	0	2	8	8	2

Exhibit 2-1 (continued)

| Part 2: Area Ratings | | | | Part 3: Summary Index | | |
Money and Inflation	Govern-ment Operations	Takings	Inter-national Sector	Summary Rating	Grade	
						AFRICA
2.5	1.7	0.0	2.3	1.9	(F-)	Algeria
3.4	4.9	0.0	3.8	4.1	(F)	Benin
6.6	5.4	6.6	5.0	5.8	(D)	Botswana
2.8	2.7	10.0	0.8	2.7	(F-)	Burundi
3.0	3.8	4.9	3.3	3.9	(F-)	Cameroon
1.9	4.8	0.0	3.4	3.6	(F-)	C African Rep
3.3	3.8	7.5	5.2	4.7	(F)	Chad
6.4	1.7	4.5	4.5	3.7	(F-)	Congo Rep
2.2	4.2	2.3	4.8	3.6	(F-)	Cote d' Ivoire
3.3	4.3	5.8	3.9	4.5	(F)	Gabon
0.6	4.7	7.4	3.0	4.4	(F)	Ghana
3.8	4.0	6.3	7.1	5.3	(D)	Kenya
0.6	5.6	7.5	3.5	4.4	(F)	Madagascar
1.0	4.4	7.7	4.8	4.5	(F)	Malawi
2.5	4.7	0.0	5.8	4.2	(F)	Mali
9.4	7.1	7.9	6.9	7.6	(B)	Mauritius
6.4	3.7	4.6	4.6	4.6	(F)	Morocco
3.0	4.5	0.0	3.6	3.7	(F-)	Niger
0.6	2.7	7.7	1.2	3.0	(F-)	Nigeria
3.9	3.2	8.5	1.7	3.8	(F-)	Rwanda
3.4	5.4	0.0	4.3	3.8	(F-)	Senegal
2.2	4.3	7.7	3.0	4.2	(F)	Sierra Leone
0.0	2.0	0.0	0.0	N/R		Somalia
3.9	5.8	5.6	6.9	5.7	(D)	South Africa
3.2	4.2	6.2	5.5	4.6	(F)	Tanzania
4.8	4.3	0.0	3.8	4.1	(F)	Togo
6.4	4.1	3.8	5.1	4.7	(F)	Tunisia
0.6	4.7	8.4	2.6	4.3	(F)	Uganda
0.0	2.3	5.8	3.8	3.3	(F-)	Zaire
0.0	2.8	7.8	4.3	4.1	(F)	Zambia
1.3	4.2	3.1	4.6	3.6	(F-)	Zimbabwe

N/R = No rating because data were available for less than 12 of the 17 components in the index for this year.

Note: See Exhibit 1-1 for the description of each component in the index.

a The following conversion table was used to allocate the letter grades:

summary rating of 9.0 or more = A+;

summary rating of 8.0 to 8.9 = A;

summary rating of 7.0 to 7.9 = B;

summary rating of 6.0 to 6.9 = C;

summary rating of 5.0 to 5.9 = D;

summary rating of 4.0 to 4.9 = F;

summary rating less than 4.0 = F−.

Exhibit 2-1 (right side) also presents ratings for the four areas covered by our index and the aggregate summary rating. Both the area and summary ratings reflect the aggregation of the component ratings, based on the component weights presented in Exhibit 1-1. As in the case of the component ratings, higher area and summary ratings are indicative of greater economic freedom.

Let us look at the various component ratings for a few countries and consider their significance. The United States, Japan, Belgium and Denmark (and several others) received a rating of ten for component I-A, monetary expansion adjusted for the estimated growth rate of potential output. The ten rating indicates that the growth of the money supply of these countries during the last five years (1991-1995) would have placed them in the top 1/11th of the countries during the base year (1985) in terms of the *least* monetary expansion adjusted for the potential growth of real output. (Note: see Chapter 1, endnote 7 for details concerning the importance of the base year.) At the other end of the spectrum, Brazil received a rating of zero, indicating that the growth rate of its money supply during 1991-1995 would have placed it in the bottom 1/11th of countries—those with the most rapid growth rates of the money supply—during the 1985 base year. (Note: the *annual* growth rate of the money supply in Brazil was 1,111% during 1991-1995.) Of course, intermediate ratings closer to ten reflect moderate rates of money growth, while the ratings closer to zero reflect more money growth.

The second component (I-B) in the index is the instability in the price level as measured by the standard deviation in the rate of inflation during the last five years. Countries with the lowest standard deviation (least variability) in the inflation rate are given the highest ratings. The ratings of ten for the United States, Canada, Australia and Japan, for example, indicate that the small variability in the inflation rate in each of these countries during 1991-1995 would have placed them in the top 1/11th of the countries with the least variability in the inflation rate during the base year period. The zero ratings of Brazil and Nicaragua indicate that the fluctuations in the inflation rates of these countries during 1991-1995 would have placed them in the bottom 1/11th of all countries during the base year period.

The next two components, freedom to maintain a foreign currency bank account domestically (I-C) and freedom to maintain a bank account abroad (I-D) have only two possible outcomes—it is either legal or illegal for citizens to maintain these accounts. A rating of ten indicates that the accounts were legal in the mid- 1990s; a zero rating indicates that the accounts were illegal.

Using the component weights of Exhibit 1-1, the four Money and Inflation components are aggregated into an area rating. These results are presented in Part 2 of Exhibit 2-1. Of course, countries with high ratings for the four monetary components will also receive a high rating in this area. For example, the Money and Inflation *area ratings* of the United States and Japan (among others) were ten because they received a rating of ten for each of the four components in this area. The monetary area rating of Canada was slightly lower (9.7) since it received a 9 for the money expansion component (I-A) and a ten for the other three components. The area ratings are merely a reflection of the component ratings that comprise them.

Finally, the component ratings were used to derive a summary rating for each country. In the calculation of the summary rating, each component was assigned the weight indicated in Exhibit 1-1.[1] Of course, countries with high ratings for most components (and particularly for those that are weighed more heavily) will have the highest summary ratings. On the other hand, countries with a large majority of low component ratings will have the lowest summary ratings.

In order to make comparisons across countries easier, we assigned letter grades to various ranges of summary ratings. Countries with a summary rating of 8.0 or more were assigned a letter grade of "A." (A rating of 9.0 or more was assigned an A+). Countries with summary ratings in the 7.0 to 7.9 range were assigned a "B." Below that point, one letter grade was subtracted for each decline of 1.0 in the summary rating. Thus, countries with a summary rating of less than five, were given a letter grade of "F." When the summary rating for a country was less than 4.0, indicating low ratings for most of the components of our index, an F- grade was assigned.

In order to make comparisons across countries easier, we assigned letter grades to various ranges of summary ratings.

Exhibit 2-1 makes it easy to compare ratings of the industrial countries and within regions. Among the high-income industrial countries, only New Zealand earned a rating of "A" in 1995. The 7.9 rating of the United States was just below the cutoff for an "A." In addition to the United States, Australia, Switzerland, and United Kingdom earned "B" ratings. Canada's 6.9 rating was just below the "B" cutoff. Denmark, Italy, Spain, and Sweden had the lowest ratings among the industrial nations. In general, the ratings of the industrial nations were lowest in the Takings area. Most rated high in the monetary and international areas.

Taking a closer look at the summary ratings within regions, the highest ratings in South and Central America—a low B—were earned by Costa Rica and Panama. Most nations in this region earned either "C" or "D" grades. The lowest rated countries in this region were Brazil, Haiti, Nicaragua, and Venezuela—all of which were assigned grades of either F or F-.

The summary ratings of the non-industrial European and the Middle Eastern nations were quite low. Only Bahrain and Oman were able to earn grades of "C." The lowest ratings in this region went to Albania, Croatia, Iran, Romania, Russia, Slovenia, Syria, and Ukraine. All of these countries earned a grade of F-, indicating that their policies and institutions were highly inconsistent with economic freedom.

In Asia, the summary index ratings were highly diverse. Hong Kong (A+) and Singapore (A) registered the highest ratings. Malaysia, Philippines, and Thailand earned a "B" grade, while Taiwan and South Korea were assigned a high "C." At the other end of the spectrum, Bangladesh, China, India, and Pakistan posted F ratings, while Nepal registered an F-.

The economic freedom ratings of the African countries were extremely low. Except for the "B" of Mauritius and the "D" grades of Botswana, Kenya, and South Africa, the other 26 African nations included in our study earned grades of either F or F-. (Note: There was insufficient data to give Somalia a summary rating in 1995.)

1995 COUNTRY RANKINGS

By a significant margin, Hong Kong was the highest rated country in the world.

Exhibit 2-2 presents the 1995 summary ratings arranged from high to low. This makes it easy to identify the countries with the highest and lowest ratings (and therefore rankings). By a significant margin, Hong Kong was the highest rated country in the world in 1995, a spot that it also achieved during each of the four prior rating years. Singapore, New Zealand, United States, and surprisingly, Mauritius round out the Top Five. Switzerland, United Kingdom, Thailand, and Costa Rica occupy spots six through nine. Four countries—Malaysia, Philippines, Australia, and Panama—are tied for the tenth place ranking. Several of the countries in the Top Ten occupied this lofty position throughout the 1975-1995 period. Hong Kong, Singapore, United States, and Switzerland fall into this category. Malaysia has also ranked in the Top Ten since 1985. The other Top Ten members have improved their relative position substantially during the last decade. This is particularly true of Mauritius, Costa Rica, Thailand, and Philippines.

Exhibit 2-2: Summary Ratings and Rankings 1995

Summary Rating		Summary Rating	
Hong Kong 1	9.3	Trinidad/Tob. 5	5.4
Singapore 2	8.2	Jordan 59	5.4
New Zealand 3	8.0	Kenya 61	5.3
United States 4	7.9	Czech Rep 62	5.2
Mauritius 5	7.6	Hungary 63	5.1
Switzerland 6	7.4	Cyprus 64	5.0
U. K. 7	7.3	Greece 64	5.0
Thailand 8	7.2	Slovakia 66	4.9
Costa Rica 9	7.1	Chad 67	4.7
Malaysia 10	7.0	Tunisia 67	4.7
Philippines 10	7.0	Latvia 67	4.7
Australia 10	7.0	Tanzania 70	4.6
Panama 10	7.0	Israel 70	4.6
Canada 14	6.9	Morocco 70	4.6
El Salvador 14	6.9	Pakistan 70	4.6
Taiwan 16	6.8	Nicaragua 70	4.6
Paraguay 16	6.8	Gabon 75	4.5
South Korea 18	6.7	Malawi 75	4.5
Japan 18	6.7	Turkey 75	4.5
Bahrain 18	6.7	Madagascar 78	4.4
Netherlands 21	6.5	Ghana 78	4.4
Guatemala 21	6.5	India 78	4.4
Ireland 21	6.5	Uganda 81	4.3
Iceland 21	6.5	Poland 81	4.3
Bolivia 25	6.4	China 81	4.3
Argentina 25	6.4	Bangladesh 84	4.2
Chile 25	6.4	Mali 84	4.2
Germany 25	6.4	Sierra Leone 84	4.2
Oman 29	6.3	Benin 87	4.1
Belize 29	6.3	Bulgaria 87	4.1
Uruguay 29	6.3	Zambia 87	4.1
Indonesia 29	6.3	Togo 87	4.1
Peru 29	6.3	Egypt 91	4.0
Belgium 29	6.3	Cameroon 92	3.9
Bahamas 35	6.2	Venezuela 92	3.9
Mexico 35	6.1	Rwanda 94	3.8
Finland 36	6.1	Nepal 94	3.8
France 36	6.1	Slovenia 94	3.8
Fiji 36	6.1	Senegal 94	3.8
Norway 36	6.1	Niger 98	3.7
Austria 36	6.0	Brazil 98	3.7
Portugal 42	5.9	Congo Rep 98	3.7
Jamaica 42	5.9	Zimbabwe 101	3.6
Denmark 42	5.9	Cote d' Ivoire 1	3.6
Honduras 42	5.9	C African Rep 1	3.6
Spain 42	5.9	Romania 101	3.6
Sweden 42	5.9	Russia 105	3.5
Botswana 48	5.8	Albania 106	3.4
Malta 48	5.8	Ukraine 106	3.4
South Africa 50	5.7	Zaire 108	3.3
Barbados 50	5.7	Nigeria 109	3.0
Sri Lanka 52	5.6	Iran 110	2.9
Dom. Rep. 52	5.6	Haiti 110	2.9
Estonia 52	5.6	Burundi 112	2.7
Colombia 55	5.5	Syria 112	2.7
Lithuania 55	5.5	Croatia 114	2.4
Italy 55	5.5	Algeria 115	1.9
Ecuador 55	5.5		

At the other end of the spectrum, our index indicates that the economies of Algeria, Croatia, Syria, Burundi, Haiti, Iran, Nigeria, Zaire, Ukraine, and Albania were the least free in the world in 1995. In total, there were 24 countries with ratings of less than 4.0. Ratings in this range (F-) are indicative of low or middle-low ratings for all or almost all components.

CHANGES IN THE ECONOMIC FREEDOM OF COUNTRIES

As we previously mentioned, country ratings were also derived for 1975, 1980, 1985, and 1990. In many ways, the change in a country's rating is more interesting than the rating at a point in time. If our index is a good measure of economic freedom, an increase in a country's summary rating indicates that it is moving toward liberalization—that the economic freedom of the citizenry is expanding. In contrast, a reduction in the summary rating suggests a decline in economic freedom.

New Zealand registered the largest increase, a jump from 4.2 in 1975 to 8.0 in 1995.

Which countries have made the most progress toward economic freedom— Exhibit 2-3 (left frame) presents the summary ratings for 1975, 1985, and 1995 of the ten countries that registered the largest rating increases during the last two decades. The summary ratings of these countries were at least 2.6 units higher in 1995 than in 1975. New Zealand registered the largest increase, a jump from 4.2 in 1975 (and 4.1 in 1985) to 8.0 in 1995. As an inspection of the "country profile" data (see Chapter 3) for New Zealand reveals, improvement was made in most rating categories. Monetary policy was more stable, foreign currency bank accounts were legalized, privatization reduced the size of the state enterprise sector, transfers and subsidies were reduced, the top marginal tax rate was chopped (from 66% in the mid-1980s to 33% in the 1990s), and trade policies were liberalized. Interestingly, most of these changes took place during the last decade.[2]

The rating increases of Chile and Mauritius were only marginally lower than those of New Zealand. In contrast with New Zealand, Chile moved significantly toward economic liberalization during 1975-1985 and that trend continued during 1985-1995. In the mid-1970s, the Chilean economy was characterized by triple- digit annual increases in both the money supply and the price level. In recent years the money growth has fallen to the 20% range—still more rapid than ideal, but a substantial improvement compared to the 1970s—and the inflation rate has fallen to single-digit levels.

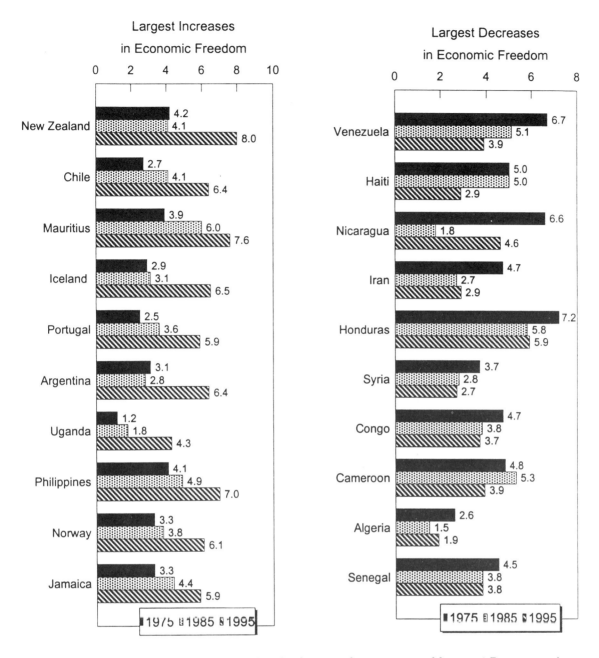

Exhibit 2-3: The Ten Countries with the Largest Increases and Largest Decreases in Economic Freedom, 1975 - 1995

Chile legalized the use of foreign currency bank accounts both domestically and abroad. Reductions in government consumption and the privatization of state enterprises also contributed to Chile's improvement. The most important factors pushing up Chile's rating were lower marginal tax rates and a reduction in the size of the transfer sector. Chile has reduced its top marginal tax rate during every five year period since 1975. In 1975 the top marginal tax rate was 80 percent. That rate was sliced to 60% in 1980, 57% in 1985, 50% in 1990 and 45% in 1995. The primary factor under- lying the

29

reduction in transfers and subsidies was the adoption of a private savings and investment plan instead of a pay-as-you-go social security system. (See country profile for Chile in Chapter 3.)

Chile has reduced its top marginal tax rate during every five year period since 1975.

Like Chile, Mauritius has moved steadily toward a freer economy throughout the last two decades. A more stable monetary policy boosted its summary rating during 1975-1985. The marginal tax rate was cut from 50% in 1980 to 35% in 1985 and 30% in 1995. More recently, legalization of foreign currency bank accounts, elimination of exchange rate controls, and liberalization of restrictions on the mobility of capital have enhanced the summary rating of Mauritius. As the result of this improvement, along with its relatively small government consumption and transfer sectors, this small country now has one of the freest economies in the world.

As Exhibit 2-3 illustrates, Portugal has registered steady movement toward a freer economy since 1975 and the summary ratings of both Iceland and Argentina have increased substantially during the last decade. Uganda, Philippines, Norway, and Jamaica round out the list of ten recording the largest gains during the last two decades. Interestingly, with the exception of New Zealand and Norway, all of these countries were low-income, less developed nations at the beginning of the period.

Exhibit 2-3 also presents data for the ten countries that recorded the largest reductions in economic freedom during the last two decades. Venezuela has the dubious distinction of heading this list. In 1975 our index ranked Venezuela as the fifth freest economy in the world. Since that time, monetary policy has become more erratic; foreign currency bank accounts have been restricted; and price controls—including those imposed on the financial and foreign exchange markets—have become more restrictive. At a time when most of Latin America was moving toward economic liberalism, Venezuela moved in the opposite direction. In 1995, it ranked 92nd (among the 115 economies of our study), quite a plunge from its lofty position of 1975. (See country profile in Chapter 3 for additional details.)

Haiti, Nicaragua (despite a significant rating increase in the 1990s), Iran, Honduras, and Syria are also among the economies that have become substantially less free during the last two decades. Interestingly, all of the countries that have regressed during this period are from three regions—Latin America, Africa, and the Middle East.

Exhibit 2-4 presents the "honor roll" of most improved countries during the last decade (left frame) and during the most recent five years (right frame). Of course, there will be some overlap of these groups with the most improved economies for the entire 20-year period. But there are several "new entrants" into the most improved category. The ratings of both Peru and Poland rose significantly during both the late 1980s and the early 1990s. These economies are now considerably more free than during the mid-1980s. The rating of Costa Rica rose sharply during the last half of the 1980s and the improvement was maintained and improved slightly during the 1990s. The ratings of Nicaragua, El Salvador, and Tanzania have also jumped sharply, but most of their improvement was during the 1990s. Russia, Bulgaria, Hungary, and Dominican Republic are also among the countries registering the largest rating increases during the last five years.

With the collapse of communism, the economies of Eastern Europe and the former Soviet Union are currently going through a dramatic period of transition. In 1990 most countries in this region ranked among the world's 15 least free economies. Croatia, Ukraine, Albania, Russia, and Romania still fall into this category. As Exhibit 2-5 illustrates, these economies have made significant moves toward economic liberalism in the 1990s. Our index indicates they were "more free" in 1995 than in 1990. Several of the rating increases are substantial. For example, the ratings of the Czech and Slovak Republics were 5.2 and 4.9 respectively in 1995, compared to a 2.4 rating in 1990 for the former Czechoslovakia. The summary ratings of both Hungary and Bulgaria rose by more than 2 units between 1990 and 1995; Poland registered a 1.5 unit increase during the same period. Except for Romania, all of the rated former Soviet bloc countries recorded summary rating increases of at least 1.5 units between 1990 and 1995.

In spite of these rating increases, the summary ratings of these countries are still low. Two Baltic states—Estonia and Lithuania —have the highest summary ratings within this group. The ratings of the Czech Republic and Hungary are only slightly lower. None of these countries was able to make even the Top Fifty among the 115 countries of our study. Estonia ranks 52nd; Lithuania 55th; the Czech Republic 62nd; and Hungary 63rd. At the other end of the spectrum, Croatia ranks 114th; Ukraine and Albania tied for 106th; Russia ranked 105th; and Romania 101st. Almost all of these countries received a very low rating (two or less) for both the money growth and inflation variability components. Several are now in a position to improve their ratings in these two areas during the next three or four years. This improvement, along with continued moves toward liberalization in other areas, could push several of these countries into the Top Thirty in the not too distant future.

31

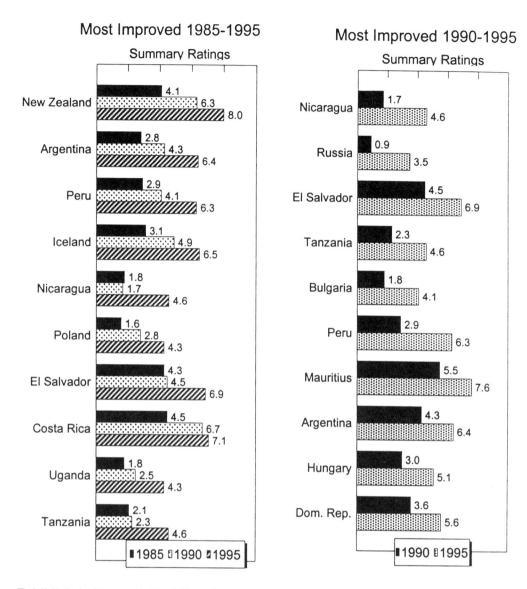

Exhibit 2-4: Honor Roll of Most Improved: 1985-1995 and 1990-1995

ECONOMIC FREEDOM, INCOME, AND GROWTH

In the last edition, we had a chapter on economic freedom and growth. We will not address that topic in detail in this report. We would, however, like to present an exhibit illustrating the basic relationship between economic freedom, per capita income, and growth. We arrayed the summary ratings for our 115 countries from the highest to the lowest and divided them into quintiles—five groups of 23 (one group had 24 and another 22 as the result of

Summary Ratings: 1990-1995

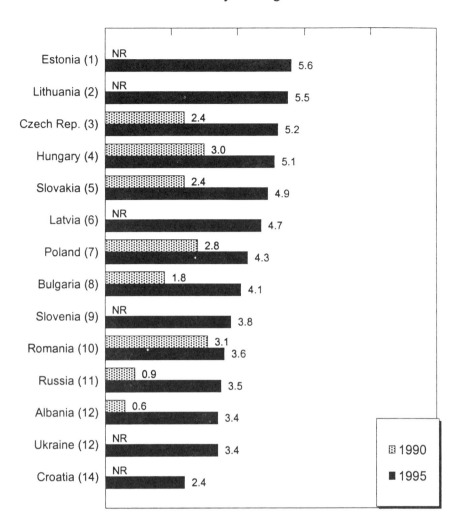

NR = no rating.
(Note: The 1995 rankings within this group are indicated in parenthesis. The summary rating in 1990 for the Czech Republic and Slovakia is for the former Czechoslovakia.)

Exhibit 2-5: Changes in Economic Freedom in Eastern Europe and the Former Soviet Union

ties). Then the average per capita GDP in 1996 and annual rate of growth during 1985-1996 were derived for each of the quintile groups. These figures are presented in Exhibit 2-6.[3] For the top quintile of "most free" economies, the average per capita GDP was $14,829. The figure for the next quintile was $12,369 and it declined for each quintile down to $2,541 for the countries comprising the "least free" quintile. Clearly, there was a strong positive relationship between per capita GDP and economic freedom as measured by our index.

(a) Per Capita GDP (1995 U.S. dollars)   (b) Growth of Real GDP Per Capita 1985-1996

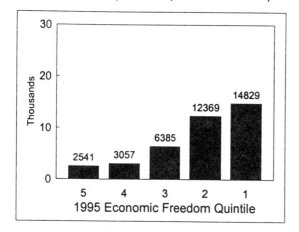 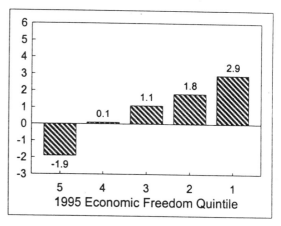

(Note: The summary ratings of the five quintiles were: top quintile = 6.5 and above; second highest quintile = 5.9 to 6.4, third highest = 4.7 to 5.8; fourth highest = 3.9 to 4.6; lowest quintile = 3.8 and lower. The per capita GDP data are updates of the Penn World Tables data of Robert Summers and Alan Heston which were derived by the purchasing power parity method.

Exhibit 2-6: Per Capita GDP and Growth of Real Income by Quintile Ratings of Economic Freedom

The growth of real GDP between 1985 and 1996 (or the most recent year available) is also presented by quintile. The top quintile registered per capita growth of 2.9%. The figure for the second quintile fell to 1.8% and it continued to decline by approximately 1% as one moved down each quintile. For the least free quintile (countries in this group had summary ratings of 3.8 or less), per capita GDP fell at an annual rate of 1.9% during 1985- 1996.[4]

Both per capita GDP and its growth rate are positively linked with economic freedom. This relationship is not an artifact of the construction of the index.

Thus, both per capita GDP and its growth rate are positively linked with economic freedom. This relationship is not an artifact of the construction of the index. The components of the index were all indicators of institutional structure and economic policy. None of them were "proxies" for level of income or development. If economic freedom did not exert a positive impact on growth and eventually the level of income achieved, there would be no reason why the income and growth figures would be positively correlated with the index rating. They could just as well have been negatively correlated. Or there could have been no relationship at all. This positive correlation suggests that countries that follow policies more consistent with economic freedom reap a payoff in the form of more rapid economic growth that leads to higher living standards.[5]

34

LOOKING AHEAD

The focal point of this Annual Report is the expanded country profile section. The following chapter presents this material.

ENDNOTES

1. If the data for a component could not be obtained for a country, the weight for that component was distributed proportionally among the other components when deriving the summary index for the country.

2. For an excellent survey of recent economic policy in New Zealand , see Lewis Evans, Arthur Grimes, Bryce Wilkinson, and David Teece, "Economic Reform in New Zealand 1984-1995: The Pursuit of Efficiency," *Journal of Economic Literature* (December 1996).

3. A similar exhibit in the last edition by grade level was widely reproduced by the media. Since there are so few countries in the grade "A" and "B" categories, this time, we thought it would be more meaningful to present the data by quintiles rather than grade level.

4. Everyone of the countries in the "most free" quintile achieved a positive growth rate of real GDP during 1985-1996. Four of the economies in the second freest quintile experienced declines in real GDP. The number of countries with a negative growth rate rose to 7 for the third quintile, 10 for the fourth quintile and 13 for the "least free" quintile. Since the growth data were unavailable for newly-formed countries (Slovenia, Ukraine, Russia, and Croatia) during this period, they were omitted from the average growth rate calculation. Thus, the growth figures were available for only 18 countries in the least free quintile. Thirteen of the 18 experienced reductions in per capita GDP.

5. In some ways, the strong linkage between level of economic freedom and growth of per capita GDP is a bit surprising because both economic theory and more detailed analysis indicate that *changes* in economic freedom will also influence growth. Some of the low rated countries have experienced significant increases in economic freedom, which would tend to increase their growth rate. Correspondingly, some countries with a relatively high rating have experienced recent reductions in economic freedom, which tend to adversely affect their growth. Both of these factors would weaken the simple relationship between economic freedom and growth. Of course, as a country shifts toward policies more consistent with economic freedom, it will take time to convince potential investors and other decision-makers that the shift is permanent. Thus, there may often be a time lag between a move to a freer economy and a significant positive impact on economic growth. See Chapter 4 of *Economic Freedom of the World: 1975-1995* for additional analysis of these topics.

CHAPTER 3

Country Profiles

This chapter presents detailed data covering both economic freedom and the recent economic performance for 81 of the 115 countries included in this study.

For each country, we present a bar chart of both the summary economic freedom rating and total government expenditures as a share of GDP for 1975, 1980, 1985, 1990, and 1995.[1] For years, the government expenditure/GDP ratio was considered the most objective measure of the size of the government sector compared to the market sector. In addition to government expenditures (including both government consumption and size of the transfer sector), our economic freedom index highlights the importance of several other factors including monetary stability and institutions, price controls, discriminatory taxation, and freedom of international exchange. Some would argue that these "other factors" should have less (or more) weight in the measurement of economic freedom. Observation of changes in both economic freedom and government expenditures will help us better interpret the trends in, and meaning of, these two different but interrelated indicators.

Part 1 of each country profile shows the ratings for each of the seventeen components of the economic freedom index, as well as the accompanying area and summary ratings. When they can be easily denoted, the underlying raw data upon which the component rating was based are reported in parentheses. Since this information is presented for each rating year, it makes it easy to observe the specific component factors causing a country's rating to change over time. The country rankings for each year are also reported in the final line of Part 1.

The International Monetary Fund *(International Financial Statistics* and *Government Finance Statistics Yearbook)* and the World Bank *(World Tables)* provided the primary data sources for money supply, GDP deflator, government consumption as a share of total consumption, interest rates, transfers and subsidies, taxes on international trade, and the size of the trade sector used to derive the related components presented in Part 1. The precise sources used to derive each component of the index and a complete explanation of the procedures used to determine the component ratings are indicated in the source notes accompanying the tables of Appendix II.

Part 2 of each country profile presents annual data for various key indicators of economic policy and performance for the 1988- 1996 period. Population and per capita real GDP figures are reported at the beginning of Part 2. The per capita GDP figure (in 1995 U.S. dollars) is an update of the Summers and Heston, *Penn World Tables* (Cambridge: National Bureau of Economic Research, 1994) income data which were derived by the purchasing power parity method. The original data were in 1985 dollars and they generally ran through 1992. We used real per capita GDP growth rates as measured in local currencies to update the Summers and Heston data to 1996, and the U.S. GDP deflator to convert from 1985 to 1995 dollars. While purchasing power parity estimates of GDP are less widely reported than estimates derived by the exchange rate conversion method, most economists believe that the former are more accurate. Furthermore, the Summers and Heston data are widely accepted as the best available set of income comparisons across countries.

The growth rates of per capita real GDP for 1980-1990 and 1990-1996 are also presented in Part 2. These figures were derived from real GDP (measured in local currency) and population data. Annual growth rates for real GDP are also shown for 1988-1996.

Part 2 also presents annual data for the rate of inflation (as measured by the CPI), money supply (both M1 and M2) growth rates, gross investment/GDP ratio, size of trade sector (defined as exports + imports divided by two as a percent of GDP), government expenditure/GDP ratio, deficit (or surplus) of the central government as a share of GDP, and the rate of unemployment. Except for the unemployment data for OECD countries, the source for all the annual data in Part 2 was the International Monetary Fund, *International Financial Statistics*, (either the annual yearbook or the monthly publication). Since the *OECD Economic Outlook* provides unemployment figures based on a standardized definition, these figures were used for OECD members. When we were unable to obtain the necessary data from international sources, the institutes of the Economic Freedom Network were sometimes able to obtain the figures for us from national sources.

Finally, each country profile includes a written description of the country's economic freedom and performance. Many of the member institutes of the Economic Freedom Network helped us in the preparation of this text and in checking the accuracy of the data. Of course, we bear complete responsibility for any errors.

ENDNOTE

1. We made a special effort to obtain figures for total government expenditures for all purposes, including government consumption, investment, transfers and subsidies, and net interest cost. We also sought to include expenditures for all levels of government. Grants and aid from a central government to lower levels were counted only once. As we discovered, this comprehensive measure for size of government is not an easy figure to obtain. The reported figures are often for the central government only or they often omit important categories of government expenditures such as income transfers, capital expenditures, or interest. For OECD countries, the primary source of this figure was *OECD Historical Statistics*, Table 6.5. The institutes of the Economic Freedom Network often helped us obtain this figure for the countries they represent.

ALBANIA

Economic Freedom Rating

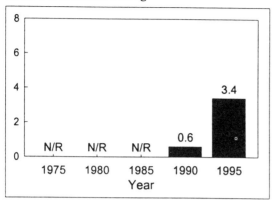

Total Government Expenditures As a Percent of GDP

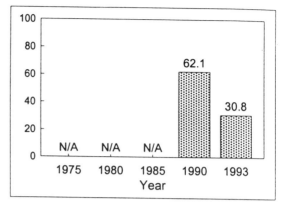

Part 1: The Economic Freedom Ratings for the Components and Various Area and Summary Indexes: 1975, 1980, 1985, 1990 and 1995.

(The numbers in parentheses indicate the actual values for the components.)

Components of Economic Freedom	1990		1995	
I. Money and Inflation	**0.0**		**1.9**	
(a) Annual Money Growth (last 5 yrs.)	-		0	(78.9)
(b) Inflation Variablity (last 5 yrs.)	-		0	(86.2)
(c) Ownership of Foreign Currency	0		10	
(d) Maint. of Bank Account Abroad	0		0	
II. Government Operation	**0.3**		**3.6**	
(a) Gov't Consump. (% of Total Consump.)	1	(29.1)	5	(22.0)
(b) Government Enterprises	0		0	
(c) Price Controls	0		4	
(d) Entry Into Business	-		5.0	
(e) Legal System	-		2.5	
(f) Avoidance of Neg. Interest Rates	0		6	
III. Takings	**0.8**		**2.3**	
(a) Transfers and Subsidies (% of GDP)	1	(24.3)	3	(14.9)
(b) Marginal Tax Rates (Top Rate)	-		-	
(c) Conscription	0		0	
IV. International Sector	**1.2**		**5.4**	
(a) Taxes on International Trade (Avg.)	-		-	
(b) Black Market Exchange Rates (Prem.)	0	(800)	10	(0)
(c) Size of Trade Sector (% of GDP)	5	(42.0)	3	(38.0)
(d) Capital Transactions with Foreigners	0		2	
Economic Freedom Rating	**0.6**		**3.4**	
Ranking of Country	**109**		**106**	

Part 2: Recent Economic Indicators:

Population 1996:	3.4		**Real Per Capita GDP** :	1996 =	$475	
(in millions)			(in 1995 U.S. dollars)			
Annual Rate of Change (1980-96):	-0.6%		Avg. Growth Rate:	1980-90=	-	
				1990-96=	-4.0%	

Economic Indicators:*	1990	1991	1992	1993	1994	1995	1996
Change in Real GDP: Aggregate	-10.0	-27.7	-9.7	-11.0	9.4	8.6	8.5
: Per Capita	-9.4	-27.1	-9.1	-10.4	10.0	9.2	9.1
Inflation Rate (CPI)	0.0	35.5	226.0	85.0	22.6	7.8	12.7
Change in Money Supply: (M1)	-	-	-	-	-	51.8	50.8
: (M2)	-	-	-	-	-	23.8	32.6
Investment/GDP Ratio	34.6	-	-	-	-	-	-
Size of Trade Sector (% of GDP)	42.0	-	-	-	-	38.0	-
Total Gov't Exp./GDP Ratio	62.1	61.9	46.9	44.0	28.5	30.8	29.4
Central Government Budget Deficit (-) or Surplus (+) As a Percent of GDP	-3.7	-44.0	-22.0	-16.0	-14.0	-9.4	-15.0
Unemployment Rate	7.6	11.7	30.3	22.4	19.2	13.0	11.0

* The figures in this table are in percent form.

In 1990 Albania ranked last among the 109 countries that we were able to rate. Its 1995 ranking was slightly better, 106th (out of 115).

Like so many transitional economies, Albania ran large budget deficits which were financed with money creation. In turn, this led to hyperinflation, economic chaos, and high rates of unemployment. Subsequently, a few positive steps were taken. Some control was exerted over the growth of the money supply and the inflation rate was reduced to the 10% range in 1995. Citizens were allowed to maintain foreign currency bank accounts domestically, which provided them with some means of protection against inflation. Exchange rate controls were liberalized. The economy began to stabilize and impressive growth was achieved during 1994-1996. However, the collapse of several pyramid investment schemes in early 1997 led to civil unrest and once again thrust the country into a chaotic situation.

All of this highlights the importance of institutional structures for the smooth operation of a market economy. Monetary arrangements must provide for price stability and legal structures must protect people against fraud. Unfortunately, development of sensible monetary and legal arrangements, including a judicial system capable of protecting property rights and enforcing contacts, is not easy. This is precisely the task that confronts the proponents of a market economy in this, the poorest country in Europe.

ARGENTINA

Economic Freedom Rating

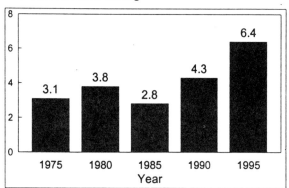

**Total Government Expenditures
As a Percent of GDP**

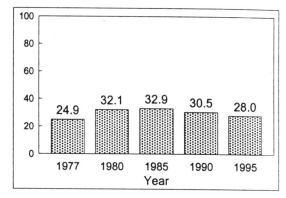

Part 1: The Economic Freedom Ratings for the Components and Various Area and Summary Indexes: 1975, 1980, 1985, 1990 and 1995.
(The numbers in parentheses indicate the actual values for the components.)

Components of Economic Freedom	1975		1980		1985		1990		1995	
I. Money and Inflation	3.6		3.6		3.6		3.6		3.6	
(a) Annual Money Growth (last 5 yrs.)	0	(78.2)	0	(146.0)	0	(296.1)	0	(514.4)	0	(52.5)
(b) Inflation Variablity (last 5 yrs.)	0	(61.8)	0	(119.8)	0	(207.6)	0	(1185.0)	0	(54.0)
(c) Ownership of Foreign Currency	10		10		10		10		10	
(d) Maint. of Bank Account Abroad	10		10		10		10		10	
II. Government Operation	6.0		4.7		5.5		4.9		7.8	
(a) Gov't Consump. (% of Total Consump.)	6	(17.8)	6	(16.5)	8	(13.0)	10	(4.7)	-	
(b) Government Enterprises	6		6		6		8		8	
(c) Price Controls	-		-		-		0		8	
(d) Entry Into Business	-		-		-		-		10.0	
(e) Legal System	-		-		-		-		2.5	
(f) Avoidance of Neg. Interest Rates	-		0		0		0		10	
III. Takings	3.9		4.4		2.5		5.3		5.8	
(a) Transfers and Subsidies (% of GDP)	5	(7.9)	4	(9.7)	4	(11.7)	5	(7.2)	4	(9.4)
(b) Marginal Tax Rates (Top Rate)	4	(51)	6	(45)	2	(62)	7	(35)	9	(30)
(c) Conscription	0		0		0		0		0	
IV. International Sector	0.3		2.5		0.7		3.1		7.2	
(a) Taxes on International Trade (Avg.)	0	(12.9)	1	(9.5)	0	(12.7)	1	(9.9)	6	(4.8)
(b) Black Market Exchange Rates (Prem.)	1	(124)	8	(1)	2	(40)	10	(0)	10	(0)
(c) Size of Trade Sector (% of GDP)	0	(5.9)	0	(5.8)	1	(9.0)	0	(7.7)	0	(8.0)
(d) Capital Transactions with Foreigners	0		0		0		0		10	
Economic Freedom Rating	3.1		3.8		2.8		4.3		6.4	
Ranking of Country	79		57		91		62		25	

42

Part 2: Recent Economic Indicators:

Population 1996:	35.0	**Real Per Capita GDP** :		1996=	$8,698
(in millions)		(in 1995 U.S. dollars)			
Annual Rate of Change (1985-96):	1.4%	Avg. Growth Rate:	1980-90 =	-2.3%	
			1990-96 =	3.5%	

Economic Indicators:*	1988	1989	1990	1991	1992	1993	1994	1995	1996
Change in Real GDP:Aggregate	-1.9	-6.2	0.1	8.9	8.7	6.0	7.4	-3.2	6.6
: Per Capita	-3.3	-7.6	-1.3	7.5	7.3	4.6	6.0	-4.6	5.2
Inflation Rate (CPI)	343.0	3079.8	2314.0	171.7	24.9	10.6	4.2	3.4	0.3
Change in Money Supply: (M1)	351.4	4168.2	1023.2	148.6	49.0	33.0	8.2	1.7	-
: (M2)	443.3	2226.2	1099.3	141.3	62.5	46.5	17.6	-2.7	-
Investment/GDP Ratio	18.6	15.5	14.0	14.6	16.7	18.2	19.9	20.7	-
Size of Trade Sector (% of GDP)	7.9	9.8	7.7	7.0	7.4	7.3	8.0	8.0	-
Total Gov't Exp./GDP Ratio	33.1	36.2	30.5	29.7	28.8	28.6	27.9	28.0	
Central Government Budget Deficit (-) or Surplus (+) As a Percent of GDP	-1.9	-0.4	-1.6	-1.6	+0.5	+1.0	-0.1	-0.9	-
Unemployment Rate	6.0	7.4	7.4	5.8	6.7	10.1	12.1	18.8	-

* The figures in this table are in percent form.

After stagnating among the lowest rated countries in the world during 1975-1985, Argentina has made substantial moves toward economic freedom during the last decade. Its summary rating rose from 2.8 in 1985 to 6.4 in 1995. Only New Zealand registered a larger increase during this period. Argentina's *ranking* also soared from 91st in 1985 to 62nd in 1990 and 25th in 1995. Even though Argentina has moved toward monetary restraint and achieved a low stable rate of inflation during 1994-1996, its marks in these two areas are still low because they cover a five-year time period. If it continues to follow a stable monetary policy, higher ratings in these two areas in the next couple of years are sure to boost its summary rating and ranking even higher.

Argentina started the deregulation process and move toward a market economy in the late 1980s. Exchange rate controls were eliminated and a currency board structure was used to anchor the Argentine peso to the U.S. dollar (1 peso = $1). Several government enterprises were privatized; credit market restrictions were relaxed; marginal tax rates were reduced (the top rate was cut from 62% in 1985 to 35% in 1990 and 30% in 1995).

Most restrictions on capital transactions with foreigners were also eliminated.

The currency board and accompanying reduction of monetary growth reduced the inflation rate from over 2000% in 1990 to 4% in 1994. The Mexican peso crisis of late-1994 severely tested Argentina's resolve to escape the vicious cycle of monetary expansion and hyper-inflation. In order to maintain the one-to-one conversion rate with the dollar, Argentina had to sharply reduce its domestic money supply. The fall-out of the crisis threw the economy into a recession during 1995, but Argentina weathered the storm and enhanced its credibility both at home and abroad. The economy has rebounded strongly in 1996 and returned to the impressive growth path of 1991-1994.

Perhaps Argentina's most serious current problem is a highly inflexible labor market. The rate of unemployment rate soared to 18% during the recession of 1995. Wage setting in Argentina is highly centralized and therefore wages adjust slowly to dynamic change. Decentralization of collective bargaining units and deregulation of the labor market would help Argentina maintain strong growth and achieve its full potential in the future.

43

AUSTRALIA

Economic Freedom Rating

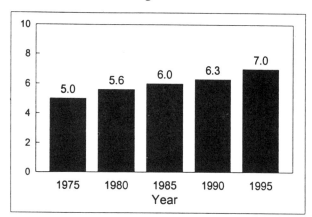

Total Government Expenditures
As a Percent of GDP

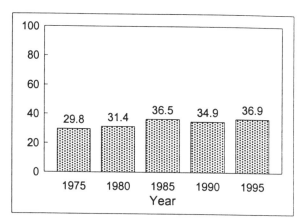

Part 1: The Economic Freedom Ratings for the Components and Various Area and Summary Indexes: 1975, 1980, 1985, 1990 and 1995.
(The numbers in parentheses indicate the actual values for the components.

Components of Economic Freedom	1975		1980		1985		1990		1995	
I. Money and Inflation	**7.1**		**8.5**		**9.0**		**8.2**		**9.1**	
(a) Annual Money Growth (last 5 yrs.)	6	(11.8)	6	(11.4)	9	(5.9)	5	(13.5)	7	(9.4)
(b) Inflation Variablity (last 5 yrs.)	5	(4.2)	9	(1.6)	8	(2.2)	9	(1.9)	10	(0.6)
(c) Ownership of Foreign Currency	10		10		10		10		10	
(d) Maint. of Bank Account Abroad	10		10		10		10		10	
II. Government Operation	**4.4**		**5.7**		**5.7**		**6.1**		**7.2**	
(a) Gov't Consump. (% of Total Consump.)	3	(23.0)	3	(23.4)	3	(23.9)	4	(22.1)	4	(21.9)
(b) Government Enterprises	6		6		6		6		6	
(c) Price Controls	-		-		-		6		7	
(d) Entry Into Business	-		-		-		-		10.0	
(e) Legal System	-		-		-		-		7.5	
(f) Avoidance of Neg. Interest Rates	4		10		10		10		10	
III. Takings	**3.9**		**3.9**		**3.5**		**4.3**		**4.4**	
(a) Transfers and Subsidies (% of GDP)	4	(8.5)	4	(10.1)	3	(11.9)	4	(10.7)	3	(14.2)
(b) Marginal Tax Rates (Top Rate)	2	(64)	2	(62)	2	(60)	3	(49)	4	(47)
(c) Conscription	10		10		10		10		10	
IV. International Sector	**5.2**		**5.5**		**7.1**		**7.8**		**8.2**	
(a) Taxes on International Trade (Avg.)	6	(4.4)	7	(3.6)	7	(3.2)	7	(3.1)	8	(1.9)
(b) Black Market Exchange Rates (Prem.)	8	(1)	8	(1)	10	(0)	10	(0)	10	(0)
(c) Size of Trade Sector (% of GDP)	4	(14.4)	4	(17.0)	6	(17.6)	5	(17.2)	6	(20.3)
(d) Capital Transactions with Foreigners	2		2		5		8		8	
Economic Freedom Rating	**5.0**		**5.6**		**6.0**		**6.3**		**7.0**	
Ranking of Country	**24**		**19**		**15**		**15**		**10**	

44

Part 2: Recent Economic Indicators

Population 1996:	18.3	**Real Per Capita GDP** :	1996 =	$22,809	
(in millions)		(in 1995 U.S. dollars)			
Annual Rate of Change (1985-96):	1.4%	A vg. Growth Rate:	1980-90 =	1.5%	
			1990-96 =	1.3%	

Economic Indicators:*	1988	1989	1990	1991	1992	1993	1994	1995	1996
Change in Real GDP: Aggregate	4.3	4.2	1.4	-1.6	2.6	4.0	5.2	3.1	3.8
: Per Capita	2.9	2.8	0.0	-3.0	1.2	2.6	3.8	1.7	2.5
Inflation Rate (CPI)	7.2	7.6	7.3	3.2	1.0	1.8	1.9	4.6	1.5
Change in Money Supply: (M1)	29.6	7.5	7.3	7.0	20.1	17.8	11.1	6.3	8.4
: (M2)	20.1	28.1	12.6	0.7	7.6	6.0	9.7	8.6	5.7
Investment/GDP Ratio	25.3	26.8	22.8	19.8	19.7	20.4	21.5	21.4	19.5
Size of Trade Sector (% of GDP)	17.0	17.2	17.2	17.6	18.7	19.3	19.4	20.3	20.2
Total Gov't Exp./GDP Ratio	34.7	35.4	37.7	39.6	39.8	39.5	39.0	39.0	38.5 [p]
General Government Budget Deficit (-) or Surplus (+) As a Percent of GDP	+1.0	+1.0	+0.6	-2.7	-4.0	-3.7	-4.0	-2.2	-1.7
Unemployment Rate	7.2	6.1	6.9	9.5	10.7	11.0	9.8	8.6	8.8 [a]

* The figures in this table are in percent form.

[a] October, 1996.

[p] Preliminary.

Australia's economic freedom rating has registered modest but steady increases during the last two decades. It ranking has also risen. In 1995 the Australian economy ranked 10th, compared to 24th in 1975 and 15th in 1985.

Several factors have contributed to the improvement in Australia's economic freedom rating. Tariffs have been reduced and other trade barriers relaxed. The size of the trade sector has expanded from 14% of GDP in 1975 to 20% in 1995 and 1996. During the last six years, the inflation rate has averaged 2.3%, and it has been relatively stable. While government consumption accounted for 21.9% of total consumption (government plus private) in 1995, even this figure has declined slightly during the last decade. The top marginal tax rate on personal income has been reduced modestly from the high levels of the 1975-1985 period.

The major weakness of this economy is its large and growing transfer sector. Total government expenditures rose from 30% of GDP in 1975 to 37% in 1995. The growth of transfer payments fully account for the growth of government during this period. In 1995, 15% of GDP was transferred from one citizen to another, up from 8.5% of GDP in 1975. Generally, the growth of transfers leads to large budget deficits, reductions in investment (as a share of GDP) and high rates of unemployment. All of these factors have plagued the Australian economy during the 1990s. Since 1990, the budget deficits of the central government have averaged 3% of GDP, the investment rate has declined, and the rate of unemployment has hovered around 10% of the labor force. Like several other high-income industrial nations, Australia must reduce the size of its income transfers and provide citizens with private sector options that will encourage saving and investment if it wants to achieve strong growth and continued prosperity in the future.

AUSTRIA

Economic Freedom Rating

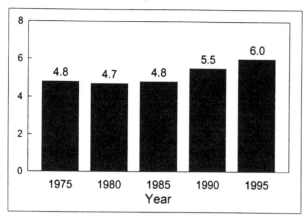

Total Government Expenditures As a Percent of GDP

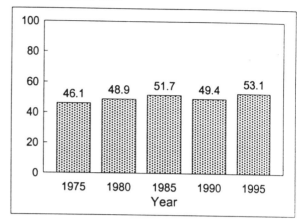

Part 1: The Economic Freedom Ratings for the Components and Various Area and Summary Indexes: 1975, 1980, 1985, 1990 and 1995.

(The numbers in parentheses indicate the actual values for the components.)

Components of Economic Freedom	1975		1980		1985		1990		1995	
I. Money and Inflation	**7.1**		**8.3**		**8.3**		**9.7**		**9.4**	
(a) Annual Money Growth (last 5 yrs.)	6	(12.1)	10	(4.5)	10	(4.4)	9	(4.9)	8	(7.0)
(b) Inflation Variablity (last 5 yrs.)	10	(1.1)	10	(0.6)	10	(1.3)	10	(0.9)	10	(0.7)
(c) Ownership of Foreign Currency	10		10		10		10		10	
(d) Maint. of Bank Account Abroad	0		0		0		10		10	
II. Government Operation	**3.2**		**3.3**		**3.7**		**4.1**		**5.6**	
(a) Gov't Consump. (% of Total Consump.)	3	(23.5)	2	(24.4)	2	(24.7)	2	(24.3)	2	(25.5)
(b) Government Enterprises	2		2		2		2		2	
(c) Price Controls	-		-		-		5		8	
(d) Entry Into Business	-		-		-		-		7.5	
(e) Legal System	-		-		-		-		7.5	
(f) Avoidance of Neg. Interest Rates	6		8		10		10		8	
III. Takings	**2.7**		**1.3**		**1.3**		**2.3**		**2.3**	
(a) Transfers and Subsidies (% of GDP)	2	(19.4)	1	(22.1)	1	(23.1)	1	(22.4)	1	(24.4)
(b) Marginal Tax Rates (Top Rate)	4	(54)	2	(62)	2	(62)	4	(50)	4	(50)
(c) Conscription	0		0		0		0		0	
IV. International Sector	**6.8**		**7.3**		**7.4**		**8.1**		**8.5**	
(a) Taxes on International Trade (Avg.)	8	(1.7)	9	(0.7)	9	(0.6)	9	(0.7)	9	(0.6)
(b) Black Market Exchange Rates (Prem.)	10	(0)	10	(0)	10	(0)	10	(0)	10	(0)
(c) Size of Trade Sector (% of GDP)	7	(31.5)	8	(37.8)	9	(40.6)	8	(39.6)	6	(36.1)
(d) Capital Transactions with Foreigners	2		2		2		5		8	
Economic Freedom Rating	**4.8**		**4.7**		**4.8**		**5.5**		**6.0**	
Ranking of Country	**28**		**29**		**32**		**31**		**41**	

Part 2: Recent Economic Indicators

Population 1996:	8.1	**Real Per Capita GDP :** [a]	1996 =	$18,509
(in millions)		(in 1995 U.S. dollars)		
Annual Rate of Change (1985-96):	1.2%	Avg. Growth Rate:	1980-90=	1.9%
			1990-96=	1.1%

Economic Indicators:*	1988	1989	1990	1991	1992	1993	1994	1995	1996 [p]
Change in Real GDP: Aggregate	4.1	3.8	4.2	2.8	2.0	0.4	3.0	1.8	0.8
: Per Capita	2.9	2.6	3.0	1.6	0.8	-0.8	1.8	0.6	0.5
Inflation Rate (CPI)	1.9	2.6	3.3	3.3	4.0	3.6	3.0	2.3	1.9
Change in Money Supply: (M1)	8.8	1.2	5.2	7.5	6.5	9.1	8.4	15.6	10.8
: (M2)	5.8	7.1	9.7	7.4	6.9	5.5	5.3	5.0	7.3
Investment/GDP Ratio	24.7	25.0	25.5	25.9	25.9	24.7	26.3	27.0	26.9
Size of Trade Sector (% of GDP)	37.2	39.3	39.6	39.6	38.9	36.7	37.1	36.1	36.8
Total Gov't Exp./GDP Ratio	50.9	49.7	49.4	50.5	51.1	53.8	52.4	53.1	52.8
General Government Budget Deficit (-) or Surplus (+) As a Percent of GDP	-3.0	-2.8	-2.2	-2.7	-1.9	-4.2	-4.4	-5.9	-3.7
Unemployment Rate [b]	3.6	3.1	3.2	3.5	3.6	4.2	3.7	3.8	4.1 [c]

* The figures in this table are in percent form.

[a] Derived by purchasing power parity method.

[b] These rates are the OECD standardized unemployment rates. They are comparable with the rates for other OECD countries. See *OECD Main Economic Indicators*, January, 1997, p. 24.

[c] October, 1996.

[p] Preliminary.

In 1995 Austria ranked 41st among the 115 countries in our study. While its *rating* improved slightly during the last decade, its *ranking* declined as other countries moved more rapidly toward liberalization.

A stable monetary policy, well established legal system, and relatively free trade policies are the strengths of this economy. In recent years, the inflation rate has fluctuated in a narrow range around 3%. The Austrian shilling is a strong, fully convertible currency and citizens are free to maintain foreign currency bank accounts both domestically and abroad. During the last decade, the top marginal tax rate was reduced from 62% to 50% and several restrictions limiting the mobility of capital were relaxed. There have also been modest moves toward deregulation. Limitations on hours worked during busy periods and the hours that businesses are allowed to remain open have been liberalized.

Despite these positive developments, the Austrian economy continues to be dominated by government. Government consumption accounts for 25% of the total and a huge transfer sector takes 25% of GDP away from the person that earned it and transfers it to others. Total government expenditures have grown and they now account for more than one-half of GDP. While there has been some privatization in the oil, energy and steel industries, Austria (unlike most other European countries) has made little progress toward privatization in the telecommunication sector. However, liberalization in telecommunications and energy was initiated in accordance with EU rules. During the last 4 years, the budget deficit has averaged more than 4% of GDP, a level that is unsustainable. A budgetary consolidation program to reduce the deficit below 3% in 1997 has been adopted. Nevertheless, Austria will be forced to make some difficult decisions concerning the size and functions of government in the near future.

BAHAMAS

Economic Freedom Rating

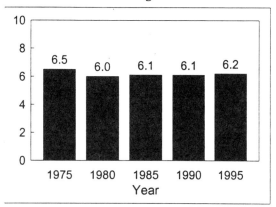

Total Government Expenditures As a Percent of GDP

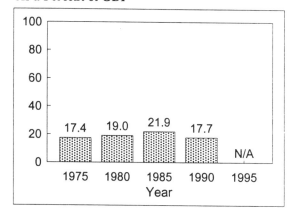

Part 1: The Economic Freedom Ratings for the Components and Various Area and Summary Indexes: 1975, 1980, 1985, 1990 and 1995.

(The numbers in parentheses indicate the actual values for the components.)

Components of Economic Freedom	1975		1980		1985		1990		1995	
I. Money and Inflation	**5.0**		**3.8**		**5.1**		**6.1**		**5.7**	
(a) Annual Money Growth (last 5 yrs.)	10	(-4.0)	6	(10.6)	9	(5.9)	9	(6.0)	10	(2.8)
(b) Inflation Variablity (last 5 yrs.)	6	(3.1)	6	(3.3)	7	(2.6)	10	(0.5)	8	(2.2)
(c) Ownership of Foreign Currency	0		0		0		0		0	
(d) Maint. of Bank Account Abroad	0		0		0		0		0	
II. Government Operation	**6.4**		**5.6**		**5.2**		**5.1**		**5.7**	
(a) Gov't Consump. (% of Total Consump.)	6	(17.6)	6	(16.9)	6	(16.5)	7	(15.6)	6	(16.5)
(b) Government Enterprises	6		4		2		2		6	
(c) Price Controls	-		-		-		4		4	
(d) Entry Into Business	-		-		-		-		5.0	
(e) Legal System	-		-		-		-		5.0	
(f) Avoidance of Neg. Interest Rates	8		8		10		10		10	
III. Takings	**10.0**		**10.0**		**10.0**		**10.0**		**9.6**	
(a) Transfers and Subsidies (% of GDP)	10	(0.5)	10	(0.5)	10	(0.1)	10	(1.0)	9	(1.6)
(b) Marginal Tax Rates (Top Rate)	10	(0)	10	(0)	10	(0)	10	(0)	10	(0)
(c) Conscription	10		10		10		10		10	
IV. International Sector	**3.2**		**3.0**		**2.9**		**2.3**		**3.1**	
(a) Taxes on International Trade (Avg.)	2	(8.8)	2	(8.1)	1	(9.3)	1	(9.6)	1	(10.3)
(b) Black Market Exchange Rates (Prem.)	4	(14)	4	(20)	4	(11)	4	(13)	7	(2)
(c) Size of Trade Sector (% of GDP)	6	(76.0)	5	(74.8)	6	(75.2)	2	(53.5)	2	(51.2)
(d) Capital Transactions with Foreigners	2		2		2		2		2	
Economic Freedom Rating	**6.5**		**6.0**		**6.1**		**6.1**		**6.2**	
Ranking of Country	**7**		**10**		**13**		**22**		**35**	

Part 2: Recent Economic Indicators:

Population 1996: 0.3   **Real Per Capita GDP** : 1993 = $16,222

  (in millions)   (in 1995 U.S. dollars)

Annual Rate of Change (1985-96):   2.0%   Avg. Growth Rate: 1980-90=   1.3%

                                                   1990-96=   -1.7%

Economic Indicators:*		1988	1989	1990	1991	1992	1993	1994	1995	1996
Change in Real GDP: Aggregate	a	2.0	2.9	-0.9	-3.5	0.2	1.9	2.1	2.1	2.3
: Per Capita	a	-0.1	1.1	-3.2	-4.9	-1.7	0.0	0.6	0.7	0.9
Inflation Rate (CPI)		4.4	5.4	4.7	7.1	5.7	2.7	1.4	2.0	1.3
Change in Money Supply: (M1)		7.0	0.4	9.8	8.3	2.8	2.0	10.6	7.1	6.0
: (M2)		8.0	8.7	14.6	7.8	5.6	16.0	8.8	8.8	3.8
Investment/GDP Ratio		20.9	24.1	22.0	20.5	20.9	21.0	-	-	-
Size of Trade Sector (% of GDP)		70.9	53.4	53.5	51.4	50.6	50.2	50.5	51.2	-
Total Gov't Exp./GDP Ratio		19.9	19.3	17.7	18.9	19.5	19.0	-	-	-
Central Government Budget Deficit (-) or Surplus (+) As a Percent of GDP		-2.9	-4.1	-2.4	-4.3	-2.9	-2.8	-	-	-
Unemployment Rate		-	-	-	12.3	14.8	13.1	13.0	-	-

* The figures in this table are in percent form.

a Since the Bahamas does not calculate a GDP deflator, the CPI was used to adjust the nominal GDP figures for inflation.

In 1995 the Bahamas ranked 35th among the 115 countries in our study. At first glance this economy appears to be quite free. Government expenditures and taxes are relatively low. There is no income tax. Direct income transfers and subsidies are small and most businesses are privately owned.

Probing beneath the surface, however, one discovers that this is a highly regulated, central-managed economy. The business sector is characterized by a complex and contradictory set of entry restraints, targeted tax breaks, and indirect subsidies. A bureaucratic licensing system restrains entry into many business activities and exerts political control over the economy. While foreigners are virtually excluded from the wholesale and retail business sector, they qualify for attractive tax breaks in other areas (export manufacturing and light industry, for example). When they meet certain criteria, new hotels are exempted from property taxes for up to ten years and granted other tax concessions for even longer periods of time. The government also uses both regulatory power and tax concessions to promote the offshore banking industry.

Regulations abound in other areas. A residency and work permit system controls and taxes foreign-

ers. Price controls are imposed on petroleum and food products. Domestic citizens are not allowed to maintain foreign currency bank accounts. Foreign exchange controls limit the movement of capital. Tariff rates vary widely among product categories, distorting relative prices and reducing the gains from international trade.

During the 1980s, the employment of state-operated enterprises expanded and the government became a major hotel owner and operator A reform government elected in August 1992 and re-elected in 1997 has privatized the largest part of these holdings.

Nevertheless, state enterprises and excessive regulations continue to exert a major impact on the economy. While the new government has speeded the investment approval process, regulations limiting the entry and development of business remain on the books. Residents dealing with the government telephone monopoly often confront lengthy waiting periods. The government-operated airline has 635 employees, while operating only 9 planes. Hopefully, a decade of economic stagnation is ending and this country will move toward deregulation and economic liberalism in the near future.

49

BAHRAIN

Economic Freedom Rating

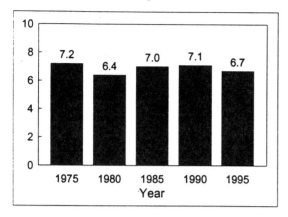

**Total Government Expenditures
As a Percent of GDP**

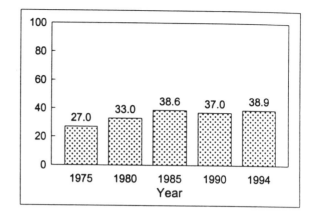

Part 1: The Economic Freedom Ratings for the Components and Various Area and Summary Indexes: 1975, 1980, 1985, 1990 and 1995.
(The numbers in parentheses indicate the actual values for the components.)

Components of Economic Freedom	1975		1980		1985		1990		1995	
I. Money and Inflation	**6.7**		**6.6**		**6.7**		**7.3**		**9.3**	
(a) Annual Money Growth (last 5 yrs.)	7	(9.3)	2	(18.1)	8	(7.7)	10	(-1.7)	10	(-0.5)
(b) Inflation Variablity (last 5 yrs.)	3	(7.2)	7	(2.6)	2	(8.2)	2	(8.2)	8	(2.5)
(c) Ownership of Foreign Currency	10		10		10		10		10	
(d) Maint. of Bank Account Abroad	10		10		10		10		10	
II. Government Operation	**1.0**		**1.5**		**1.0**		**3.3**		**3.0**	
(a) Gov't Consump. (% of Total Consump.)	-		1	(29.0)	0	(41.0)	0	(41.9)	0	(45.5)
(b) Government Enterprises	2		2		2		2		2	
(c) Price Controls	-		-		-		4		4	
(d) Entry Into Business	-		-		-		-		5.0	
(e) Legal System	-		-		-		-		0.0	
(f) Avoidance of Neg. Interest Rates	-		-		-		10		8	
III. Takings	**10.0**		**10.0**		**10.0**		**10.0**		**10.0**	
(a) Transfers and Subsidies (% of GDP)	-		-		10	(0.0)	10	(0.5)	10	(0.0)
(b) Marginal Tax Rates (Top Rate)	10	(0)	10	(0)	10	(0)	10	(0)	10	(0)
(c) Conscription	10		10		10		10		10	
IV. International Sector	**6.8**		**6.5**		**6.9**		**7.3**		**6.8**	
(a) Taxes on International Trade (Avg.)	-		-		9	(0.7)	9	(1.1)	9	(1.5)
(b) Black Market Exchange Rates (Prem.)	10	(0)	10	(0)	10	(0)	10	(0)	10	(0)
(c) Size of Trade Sector (% of GDP)	9	(120.6)	8	(117.7)	6	(95.8)	8	(110.8)	5	(95.5)
(d) Capital Transactions with Foreigners	2		2		2		2		2	
Economic Freedom Rating	**7.2**		**6.4**		**7.0**		**7.1**		**6.7**	
Ranking of Country	**2**		**8**		**4**		**5**		**18**	

Part 2: Recent Economic Indicators:

Population 1996:   0.6   **Real Per Capita GDP**   :   1994 = $14,926

   (in millions)   (in 1995 U.S. dollars)

Annual Rate of Change (1985-96):   3.7%   Avg. Growth Rate: 1980-90 =   -2.5%

                                                 1990-94 =   1.8%

Economic Indicators:*	1988	1989	1990	1991	1992	1993	1994	1995	1996
Change in Real GDP: Aggregate	9.0	2.4	4.6	4.6	7.8	8.3	2.3	-	-
: Per Capita	5.3	-1.3	0.9	0.9	4.1	4.6	-1.5	-	-
Inflation Rate (CPI)	0.3	1.5	0.9	0.8	-0.2	2.5	0.8	-	-
Change in Money Supply: (M1)	-1.0	-2.3	22.2	1.7	13.6	5.4	-3.9	-6.4	-
: (M2)	4.0	4.4	-11.6	20.5	4.1	5.5	6.2	6.9	-
Investment/GDP Ratio	26.5	26.5	25.1	27.7	29.8	31.2	30.0	-	-
Size of Trade Sector (% of GDP)	84.5	96.9	110.8	107.5	109.4	103.8	95.5	-	-
Total Gov't Exp./GDP Ratio	38.1	37.4	37.0	35.0	36.2	37.4	38.9	-	-
Central Government Budget Deficit (-) or Surplus (+) As a Percent of GDP	+3.8	-8.4	-6.8	-4.2	-6.9	-0.1	-3.2	-	-
Unemployment Rate									

* The figures in this table are in percent form.

Our index ranked Bahrain as the 18th freest economy in the world in 1995. Its ranking for the earlier years was even higher, but this was because data limitations prevented the inclusion prior to 1995 of the components on entry into business and legal structure—two areas where Bahrain earns poor marks.

Monetary stability (including the freedom to maintain foreign currency bank accounts), low taxes, a small transfer sector, and sound financial markets are the strengths of this economy. But focus on these features paints a very deceptive picture. Government dominates the spending and consumption of this economy. Total government expenditures sum to just under 40% of GDP—a figure similar to that of European welfare states. Even more revealing, 45% of the consumption expenditures are undertaken by the government. *This is the highest government consumption rate in the world.* These figures are not indicative of a free market economy directed by prices that coordinate the consumption choices of individuals. Rather they reflect that Bahrain is a big government welfare state financed with oil revenues. Given these factors, if anything, we believe that our index overstates its economic freedom.

51

BANGLADESH

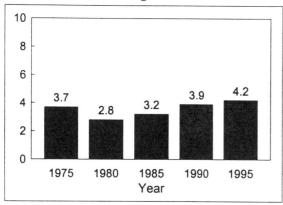

Economic Freedom Rating

Total Government Expenditures
As a Percent of GDP

No Data

Part 1: The Economic Freedom Ratings for the Components and Various Area and Summary Indexes: 1975, 1980, 1985, 1990 and 1995.
(The numbers in parentheses indicate the actual values for the components.)

Components of Economic Freedom	1975		1980		1985		1990		1995	
I. Money and Inflation	**2.1**		**0.9**		**3.0**		**5.4**		**4.2**	
(a) Annual Money Growth (last 5 yrs.)	6	(10.9)	2	(19.0)	2	(17.5)	9	(5.4)	6	(11.4)
(b) Inflation Variablity (last 5 yrs.)	1	(31.5)	1	(14.4)	7	(3.0)	8	(2.1)	7	(2.8)
(c) Ownership of Foreign Currency	0		0		0		0		0	
(d) Maint. of Bank Account Abroad	0		0		0		0		0	
II. Government Operation	**8.0**		**7.5**		**7.5**		**5.0**		**4.8**	
(a) Gov't Consump. (% of Total Consump.)	10	(3.5)	10	(6.5)	10	(7.5)	7	(14.4)	7	(15.0)
(b) Government Enterprises	6		6		6		6		6	
(c) Price Controls	-		-		-		0		0	
(d) Entry Into Business	-		-		-		-		5.0	
(e) Legal System	-		-		-		-		5.0	
(f) Avoidance of Neg. Interest Rates	-		6		6		10		8	
III. Takings	**10.0**		**3.0**		**3.0**		**10.0**		**10.0**	
(a) Transfers and Subsidies (% of GDP)	-		-		-		-		-	
(b) Marginal Tax Rates (Top Rate)	-		1	(60)	1	(60)	-		-	
(c) Conscription	10		10		10		10		10	
IV. International Sector	**1.4**		**0.4**		**0.4**		**0.7**		**1.6**	
(a) Taxes on International Trade (Avg.)	3	(7.9)	0	(13.4)	0	(17.9)	1	(12.1)	-	
(b) Black Market Exchange Rates (Prem.)	2	(51)	1	(111)	1	(168)	1	(165)	3	(28)
(c) Size of Trade Sector (% of GDP)	0	(5.5)	1	(12.0)	1	(12.9)	1	(13.5)	2	(18.3)
(d) Capital Transactions with Foreigners	0		0		0		0		0	
Economic Freedom Rating	**3.7**		**2.8**		**3.2**		**3.9**		**4.2**	
Ranking of Country	**63**		**94**		**84**		**77**		**84**	

Part 2: Recent Economic Indicators:

Population 1996: (in millions)	123.2	**Real Per Capita GDP** : (in 1995 U.S. dollars)	1995 = $2,295
Annual Rate of Change (1985-96):	1.9%	Avg. Growth Rate:	1980-90= 2.6%
			1990-95= 2.6%

Economic Indicators:*	1988	1989	1990	1991	1992	1993	1994	1995	1996
Change in Real GDP: Aggregate	2.9	2.5	6.6	3.4	4.2	4.5	4.2	4.4	-
: Per Capita	1.0	0.6	4.7	1.5	2.3	2.6	2.3	2.3	
Inflation Rate (CPI)	9.3	10.0	8.1	7.2	4.3	0.0	3.6	5.8	-
Change in Money Supply: (M1)	4.2	12.9	9.6	7.7	13.6	16.0	24.3	16.7	-
: (M2)	13.6	18.7	10.2	13.4	12.2	10.5	19.3	12.2	-
Investment/GDP Ratio	14.5	12.9	12.8	11.5	12.1	14.3	13.8	16.1	-
Size of Trade Sector (% of GDP)	12.4	12.9	13.5	12.6	13.3	14.8	15.0	18.3	-
Total Gov't Exp./GDP Ratio									
Central Government Budget Deficit (-) or Surplus (+) As a Percent of GDP									
Unemployment Rate									

* The figures in this table are in percent form.

In 1995, Bangladesh ranked 84th among the 115 countries of our study. Its economic freedom rating declined slightly between 1975 and 1980. Since 1980, it has increased marginally.

Even though government expenditures as a share of GDP are modest, this economy is characterized by excessive regulation and a weak institutional structure. Regulations prohibit citizens from maintaining foreign currency bank accounts, limit entry and increase the cost of doing business, and control the exchange rate market. Both investments abroad by citizens and foreign investment within the country are highly regulated. Price controls are imposed on many products.

Neither the legal nor monetary institutions reflect rule of law principles. Government officials have a great deal of discretionary authority to both provide favors and impose costs on citizens engaging in economic activities. Arrangements of this type stifle entrepreneurship and promote discriminatory treatment and corruption. While monetary growth has been modest in recent years, the institutional structure fails to provide the central bank with a clearly defined objective (for example, a low and stable rate of inflation). When the objectives are ambiguous, accountability is absent.

Given the low level of economic freedom and institutional weaknesses of this economy, the growth rate has been quite good during the last 15 years. If it is going to do better in the future, movement toward greater economic freedom is essential.

BARBADOS

Economic Freedom Rating

Total Government Expenditures As a Percent of GDP

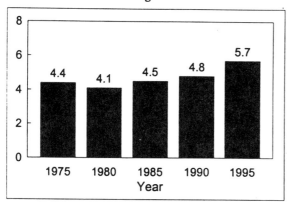

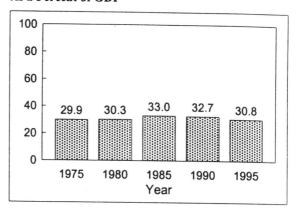

Part 1: The Economic Freedom Ratings for the Components and Various Area and Summary Indexes: 1975, 1980, 1985, 1990 and 1995.
(The numbers in parentheses indicate the actual values for the components.)

Components of Economic Freedom	1975		1980		1985		1990		1995	
I. Money and Inflation	**2.8**		**1.6**		**2.3**		**1.6**		**5.1**	
(a) Annual Money Growth (last 5 yrs.)	6	(10.6)	3	(16.4)	1	(21.3)	2	(18.5)	9	(-5.0)
(b) Inflation Variablity (last 5 yrs.)	3	(7.7)	2	(11.0)	6	(3.2)	3	(7.0)	7	(2.6)
(c) Ownership of Foreign Currency	0		0		0		0		0	
(d) Maint. of Bank Account Abroad	0		0		0		0		0	
II. Government Operation	**4.5**		**4.4**		**4.9**		**5.2**		**5.3**	
(a) Gov't Consump. (% of Total Consump.)	5	(18.3)	4	(21.6)	3	(23.4)	3	(22.7)	2	(24.2)
(b) Government Enterprises	4		4		4		4		4	
(c) Price Controls	-		-		-		6		6	
(d) Entry Into Business	-		-		-		-		5.0	
(e) Legal System	-		-		-		-		7.5	
(f) Avoidance of Neg. Interest Rates	-		6		10		10		10	
III. Takings	**5.8**		**5.8**		**5.8**		**7.2**		**7.7**	
(a) Transfers and Subsidies (% of GDP)	10	(0.2)	10	(0.2)	10	(0.0)	10	(0.5)	10	(0.0)
(b) Marginal Tax Rates (Top Rate)	1	(65)	1	(60)	1	(60)	4	(50)	5	(40)
(c) Conscription	10		10		10		10		10	
IV. International Sector	**3.7**		**3.7**		**4.0**		**3.9**		**4.3**	
(a) Taxes on International Trade (Avg.)	6	(4.4)	6	(3.7)	7	(3.4)	7	(3.6)	7	(3.3)
(b) Black Market Exchange Rates (Prem.)	4	(20)	4	(11)	4	(11)	4	(10)	6	(3)
(c) Size of Trade Sector (% of GDP)	2	(63.1)	2	(71.1)	2	(63.9)	1	(50.4)	0	(47.8)
(d) Capital Transactions with Foreigners	2		2		2		2		2	
Economy Freedom Rating	**4.4**		**4.1**		**4.5**		**4.8**		**5.7**	
Ranking of Country	**38**		**48**		**39**		**43**		**50**	

Part 2: Recent Economic Indicators:

Population 1996:	0.3	**Real Per Capita GDP** :	1994 =	$8,065
(in millions)		(in 1995 U.S. dollars)		
Annual Rate of Change (1985-96):	0.4%	Avg. Growth Rate:	1980-90=	0.5%
			1990-94=	-2.6%

Economic Indicators:*	1988	1989	1990	1991	1992	1993	1994	1995	1996
Change in Real GDP: Aggregate	3.5	3.6	-3.3	-4.0	-11.9	2.9	5.2	-	-
: Per Capita	3.1	3.2	-3.7	-4.4	-12.3	2.5	4.8	-	
Inflation Rate (CPI)	4.9	6.2	3.1	6.3	6.1	1.1	0.1	1.9	-
Change in Money Supply: (M1)	12.4	-12.5	14.6	-5.9	1.5	-5.1	8.3	-17.0	-
: (M2)	11.1	1.1	13.8	-1.1	5.0	2.9	8.9	4.9	-
Investment/GDP Ratio	17.5	17.9	18.8	17.1	9.5	12.7	13.3	-	
Size of Trade Sector (% of GDP)	48.6	51.6	50.4	48.8	46.2	49.2	47.8	-	-
Total Gov't Exp./GDP Ratio	31.2	33.2	32.7	-	-	33.4	30.8	-	-
Central Government Budget Deficit (-) or Surplus (+) As a Percent of GDP	-2.6	-0.9	-8.2	-2.4	-2.5	-2.6	-2.3	-	-
Unemployment Rate	17.4	16.5	15.0	17.3	23.0	24.3	21.7	19.7	-

* The figures in this table are in percent form.

Even though its economic freedom *rating* has improved slightly during the last decade, Barbados's *ranking* has actual fallen. In 1995 this economy ranked 50th, down from 39th in 1985 and 43rd in 1990.

The weaknesses of this economy are excessive regulation, a large government enterprise sector, and protectionist trade policies. Citizens are not allowed to maintain foreign currency bank accounts; price controls are imposed on several product lines; and a complex web of regulations,

tax breaks, and subsidies distort markets and reduce the mobility of capital. State-owned enterprises are present in several non-traditional areas, including housing, hotels, petroleum, and agricultural development. Exchange rate controls and other regulations reduce the size of the trade sector, which is exceedingly small (as a share of the economy) for a country of this size.

Government expenditures consume approximately 30% of GDP. This is a very high figure for a country with a negligible transfer sector.

BELGIUM

Economic Freedom Rating

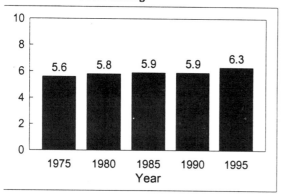

**Total Government Expenditures
As a Percent of GDP**

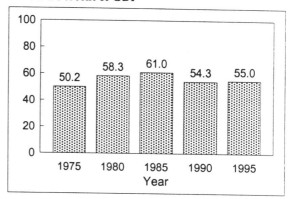

Part 1: The Economic Freedom Ratings for the Components and Various Area and Summary Indexes: 1975, 1980, 1985, 1990 and 1995.

(The numbers in parentheses indicate the actual values for the components.)

Components of Economic Freedom	1975		1980		1985		1990		1995	
I. Money and Inflation	**7.8**		**9.7**		**10.0**		**10.0**		**10.0**	
(a) Annual Money Growth (last 5 yrs.)	6	(11.0)	10	(4.5)	10	(3.5)	10	(3.3)	10	(3.8)
(b) Inflation Variablity (last 5 yrs.)	7	(3.0)	9	(1.6)	10	(0.8)	10	(1.0)	10	(0.6)
(c) Ownership of Foreign Currency	10		10		10		10		10	
(d) Maint. of Bank Account Abroad	10		10		10		10		10	
II. Government Operation	**5.2**		**6.1**		**6.1**		**5.1**		**6.8**	
(a) Gov't Consump. (% of Total Consump.)	4	(21.2)	4	(22.0)	4	(20.7)	5	(18.8)	5	(19.2)
(b) Government Enterprises	6		6		6		6		6	
(c) Price Controls	-		-		-		2		5	
(d) Entry Into Business	-		-		-		-		7.5	
(e) Legal System	-		-		-		-		10.0	
(f) Avoidance of Neg. Interest Rates	6		10		10		10		10	
III. Takings	**0.9**		**0.0**		**0.0**		**0.9**		**0.5**	
(a) Transfers and Subsidies (% of GDP)	0	(28.5)	0	(26.0)	0	(27.6)	0	(25.0)	0	(26.5)
(b) Marginal Tax Rates (Top Rate)	2	(64)	0	(76)	0	(76)	2	(55-65)	1	(58-68)
(c) Conscription	0		0		0		0		0	
IV. International Sector	**10.0**		**10.0**		**10.0**		**10.0**		**10.0**	
(a) Taxes on International Trade (Avg.)	10	(0.0)	10	(0.0)	10	(0.0)	10	(0.0)	10	(0.0)
(b) Black Market Exchange Rates (Prem.)	10	(0)	10	(0)	10	(0)	10	(0)	10	(0)
(c) Size of Trade Sector (% of GDP)	10	(53.5)	10	(64.2)	10	(75.6)	10	(72.5)	10	(70.2)
(d) Capital Transactions with Foreigners	10		10		10		10		10	
Economic Freedom Rating	**5.6**		**5.8**		**5.9**		**5.9**		**6.3**	
Ranking of Country	**15**		**16**		**18**		**24**		**29**	

Part 2: Recent Economic Indicators

Population 1996:	10.1		Real Per Capita GDP :		1996=	$19,765
(in millions)			(in 1995 U.S. dollars)			
Annual Rate of Change (1985-96):	0.2%		Avg. Growth Rate:		1980-90=	1.8%
					1990-96=	1.5%

Economic Indicators:*	1988	1989	1990	1991	1992	1993	1994	1995	1996
Change in Real GDP: Aggregate	4.9	3.5	3.2	2.2	1.8	-1.6	2.2	1.9	1.9
: Per Capita	4.7	3.3	3.0	2.0	1.6	-1.8	2.0	1.7	1.7
Inflation Rate (CPI)	1.2	3.1	3.5	3.2	2.4	2.8	2.4	1.5	2.4
Change in Money Supply: (M1)	5.5	5.4	0.8	1.3	-1.1	7.7	1.5	4.8	1.2
: (M2)	5.3	10.1	4.1	5.2	3.3	4.4	2.8	4.9	8.3
Investment/GDP Ratio	18.1	19.5	20.4	19.5	19.2	17.3	17.6	17.9	-
Size of Trade Sector (% of GDP	70.6	75.5	72.5	70.9	67.8	66.2	69.0	70.2	-
Total Gov't Exp./GDP Ratio	57.3	55.3	55.3	56.6	56.7	57.1	56.5	55.4	54.9 p
General Government Budget Deficit (-) or Surplus (+) As a Percent of GDP	-7.0	-6.4	-5.6	-6.5	-7.2	-7.5	-5.1	-4.1	-3.2
Unemployment Rate	9.7	8.0	7.2	7.2	7.7	8.9	10.0	9.9	9.6 a

* The figures in this table are in percent form.

a October, 1996.

p Preliminary.

While Belgium's summary rating of economic freedom has been relatively constant, its *ranking* has declined. In 1975, it ranked 15th, but it slipped to 24th in 1990 and 29th in 1995.

A stable monetary regime and free trade policies are the strengths of this economy. Monetary restraint, a low and stable rate of inflation, and the freedom of citizens to maintain foreign currency bank accounts has earned Belgium a "perfect ten" in the monetary area for the last three rating years. Similarly, low tariffs, a fully convertible currency, a large trade sector, and liberal policies with regard to the mobility of capital earned it a 10 in the international area during each of our five rating years.

Like so many other European countries, Belgium's downfall is a huge transfer sector, high level of government expenditures, and high taxes. Transfers and subsidies summed to 26.5% of GDP in 1995, a level exceeded only by Sweden, Netherlands, France, and Ireland. Total government expenditures consumed 55% of GDP, a figure that is actually slightly lower than that of the mid-1980s. Of course, large government expenditures generally lead to high taxes, large budget deficits, and high unemployment. Belgium is now experiencing all three. Its top marginal tax rate is one of the highest in the world. The top rate ranging between 58% and 68% takes effect at an income level equivalent to approximately 75,000 US dollars. In the 1990s, budget deficits have averaged 5.5% of GDP and the unemployment rate is now hovering around 10%. Belgium is a high income country—its real per capita GDP in 1996 was almost $20,000. Unless it is willing to reduce the size of government and move toward a freer economy, it is unlike to maintain its current relative economic position.

BELIZE

Economic Freedom Rating

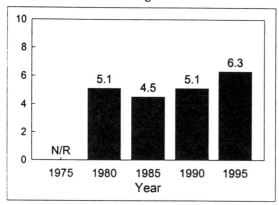

Total Government Expenditures
As a Percent of GDP

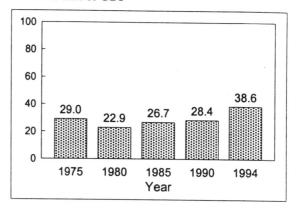

Part 1: The Economic Freedom Ratings for the Components and Various Area and Summary Indexes: 1975, 1980, 1985, 1990 and 1995.

(The numbers in parentheses indicate the actual values for the components.)

Components of Economic Freedom	1975		1980		1985		1990		1995	
I. Money and Inflation	**2.0**		**2.9**		**3.4**		**4.5**		**6.4**	
(a) Annual Money Growth (last 5 yrs.)	-		3	(16.2)	8	(7.0)	7	(8.1)	10	(1.0)
(b) Inflation Variablity (last 5 yrs.)	2	(8.3)	6	(3.6)	3	(6.5)	7	(2.8)	10	(1.2)
(c) Ownership of Foreign Currency	-		0		0		0		0	
(d) Maint. of Bank Account Abroad	-		0		0		0		0	
II. Government Operation	**7.0**		**6.8**		**5.7**		**5.0**		**7.1**	
(a) Gov't Consump. (% of Total Consump.)	6	(16.4)	5	(19.3)	2	(23.1)	5	(20.2)	5	(19.7)
(b) Government Enterprises	8		8		8		8		8	
(c) Price Controls	-		-		-		0		6	
(d) Entry Into Business	-		-		-		-		7.5	
(e) Legal System	-		-		-		-		7.5	
(f) Avoidance of Neg. Interest Rates	-		8		8		10		10	
III. Takings	**0.0**		**8.5**		**6.0**		**7.2**		**7.7**	
(a) Transfers and Subsidies (% of GDP)	-		8	(2.6)	7	(3.6)	10	(1.2)	10	(1.2)
(b) Marginal Tax Rates (Top Rate)	-		-		4	(50)	4	(45)	5	(45)
(c) Conscription	-		10		10		10		10	
IV. International Sector	**4.5**		**3.2**		**2.4**		**3.1**		**3.6**	
(a) Taxes on International Trade (Avg.)	-		2	(8.7)	1	(10.9)	1	(10.8)	1	(10.9)
(b) Black Market Exchange Rates (Prem.)	3	(32)	3	(34)	1	(63)	3	(25)	6	(3)
(c) Size of Trade Sector (% of GDP)	7	(80.8)	3	(62.0)	3	(54.9)	4	(63.7)	2	(53.6)
(d) Capital Transactions with Foreigners	-		5		5		5		5	
Economic Freedom Rating			**5.1**		**4.5**		**5.1**		**6.3**	
Ranking of Country			**25**		**39**		**37**		**29**	

58

Part 2: Recent Economic Indicators:

Population 1996:	0.2	**Real Per Capita GDP** :	1995= $5,993
(in millions)		(in 1995 U.S. dollars)	
Annual Rate of Change (1985-96):	2.8%	Avg. Growth Rate:	1980-90= 2.1%
			1990-95= 2.5%

Economic Indicators:*	1988	1989	1990	1991	1992	1993	1994	1995	1996
Change in Real GDP: Aggregate	9.2	13.1	10.7	3.0	7.7	4.2	2.2	3.7	-
: Per Capita	6.4	10.3	7.9	0.2	4.9	1.4	-0.6	0.9	
Inflation Rate (CPI)	5.3	-	3.0	2.3	2.3	1.4	2.6	2.9	-
Change in Money Supply: (M1)	-3.0	22.1	6.1	11.6	6.8	7.9	5.7	7.8	-
: (M2)	4.3	13.9	15.2	10.1	13.0	3.3	8.4	18.2	-
Investment/GDP Ratio	25.4	30.3	28.5	30.5	28.8	30.8	23.2	22.3	-
Size of Trade Sector (% of GDP)	64.9	64.4	63.7	63.7	64.1	62.1	55.7	53.6	-
Total Gov't Exp./GDP Ratio	23.8	27.9	28.4	32.3	33.4	35.7	38.6	-	
Central Government Budget Deficit (-) or Surplus (+) As a Percent of GDP	+7.1	-0.8	+0.7	-3.2	-3.4	-8.9	-10.6	-	-
Unemployment Rate	-	-	-	-	-	9.8	11.1	-	

* The figures in this table are in percent form.

Belize's economic freedom rating has improved since the mid-1980's. Our 1995 index ranks it 29th (out of 115), up from 39th in 1985.

The strengths of this economy are:

- A relatively stable monetary policy (note the low rate of monetary growth and the price stability of the 1990s);
- Few government enterprises;
- A small transfer sector; and
- The absence of conscription.

Its primary weaknesses are excessive regulation (note the legal restrictions on foreign currency bank accounts and limitations on the mobility of capital) and protectionist trade policies. The growth of government expenditures during the last decade is also a troublesome sign. As a share of GDP, government expenditures rose to 38% in 1994, up from 23% in 1980.

BOLIVIA

Economic Freedom Rating

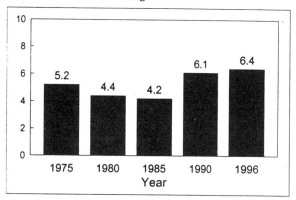

Total Government Expenditures
As a Percent of GDP

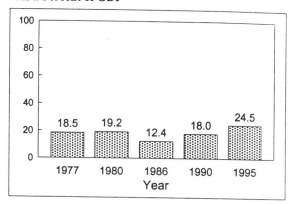

Part 1: The Economic Freedom Ratings for the Components and Various Area and Summary Indexes: 1975, 1980, 1985, 1990 and 1995.
(The numbers in parentheses indicate the actual values for the components.)

Components of Economic Freedom	1975		1980		1985		1990		1993-95	
I. Money and Inflation	4.3		4.6		0.0		3.9		4.3	
(a) Annual Money Growth (last 5 yrs.)	1	(26.3)	1	(25.2)	0	(570.0)	1	(37.3)	1	(28.5)
(b) Inflation Variablity (last 5 yrs.)	1	(21.0)	2	(11.0)	0	(4349.2)	0	(91.2)	1	(16.9)
(c) Ownership of Foreign Currency	10		10		0		10		10	
(d) Maint. of Bank Account Abroad	10		10		0		10		10	
II. Government Operation	5.5		5.2		4.3		6.0		5.9	
(a) Gov't Consump. (% of Total Consump.)	7	(15.1)	6	(17.4)	7	(14.6)	7	(15.5)	7	(15.5)
(b) Government Enterprises	4		4		4		4		4	
(c) Price Controls	-		-		-		6		8	
(d) Entry Into Business	-		-		-		-		7.5	
(e) Legal System	-		-		-		-		0.0	
(f) Avoidance of Neg. Interest Rates	-		6		0		8		8	
III. Takings	7.5		5.0		7.3		7.9		7.9	
(a) Transfers and Subsidies (% of GDP)	10	(1.3)	9	(1.6)	9	(1.8)	8	(2.8)	8	(2.5)
(b) Marginal Tax Rates (Top Rate)	-		3	(48)	8	(30)	10	(10)	10	(13)
(c) Conscription	0		0		0		0		0	
IV. International Sector	4.2		3.0		3.4		5.4		6.7	
(a) Taxes on International Trade (Avg.)	2	(8.9)	3	(7.8)	4	(7.0)	8	(2.3)	8	(2.1)
(b) Black Market Exchange Rates (Prem.)	6	(5)	4	(22)	5	(9)	6	(3)	8	(1)
(c) Size of Trade Sector (% of GDP)	8	(29.1)	3	(18.8)	2	(15.1)	5	(23.4)	5	(24.7)
(d) Capital Transactions with Foreigners	2		2		2		2		5	
Economic Freedom Rating	5.2		4.4		4.2		6.1		6.4	
Ranking of Country	20		40		55		22		25	

Part 2: Recent Economic Indicators

Population 1996:	8.8		**Real Per Capita GDP**	:	1996 =	$2,544
(in millions)			(in 1995 U.S. dollars)			
Annual Rate of Change (1985-96):	2.9%		Avg. Growth Rate:	1980-90=	-2.7%	
				1990-96=	1.2%	

Economic Indicators:*	1988	1989	1990	1991	1992	1993	1994	1995	1996
Change in Real GDP: Aggregate	3.0	2.8	4.1	5.3	1.6	4.7	5.0	3.7	4.0
: Per Capita	0.1	-0.1	1.2	2.4	-1.3	1.8	2.1	0.8	1.1
Inflation Rate (CPI)	16.0	15.2	17.1	21.4	12.1	8.5	7.9	10.2	13.1
Change in Money Supply: (M1)	35.3	2.4	39.5	45.1	32.9	30.0	29.3	21.2	20.6
: (M2)	28.6	22.2	52.8	50.5	34.5	33.7	24.2	7.7	-
Investment/GDP Ratio	14.0	13.0	12.5	15.6	16.7	17.6	16.5	19.5	-
Size of Trade Sector (% of GDP)	18.0	21.0	23.4	24.2	24.6	24.7	25.3	24.7	-
Total Gov't Exp/GDP Ratio	14.1	15.2	18.0	18.5	22.2	25.2	24.5	-	-
Central Government Budget Deficit (-) or Surplus (+) As a Percent of GDP	-0.6	-1.2	-1.5	-0.1	-1.8	-	-	-	-
Unemployment Rate	18.0	20.0	19.0	-	-	-	-	-	-

* The figures in this table are in percent form.

Bolivia's economic freedom rating fell during 1975-1985, but it has rebounded during the last decade. In 1995, Bolivia ranked 25th, up from 55th in 1985. Historically, the potential of this country has been stifled by monetary instability and hyperinflation. In 1985 Bolivia's inflation rate soared to over 13,000% (this means that prices increased by a factor of 130 in one year). Inflation rates of this magnitude undermine economic progress, pretty much regardless of the policies in other areas.

Seeking to rebound from this catastrophic situation, Bolivia has taken a number of constructive steps. The freedom to maintain foreign currency bank accounts which was denied during the inflation of the mid-1980s has been restored. The top marginal tax rate was reduced from 48% in 1980 to 10% in 1990 and 13% in 1995. Tariff rates were reduced sharply and most of the discriminatory treatment among product categories was eliminated. Relaxation of exchange rate controls has virtually eliminated the black market in this area. There has also been some liberalization of the restrictions on the movement of capital.

The potential of this economy continues to be limited by two major problems: monetary instability and a discriminatory legal structure. While recent monetary policy has been less expansionary than during the 1980s, the monetary authorities continue to expand the money supply too rapidly. Given its monetary history, more stable policies and/or changes in monetary institutions (for example, adoption of a currency board) are needed to supply credibility in this area. The legal structure as it relates to business activity is a maze of complex tax concessions, protected markets, government favors, and both direct and indirect subsidies. Pure and simple, it is a regulatory system that breeds corruption and stifles real entrepreneurship. Deregulation is badly needed in this area.

BOTSWANA

Economic Freedom Rating

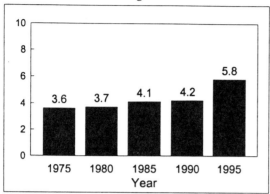

Total Government Expenditures As a Percent of GDP

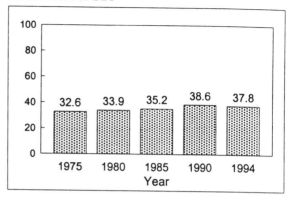

Part 1: The Economic Freedom Ratings for the Components and Various Area and Summary Indexes: 1975, 1980, 1985, 1990 and 1995.

(The numbers in parentheses the actual values for the components.)

Components of Economic Freedom	1975		1980		1985		1990		1995	
I. Money and Inflation	**1.4**		**2.5**		**1.6**		**1.3**		**6.6**	
(a) Annual Money Growth (last 5 yrs.)	-		6	(11.9)	3	(15.0)	2	(20.6)	10	(-2.9)
(b) Inflation Variablity (last 5 yrs.)	3	(7.7)	2	(8.8)	2	(8.8)	2	(8.7)	5	(3.9)
(c) Ownership of Foreign Currency	0		0		0		0		10	
(d) Maint. of Bank Account Abroad	0		0		0		0		0	
II. Government Operation	**5.6**		**4.5**		**4.9**		**4.1**		**5.4**	
(a) Gov't Consump. (% of Total Consump.)	3	(24.0)	1	(26.7)	0	(36.1)	0	(30.5)	0	(41.9)
(b) Government Enterprises	8		8		8		6		6	
(c) Price Controls	-		-		-		6		6	
(d) Entry Into Business	-		-		-		-		7.5	
(e) Legal System	-		-		-		-		7.5	
(f) Avoidance of Neg. Interest Rates	-		4		8		4		6	
III. Takings	**3.7**		**3.7**		**4.3**		**4.7**		**6.6**	
(a) Transfers and Subsidies (% of GDP)	6	(5.5)	6	(4.9)	5	(7.3)	5	(6.6)	5	(7.8)
(b) Marginal Tax Rates (Top Rate)	0	(75)	0	(75)	2	(60)	3	(50)	7	(35)
(c) Conscription	10		10		10		10		10	
IV. International Sector	**3.4**		**4.1**		**5.0**		**5.5**		**5.0**	
(a) Taxes on International Trade (Avg.)	1	(10.4)	0	(12.8)	3	(7.1)	4	(6.6)	1	(9.9)
(b) Black Market Exchange Rates (Prem.)	2	(44)	4	(10)	4	(22)	5	(7)	7	(2)
(c) Size of Trade Sector (% of GDP)	10	(54.6)	10	(58.2)	10	(57.5)	10	(59.1)	9	(51.7)
(d) Capital Transactions with Foreigners	-		5		5		5		5	
Economic Freedom Rating	**3.6**		**3.7**		**4.1**		**4.2**		**5.8**	
Ranking of Country	**67**		**65**		**60**		**69**		**48**	

62

Part 2: Recent Economic Indicators:

Population 1996:	1.5	**Real Per Capita GDP** :	1994= $4,840
(in millions)		(in 1995 U.S. dollars)	
Annual Rate of Change (1985-96):	3.0%	Avg. Growth Rate: 1980-90 =	6.1%
		1990-94 =	2.0%

Economic Indicators:*	1988	1989	1990	1991	1992	1993	1994	1995	1996
Change in Real GDP:Aggregate	15.3	13.1	5.7	8.8	6.5	-0.3	4.1	-	-
: Per Capita	12.3	10.1	2.7	5.8	3.5	-3.3	1.1	-	-
Inflation Rate (CPI)	8.4	11.6	11.4	11.8	16.2	14.3	10.5	10.5	-
Change in Money Supply: (M1)	30.2	24.6	15.7	4.7	-1.1	14.7	11.1	7.2	-
: (M2)	21.2	46.3	-14.0	41.6	13.3	2.3	15.0	9.4	-
Investment/GDP Ratio	7.3	32.0	31.8	31.7	31.5	30.0	-	-	-
Size of Trade Sector (%of GDP)	64.4	61.0	59.1	56.8	53.0	47.4	51.7	-	-
Total Gov't Exp./GDP Ratio									
Central Government Budget Deficit (+) or Surplus (+) As a Percent of GDP	+15.6	+9.6	+11.7	+10.0	-	-	-	-	-
Unemployment Rate									

* The figures in this table are in percent form.

This relatively small country is the freest among those on the African continent. Its 5.8 rating placed it 48th among the 115 economies of our study.

Botswana's economic freedom rating has increased significantly, particularly during the 1990s. During the 1990s monetary policy has been more stable, regulations prohibiting the maintenance of foreign currency bank accounts have been removed, and the top marginal tax rate has been reduced to 35% (down from 50% in 1990 and 75% in 1980).

The primary weaknesses of this economy are:

- A very high level of government consumption; only Bahrain had a higher rate of government consumption as a share of the total in 1995;
- High tariffs: the revenues from taxes on international trade summed to 10% of the total trade sector in 1995; and
- Excessive regulation (note the restrictions on foreign currency accounts abroad, presence of interest rate controls, and limitations on the mobility of capital.)

Botswana's per capita GDP grew rapidly during the 1980s but its growth rate has slowed considerably in the 1990s.

63

BRAZIL

Economic Freedom Rating

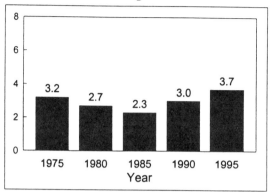

Total Government Expenditures
As a Percent of GDP

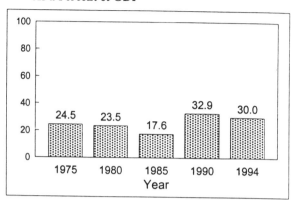

Part 1: The Economic Freedom Ratings for the Components and Various Area and Summary Indexes: 1975, 1980, 1985, 1990 and 1995.

(The numbers in parentheses indicate the actual values for the components.)

Components of Economic Freedom	1975		1980		1985		1990		1995	
I. Money and Inflation	1.3		0.6		0.0		0.0		0.0	
(a) Annual Money Growth (last 5 yrs.)	1	(28.9)	1	(41.6)	0	(137.8)	0	(647.7)	0	(1111.6)
(b) Inflation Variablity (last 5 yrs.)	3	(6.9)	1	(16.6)	0	(53.1)	0	(909.8)	0	(996.6)
(c) Ownership of Foreign Currency	0		0		0		0		0	
(d) Maint. of Bank Account Abroad	0		0		0		0		0	
II. Government Operation	6.0		6.4		3.9		1.9		4.3	
(a) Gov't Consump. (% of Total Consump.)	8	(13.8)	9	(11.7)	8	(13.1)	5	(20.1)	5	(19.7)
(b) Government Enterprises	4		4		2		2		4	
(c) Price Controls	-		-		-		0		6	
(d) Entry Into Business	-		-		-		-		7.5	
(e) Legal System	-		-		-		-		0.0	
(f) Avoidance of Neg. Interest Rates	-		-		0		0		0	
III. Takings	3.9		3.1		2.1		5.8		4.9	
(a) Transfers and Subsidies (% of GDP)	-		3	(12.4)	4	(10.0)	4	(10.7)	3	(14.9)
(b) Marginal Tax Rates (Top Rate)	5	(50)	4	(55)	1	(60)	9	(25)	8	(35)
(c) Conscription	0		0		0		0		0	
IV. International Sector	2.4		1.7		3.0		2.9		3.9	
(a) Taxes on International Trade (Avg.)	5	(5.7)	1	(10.0)	7	(3.2)	6	(3.7)	7	(2.6)
(b) Black Market Exchange Rates (Prcm.)	2	(49)	4	(18)	2	(49)	4	(10)	6	(3)
(c) Size of Trade Sector (% of GDP)	2	(9.5)	2	(10.2)	2	(9.7)	0	(6.3)	1	(7.3)
(d) Capital Transactions with Foreigners	0		0		0		0		0	
Economic Freedom Rating	3.2		2.7		2.3		3.0		3.7	
Ranking of Country	78		95		100		96		98	

64

Part 2: Recent Economic Indicators:

Population 1996:	168.4	**Real Per Capita GDP:**	1996=	$6,313
(in millions)		(in 1995 U.S. dollars)		
Annual Rate of Change (1985-96):	1.4%	Avg. Growth Rate:	1980-90=	-0.3%
			1990-96=	0.8%

Economic Indicators:*	1988	1989	1990	1991	1992	1993	1994	1995	1996
Change in Real GDP: Aggregate	-0.1	3.2	-4.6	0.3	-0.8	4.2	5.7	4.1	3.1
: Per Capita	-1.5	1.8	-6.0	-1.1	-2.2	2.8	4.3	2.7	1.7
Inflation Rate (CPI)	682.3	1287.0	2937.8	440.9	1008.7	2148.4	2668.5	84.4	18.2
Change in Money Supply: (M1)	426.9	1337.0	2333.6	429.4	981.8	2017.8	2098.7	31.2	25.4
: (M2)	1019.3	1462.7	1289.2	633.6	1606.6	2936.6	1146.4	38.9	66.3
Investment/GDP Ratio	22.7	28.6	22.9	19.3	19.5	20.0	20.8	21.6	16.9
Size of Trade Sector (%of GDP)	8.3	6.6	6.3	7.5	8.3	8.7	8.0	7.3	7.1
Total Gov't Exp./GDP Ratio	26.1	28.2	32.9	29.1	33.8	42.1	27.7	30.0	29.0
Central Government Budget Deficit (-) or Surplus (+) As a Percent of GDP	-15.2	-16.1	-5.7	-0.4	-3.6	-3.4	-1.1	-5.9	-3.9
Unemployment Rate	3.8	3.3	4.3	4.8	4.5	5.3	5.1	4.6	6.2

* The figures in this table are in percent form.

In 1995, Brazil ranked 98th among the 115 countries in our study. Its economic freedom rating and ranking have been low throughout the last two decades. The reason for Brazil's low rating is clear—its policies conflict with economic freedom in almost every area. Until very recently, its monetary policy was a disaster, characterized by excessive monetary growth and the consequent hyperinflation. Furthermore, it is illegal to maintain foreign currency bank accounts. Despite some recent privatization, government enterprises are still widespread throughout the economy. The legal system is often ambiguous and it grants a great deal of discretionary authority to government officials. The transfer sector is large, particularly for a country with a low per capita income level. Brazil's trade policies are highly protectionist—it has the smallest trade sector of any country in our study. Restrictions limiting the mobility of capital are also widespread.

In recent years, there have been some moves toward economic freedom. The top marginal tax rate has been cut. It is now 35%, down from 60% in 1985. Taxes on international trade have also been reduced (from 10.0% in 1980 to 2.6% in 1995). Finally, there is some reason for optimism that Brazil is now willing to break the vicious cycle of monetary expansion and hyperinflation. Restrictive monetary policy during 1995-1996 has reduced the inflation rate to single digits. Credibility is important. If Brazil is going to reap the full benefit of a more stable monetary policy, it would be helpful if the political authorities committed the government to a low and stable rate of inflation. For example, inflation rate targets that held the monetary authorities accountable might be adopted.

As might be expected from its pattern of economic freedom, Brazil's growth record has been dismal. Its real GDP per capita in 1996 was virtually unchanged from the level of 1980.

BULGARIA

Economic Freedom Rating

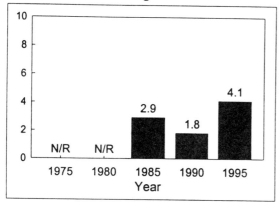

Total Government Expenditures As a Percent of GDP

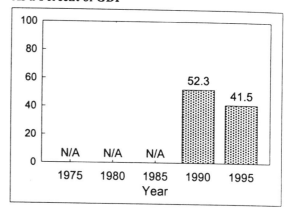

Part 1: The Economic Freedom Ratings for the Components and Various Area and Summary Indexes: 1975, 1980, 1985, 1990 and 1995.

(The numbers in parentheses indicate the actual values for the components.)

Components of Economic Freedom	1975		1980		1985		1990		1995	
I. Money and Inflation	0.0		0.0		3.4		2.2		3.6	
(a) Annual Money Growth (last 5 yrs.)	-		-		-		5	(13.1)	0	(67.0)
(b) Inflation Variablity (last 5 yrs.)	-		-		7	(2.5)	2	(11.3)	0	(83.9)
(c) Ownership of Foreign Currency	0		0		0		0		10	
(d) Maint. of Bank Account Abroad	0		0		0		0		10	
II. Government Operation	0.0		4.9		4.4		0.9		4.0	
(a) Gov't Consump. (% of Total Consump.)	-		10	(9.3)	9	(12.4)	3	(23.3)	5	(19.0)
(b) Government Enterprises	0		0		0		0		0	
(c) Price Controls	-		-		-		0		4	
(d) Entry Into Business	-		-		-		-		7.5	
(e) Legal System	-		-		-		-		5.0	
(f) Avoidance of Neg. Interest Rates	-		-		-		-		2	
III. Takings	0.0		0.0		1.5		0.0		2.6	
(a) Transfers and Subsidies (% of GDP)	-		-		2	(17.5)	0	(27.2)	3	(15.6)
(b) Marginal Tax Rates (Top Rate)	-		-		-		-		3	(50)
(c) Conscription	0		0		0		0		0	
IV. International Sector	0.5		1.4		2.8		3.4		6.3	
(a) Taxes on International Trade (Avg.)	-		-		6	(5.4)	9	(1.3)	8	(2.2)
(b) Black Market Exchange Rates (Prem.)	1	(175)	1	(175)	0	(435)	1	(100)	6	(5)
(c) Size of Trade Sector (% of GDP)	-		3	(33.2)	6	(43.0)	3	(34.9)	6	(52.2)
(d) Capital Transactions with Foreigners	0		0		0		0		5	
Economic Freedom Rating	--		--		2.9		1.8		4.1	
Ranking of Country	97		106		89		105		87	

66

Part 2: Recent Economic Indicators:

Population 1996:	8.4		**Real Per Capita GDP:**	1996=	$4,274
(in millions)			(in 1995 U.S. dollars)		
Annual Rate of Change (1985-96):	-0.7%		Avg. Growth Rate:	1980-90=	3.2%
				1990-96=	-4.3%

Economic Indicators:*	1988	1989	1990	1991	1992	1993	1994	1995	1996
Change in Real GDP: Aggregate	2.6	-1.9	-9.0	-9.1	-6.9	-5.7	1.8	2.6	-9.0
: Per Capita	2.5	-2.0	-8.3	-8.4	-6.2	-5.0	2.5	3.3	-8.3
Inflation Rate (CPI)	1.2	5.6	26.0	334.0	79.4	84.3	96.0	62.0	220.0
Change in Money Supply: (M1)	13.1	15.2	31.0	125.0	41.0	27.7	55.2	43.7	122.1
: (M2)	-	-	-	120.4	41.6	47.6	78.6	39.4	123.7
Investment/GDP Ratio	-	-	-	22.6	19.9	15.2	9.4	14.4	7.5
Size of Trade Sector (% of GDP)	45.8	47.3	34.9	45.5	48.6	52.2	-	-	-
Total Gov't Exp./GDP Ratio	-	52.3	55.1	40.1	40.6	44.8	45.2	41.5	-
Central Government Budget Deficit (-) or Surplus (+) As a Percent of GDP	-	-1.1	-8.3	-4.5	-4.9	-12.1	-4.7	-5.3	-8.9
Unemployment Rate	-	-	1.5	10.0	15.0	16.0	12.8	10.5	10.4

* The figures in this table are in percent form.

In 1995 Bulgaria ranked 87th (among the 115 countries rated), up from 105th in 1990. As in the case of most other former socialist economies, the development of a market economy in Bulgaria has been hampered by budget deficits, monetary instability, and the absence of appropriate economic institutions. Actually, liberal reforms got off to a fairly good start. In February 1991 most prices, including the exchange and interest rates, were freed as part of a "shock-therapy" inspired by the example of Poland. Political factors, however, slowed the institution of a sensible privatization program and resulted in the use of money creation as a means of financing a bloated government. This loss of momentum was followed by the return to power of the former communist party (re-named socialist) and some reversal of earlier liberaliza-

tion. Thus, the scope of economic liberalization in Bulgaria currently lags well behind that of other Eastern European former socialist countries.

Despite these disasters and the economic decline of recent years, there are some reasons for future optimism. The size of government expenditures as a share of GDP has been reduced. Citizens are now permitted to maintain foreign currency bank accounts. Furthermore, the Bulgarian government recently adopted a currency board, which is supposed to be established in 1997. This reform should tie the hands of politicians seeking to finance government programs with printing press money and thereby help bring inflation under control. In turn, political officials will be forced to adopt more sensible budget priorities and consider privatization alternatives more seriously.

CAMEROON

Economic Freedom Rating

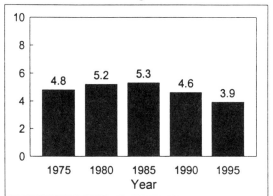

**Total Government Expenditures
As a Percent of GDP**

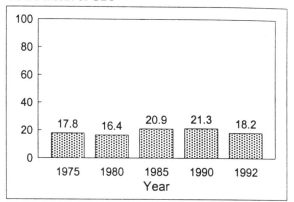

Part 1: The Economic Freedom Ratings for the Components and Various Area and Summary Indexes: 1975, 1980, 1985, 1990 and 1995.
(The numbers in parentheses indicate the actual values for the components.)

Components of Economic Freedom	1975	1980	1985	1990	1995
I. Money and Inflation	3.1	3.3	4.2	4.7	3.0
(a) Annual Money Growth (last 5 yrs.)	6 (12.3)	1 (22.2)	4 (14.8)	10 (0.3)	9 (-6.2)
(b) Inflation Variablity (last 5 yrs.)	4 (5.3)	9 (1.9)	9 (1.5)	5 (4.2)	1 (14.5)
(c) Ownership of Foreign Currency	0	0	0	0	0
(d) Maint. of Bank Account Abroad	0	0	0	0	0
II. Government Operation	6.0	6.3	6.0	4.8	3.8
(a) Gov't Consump. (% of Total Consump.)	8 (13.1)	9 (10.4)	8 (14.0)	7 (14.5)	7 (15.1)
(b) Government Enterprises	4	4	4	4	4
(c) Price Controls	-	-	-	2	2
(d) Entry Into Business	-	-	-	-	5.0
(e) Legal System	-	-	-	-	0.0
(f) Avoidance of Neg. Interest Rates	-	6	6	8	4
III. Takings	9.2	10.0	6.3	5.0	4.9
(a) Transfers and Subsidies (% of GDP)	9 (1.4)	10 (0.8)	10 (0.6)	8 (2.7)	9 (1.9)
(b) Marginal Tax Rates (Top Rate)	-	-	2 (60)	1 (60)	0 (66)
(c) Conscription	10	10	10	10	10
IV. International Sector	2.4	2.7	4.5	3.8	3.3
(a) Taxes on International Trade (Avg.)	0 (13.4)	1 (11.0)	5 (6.1)	6 (5.4)	3 (7.7)
(b) Black Market Exchange Rates (Prem.)	7 (2)	7 (2)	8 (1)	6 (4)	8 (1)
(c) Size of Trade Sector (% of GDP)	3 (24.1)	3 (25.7)	5 (28.8)	2 (20.8)	1 (20.1)
(d) Capital Transactions with Foreigners	0	0	0	0	0
Economic Freedom Rating	4.8	5.2	5.3	4.6	3.9
Ranking of Country	28	24	26	56	92

Part 2: Recent Economic Indicators:

Population 1996:	13.7	**Real Per Capita GDP** :	1995=	$1,098
(in millions)		(in 1995 U.S. dollars)		
Annual Rate of Change (1985-96):	2.7%	Avg. Growth Rate:	1980-90 =	-0.6%
			1990-95 =	-4.0%

Economic Indicators:*	1988	1989	1990	1991	1992	1993	1994	1995	1996
Change in Real GDP:Aggregate	-7.2	-6.0	2.1	-0.4	-4.4	1.0	-18.0	5.8	-
: Per Capita	-9.9	-8.7	-0.6	3.1	-7.1	-1.7	-20.7	3.1	-
Inflation Rate (CPI)	1.7	-1.7	1.1	0.1	-0.1	-3.2	35.1	13.9	-
Change in Money Supply: (M1)	0.4	7.2	-7.5	2.7	-27.9	-14.1	35.1	-11.6	-
: (M2)	2.0	6.1	-1.7	1.8	-21.9	-9.2	26.5	-6.2	-
Investment/GDP Ratio	27.7	27.2	29.0	-	-	-	-	-	-
Size of Trade Sector (% of GDP)	19.4	21.0	20.8	19.9	20.3	20.1	-	-	-
Total Gov't Exp./GDP Ratio	-	20.1	21.3	21.7	18.2	-	-	-	-
Central Government Budget Deficit (+) or Surplus (+) As a Percent of GDP	-	-3.2	-5.8	-5.2	-2.1	-	-	-	-
Unemployment Rate									

* The figures in this table are in percent form.

After increasing from 4.8 to 5.3 between 1975 and 1985, Cameroon's economic freedom rating plunged to 3.9 during the last decade. It ranked 92nd among the 115 countries of our study in 1995.

From the viewpoint of economic freedom, the major strengths of this economy are the absence of conscription and a largely convertible currency—the black market premium in the foreign exchange market has generally been small.

The major weaknesses are:
- The widespread presence of government enterprises;
- A weak, often discriminatory legal system;
- High marginal tax rates (the 66% top marginal rate was exceeded only by Italy in 1995);
- Restrictive trade practices (high tariffs and a small trade sector); and
- Restrictions on the mobility of capital (direct investments abroad must be approved by the Ministry of Finance).

As Cameroon has moved to a more restrictive economy, its growth rate has plunged. Real per capita GDP has fallen at an annual rate of 4% thus far in the 1990s.

CANADA

Economic Freedom Rating

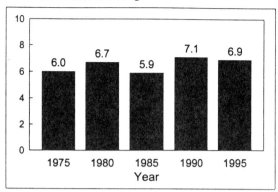

Total Government Expenditures
As a Percent of GDP

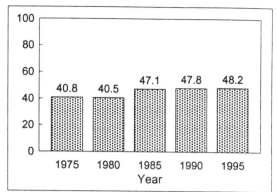

Part 1: The Economic Freedom Ratings for the Components and Various Area and Summary Indexes: 1975, 1980, 1985, 1990 and 1995.
(The numbers in parentheses indicate the actual values for the components.)

Components of Economic Freedom	1975		1980		1985		1990		1995	
I. Money and Inflation	7.1		9.4		6.9		9.7		9.7	
(a) Annual Money Growth (last 5 yrs.)	6	(10.4)	9	(5.4)	4	(14.2)	9	(5.5)	9	(4.7)
(b) Inflation Variablity (last 5 yrs.)	5	(4.0)	9	(1.9)	6	(3.2)	10	(1.0)	10	(0.6)
(c) Ownership of Foreign Currency	10		10		10		10		10	
(d) Maint. of Bank Account Abroad	10		10		10		10		10	
II. Government Operation	4.5		5.3		4.9		6.1		6.4	
(a) Gov't. Consump. (% of Total Consump.)	2	(25.6)	2	(25.8)	1	(26.0)	2	(25.6)	2	(24.5)
(b) Government Enterprises	6		6		6		6		6	
(c) Price Controls	-		-		-		8		7	
(d) Entry Into Business	-		-		-		-		7.5	
(e) Legal System	-		-		-		-		7.5	
(f) Avoidance of Neg. Interest Rates	6		10		10		10		10	
III. Takings	4.8		4.4		3.5		4.9		4.0	
(a) Transfers and Subsidies (% of GDP)	4	(9.1)	3	(14.5)	2	(16.3)	3	(15.6)	2	(17.7)
(b) Marginal Tax Rates (Top Rate)	4	(43-61)	4	(47-62)	3	(49-60)	5	(42-47)	4	(44-54)
(c) Conscription	10		10		10		10		10	
IV. International Sector	8.0		8.7		8.7		8.8		9.2	
(a) Taxes on International Trade (Avg.)	6	(3.7)	8	(2.4)	8	(1.7)	9	(1.2)	9	(0.7)
(b) Black Market Exchange Rates (Prem.)	10	(0)	10	(0)	10	(0)	10	(0)	10	(0)
(c) Size of Trade Sector (% of GDP)	8	(23.6)	9	(27.5)	9	(27.2)	8	(25.6)	10	(36.2)
(d) Capital Transactions with Foreigners	8		8		8		8		8	
Economic Freedom Rating	6.0		6.7		5.9		7.1		6.9	
Ranking of Country	12		5		18		5		14	

Part 2: Recent Economic Indicators:

Population 1996:	30.0		Real Per Capita GDP:	1996 =	$24,115
(in millions)			(in 1995 U.S. dollars)		
Annual Rate of Change (1985-96):	1.6%		Avg. Growth Rate:	1980-90 =	1.9%
				1990-96 =	-0.3%

Economic Indicators:*	1988	1989	1990	1991	1992	1993	1994	1995	1996
Change in Real GDP: Aggregate	4.9	2.4	-0.2	-1.8	0.8	2.2	4.1	2.3	1.6
: Per Capita	3.3	0.8	-1.8	-3.4	-0.8	0.6	2.5	0.7	0.0
Inflation Rate (CPI)	4.0	5.0	4.8	5.6	1.5	1.8	0.2	2.2	2.2
Change in Money Supply: (M1)	5.8	5.9	0.8	4.4	7.5	5.9	6.5	10.5	17.0
: (M2)	10.6	13.5	7.7	4.9	9.5	10.9	8.0	6.2	5.6
Investment/GDP Ratio	22.5	23.0	20.7	19.0	18.1	18.2	19.0	18.2	-
Size of Trade Sector (% of GDP)	26.3	25.6	25.6	25.2	27.0	29.6	33.3	36.2	-
Total Gov't Exp./GDP Ratio	44.2	44.8	47.8	51.1	52.1	52.2	48.9	48.2	47.3 P
General Government Budget Deficit (-) or Surplus (+) As a Percent of GDP	-2.5	-2.9	-4.1	-6.6	-7.4	-7.3	-5.3	-4.1	-2.7
Unemployment Rate	7.7	7.5	8.1	10.3	11.3	11.2	10.4	9.5	9.7 a

* The figures in this table are in percent form.

a December, 1996.

P Preliminary.

Canada's economic freedom rating has increased slightly during the last decade after experiencing a modest decline during 1975-1985. In 1995 its ranking was 14th, up from an 18th place finish in 1985 and a notch below its 12th place position in 1975.

Canada rates high marks in both the monetary and international areas. In recent years, the inflation rate has been low and relatively stable and Canadians are free to maintain bank accounts in other currencies. Tariff rates have declined and they are relatively low. The currency is fully convertible and the international trade sector is large for a country of this size.

Its major shortcomings are government consumption and the transfer sector. Expenditure levels in these areas are looking more and more like those of the European welfare states and less like the United States. Like France, Germany, and the United Kingdom, Canada channelled one-fourth of the total consumption expenditures through government in 1995. Income transfers and subsidies summed to 17.7% of GDP in 1995, nearly twice the level of 1975. Government expenditures increased to 48.2% of GDP in 1995, up from 40.5% in 1980. As a share of GDP, total government expenditures in Canada are now one-third higher (48% compared to 36%) than in the United States.

The growth of government expenditures generally leads to budget deficits, stagnating investment, and unemployment. The Canadian experience fits this general pattern. During the 1990s, budget deficits averaged more than 5% of GDP. The investment/ GDP ratio, which was persistently greater than 20% during the 1980s, has averaged only 18.5% during the last five years. The Canadian unemployment rate continues to hover around 10%, a rate that is currently more than 4% higher than that of the United States. Canada needs to shrink the size of its transfer sector, move toward a balanced budget, and deregulate its labor market. Effective action in these areas would promote both economic freedom and prosperity.

CHILE

Economic Freedom Rating

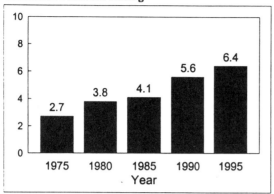

**Total Government Expenditures
As a Percent of GDP**

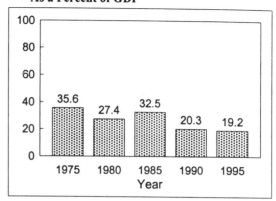

Part 1: The Economic Freedom Ratings for the Components and Various Area and Summary Indexes: 1975, 1980, 1985, 1990 and 1995.

(The numbers in parentheses indicate the actual values for the components.)

Components of Economic Freedom	1975		1980		1985		1990		1995	
I. Money and Inflation	**0.0**		**1.9**		**6.1**		**6.0**		**6.3**	
(a) Annual Money Growth (last 5 yrs.)	0	(213.3)	0	(95.6)	6	(10.6)	1	(25.2)	2	(19.9)
(b) Inflation Variablity (last 5 yrs.)	0	(234.0)	0	(80.6)	2	(9.6)	6	(3.2)	6	(3.6)
(c) Ownership of Foreign Currency	0		10		10		10		10	
(d) Maint. of Bank Account Abroad	0		0		10		10		10	
II. Government Operation	**4.5**		**6.0**		**6.4**		**7.4**		**8.8**	
(a) Gov't Consump. (% of Total Consump.)	5	(18.4)	7	(15.7)	6	(16.7)	8	(13.3)	9	(12.4)
(b) Government Enterprises	4		4		6		6		8	
(c) Price Controls	-		-		-		8		10	
(d) Entry Into Business	-		-		-		-		10.0	
(e) Legal System	-		-		-		-		5.0	
(f) Avoidance of Neg. Interest Rates	-		8		8		8		10	
III. Takings	**1.6**		**2.5**		**1.7**		**3.4**		**3.9**	
(a) Transfers and Subsidies (% of GDP)	4	(9.4)	4	(10.4)	3	(12.8)	5	(6.3)	5	(6.7)
(b) Marginal Tax Rates (Top Rate)	0	(80)	2	(60)	1	(57)	3	(50)	4	(45)
(c) Conscription	0		0		0		0		0	
IV. International Sector	**4.8**		**4.9**		**3.9**		**6.2**		**6.0**	
(a) Taxes on International Trade (Avg.)	6	(5.6)	7	(2.8)	5	(5.7)	6	(3.7)	7	(3.5)
(b) Black Market Exchange Rates (Prem.)	6	(5)	6	(6)	4	(22)	10	(0)	7	(2)
(c) Size of Trade Sector (% of GDP)	5	(26.4)	4	(24.9)	5	(26.9)	7	(32.7)	4	(28.3)
(d) Capital Transactions with Foreigners	2		2		2		2		5	
Economic Freedom Rating	**2.7**		**3.8**		**4.1**		**5.6**		**6.4**	
Ranking of Country	**87**		**57**		**60**		**28**		**25**	

Part 2: Recent Economic Indicators:

Population 1996:   14.4
  (in millions)
Annual Rate of Change (1985-96):   1.6%

Real Per Capita GDP: 1996= $8,316
(in 1995 U.S. dollars)
    Avg. Growth Rate: 1980-90=   2.0%
                          1990-96=   5.2%

Economic Indicators:*	1988	1989	1990	1991	1992	1993	1994	1995	1996
Change in Real GDP: Aggregate	7.3	9.9	3.3	7.3	11.0	6.3	4.2	8.5	7.0
: Per Capita	5.7	8.3	1.7	5.7	9.4	4.7	2.6	6.9	5.4
Inflation Rate (CPI)	14.7	17.0	26.0	21.8	15.4	12.7	11.4	8.2	6.6
Change in Money Supply: (M1)	46.5	17.2	23.3	44.7	26.3	21.2	16.2	22.2	21.5
: (M2)	27.1	31.2	23.5	28.1	23.3	23.4	11.3	25.8	-
Investment/GDP Ratio	22.8	25.5	26.3	24.5	26.8	28.8	26.8	27.4	-
Size of Trade Sector (% of GDP)	31.1	32.9	32.7	31.0	30.0	29.0	27.5	28.3	-
Total Gov't Exp./GDP Ratio [a]	24.0	20.4	20.3	21.1	20.3	20.8	20.5	19.2	21.0
Central Government Budget Deficit (-) or Surplus (+) As a Percent of GDP	+1.0	+1.4	+0.8	+1.5	+2.2	+1.9	+1.7	+2.5	+2.2
Unemployment Rate	8.1	5.3	5.6	5.3	4.4	4.5	5.9	4.7	6.6 [b]

* The figures in this table are in percent form.

[a] These data are from the Ministry of Public Finances Statistical Report, 1996, and Monthly Report, Central Bank of Chile, 1997. They exclude the expenditures of local governments, which were approximately 1.5% of GDP during this period.

[b] June, 1996.

During the last two decades, no economy has undergone more fundamental economic change and moved more persistently toward economic freedom than Chile. In 1975 this was one of the least free economies in the world, ranking 87th among the 96 countries that we were able to rate. By 1985 it had risen to 60th and it continued the climb to 25th in 1995. The figures on total government expenditures also reflect the dramatic change. In 1975, total government expenditures consumed 37% of GDP, but by 1985 this figure had fallen to 30% and by 1995 it was down to 20% of GDP.

The key elements of this economic transformation were a move toward monetary restraint, legalization of foreign currency bank accounts, a reduction of government consumption, privatization of state enterprises, social security reform, lower marginal tax rates, lower tariffs, and a more liberal exchange rate system. Perhaps the most important reform was that of social security. Under the Chilean plan, rather than pay into a social security system, individuals were allowed to channel their funds into private sector savings and investment funds. Most chose to do so, and this essentially led to the privatization of the government-operated system. Several other countries are now considering options similar to the Chilean plan.

Chile's economic record speaks for itself. It has become the first non-Asia country to achieve Asian-like growth rates. During the 1984-1996 period, the Chilean growth of real GDP has averaged 6.5%. More needs to be done. Chile needs to make its currency completely convertible and adopt a more stable monetary policy (Note the growth rate of the money supply continues to exceed 20%). If it follows this course, it will become one the ten freest countries in the world and will surely continue to experience growth and prosperity.

CHINA

Economic Freedom Rating

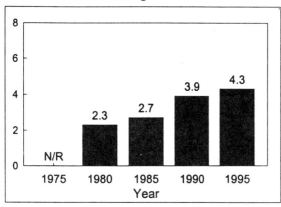

Total Government Expenditures
As a Percent of GDP

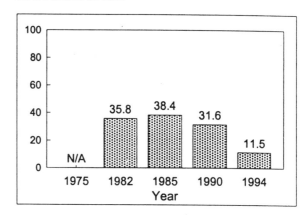

Part 1: The Economic Freedom Ratings for the Components and Various Area and Summary Indexes: 1975, 1980, 1985, 1990 and 1995.

(The numbers in parentheses indicate the actual values for the components.)

Components of Economic Freedom	1975		1980		1985		1990		1995	
I. Money and Inflation	0.0		4.0		2.6		5.8		3.8	
(a) Annual Money Growth (last 5 yrs.)	-		2	(20.0)	2	(20.3)	5	(13.8)	3	(16.2)
(b) Inflation Variablity (last 5 yrs.)	-		10	(1.1)	6	(3.2)	7	(2.7)	3	(7.4)
(c) Ownership of Foreign Currency	0		0		0		10		10	
(d) Maint. of Bank Account Abroad	0		0		0		0		0	
II. Government Operation	0.0		0.0		0.0		0.8		2.5	
(a) Gov't Consump. (% of Total Consump.)	-		-		-		-		3	(23.0)
(b) Government Enterprises	0		0		0		0		0	
(c) Price Controls	-		-		-		2		3	
(d) Entry Into Business	-		-		-		-		5.0	
(e) Legal System	-		-		-		-		0.0	
(f) Avoidance of Neg. Interest Rates	-		0		0		0		4	
III. Takings	0.0		0.0		4.7		3.9		4.7	
(a) Transfers and Subsidies (% of GDP)	-		-		-		-		-	
(b) Marginal Tax Rates (Top Rate)	-		-		6	(45)	5	(45)	6	(45)
(c) Conscription	0		0		0		0		0	
IV. International Sector	1.5		2.5		3.2		5.0		7.0	
(a) Taxes on International Trade (Avg.)	-		5	(5.7)	1	(10.0)	6	(3.7)	9	(1.2)
(b) Black Market Exchange Rates (Prem.)	3	(24)	3	(25)	4	(11)	1	(159)	5	(7)
(c) Size of Trade Sector (% of GDP)	-		1	(6.5)	8	(13.1)	10	(17.1)	10	(20.9)
(d) Capital Transactions with Foreigners	0		0		2		5		5	
Economic Freedom Rating			2.3		2.7		3.9		4.3	
Ranking of Country			99		95		77		81	

Part 2: Recent Economic Indicators:

Population 1996:	1234	**Real Per Capita GDP** :	1996=	$3,383
(in millions)		(in 1995 U.S. dollars)		
Annual Rate of Change (1985-96):	1.2%	Avg. Growth Rate:	1980-90=	7.3%
			1990-96=	8.9%

Economic Indicators:*	1988	1989	1990	1991	1992	1993	1994	1995	1996
Change in Real GDP: Aggregate	11.2	4.3	3.9	8.0	13.2	13.8	11.9	10.2	9.7
: Per Capita	10.0	3.1	2.7	6.8	12.0	12.6	10.7	9.0	8.7
Inflation Rate (CPI)	18.7	18.3	3.1	3.5	6.2	14.6	24.2	16.9	6.1
Change in Money Supply: (M1)	20.0	6.3	20.1	23.2	35.7	38.9	26.2	16.8	18.9
: (M2)	20.7	18.3	28.7	26.5	31.3	37.3	34.5	29.5	25.3
Investment/GDP Ratio	30.6	25.1	24.3	25.9	30.4	36.1	35.2	32.7	34.9
Size of Trade Sector (% of GDP)	17.3	16.5	17.1	18.3	19.8	17.9	22.5	20.9	18.6
Total Gov't Exp./GDP Ratio [a]	31.5	32.3	31.6	30.4	28.6	17.3	16.2	11.5	11.3
Central Government Budget Deficit (-) or Surplus (+) As a Percent of GDP	-0.6	-0.6	-0.8	-1.0	-1.0	-0.6	-1.3	-1.0	-1.0
Unemployment Rate	-	2.6	2.5	2.3	2.3	2.6	2.8	2.9	3.0

* The figures in this table are in percent form.

[a] Both budgetary and extra budgetary government expenditures are included in these figures (1988-1994). The extra budgetary accounts were abolished after 1994. The data for 1995 and 1996 are for the budgetary accounts.

Source: Money supply data are from the Peoples Bank of China, *Quarterly Statistical Bulletin*. The other data are from *China's Statistical Yearbook*.

Prior to the Communist Party Congress of 1978, the Chinese economy was operated and controlled by the government. Under the leadership of Deng Xiaoping, the Congress adopted several reforms designed to accelerate development and move the economy in a new direction. The reforms affected the agricultural sector, industrial enterprises, foreign trade management, taxation, banking and financial markets. The establishment of Special Economic Zones (SEZs) in several coastal areas increased the openness of the Chinese economy. With time, this experiment was extended to 14 coastal cities, then to other border cities and towns, and finally to major cities all over China. The preferential treatment and special policies granted to SEZs (for example, lower tax rates and customs, autonomy for local governments to approve foreign investments and to develop foreign trade activities) are now enjoyed by most Chinese cities.

The impact of economic reform and increased openness led to the emergence of, and increased reliance on, markets in China. Under the rural reforms adopted in 1979, the collective farms were dismantled and the arable land allocated to farmers under the "household contract responsibility system." In essense, the long-term leases accompanying this system provided farmers with a property right to land and the produce derived from it. Farmers were allowed to retain the excess output for sale in the free market after supplying the state with a fixed amount of production. The system provided farmers with a strong incentive to maximize output and to adjust the products supplied in response to changing demand conditions. As the result of these reforms, leasing of agricultural land for up to 20 years to local farmers, migrant labor from other provinces, or even investors from Hong Kong is now common in several regions.

(Continued on page 202.)

75

COLOMBIA

Economic Freedom Rating

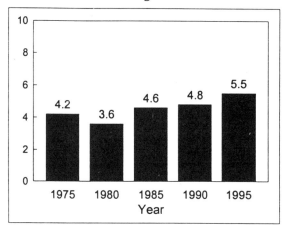

Total Government Expenditures
As A Percent of GDP

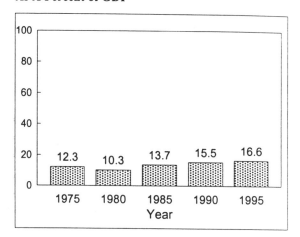

Part 1: The Economic Freedom Ratings for the Components and Various Area and Summary Indexes: 1975, 1980, 1985, 1990 and 1995.

(The numbers in parentheses indicate the actual values for the components.)

Components of Economic Freedom	1975		1980		1985		1990		1995	
I. Money and Inflation	**1.6**		**2.0**		**5.5**		**3.0**		**6.3**	
(a) Annual Money Growth (last 5 yrs.)	1	(20.9)	1	(28.9)	2	(20.4)	1	(28.9)	1	(26.2)
(b) Inflation Variablity (last 5 yrs.)	4	(5.7)	5	(4.2)	9	(1.7)	8	(2.2)	7	(2.5)
(c) Ownership of Foreign Currency	0		0		10		0		10	
(d) Maint. of Bank Account Abroad	0		0		0		0		10	
II. Government Operation	**7.5**		**6.4**		**6.0**		**6.3**		**4.6**	
(a) Gov't Consump. (% of Total Consump.)	9	(11.0)	9	(12.6)	8	(13.4)	8	(13.6)	1	(28.4)
(b) Government Enterprises	6		4		4		4		6	
(c) Price Controls	-		-		-		6		5	
(d) Entry Into Business	-		-		-		-		7.5	
(e) Legal System	-		-		-		-		0.0	
(f) Avoidance of Neg. Interest Rates	-		-		-		8		8	
III. Takings	**6.0**		**4.1**		**5.1**		**6.5**		**6.5**	
(a) Transfers and Subsidies (% of GDP)	8	(3.0)	8	(2.9)	7	(4.4)	7	(3.7)	7	(4.1)
(b) Marginal Tax Rates (Top Rate)	6	(41)	2	(56)	5	(49)	8	(30)	8	(30)
(c) Conscription	0		0		0		0		0	
IV. International Sector	**2.0**		**2.3**		**2.4**		**2.5**		**5.0**	
(a) Taxes on International Trade (Avg.)	3	(7.4)	3	(7.8)	3	(7.5)	3	(7.1)	6	(4.0)
(b) Black Market Exchange Rates (Prem.)	3	(29)	4	(16)	5	(9)	4	(17)	5	(7)
(c) Size of Trade Sector (% of GDP)	2	(14.9)	2	(15.9)	1	(13.2)	3	(17.7)	3	(18.4)
(d) Capital Transactions with Foreigners	0		0		0		0		5	
Economic Freedom Rating	**4.2**		**3.6**		**4.6**		**4.8**		**5.5**	
Ranking of Country	**44**		**68**		**37**		**43**		**58**	

Part 2: Recent Economic Indicators:

Population 1996:	35.7	**Real Per Capita GDP** :	1996=	$5,310
(in millions)		(in 1995 U.S. dollars)		
Annual Rate of Change (1985-96):	2.1%	Avg. Growth Rate:	1980-90=	1.2%
			1990-96=	2.0%

Economic Indicators:*	1988	1989	1990	1991	1992	1993	1994	1995	1996
Change in Real GDP: Aggregate	4.1	3.4	4.3	2.0	4.0	5.4	5.7	5.3	2.4
: Per Capita	2.0	1.3	2.2	-0.1	1.9	3.3	3.6	3.1	0.3
Inflation Rate (CPI)	28.1	25.8	29.1	30.4	27.0	22.6	23.8	21.0	20.0
Change in Money Supply: (M1)	25.7	-	-	31.7	44.3	27.7	27.4	23.1	16.5
: (M2)	21.6	-	-	20.8	45.0	37.5	34.6	21.7	14.6
Investment/GDP Ratio	22.0	20.0	18.5	16.0	17.2	21.2	21.1	21.1	-
Size of Trade Sector (% of GDP)	15.1	15.9	17.7	17.3	17.7	18.3	17.8	18.4	-
Total Gov't Exp./GDP Ratio	14.1	15.1	15.5	16.7	21.5	17.2	20.0	16.6	-
Central Government Budget Deficit (-) or Surplus (+) As a Percent of GDP	+0.3	-0.4	-0.1	+0.3	0.0	+0.3	+0.4	1.9	-
Unemployment Rate	-	8.9	10.2	9.8	10.3	8.7	8.9	8.9	11.7 [a]

* The figures in this table are in percent form.

[a] June, 1996.

While Colombia's rating has improved slightly, its ranking has actually declined because other countries have moved more rapidly toward liberalization. In 1995 it ranked 55th (among 115 countries), down from 37th in 1985 and 44th in 1975. It has ranked among the middle group of countries throughout the last decade.

Clearly the moves toward economic freedom have been modest. There has been some deregulation. Citizens are now permitted to maintain foreign currency bank accounts. Restrictions on the mobility of capital have been liberalized a little and there has been some privatization of state enterprises. But there is no comprehensive plan for economic liberalization. The government continues to regulate prices in several areas and impose exchange rate controls. Monetary growth continues at a rate that is far too expansionary for the achievement of price stability (a low and stable rate of inflation). Perhaps the major weakness of this economy is the absence of rule of law principles. Laws are often complex and ambiguous, which provides government officials with substantial discretionary authority. Not surprisingly, this authority is often exercised in a discriminatory manner and the process breeds corruption.

Among Latin American nations, Colombia has had one of the stronger rate of economic growth during the last 15 years. Deregulation of markets, reform of the legal structure, and adoption of policies (and institutions) consistent with monetary and price stability would greatly improve the performance of this economy and lay the foundation for solid growth and prosperity.

COSTA RICA

Economic Freedom Rating

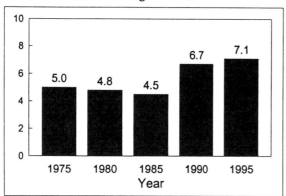

**Total Government Expenditures
As a Percent of GDP**

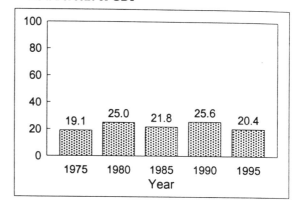

**Part 1: The Economic Freedom Ratings for the Components and Various Area and
Summary Indexes: 1975, 1980, 1985, 1990 and 1995.**

(The numbers in parentheses indicate the actual values for the components.)

Components of Economic Freedom	1975		1980		1985		1990		1995	
I. Money and Inflation	**4.6**		**5.9**		**4.3**		**7.2**		**6.5**	
(a) Annual Money Growth (last 5 yrs.)	1	(23.1)	2	(20.5)	1	(34.8)	5	(13.2)	5	(13.4)
(b) Inflation Variablity (last 5 yrs.)	2	(8.9)	5	(4.5)	1	(24.2)	6	(3.3)	4	(5.8)
(c) Ownership of Foreign Currency	10		10		10		10		10	
(d) Maint. of Bank Account Abroad	10		10		10		10		10	
II. Government Operation	**6.0**		**5.0**		**5.2**		**6.1**		**7.0**	
(a) Gov't Consump. (% of Total Consump.)	6	(17.5)	4	(21.8)	4	(20.8)	3	(22.8)	3	(22.2)
(b) Government Enterprises	6		6		6		8		8	
(c) Price Controls	-		-		-		6		6	
(d) Entry Into Business	-		-		-		-		10.0	
(e) Legal System	-		-		-		-		7.5	
(f) Avoidance of Neg. Interest Rates	-		-		6		8		8	
III. Takings	**6.1**		**5.7**		**4.7**		**7.9**		**7.5**	
(a) Transfers and Subsidies (% of GDP)	-		5	(6.0)	5	(7.2)	6	(5.0)	5	(7.0)
(b) Marginal Tax Rates (Top Rate)	5	(50)	5	(50)	3	(50)	9	(25)	9	(25)
(c) Conscription	10		10		10		10		10	
IV. International Sector	**3.9**		**2.9**		**3.8**		**5.8**		**7.3**	
(a) Taxes on International Trade (Avg.)	5	(5.9)	6	(5.3)	4	(6.9)	4	(7.0)	6	(4.6)
(b) Black Market Exchange Rates (Prem.)	5	(8)	1	(69)	3	(24)	10	(0)	10	(0)
(c) Size of Trade Sector (% of GDP)	3	(34.3)	2	(31.7)	3	(31.6)	3	(37.7)	4	(41.5)
(d) Capital Transactions with Foreigners	2		2		5		5		8	
Economic Freedom Rating	**5.0**		**4.8**		**4.5**		**6.7**		**7.1**	
Ranking of Country	**24**		**28**		**39**		**9**		**9**	

Part 2: Recent Economic Indicators:

Population 1996:   3.2   **Real Per Capita GDP:**   1995= $5,238
 (in millions)   (in 1985 U.S. dollars)
Annual Rate of Change (1985-96): 2.3%   Avg. Growth Rate: 1980-90= 0.2%
                                            1990-95= 2.2%

Economic Indicators:*	1988	1989	1990	1991	1992	1993	1994	1995	1996
Change in Real GDP: Aggregate	3.4	5.7	3.6	2.3	7.7	6.3	4.5	2.5	-
: Per Capita	1.1	4.4	1.3	0.0	5.4	4.0	2.2	0.2	-
Inflation Rate (CPI)	20.8	16.5	19.0	28.7	21.8	9.8	13.5	23.2	17.4
Change in Money Supply: (M1)	53.2	2.0	3.9	20.0	37.2	7.0	37.7	-6.0	-
: (M2)	40.2	16.4	27.5	33.7	24.5	15.2	22.0	4.8	-
Investment/GDP Ratio	24.5	26.5	27.4	25.2	29.3	29.9	26.8	25.5	-
Size of Trade Sector (% of GDP)	34.9	36.7	37.7	39.4	41.0	42.4	41.3	41.5	-
Total Gov't Exp./GDP Ratio	24.5	26.1	25.6	24.8	23.9	26.2	30.6	20.4	-
Central Government Budget Deficit (-) or Surplus (+) As a Percent of GDP	-	-2.1	-3.1	-1.3	+0.9	-0.2	-5.7	-5.1	-
Unemployment Rate	-	3.8	4.6	5.5	4.1	4.1	4.2	-	-

* The figures in this table are in percent form.

The experience of Costa Rica illustrates the importance of economic freedom as a source of progress. Between 1975 and 1985 Costa Rica's economic freedom rating declined and it fell to a 39th place ranking among the 107 countries rated in 1985. Between 1985 and 1990, its economic freedom rating rose substantially and it moved up to a 9th place ranking in both 1990 and 1995.

Several factors contributed to the jump in Costa Rica's rating. The top marginal tax rate was sliced from 50% to 25%. Various restraints on international trade were liberalized. The average tariff rate was cut from 6.9% in 1985 to 4.6% in 1995. Exchange rate controls were relaxed and eventually eliminated. Responding to trade liberalization, the size of the trade sector increased from 30% of GDP in the mid-1980s to more than 40% in the 1990s. Perhaps excessive monetary growth is the major current shortcoming of this economy. The annual rate of monetary growth during the 1985-1994 period averaged approximately 20%, a rate that is far too expansionary for the achievement of stable prices.

The increase in economic freedom has fueled economic growth. During the 1985-1995 period, the real GDP of Costa Rica expanded at an average annual rate of 4%, more than twice the rate of the 1975-1985 period. Costa Rica has now experienced 12 straight years of growth in real GDP. Continued movement toward economic freedom will keep this country on a solid growth path.

CZECH REPUBLIC (Data prior to 1993 are for former Czechoslovakia)

Economic Freedom Rating

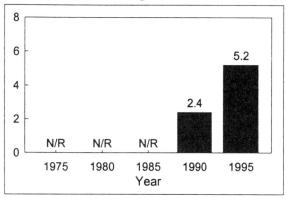

**Total Government Expenditures
As a Percent of GDP**

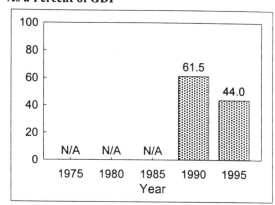

Part 1: The Economic Freedom Ratings for the Components and Various Area and Summary Indexes: 1975, 1980, 1985, 1990 and 1995.

(The numbers in parentheses indicate the actual values for the components.)

Components of Economic Freedom	1975	1980	1985	1990	1995
I. Money and Inflation	**0.0**	**0.0**	**5.7**	**4.7**	**4.6**
(a) Annual Money Growth (last 5 yrs.)	-	-	10 (3.0)	10 (0.4)	2 (20.0)
(b) Inflation Variablity (last 5 yrs.)	-	-	8 (2.2)	5 (4.0)	1 (13.9)
(c) Ownership of Foreign Currency	0	0	0	0	10
(d) Maint. of Bank Account Abroad	0	0	0	0	10
II. Government Operation	**0.5**	**0.5**	**0.5**	**0.3**	**5.5**
(a) Gov't Consump. (% of Total Consump.)	1 (26.6)	1 (27.3)	1 (30.1)	1 (29.9)	2 (25.9)
(b) Government Enterprises	0	0	0	0	4
(c) Price Controls	-	-	-	0	6
(d) Entry Into Business	-	-	-	-	10.0
(e) Legal System	-	-	-	-	5.0
(f) Avoidance of Neg. Interest Rates	-	-	-	-	6
III. Takings	**0.0**	**0.0**	**0.0**	**1.9**	**2.3**
(a) Transfers and Subsidies (% of GDP)	-	-	-	0 (37.2)	0 (28.4)
(b) Marginal Tax Rates (Top Rate)	-	-	-	4 (55)	5 (43)
(c) Conscription	0	0	0	0	0
IV. International Sector	**0.0**	**0.0**	**1.6**	**3.2**	**8.4**
(a) Taxes on International Trade (Avg.)	-	-	-	6 (4.0)	9 (1.1)
(b) Black Market Exchange Rates (Prem.)	0 (359)	0 (387)	0 (423)	2 (61)	10 (0)
(c) Size of Trade Sector (% of GDP)	-	-	7 (34.9)	5 (34.4)	10 (61.6)
(d) Capital Transactions with Foreigners	0	0	0	0	5
Economic Freedom Rating				2.4	5.2
Ranking of Country				101	62

Part 2: Recent Economic Indicators: [a]

Population 1996:   10.3   **Real Per Capita GDP:**   1996 = $9,930
  (in millions)   (in 1995 U.S. dollars)
Annual Rate of Change (1990-96):   0.0%   Avg. Growth Rate: 1990-96 =   -1.6%

Economic Indicators:*	1988	1989	1990	1991	1992	1993	1994	1995	1996
Change in Real GDP:Aggregate	2.3	0.7	-1.5	-14.0	-6.9	0.0	2.1	4.8	4.0
: Per Capita	2.3	0.7	-1.5	-14.0	-6.9	0.0	2.1	4.8	4.0
Inflation Rate (CPI)	0.1	1.4	10.0	57.7	10.8	20.8	10.1	9.1	9.0
Change in Money Supply: (M1)	6.1	4.7	0.2	4.2	25.7	24.0	50.3	6.7	-
: (M2)	6.7	6.3	3.8	10.7	27.6	22.5	20.4	29.3	-
Investment/GDP Ratio	13.5	12.9	15.7	13.3	-	18.4	20.4	28.0	-
Size of Trade Sector (% of GDP)	-	-	-	54.2	56.0	55.6	52.7	61.6	-
Total Gov't Exp./GDP Ratio	-	72.3	61.5	57.1	60.1	47.5	44.2	44.0	-
Central Government Budget Deficit (+) or Surplus (+) As a Percent of GDP	-	-2.4	+0.1	-2.0	-3.3	+0.0	+1.0	+0.6	0.0
Unemployment Rate	-	-	1.2	4.0	3.0	3.7	3.3	2.9	3.5

* The figures in this table are in percent form.

[a] All data prior to 1993 are for the former Czechoslovakia. The 1993-96 data are for the Czech Republic only. The Czech Republic comprised approximately two-thirds of the former Czechoslovakia.

Our index indicates that the Czech Republic has made significant moves toward economic freedom since the fall of communism and the Velvet Revolution of 1989. Its summary rating increased from 2.4 in 1990 to 5.2 in 1995. Similarly, its ranking rose from 101th in 1990 to 62nd in 1995. (Note: the 1990 figures are for the former Czechoslovakia.) Its 1995 rating was slightly higher than that of Greece and Hungary, for example.

The Czech Republic has made the transition to a market economy smoother than the other former socialist countries. Because it exercised greater monetary restraint prior to the decontrol of prices, it was spared the hyperinflation that beset most other transitional economies. Institutional change accounts for much of the improvement since 1990. Price controls have been eliminated from most products. Various types of privatization programs, including a voucher plan that privatized many large firms, have reduced the size and scope of state-operated enterprises. Exchange rate controls have been eliminated and the Czech koruna is now a fully convertible currency. As trade bar-

riers have fallen, the size of the trade sector has grown and it is now quite large for a country the size of the Czech Republic. Finally, government expenditures for both consumption and income transfers have been curtailed. In 1995 total government expenditures summed to 44% of GDP, down from 61.5% in 1990.

Problems remain. Monetary policy is too expansionary for the achievement of stable prices; therefore the inflation rate continues to hover around 10%. In the case of recently privatized assets, the legal system is often unable to protect the property rights of the new owners against the actions of holdover managers. Both employment and income taxes are high and compliance is low and difficult to enforce in an economy where most transactions are conducted with cash rather than checks. Nonetheless, the foundation for a market economy has been laid and the Czech Republic is now on a solid, sustainable growth path. If it continues to move toward economic freedom, its future will be bright.

81

DENMARK

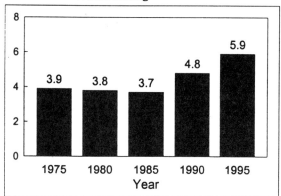

Total Government Expenditures As a Percent of GDP

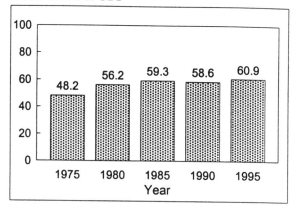

Part 1: The Economic Freedom Ratings for the Components and Various Area and Summary Indexes: 1975, 1980, 1985, 1990 and 1995.
(The numbers in parentheses indicate the actual values for the components.)

Components of Economic Freedom	1975		1980		1985		1990		1995	
I. Money and Inflation	**4.8**		**5.5**		**3.9**		**9.1**		**10.0**	
(a) Annual Money Growth (last 5 yrs.)	6	(12.2)	7	(8.8)	4	(14.7)	7	(8.6)	10	(1.8)
(b) Inflation Variablity (last 5 yrs.)	9	(2.1)	10	(0.8)	8	(2.4)	10	(0.8)	10	(0.3)
(c) Ownership of Foreign Currency	0		0		0		10		10	
(d) Maint. of Bank Account Abroad	0		0		0		10		10	
II. Government Operation	**3.3**		**3.7**		**3.7**		**4.4**		**6.9**	
(a) Gov't Consump. (% of Total Consump.)	0	(30.7)	0	(32.3)	0	(31.6)	0	(32.8)	0	(31.8)
(b) Government Enterprises	4		4		4		4		4	
(c) Price Controls	-		-		-		6		9	
(d) Entry Into Business	-		-		-		-		10.0	
(e) Legal System	-		-		-		-		10.0	
(f) Avoidance of Neg. Interest Rates	8		10		10		10		10	
III. Takings	**1.3**		**0.4**		**0.4**		**0.4**		**0.5**	
(a) Transfers and Subsidies (% of GDP)	2	(17.8)	1	(20.8)	1	(20.4)	1	(22.6)	0	(26.5)
(b) Marginal Tax Rates (Top Rate)	1	(63)	0	(66)	0	(73)	0	(68)	1	(63.5)
(c) Conscription	0		0		0		0		0	
IV. International Sector	**6.7**		**6.7**		**7.7**		**7.5**		**8.2**	
(a) Taxes on International Trade (Avg.)	9	(0.9)	10	(0.1)	10	(0.0)	10	(0.0)	10	(0.0)
(b) Black Market Exchange Rates (Prem.)	8	(1)	7	(2)	10	(0)	10	(0)	10	(0)
(c) Size of Trade Sector (% of GDP)	3	(30.6)	3	(33.3)	4	(36.5)	3	(32.8)	2	(32.4)
(d) Capital Transactions with Foreigners	5		5		5		5		8	
Economic Freedom Rating	**3.9**		**3.8**		**3.7**		**4.8**		**5.9**	
Ranking of Country	**55**		**57**		**73**		**43**		**42**	

Part 2: Recent Economic Indicators:

Population 1996:	5.3	**Real Per Capita GDP** :	1996=	$21,777
(in millions)		(in 1995 U.S. dollars)		
Annual Rate of Change (1985-96):	0.2%	Avg. Growth Rate:	1980-90=	2.0%
			1990-96=	1.8%

Economic Indicators:*	1988	1989	1990	1991	1992	1993	1994	1995	1996
Change in Real GDP: Aggregate	1.2	0.6	1.4	1.3	0.2	1.5	4.4	2.6	2.7
: Per Capita	1.0	0.4	1.2	1.1	0.0	1.3	4.2	2.4	2.5
Inflation Rate (CPI)	4.6	4.8	2.6	2.4	2.1	1.3	2.0	2.1	2.3
Change in Money Supply: (M1)	19.5	0.4	8.1	9.2	-0.9	10.5	-1.4	4.6	8.9
: (M2)	5.4	1.3	6.5	6.1	-0.7	19.7	-10	6.2	7.9
Investment/GDP Ratio	17.9	18.4	17.3	16.4	15.4	14.2	14.8	17.5	-
Size of Trade Sector (% of GDP)	31.0	32.8	32.8	34.1	33.2	30.8	32.0	32.4	-
Total Gov't Exp./GDP Ratio	59.4	59.6	58.6	59.2	61.1	63.7	63.6	60.9	61.6 ᵖ
General Government Budget Deficit (-) or Surplus (+) As a Percent of GDP	0.6	-0.5	-1.5	-2.1	-2.9	-3.9	-3.5	-1.6	-1.5
Unemployment Rate	8.6	9.3	9.6	10.5	11.4	10.1	8.2	7.1	5.6 ᵃ

* The figures in this table are in percent form.

ᵃ October, 1996

ᵖ Preliminary

Denmark's 5.9 rating in 1995 placed it 42nd among the 115 countries in our study.

Denmark's rating has improved during the last decade, primarily as the result of a freer and more stable monetary regime. During the last five years, monetary expansion has been low (less than 5%) and the inflation rate has been steady at an annual rate of approximately 2%. The former restrictions on the maintenance of foreign currency bank accounts have been abolished. Removal of prior restrictions limiting the mobility of capital have also contributed to Denmark's recent improvement.

The strengths of this economy are monetary stability and relatively free international exchange. (Note the high ratings in each of these areas.) Its major deficiencies are huge government consumption and transfer sectors and the high taxes required for their finance. Government now takes 60% of the Danish GDP, up from 48% in 1975. The current top marginal tax rate of 63.5% is one of the highest in the world. Even though the legal and economic institutions of this country are strong, economic freedom is limited when 60% of the income is channelled by the government, rather than by markets reflecting the personal choices of individuals.

83

DOMINICAN REPUBLIC

Economic Freedom Rating

Total Government Expenditures As a Percent of GDP

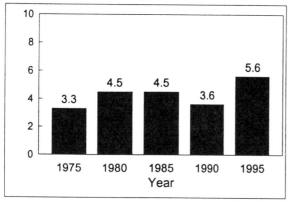

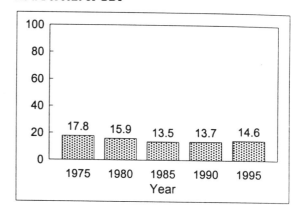

Part 1: The Economic Freedom Ratings for the Components and Various Area and Summary Indexes: 1975, 1980, 1985, 1990 and 1995.

(The numbers in parentheses indicate the actual values for the components.)

Components of Economic Freedom	1975		1980		1985		1990		1995	
I. Money and Inflation	**1.9**		**5.2**		**3.3**		**0.6**		**2.6**	
(a) Annual Money Growth (last 5 yrs.)	3	(16.6)	6	(10.6)	3	(17.4)	1	(38.2)	3	(17.3)
(b) Inflation Variablity (last 5 yrs.)	3	(6.8)	5	(4.7)	2	(13.1)	1	(16.7)	5	(4.1)
(c) Ownership of Foreign Currency	0		0		0		0		0	
(d) Maint. of Bank Account Abroad	0		10		10		0		0	
II. Government Operation	**8.0**		**8.0**		**8.0**		**5.6**		**5.9**	
(a) Gov't Consump. (% of Total Consump.)	10	(8.2)	10	(9.0)	10	(8.1)	10	(6.9)	10	(9.0)
(b) Government Enterprises	6		6		6		6		6	
(c) Price Controls	-		-		-		4		6	
(d) Entry Into Business	-		-		-		-		5.0	
(e) Legal System	-		-		-		-		0.0	
(f) Avoidance of Neg. Interest Rates	-		-		-		0		8	
III. Takings	**3.2**		**4.9**		**4.5**		**4.9**		**9.1**	
(a) Transfers and Subsidies (% of GDP)	8	(2.5)	9	(1.6)	8	(2.5)	9	(1.5)	9	(1.4)
(b) Marginal Tax Rates (Top Rate)	0	(73)	0	(73)	0	(73.1)	0	(73)	9	(25)
(c) Conscription	0		10		10		10		10	
IV. International Sector	**1.8**		**1.5**		**3.3**		**2.2**		**3.1**	
(a) Taxes on International Trade (Avg.)	0	(16.1)	1	(9.2)	4	(6.5)	3	(7.8)	1	(12.2)
(b) Black Market Exchange Rates (Prem.)	3	(28)	2	(37)	4	(14)	1	(66)	7	(2)
(c) Size of Trade Sector (% of GDP)	3	(28.0)	1	(24.1)	3	(28.5)	3	(31.2)	2	(27.8)
(d) Capital Transactions with Foreigners	2		2		2		2		2	
Economic Freedom Rating	**3.3**		**4.5**		**4.5**		**3.6**		**5.6**	
Ranking of Country	72		37		39		84		52	

84

Part 2: Recent Economic Indicators:

Population 1996:   8.1   **Real Per Capita GDP** :   1996= $3,460
  (in millions)   (in 1995 U.S. dollars)
Annual Rate of Change (1985-96): 2.1%   Avg. Growth Rate: 1980-90= -1.0%
    1990-96= 0.9%

Economic Indicators:*	1988	1989	1990	1991	1992	1993	1994	1995	1996
Change in Real GDP: Aggregate	1.6	4.1	-5.8	1.0	8.0	3.0	4.3	4.8	7.3
: Per Capita	-0.5	2.0	-7.7	-1.4	5.5	0.0	2.2	2.6	5.0
Inflation Rate (CPI)	48.4	34.6	79.9	7.9	5.2	2.8	14.3	4.2	4.0
Change in Money Supply: (M1)	51.3	25.9	40.5	27.4	26.0	16.6	-3.9	20.3	25.3
: (M2)	51.4	28.9	38.8	40.9	32.2	22.8	6.3	18.9	20.1
Investment/GDP Ratio	39.0	28.0	21.9	20.3	20.3	22.0	22.7	24.2	23.2
Size of Trade Sector (% of GDP)	34.4	33.7	31.2	26.9	26.1	25.3	25.8	27.8	-
Total Gov't Exp./GDP Ratio	18.9	16.6	13.7	12.6	14.2	16.4	17.5	14.6	14.9
Central Government Budget Deficit (-) or Surplus (+) As a Percent of GDP	-0.7	0.7	1.0	1.5	1.0	-0.6	-2.1	0.3	0.2
Unemployment Rate	19.1	18.9	21.0	19.6	20.3	19.9	16.0	15.8	16.7

* The figures in this table are in percent form.

After years of monetary instability, regulatory restrictions, discriminatory taxes and economic stagnation, the Dominican Republic has taken some modest steps toward economic freedom in the 1990s. The economic freedom rating of this country rose from 3.6 in 1990 to 5.6 in 1995. During the same period, its ranking jumped from 84th to 52nd.

The primary reasons for the improvement of the 1990s were:

- increased monetary and price stability (note the sharp reduction in the growth rate of the money supply between 1990 and 1995 and the accompanying lower and more stable rate of inflation);
- relaxation of both interest rate and exchange rate controls; and
- a reduction in tax rates—the top marginal rate was cut from 73% in 1990 to 25% in 1995.

Much more needs to be done. Regulatory restrictions limiting entry into business should be relaxed. Lower tariffs and liberalization of trade is badly needed. (Note that the size of the trade sector is much smaller than would be expected for a country of this size and location.) Citizens should be permitted to maintain foreign currency bank accounts and institutional changes designed to reinforce and add credibility to the recent moves toward monetary and price stability would also be helpful. The major weakness of this economy, however, is its highly discretionary and often ambiguous legal structure. Moves toward greater transparency and more clearly defined rule of law would do a great deal to promote both economic freedom and progress.

Perhaps the climate for such changes is improving. The modest moves toward economic freedom during the 1990s were accompanied by improved economic performance. In contrast with the economic decline of the 1980s, real GDP has grown at a robust 5.5% during the last five years.

ECUADOR

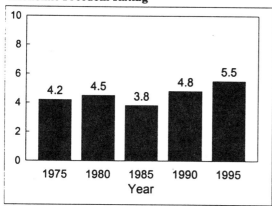

Economic Freedom Rating

Total Government Expenditures As a Percent of GDP

No Data

Part 1: The Economic Freedom Ratings for the Components and Various Area and Summary Indexes: 1975, 1980, 1985, 1990 and 1995.
(The numbers in parentheses indicate the actual values for the components.)

Components of Economic Freedom	1975		1980		1985		1990		1995	
I. Money and Inflation	**4.3**		**5.6**		**4.6**		**4.3**		**4.6**	
(a) Annual Money Growth (last 5 yrs.)	1	(24.8)	1	(23.5)	1	(23.0)	1	(40.0)	1	(34.5)
(b) Inflation Variablity (last 5 yrs.)	1	(14.6)	5	(4.3)	2	(10.2)	1	(16.7)	2	(10.6)
(c) Ownership of Foreign Currency	10		10		10		10		10	
(d) Maint. of Bank Account Abroad	10		10		10		10		10	
II. Government Operation	**5.5**		**5.5**		**4.3**		**3.5**		**4.4**	
(a) Gov't Consump. (% of Total Consump.)	5	(18.2)	5	(19.6)	7	(15.1)	9	(11.2)	7	(15.9)
(b) Government Enterprises	6		6		4		4		4	
(c) Price Controls	-		-		-		0		0	
(d) Entry Into Business	-		-		-		-		7.5	
(e) Legal System	-		-		-		-		2.5	
(f) Avoidance of Neg. Interest Rates	-		-		0		0		6	
III. Takings	**3.9**		**4.7**		**3.7**		**5.5**		**7.8**	
(a) Transfers and Subsidies (% of GDP)	-		6	(4.9)	7	(4.0)	8	(2.3)	9	(1.5)
(b) Marginal Tax Rates (Top Rate)	5	(50)	5	(50)	2	(58)	5	(40)	9	(25)
(c) Conscription	0		0		0		0		0	
IV. International Sector	**3.6**		**3.0**		**3.1**		**3.0**		**5.0**	
(a) Taxes on International Trade (Avg.)	2	(8.9)	3	(7.2)	5	(6.2)	6	(4.0)	7	(3.5)
(b) Black Market Exchange Rates (Prem.)	6	(5)	4	(13)	2	(48)	0	(10)	4	(12)
(c) Size of Trade Sector (% of GDP)	5	(29.5)	3	(25.3)	3	(23.8)	4	(30.1)	3	(27.8)
(d) Capital Transactions with Foreigners	2		2		2		2		5	
Economic Freedom Rating	**4.2**		**4.5**		**3.8**		**4.8**		**5.5**	
Ranking of Country	**44**		**37**		**69**		**43**		**55**	

Part 2: Recent Economic Indicators:

Population 1996: (in millions)	11.7	**Real Per Capita GDP** : (in 1995 U.S. dollars)	1995= $4,055
Annual Rate of Change (1985-96):	2.3%	Avg. Growth Rate:	1980-90= -0.3% 1990-95= 1.1%

Economic Indicators:*	1988	1989	1990	1991	1992	1993	1994	1995	1996
Change in Real GDP: Aggregate	10.5	0.3	3.0	5.0	3.6	2.0	4.4	2.3	-
: Per Capita	8.2	-2.0	0.7	2.7	1.3	-0.3	2.1	0.0	-
Inflation Rate (CPI)	58.2	75.6	48.5	48.7	54.6	45.0	27.3	22.9	22.8
Change in Money Supply: (M1)	52.7	43.8	59.0	46.7	48.4	63.7	32.5	2.7	-
: (M2)	56.4	38.0	52.6	54.1	52.2	63.0	51.6	36.7	-
Investment/GDP Ratio	20.7	17.5	22.2	21.2	20.2	18.9	18.6	20.9	-
Size of Trade Sector (% of GDP)	29.5	30.3	30.1	30.6	29.6	25.9	25.2	27.8	-
Total Gov't Exp./GDP Ratio									
Central Government Budget Deficit (-) or Surplus (+) As a Percent of GDP	-	+1.9	+1.8	+1.5	+2.3	+2.6	+0.3	-1.2	-
Unemployment Rate	-	-	6.1	8.5	8.9	8.3	7.1	-	-

* The figures in this table are in percent form.

In 1995 Ecuador ranked 55th among the 115 countries of our study. It has persistently ranked in the middle group during each of our rating years.

On the positive side, government consumption and income transfers are both relatively low. Taxes are also low and the current top marginal tax rate (25%) is substantially lower than the 58% rate of the mid-1980s. Citizens are permitted to maintain foreign currency bank accounts which provides them with some measure of protection against the inflation policies that have historically beset this economy.

Excessive regulation and a weak institutional structure are the major weaknesses of this econ-

omy. Regulations control both exchange rates and interest rates, restrict the mobility of capital, and often limit entry and increase the cost of doing business. The central bank is controlled by the politicians and the monetary institutions do little to breed confidence that price stability is an important goal. The legal institutions are also highly politicized and provide government officials with discretionary authority, which inevitably leads to both discrimination and corruption.

This economy has stagnated for two decades. Perhaps the poor performance will soon create an environment that will facilitate needed institutional reforms and movement toward economic freedom.

EGYPT

Economic Freedom Rating

**Total Government Expenditures
As a Percent of GDP**

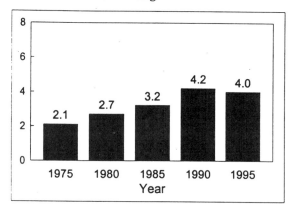

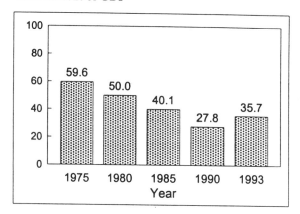

Part 1: The Economic Freedom Ratings for the Components and Various Area and Summary Indexes: 1975, 1980, 1985, 1990 and 1995.

(The numbers in parentheses indicate the actual values for the components.)

Components of Economic Freedom	1975	1980	1985	1990	1995
I. Money and Inflation	**2.9**	**5.6**	**6.6**	**8.5**	**7.4**
(a) Annual Money Growth (last 5 yrs.)	3 (16.8)	1 (28.9)	3 (16.1)	6 (10.8)	8 (7.0)
(b) Inflation Variablity (last 5 yrs.)	6 (3.5)	5 (4.4)	6 (3.4)	9 (1.6)	4 (5.7)
(c) Ownership of Foreign Currency	0	10	10	10	10
(d) Maint. of Bank Account Abroad	0	10	10	10	10
II. Government Operation	**0.5**	**2.8**	**3.2**	**3.9**	**3.3**
(a) Gov't Consump. (% of Total Consump.)	1 (28.4)	5 (18.5)	5 (20.2)	9 (12.3)	8 (12.6)
(b) Government Enterprises	0	0	0	0	0
(c) Price Controls	-	-	-	2	2
(d) Entry Into Business	-	-	-	-	2.5
(e) Legal System	-	-	-	-	0.0
(f) Avoidance of Neg. Interest Rates	-	4	6	6	10
III. Takings	**0.0**	**0.8**	**2.1**	**2.5**	**3.0**
(a) Transfers and Subsidies (% of GDP)	0 (25.0)	2 (17.2)	3 (13.9)	4 (8.9)	4 (8.9)
(b) Marginal Tax Rates (Top Rate)	-	0 (80)	2 (65)	2 (65)	3 (50)
(c) Conscription	0	0	0	0	0
IV. International Sector	**3.8**	**3.0**	**2.1**	**3.7**	**4.0**
(a) Taxes on International Trade (Avg.)	0 (16.7)	0 (13.1)	1 (12.1)	5 (5.9)	5 (6.1)
(b) Black Market Exchange Rates (Prem.)	8 (1)	5 (9)	1 (146)	2 (56)	6 (3)
(c) Size of Trade Sector (% of GDP)	10 (30.7)	10 (36.7)	9 (26.0)	10 (32.5)	5 (23.1)
(d) Capital Transactions with Foreigners	0	0	0	0	0
Economic Freedom Rating	**2.1**	**2.7**	**3.2**	**4.2**	**4.0**
Ranking of Country	**93**	**95**	**84**	**69**	**91**

Part 2: Recent Economic Indicators:

Population 1996:	60.1	**Real Per Capita GDP :**	1995=	$2,654
(in millions)		(in 1995 U.S. dollars)		
Annual Rate of Change (1985-96):	2.5%	Avg. Growth Rate:	1980-90=	2.6%
			1990-95=	1.3%

Economic Indicators:*	1988	1989	1990	1991	1992	1993	1994	1995	1996
Change in Real GDP: Aggregate	5.4	5.0	5.7	1.1	4.4	2.9	3.9	4.6	-
: Per Capita	2.9	2.5	3.2	-1.4	1.9	0.4	1.4	2.1	-
Inflation Rate (CPI)	17.7	21.3	16.8	19.7	13.6	12.1	8.2	8.3	-
Change in Money Supply: (M1)	12.8	9.2	16.6	8.1	8.8	12.1	10.7	8.5	-
: (M2)	21.5	17.5	28.7	19.3	19.4	13.2	11.2	9.9	-
Investment/GDP Ratio	33.2	31.3	29.4	24.0	19.8	19.7	20.3	19.2	-
Size of Trade Sector (% of GDP)	31.7	30.1	32.5	37.1	32.6	30.6	25.5	23.1	-
Total Gov't Exp./GDP Ratio	36.6	31.1	27.8	31.9	39.3	35.7	-	-	-
Central Government Budget Deficit (-) or Surplus (+) As a Percent of GDP	-7.7	-5.4	-5.7	-1.0	-3.5	-	-	-	-
Unemployment Rate	-	6.9	8.6	9.6	9.0	-	-	-	-

* The figures in this table are in percent form.

Source: United Nations, Statistical Yearbook, 1992 (New York 1994).

Only three countries (Uganda, Israel, and Russia) had lower economic freedom ratings than Egypt in 1975. Between 1975 and 1990, Egypt's economic freedom rating rose slowly from 2.1 to 4.2, prior to receding to 4.0 in 1995. Egypt's 1995 rating places it 91st (out of 115), down from a ranking of 68th in 1990. Interestingly, the changes in government expenditures are highly consistent with the changes in the economic freedom. As a share of GDP, total government expenditures declined during 1975-1990, but they have been increasing in the 1990s.

The improvement in Egypt's rating compared to the rating it had in the mid-1970s is the result of greater monetary stability, a sharp reduction in both government consumption and the size of the transfer sector, lower marginal tax rates (the top marginal rate is now 50% down from 80% in 1980.), and relaxation of exchange rate controls. Despite these improvements, this economy still has a long way to go. It is still plagued with numerous government enterprises, price controls, high taxes, a legal system that often fails to support private property rights, conscription, and capital market restrictions.

Egypt has made some progress. A decisive move toward a freer economy could well lead to strong economic growth.

EL SALVADOR

Economic Freedom Rating

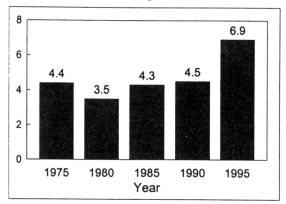

Total Government Expenditures As a Percent of GDP

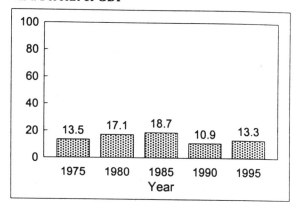

Part 1: The Economic Freedom Ratings for the Components and Various Area and Summary Indexes: 1975, 1980, 1985, 1990 and 1995.
(The numbers in parentheses indicate the actual values for the components.)

Components of Economic Freedom	1975		1980		1985		1990		1995	
I. Money and Inflation	2.3		1.9		3.8		2.5		8.5	
(a) Annual Money Growth (last 5 yrs.)	2	(18.4)	3	(16.9)	7	(9.8)	6	(11.5)	6	(12.3)
(b) Inflation Variablity (last 5 yrs.)	5	(4.5)	3	(7.5)	5	(4.7)	2	(8.2)	9	(1.8)
(c) Ownership of Foreign Currency	0		0		0		0		10	
(d) Maint. of Bank Account Abroad	0		0		0		0		10	
II. Government Operation	6.0		5.0		6.8		8.4		6.8	
(a) Gov't Consump. (% of Total Consump.)	8	(13.5)	6	(16.3)	7	(16.0)	9	(11.4)	10	(8.1)
(b) Government Enterprises	4		4		6		8		8	
(c) Price Controls	-		-		-		-		6	
(d) Entry Into Business	-		-		-		-		5.0	
(e) Legal System	-		-		-		-		2.5	
(f) Avoidance of Neg. Interest Rates	-		-		8		8		10	
III. Takings	5.8		4.6		5.0		4.5		6.9	
(a) Transfers and Subsidies (% of GDP)	8	(2.5)	8	(2.7)	9	(2.0)	9	(1.4)	8	(3.2)
(b) Marginal Tax Rates (Top Rate)	4	(55)	3	(60)	3	(48)	2	(60)	8	(30)
(c) Conscription	-		0		0		0		0	
IV. International Sector	3.5		2.3		1.9		3.1		5.8	
(a) Taxes on International Trade (Avg.)	4	(6.4)	4	(6.2)	3	(7.1)	6	(4.1)	7	(3.6)
(b) Black Market Exchange Rates (Prem.)	4	(20)	1	(100)	1	(195)	3	(24)	8	(1)
(c) Size of Trade Sector (% of GDP)	4	(35.7)	2	(33.7)	1	(26.1)	0	(21.5)	1	(29.6)
(d) Capital Transactions with Foreigners	2		2		2		2		5	
Economic Freedom Rating	4.4		3.5		4.3		4.5		6.9	
Ranking of Country	38		74		51		60		14	

Part 2: Recent Economic Indicators:

Population 1996:	5.9	**Real Per Capita GDP** :	1995=	$2,911
(in millions)		(in 1995 U.S. dollars)		
Annual Rate of Change (1985-96):	1.7%	Avg. Growth Rate:	1980-90=	-1.3%
			1990-95=	4.0%

Economic Indicators:*	1988	1989	1990	1991	1992	1993	1994	1995	1996
Change in Real GDP: Aggregate	1.6	1.1	3.4	3.6	7.5	7.4	6.0	6.1	-
: Per Capita	-0.1	-0.6	1.7	1.9	5.8	5.7	4.3	4.4	-
Inflation Rate (CPI)	19.8	17.6	24.0	14.4	11.2	18.6	10.6	10.0	7.2
Change in Money Supply: (M1)	8.1	13.5	22.3	17.9	29.6	17.2	5.0	11.8	
: (M2)	12.2	12.8	32.3	23.5	30.7	27.4	24.9	9.8	
Investment/GDP Ratio	12.8	15.3	13.9	15.4	18.5	18.6	19.8	19.7	-
Size of Trade Sector (% of GDP)	19.1	18.5	21.5	20.9	21.5	20.8	27.6	29.6	-
Total Gov't Exp./GDP Ratio	11.1	10.3	10.9	11.5	12.2	12.8	14.5	13.3	-
Central Government Budget Deficit (-) or Surplus (+) As a Percent of GDP	-0.6	-2.3	-0.1	-2.8	-3.8	-2.1	-1.5	-1.1	-
Unemployment Rate	-	8.4	10.0	7.5	7.9	-	-	-	-

* The figures in this table are in percent form.

After years of civil unrest and economic restrictions, El Salvador's economic freedom rating has improved substantially in the 1990s. Its rating jumped from 4.5 in 1990 to 6.9 in 1995, one of the largest improvements registered during this time period. Perhaps even more impressive, it ranked as the 14th freest economy in 1995, up from 60th in 1990.

The major factors underlying this dramatic gain were:

- Substantial reduction in the variability of the inflation rate;
- Legalization of foreign currency accounts;
- Reduction of the top marginal tax rate from 60% in 1990 to 30% in 1995;
- Virtual elimination of exchange rate controls (note the sharp reduction in the black market exchange rate);
- Relaxation of several restrictions limiting the mobility of capital.

More needs to be done. Monetary policy is still too expansionary and the inflation rate is too high. Perhaps most importantly, rule of law principles need to be built into the legal code. A start has been made, however, and this economy has experienced solid growth in the 1990s.

ESTONIA

Economic Freedom Rating

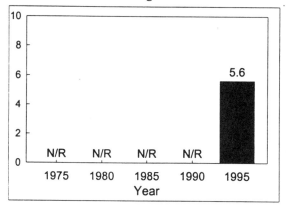

Total Government Expenditures As a Percent of GDP

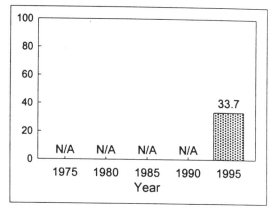

Part 1: The Economic Freedom Ratings for the Components and Various Area and Summary Indexes: 1975, 1980, 1985, 1990 and 1995.

(The numbers in parentheses indicate the actual values for the components.)

Components of Economic Freedom	1995	
I. Money and Inflation	**3.6**	
(a) Annual Money Growth (last 5 yrs.)	0	(83.3)
(b) Inflation Variablity (last 5 yrs.)	0	(395.0)
(c) Ownership of Foreign Currency	10	
(d) Maint. of Bank Account Abroad	10	
II. Government Operation	**4.7**	
(a) Gov't Consump. (% of Total Consump.)	1	(29.1)
(b) Government Enterprises	2	
(c) Price Controls	6	
(d) Entry Into Business	10.0	
(e) Legal System	7.5	
(f) Avoidance of Neg. Interest Rates	0	
III. Takings	**4.9**	
(a) Transfers and Subsidies (% of GDP)	3	(13.7)
(b) Marginal Tax Rates (Top Rate)	8	(26)
(c) Conscription	0	
IV. International Sector	**9.2**	
(a) Taxes on International Trade (Avg.)	9	(0.4)
(b) Black Market Exchange Rates (Prem.)	10	(0)
(c) Size of Trade Sector (% of GDP)	10	(87.0)
(d) Capital Transactions with Foreigners	8	
Economic Freedom Rating	**5.6**	
Ranking of Country	**52**	

92

Part 2: Recent Economic Indicators:

Population 1996:	1.5	**Real Per Capita GDP**	:	1995=	$4,760	
(in millions)		(in 1995 U.S. dollars)				
Annual Rate of Change (1992-96):	-0.2%	Avg. Growth Rate:	1980-90=	-		
			1990-95=	-6.4%		

Economic Indicators:*	1990	1991	1992	1993	1994	1995	1996
Change in Real GDP: Aggregate	-7.1	-22.1	-21.6	-6.6	6.0	4.0	2.3
: Per Capita	-6.9	-21.9	-21.4	-6.4	6.2	4.2	2.1
Inflation Rate (CPI)	23.1	210.6	1069.0	89.0	48.0	28.9	25.0
Change in Money Supply: (M1)	-	-	291.5	75.2	20.6	29.1	-
: (M2)	-	-	-	-	34.6	27.1	-
Investment/GDP Ratio	-	24.4	26.2	23.6	20.6	29.1	-
Size of Trade Sector (% of GDP)	-	29.5	51.1	71.0	84.4	87.0	-
Total Gov't Exp./GDP Ratio	-	-	31.0	33.9	33.7	-	-
Central Government Budget Deficit (-) or Surplus (+) As a Percent of GDP	-	-	-	-	1.3	0.8	-1.5
Unemployment Rate	-	-	1.0	1.7	5.1	5.0	3.0

* The figures in this table are in percent form.

Estonia's 5.6 rating in 1995 placed it 52nd among the 115 countries in our study. Its rating was a little lower than that of Sweden, but a little higher than Italy, for example. Our index indicates that Estonia (along with Lithuania which rates a tenth of a point lower) are the freest of the former socialist countries.

Estonian's are free to maintain foreign currency bank accounts. Entry restraints into business are generally low. The top marginal tax rate of 26% is also relatively low. A major strength of this economy is a relatively free trade sector. Tariffs are low and exchange rate liberalization has eliminated the black market in this area. There are also relatively few restrictions on the mobility of capital. These policies have led to a large (87% of GDP) and growing trade sector.

Rapid money growth and price level instability continue to be problem areas. Even though the inflation rate has decelerated sharply from the 1,069% rate of 1992, it continues to run in the 20% range. Monetary expansion is clearly too rapid for the achievement of a low and stable rate of inflation. Nonetheless, Estonia is off to a reasonably good start. The foundation for a market economy is now present, and its current government expenditure level (33.7% of GDP in 1995) is low by European standards. If it can move toward monetary stability, control the growth of government spending, and avoid excessive (and unnecessary) regulation, both economic freedom and income levels will expand in the decade ahead.

FINLAND

Economic Freedom Rating

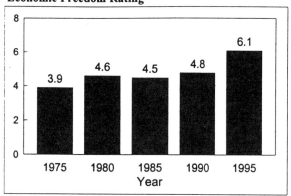

Total Government Expenditures As a Percent of GDP

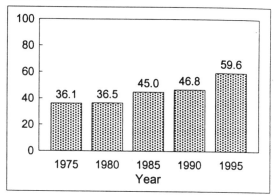

Part 1: The Economic Freedom Ratings for the Components and Various Area and Summary Indexes: 1975, 1980, 1985, 1990 and 1995.

(The numbers in parentheses indicate the actual values for the components.)

Components of Economic Freedom	1975		1980		1985		1990		1995	
I. Money and Inflation	3.6		7.0		6.4		9.1		9.4	
(a) Annual Money Growth (last 5 yrs.)	1	(22.4)	7	(8.6)	5	(12.8)	7	(8.2)	8	(6.8)
(b) Inflation Variablity (last 5 yrs.)	4	(5.5)	9	(1.9)	9	(1.9)	10	(0.9)	10	(1.1)
(c) Ownership of Foreign Currency	10		10		10		10		10	
(d) Maint.of Bank Account Abroad	0		0		0		10		10	
II. Government Operation	4.5		4.9		4.9		5.2		6.9	
(a) Gov't Consump. (% of Total Consump.)	3	(23.6)	2	(25.0)	1	(26.9)	1	(28.5)	1	(28.3)
(b) Government Enterprises	6		6		6		6		6	
(c) Price Controls	-		-		-		6		9	
(d) Entry Into Business	-		-		-		-		7.5	
(e) Legal System	-		-		-		-		10.0	
(f) Avoidance of Neg. Interest Rates	-		8		10		10		10	
III. Takings	2.1		1.7		1.3		0.8		1.3	
(a) Transfers and Subsidies (% of GDP)	3	(14.1)	3	(14.3)	2	(15.8)	2	(16.0)	1	(22.6)
(b) Marginal Tax Rates (Top Rate)	2	(61-68)	1	(65-71)	1	(64-70)	0	(63-69)	2	(55-61)
(c) Conscription	0		0		0		0		0	
IV. International Sector	5.8		6.1		6.6		6.3		7.9	
(a) Taxes on International Trade (Avg.)	8	(1.6)	9	(0.8)	9	(0.4)	9	(0.6)	9	(0.5)
(b) Black Market Exchange Rates (Prem.)	8	(1)	8	(1)	10	(0)	10	(0)	10	(0)
(c) Size of Trade Sector (% of GDP)	4	(27.0)	4	(33.6)	4	(29.1)	2	(23.8)	2	(33.7)
(d) Capital Transactions with Foreigners	2		2		2		2		8	
Economic Freedom Rating	3.9		4.6		4.5		4.8		6.1	
Ranking of Country	55		34		39		43		36	

Part 2: Recent Economic Indicators:

Population 1996:   5.1   **Real Per Capita GDP**   :   1996= $17,898
  (in millions)   (in 1995 U.S. dollars)
Annual Rate of Change (1985-96):   0.4%   Avg. Growth Rate: 1980-90=   2.7%
                                                         1990-96=   -0.6%

Economic Indicators:*	1988	1989	1990	1991	1992	1993	1994	1995	1996
Change in Real GDP: Aggregate	4.9	5.7	0.0	-7.1	-3.6	-1.2	4.4	4.2	1.6
: Per Capita	4.5	5.3	-0.4	-7.5	-4.0	-1.6	4.0	3.8	1.2
Inflation Rate (CPI)	5.1	6.6	6.1	4.1	2.6	2.1	1.1	1.0	0.7
Change in Money Supply: (M1)	18.4	15.4	7.2	-	3.2	5.1	8.9	14.0	17.9
: (M2)	23.0	9.5	5.0	7.7	-1.0	1.5	1.4	6.0	-
Investment/GDP Ratio	26.6	29.7	28.1	18.8	16.7	14.3	15.4	16.4	-
Size of Trade Sector (% of GDP)	25.2	24.8	23.8	22.6	26.3	30.4	32.6	33.7	-
Total Gov't Exp./GDP Ratio	45.3	43.3	46.8	55.5	60.6	61.8	61.0	59.6	58.7 [p]
Central Government Budget Deficit (-) or Surplus (+) As a Percent of GDP	+4.1	+6.3	+5.4	-1.5	-5.8	-8.0	-6.2	-5.4	-2.9
Unemployment Rate	4.5	3.4	3.4	7.5	13.0	17.6	17.9	16.6	15.0 [a]

* The figures in this table are in percent form.

[a] October, 1996

[p] Preliminary

Finland's 6.1 rating in 1995 placed it 36th among the 115 economies of our study. Even though its rating is higher in 1995 than 1990, this is a little deceptive. The higher rating was primarily because of the inclusion of the "entry into business" and "legal system" components into our index for the first time in 1995. The figures on government expenditures do not indicate that this economy has been moving toward economic freedom. Total government expenditures were almost 60% of GDP in 1995, up from only 36% in 1975 (and 45% in 1985).

This is a troubled economy. Like several other "big government" European nations, Finland is caught in the vicious cycle of large government expenditures, budget deficits (the government deficit has averaged 5% of GDP during the last 5 years), and rising interest costs that fuel still more government spending. Higher taxes will not solve this problem. Finland's current top marginal tax rate of approximately 60% is already one of the highest in the world. Weak private investment and high unemployment are typically side effects of large government expenditures, rising interest costs, and high taxes. Changing trade patterns associated with the collapse of the former Soviet Union created an additional transition problem that drove the Finnish unemployment rate to record levels (nearly 20%) in 1994. The situation is now improving a little—the budget deficit shrank and the unemployment rate fell to 15% in 1996. Sustainable improvement, however, is dependent on other factors, particularly a reduction in the size of government and increased reliance on markets to coordinate economic activity.

FRANCE

Economic Freedom Rating

**Total Government Expenditures
As a Percent of GDP**

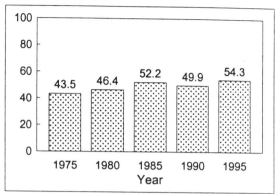

Part 1: The Economic Freedom Ratings for the Components and Various Area and Summary Indexes: 1975, 1980, 1985, 1990 and 1995.
(The numbers in parentheses indicate the actual values for the components.)

Components of Economic Freedom	1975		1980		1985		1990		1995	
I. Money and Inflation	**4.2**		**4.9**		**5.1**		**10.0**		**10.0**	
(a) Annual Money Growth (last 5 yrs.)	6	(12.4)	5	(13.4)	8	(8.0)	10	(3.7)	10	(-0.5)
(b) Inflation Variablity (last 5 yrs.)	7	(2.6)	10	(0.8)	8	(2.3)	10	(0.9)	10	(0.5)
(c) Ownership of Foreign Currency	0		0		0		10		10	
(d) Maint. of Bank Account Abroad	0		0		0		10		10	
II. Government Operation	**4.0**		**3.7**		**4.1**		**4.9**		**6.6**	
(a) Gov't Consump. (% of Total Consump.)	4	(22.0)	3	(23.6)	2	(24.1)	3	(23.1)	2	(24.6)
(b) Government Enterprises	2		2		4		4		6	
(c) Price Controls	-		-		-		6		8	
(d) Entry Into Business	-		-		-		-		7.5	
(e) Legal System	-		-		-		-		7.5	
(f) Avoidance of Negative Interest Rates	8		8		8		8		10	
III. Takings	**2.7**		**1.4**		**0.5**		**1.4**		**1.9**	
(a) Transfers and Subsidies (% of GDP)	1	(24.0)	0	(26.1)	0	(26.8)	0	(25.2)	0	(27.9)
(b) Marginal Tax Rates (Top Rate)	5	(48)	3	(60)	1	(65)	3	(53)	4	(51)
(c) Conscription	0		0		0		0		0	
IV. International Sector	**6.9**		**6.0**		**6.3**		**7.9**		**7.9**	
(a) Taxes on International Trade (Avg.)	10	(0.1)	10	(0.1)	10	(0.0)	10	(0.0)	10	(0.0)
(b) Black Market Exchange Rates (Prem.)	10	(0)	6	(3)	6	(4)	10	(0)	10	(0)
(c) Size of Trade Sector (% of GDP)	4	(18.5)	5	(22.1)	7	(23.6)	5	(22.6)	5	(22.3)
(d) Capital Transactions with Foreigners	2		2		2		5		5	
Economic Freedom Rating	**4.4**		**3.8**		**3.6**		**5.5**		**6.1**	
Ranking of Country	**38**		**57**		**73**		**31**		**36**	

Part 2: Recent Economic Indicators:

Population 1996:	58.2	**Real Per Capita GDP**	:	1996=	$20,350	
(in millions)		(in 1995 U.S. dollars)				
Annual Rate of Change (1985-96):	0.5%	Avg. Growth Rate:		1980-90=	1.9%	
				1990-96=	0.9%	

Economic Indicators:*	1988	1989	1990	1991	1992	1993	1994	1995	1996
Change in Real GDP: Aggregate	4.5	4.3	2.5	0.8	1.2	-1.3	2.8	2.2	1.4
: Per Capita	4.0	3.8	2.0	0.3	0.7	-1.8	2.3	1.7	0.9
Inflation Rate (CPI)	2.7	3.5	3.4	3.2	2.4	2.1	1.7	1.8	1.7
Change in Money Supply: (M1)	4.1	6.6	4.2	-5.5	-0.1	1.0	3.2	9.0	4.0
: (M2)	5.6	2.4	2.4	-0.9	1.2	3.8	6.8	10.9	-1.9
Investment/GDP Ratio	21.4	22.3	22.5	21.5	19.7	17.1	18.0	18.2	-
Size of Trade Sector (% of GDP)	21.3	22.8	22.6	22.6	22.5	20.9	21.7	22.3	-
Total Gov't Exp./ GDP Ratio	50.0	49.1	49.9	50.5	52.2	55.0	54.9	54.3	54.7 p
General Government Budget Deficit (-) or Surplus (+) As a Percent of GDP	-1.7	-1.2	-1.6	-2.0	-3.8	-5.6	-5.6	-4.8	-4.1
Unemployment Rate	10.0	9.4	8.9	9.4	10.4	11.7	12.3	11.6	12.5 a

* The figures in this table are in percent form.

a October, 1996.

p Preliminary.

The economic freedom rating of France has increased during the last decade, following a decline during 1975-1985. In 1995 France ranked 36th among the nations in our study, up from 75th in 1985 but virtually unchange from its 1975 position.

The improvement during the last decade was primarily the result of a reduction in monetary growth, greater price stability, and legalization of foreign currency bank accounts. Like most of the European welfare state economies, France achieved high ratings in the monetary and international sectors, but low ratings for government operations and takings, particularly the latter.

Given France's high level of government expenditures (54% of GDP in 1995), our index may overstate the economic freedom of this country. If the components affected (primarily consumption and income transfers) were given more weight, its summary rating would lower. So, too, would the degree of improvement. After all, total government expenditures are now modestly greater than 1985 and substantially higher than the 43.5% figure of 1975.

Like other European countries with large transfer sectors and government expenditures equal to 50% or more of GDP, France is now caught in the budget deficit, declining investment, and high unemployment cycle. Budget deficits have averaged 4.8% of GDP during 1992-1996. During this same period, the investment/GDP ratio has averaged approximately 18%, down from the 22% rate of the 1980s. The unemployment rate stubbornly persists at double-digit levels. France needs to reduce the size of its transfer sector and deregulate its labor market. If it fails to do so, the current economic stagnation is likely to continue.

GERMANY

Economic Freedom Rating

Total Government Expenditures As a Percent of GDP

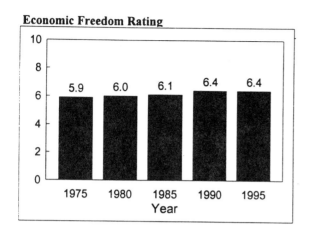

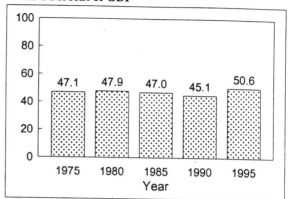

Part 1: The Economic Freedom Ratings for the Components and Various Area and Summary Indexes: 1975, 1980, 1985, 1990 and 1995.

(The numbers in parentheses indicate the actual values for the components.)

Components of Economic Freedom	1975		1980		1985		1990		1995	
I. Money and Inflation	**8.8**		**9.4**		**9.7**		**9.1**		**9.7**	
(a) Annual Money Growth (last 5 yrs.)	6	(10.5)	8	(7.0)	9	(5.1)	7	(10.2)	9	(4.8)
(b) Inflation Variablity (last 5 yrs.)	10	(0.9)	10	(0.5)	10	(1.0)	10	(0.7)	10	(1.0)
(c) Ownership of Foreign Currency	10		10		10		10		10	
(d) Maint. of Bank Account Abroad	10		10		10		10		10	
II. Government Operation	**4.5**		**4.9**		**4.9**		**6.4**		**6.8**	
(a) Gov't Consump. (% of Total Consump.)	1	(26.5)	1	(26.3)	1	(26.1)	2	(25.2)	2	(25.5)
(b) Government Enterprises	6		6		6		6		6	
(c) Price Controls	-		-		-		9		9	
(d) Entry Into Business	-		-		-		-		7.5	
(e) Legal System	-		-		-		-		7.5	
(f) Avoidance of Neg. Interest Rates	8		10		10		10		10	
III. Takings	**2.7**		**2.2**		**1.7**		**2.2**		**1.8**	
(a) Transfers and Subsidies (% of GDP)	2	(17.4)	2	(17.6)	2	(19.0)	2	(17.9)	1	(21.6)
(b) Marginal Tax Rates (Top Rate)	4	(56)	3	(56)	2	(56)	3	(56)	3	(57)
(c) Conscription	0		0		0		0		0	
IV. International Sector	**8.8**		**9.0**		**9.8**		**9.7**		**9.2**	
(a) Taxes on International Trade (Avg.)	10	(0.0)	10	(0.0)	10	(0.0)	10	(0.0)	10	(0.0)
(b) Black Market Exchange Rates (Prem.)	10	(0)	10	(0)	10	(0)	10	(0)	10	(0)
(c) Size of Trade Sector (% of GDP)	6	(23.2)	7	(26.7)	9	(30.8)	8	(29.0)	5	(22.5)
(d) Capital Transactions with Foreigners	8		8		10		10		10	
Economic Freedom Rating	**5.9**		**6.0**		**6.1**		**6.4**		**6.4**	
Ranking of Country	**13**		**10**		**14**		**14**		**25**	

Part 2: Recent Economic Indicators:

Population 1996:	81.9	**Real Per Capita GDP** :	1996 =	$21,387	
(in millions)		(in 1995 U.S. dollars)			
Annual Rate of Change (1985-96):	0.4%	Avg. Growth Rate:	1980-90=	1.8%	
			1990-96=	2.3%	

Economic Indicators:*	1988	1989	1990	1991	1992	1993	1994	1995	1996
Change in Real GDP: Aggregate	3.6	3.7	5.9	4.9	1.8	-1.7	2.3	2.5	2.5
: Per Capita	3.2	3.3	5.5	4.5	1.4	-2.1	1.9	2.3	2.5
Inflation Rate (CPI)	1.3	2.8	2.7	3.5	4.0	4.1	3.0	1.8	1.4
Change in Money Supply: (M1)	11.7	5.7	27.9	4.2	11.5	8.8	4.9	7.1	11.2
: (M2)	5.8	5.1	18.6	6.4	7.9	11.6	2.5	4.6	7.7
Investment/GDP Ratio	22.8	23.6	24.6	25.9	25.1	23.9	24.5	22.7	22.4
Size of Trade Sector (% of GDP)	27.0	28.8	29.0	30.7	30.0	21.9	22.4	22.5	-
Total Gov't Exp./GDP Ratio	46.3	44.8	45.1	47.9	48.5	49.5	48.9	50.6	51.0
General Government Budget Deficit (-) or Surplus (+) As a Percent of GDP	-2.2	+0.1	-2.1	-3.3	-2.8	-3.5	-2.4	-3.5	-3.9
Unemployment Rate	7.6	6.9	6.2	7.3	7.7	8.9	9.6	9.4	10.4

* The figures in this table are in percent form. Prior to 1991, data are for West Germany only.

While the economic freedom rating of Germany has improved slightly during the last two decades, its relative position has fallen as other countries have liberalized their economies. In 1995, the German economy ranked 25th (tied with Argentina, Bolivia and Chile), down from its 14th place ranking in 1990 and 10th place finish in 1980.

Monetary and price stability, freedom to maintain bank accounts in other currencies, a stable and competitive credit market, and a relatively free trade sector constitute the strengths of this economy. There are three major weaknesses: a high level of government consumption, a large transfer sector, and high tax rates. Throughout most of the last two decades, approximately 25% of the consumption expenditures have been allocated by the government rather than directed by markets. During the same period, 20% of GDP has been consistently taxed away from its earner and transferred to someone else. Government expenditures now account for more than half of GDP. Of course, big government means high taxes. Since many high-income countries cut taxes during the last decades, Germany's top marginal tax rate of 56% is among the highest in the world. (Note: if the surtax imposed on church membership were counted, the top rate would exceed 60%.) Several political leaders, including the finance minister, have proposed substantial reductions in tax rates, but the tax cut proposals face an uncertain future as the German economy stagnates and the budget deficit increases.

The German economy needs economic liberalization. The highly regulated German labor market is inflexible. This inflexibility, along with generous transfer benefits, has pushed the unemployment rate to its highest level in fifty years. The German social security system needs liberal reform—the provision of private sector investment options, for example. Given its price stability, strong and competitive trade sector, and high investment rate, this economy will probably continue to perform reasonably well in the future. If Germany continues on its present course, however, its future income *relative to other countries* will almost surely decline.

99

GHANA

Economic Freedom Rating

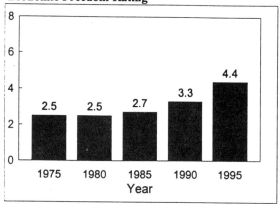

Total Government Expenditures
As a Percent of GDP

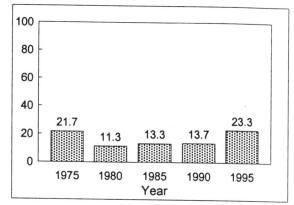

Part 1: The Economic Freedom Ratings for the Components and Various Area and Summary Indexes: 1975, 1980, 1985, 1990 and 1995.

. (The numbers in parentheses indicate the actual values for the components.)

Components of Economic Freedom	1975	1980	1985	1990	1995
I. Money and Inflation	**1.0**	**0.6**	**0.3**	**2.0**	**0.6**
(a) Annual Money Growth (last 5 yrs.)	1 (28.4)	1 (42.4)	1 (44.0)	1 (37.8)	1 (32.0)
(b) Inflation Variablity (last 5 yrs.)	2 (8.7)	1 (16.9)	0 (38.2)	5 (4.8)	1 (21.9)
(c) Ownership of Foreign Currency	0	0	0	0	0
(d) Maint. of Bank Account Abroad	0	0	0	0	0
II. Government Operation	**3.4**	**3.5**	**3.9**	**3.3**	**4.7**
(a) Gov't Consump. (% of Total Consump.)	7 (15.1)	9 (11.7)	10 (10.2)	9 (11.6)	8 (13.0)
(b) Government Enterprises	0	0	0	2	2
(c) Price Controls	-	-	-	0	6
(d) Entry Into Business	-	-	-	-	5.0
(e) Legal System	-	-	-	-	2.5
(f) Avoidance of Neg. Interest Rates	-	0	0	2	4
III. Takings	**4.5**	**5.0**	**5.4**	**5.5**	**7.4**
(a) Transfers and Subsidies (% of GDP)	8 (3.1)	8 (2.4)	9 (1.3)	8 (2.6)	7 (3.3)
(b) Marginal Tax Rates (Top Rate)	0 (70)	1 (60)	1 (60)	2 (55)	7 (35)
(c) Conscription	10	10	10	10	10
IV. International Sector	**0.6**	**0.0**	**0.3**	**1.8**	**3.0**
(a) Taxes on International Trade (Avg.)	0 (20.6)	0 (17.3)	0 (21.7)	1 (11.6)	2 (8.1)
(b) Black Market Exchange Rates (Prem.)	1 (67)	0 (304)	1 (142)	5 (7)	7 (2)
(c) Size of Trade Sector (% of GDP)	2 (18.9)	0 (8.8)	0 (10.6)	1 (19.7)	3 (27.7)
(d) Capital Transactions with Foreigners	0	0	0	0	0
Economic Freedom Rating	**2.5**	**2.5**	**2.7**	**3.3**	**4.4**
Ranking of Country	**92**	**97**	**95**	**91**	**78**

Part 2: Recent Economic Indicators:

Population 1996:	18.0	**Real Per Capita GDP** :	1996=	$1,433
(in millions)		(in 1995 U.S. dollars)		
Annual Rate of Change (1985-96):	3.2%	Avg. Growth Rate:	1980-90 =	-1.2%
			1990-96 =	1.3%

Economic Indicators:*	1988	1989	1990	1991	1992	1993	1994	1995	1996
Change in Real GDP: Aggregate	5.6	5.1	3.3	5.3	3.9	5.0	3.8	4.5	5.2
: Per Capita	2.4	1.9	0.1	2.1	0.7	1.8	0.8	1.5	2.2
Inflation Rate (CPI)	31.4	25.2	37.3	18.0	10.1	25.0	24.9	59.5	41.0
Change in Money Supply: (M1)	45.0	52.7	10.8	7.7	53.0	27.9	50.3	33.4	-
: (M2)	46.4	54.8	13.5	17.3	52.2	26.4	45.7	40.4	34.0
Investment/GDP Ratio	10.9	13.5	12.3	12.7	12.9	22.0	-	-	-
Size of Trade Sector (% of GDP)	21.4	20.7	19.7	19.7	21.4	27.7	27.7		-
Total Gov't Exp./GDP Ratio	13.7	13.9	13.7	14.4	18.2	21.5	23.4	23.3	23.2
Central Government Budget Deficit (-) or Surplus (+) As a Percent of GDP	+0.4	+0.7	+0.2	+1.6	-5.2	-3.2	+2.3	+0.7	-1.0
Unemployment Rate									

* The figures in this table are in percent form.

Throughout most of the last two decades, the economy of Ghana was one of the least free in the world. In 1985 it ranked 95th out of the 107 countries that were rated. There has been modest improvement during the 1990s. In 1995 Ghana ranked 78th among the 115 countries in our study.

The recent improvement is primarily the result of lower marginal tax rates and some liberalization of international trade. The top marginal tax rate was cut from 60% in 1985 and 55% in 1990 to 35% in 1995. Taxes on international trade are now approximately half the level of 1975-1985 and exchange rate controls have been liberalized substantially since 1985. As the result, the international trade sector as a share of GDP is now more than twice the levels of 1980 and 1985.

Much more needs to be done. During the last five years, monetary expansion has averaged 34% annually. The predictable side effect—a high and variable rate of the inflation—continues to undermine the confidence and planning of decision-makers. Trade restrictions continue to retard international exchange and the mobility of capital. Foreign investors must obtain approval from the Ghana Investment Center prior to undertaking a project; otherwise they will not be permitted to remit returns from their investment. Price controls continue to be imposed on various products and the legal system provides political officials with a great deal of discretionary authority to intrude and limit business activity. Policies of this type must be scrapped if this poor country is going to develop.

GREECE

Economic Freedom Rating

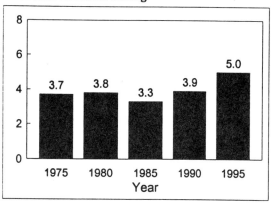

**Total Government Expenditures
As a Percent of GDP**

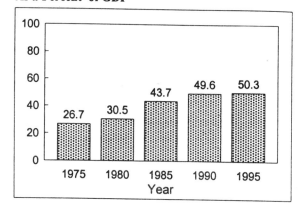

Part 1: The Economic Freedom Ratings for the Components and Various Area and Summary Indexes: 1975, 1980, 1985, 1990 and 1995.

(The numbers in parentheses indicate the actual values for the components.)

Components of Economic Freedom	1975	1980	1985	1990	1995
I. Money and Inflation	3.5	5.2	5.2	4.9	5.5
(a) Annual Money Growth (last 5 yrs.)	2 (19.0)	2 (18.5)	2 (18.9)	2 (19.2)	4 (14.0)
(b) Inflation Variablity (last 5 yrs.)	3 (7.3)	8 (2.4)	8 (2.3)	7 (2.9)	7 (2.8)
(c) Ownership of Foreign Currency	10	10	10	10	10
(d) Maint. of Bank Account Abroad	0	0	0	0	0
II. Government Operation	3.6	3.6	3.2	3.3	5.6
(a) Gov't Consump. (% of Total Consump.)	5 (18.3)	4 (21.3)	3 (23.7)	6 (17.5)	7 (15.9)
(b) Government Enterprises	2	2	2	2	2
(c) Price Controls	-	-	-	0	5
(d) Entry Into Business	-	-	-	-	7.5
(e) Legal System	-	-	-	-	5.0
(f) Avoidance of Neg. Interest Rates	4	6	6	8	8
III. Takings	3.1	2.6	1.3	2.3	2.3
(a) Transfers and Subsidies (% of GDP)	3 (12.5)	3 (13.8)	2 (17.7)	1 (23.8)	0 (24.6)
(b) Marginal Tax Rates (Top Rate)	4 (52)	3 (60)	1 (63)	4 (50)	5 (45)
(c) Conscription	0	0	0	0	0
IV. International Sector	4.6	4.3	4.5	5.6	7.2
(a) Taxes on International Trade (Avg.)	7 (3.5)	7 (3.2)	9 (0.3)	10 (0.1)	10 (0.1)
(b) Black Market Exchange Rates (Prem.)	6 (3)	5 (7)	3 (25)	6 (3)	10 (0)
(c) Size of Trade Sector (% of GDP)	2 (21.9)	2 (23.6)	3 (27.0)	3 (27.1)	1 (21.8)
(d) Capital Transactions with Foreigners	2	2	2	2	5
Economic Freedom Rating	3.7	3.8	3.3	3.9	5.0
Ranking of Country	63	57	80	77	64

Part 2: Recent Economic Indicators:

Population 1996:	10.5		Real Per Capita GDP	:	1995=	$9,939
(in millions)			(in 1995 U.S. dollars)			
Annual Rate of Change (1985-96):	0.5%		Avg. Growth Rate:	1980-90=	0.9%	
				1990-95=	0.4%	

Economic Indicators:*	1988	1989	1990	1991	1992	1993	1994	1995	1996
Change in Real GDP: Aggregate	4.5	4.0	-0.8	3.5	0.4	-1.0	1.5	2.0	-
: Per Capita	4.0	3.5	-1.3	3.0	-0.1	-1.5	1.0	1.5	-
Inflation Rate (CPI)	13.5	13.7	20.4	19.5	15.9	14.4	10.9	9.3	7.5
Change in Money Supply: (M1)	14.0	23.3	24.3	13.5	13.3	11.3	28.0	13.4	-
: (M2)	21.3	22.7	14.3	9.0	7.9	6.9	24.8	12.0	-
Investment/GDP Ratio	23.1	23.3	23.6	23.8	21.7	20.9	20.5	21.8	-
Size of Trade Sector (% of GDP)	27.0	27.4	27.1	22.5	22.0	21.5	21.8	-	-
Total Gov't Exp./GDP Ratio	44.2	46.1	49.6	49.0	48.9	51.2	52.7	50.3	49.7 P
Central Government Budget Deficit (-) or Surplus (+) As a Percent of GDP	-11.5	-14.4	-16.1	-11.5	-12.3	-14.2	-12.1	-9.1	-8.2
Unemployment Rate	6.0	6.5	6.4	7.3	8.7	9.8	10.1	-	-

* The figures in this table are in percent form.

P Preliminary.

Greece's rating stagnated at less than 4.0 throughout the 1975-1990 period. It has increased marginally during the last five years. Its 5.0 rating placed it 64th (out of 115) in 1995.

The major factors contributing to the recent improvement were the elimination of price controls in several areas, a reduction of the top marginal tax rate to 45% (down from 63% in 1985 and 50% in 1990), movement to a fully convertible currency in the foreign exchange market, and relaxation of several restrictions limiting the mobility of capital. Much more needs to be done. Monetary policy continues to be far too expansionary. (Note that the monetary aggregates have continued to grow at approximately 15% annually in recent years.) The size of the transfer sector is one of the largest in the world. In turn, this fuels the growth of government. Total government expenditures now exceed 50% of GDP, almost twice the level of 1975.

The growth of government has led to persistently large budget deficits that have averaged 12% of GDP during the 1990s. Deficits of this size increase the pressure for monetary expansion, drain funds from the capital market, and increase the rate of unemployment. This has been the case in Greece—the unemployment rate rose significantly during the 1990s. While government has grown, the economy has not. Per capita GDP has barely expanded during the last 15 years. Unless Greece is willing to reduce the size of government, particularly its huge transfer sector, it will almost surely continue to confront economic stagnation and high rates of unemployment.

103

GUATEMALA

Economic Freedom Rating

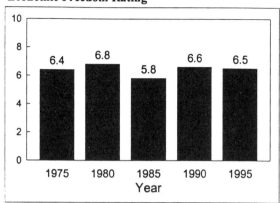

Total Government Expenditures As a Percent of GDP

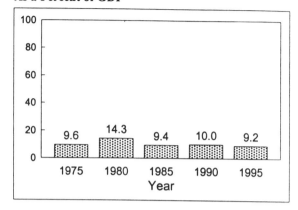

Part 1: The Economic Freedom Ratings for the Components and Various Area and Summary Indexes: 1975, 1980, 1985, 1990 and 1995.

(The numbers in parentheses indicate the actual values for the components.)

Components of Economic Freedom	1975		1980		1985		1990		1995	
I. Money and Inflation	**3.6**		**6.6**		**6.8**		**4.6**		**5.2**	
(a) Annual Money Growth (last 5 yrs.)	3	(16.0)	3	(16.3)	6	(12.4)	2	(17.8)	3	(15.5)
(b) Inflation Variablity (last 5 yrs.)	3	(7.8)	6	(3.6)	4	(5.3)	1	(15.2)	2	(9.1)
(c) Ownership of Foreign Currency	0		10		10		10		10	
(d) Maint. of Bank Account Abroad	10		10		10		10		10	
II. Government Operation	**9.0**		**8.8**		**8.8**		**7.9**		**6.3**	
(a) Gov't Consump. (% of Total Consump.)	10	(8.0)	10	(9.2)	10	(7.8)	10	(7.5)	10	(6.5)
(b) Government Enterprises	8		8		8		8		8	
(c) Price Controls	-		-		-		6		6	
(d) Entry Into Business	-		-		-		-		5.0	
(e) Legal System	-		-		-		-		0.0	
(f) Avoidance of Neg. Interest Rates	-		8		8		8		8	
III. Takings	**8.2**		**7.7**		**6.3**		**6.9**		**7.3**	
(a) Transfers and Subsidies (% of GDP)	10	(0.8)	10	(1.2)	10	(1.3)	9	(1.8)	9	(1.5)
(b) Marginal Tax Rates (Top Rate)	9	(34)	8	(40)	5	(48)	7	(34)	8	(30)
(c) Conscription	0		0		0		0		0	
IV. International Sector	**4.5**		**4.4**		**2.5**		**6.3**		**6.8**	
(a) Taxes on International Trade (Avg.)	6	(5.6)	6	(4.8)	3	(7.5)	7	(3.6)	6	(3.8)
(b) Black Market Exchange Rates (Prem.)	4	(10)	4	(10)	1	(89)	10	(0)	10	(0)
(c) Size of Trade Sector (% of GDP)	2	(22.6)	1	(23.6)	0	(12.5)	1	(21.7)	1	(22.7)
(d) Capital Transactions with Foreigners	5		5		5		5		8	
Economic Freedom Rating	**6.4**		**6.8**		**5.8**		**6.6**		**6.5**	
Ranking of Country	**8**		**3**		**20**		**11**		**21**	

Part 2: Recent Economic Indicators:

Population 1996:	10.9	**Real Per Capita GDP** :		1996=	$3,336
(in millions)		(in 1995 U.S. dollars)			
Annual Rate of Change (1985-96):	2.9%	Avg. Growth Rate:	1980-90=	-2.0%	
			1990-96=	1.1%	

Economic Indicators:*	1988	1989	1990	1991	1992	1993	1994	1995	1996
Change in Real GDP: Aggregate	3.9	3.9	3.1	3.6	4.8	3.9	4.0	4.9	3.1
: Per Capita	1.0	1.0	0.2	0.7	1.9	1.0	1.1	2.0	1.1
Inflation Rate (CPI)	10.8	11.4	41.2	33.2	10.0	11.8	10.9	8.6	10.9
Change in Money Supply: (M1)	14.4	20.7	33.0	18.6	9.1	20.4	40.1	4.3	22.1
: (M2)	19.8	16.1	25.8	48.9	31.1	15.1	12.9	11.5	11.7
Investment/GDP Ratio	13.7	13.5	13.6	14.3	18.3	17.4	16.4	14.4	-
Size of Trade Sector (% of GDP)	19.0	19.9	21.7	19.6	22.5	21.7	21.3	22.7	-
Total Gov't Exp./GDP Ratio	12.0	11.7	10.0	9.0	10.4	9.8	8.9	9.2	-
Central Government Budget Deficit (-)or Surplus (+) As a Percent of GDP	-1.7	-2.9	-2.1	0.0	0.0	-1.7	-1.4	-0.7	-0.1
Unemployment Rate									

* The figures in this table are in percent form.

In 1995, Guatemala ranked 21st among the countries in our study. Except for a decline during the mid-1980s as the result of higher trade taxes, more restrictive exchange rate controls, and a decline in the size of the trade sector, Guatemala's summary rating has been steady throughout the last two decades.

From the viewpoint of economic freedom, there are several positive attributes of this economy. Government expenditures are low—approximately 10% of GDP—and the transfer sector is small. Most of the businesses are privately owned. Both marginal tax rates and taxes on international trade have been reduced during the last decade. A 1992 reform narrowed the band of permissible tariff rates to between 5% and 20%, down from 0 to 100%. The top marginal tax rate is now 30%, down from the 48% rate of the mid-

1980s (but up from the 25% rate that was applicable in 1994).

The major weaknesses of this economy are monetary instability, insecure property rights, and an absence of the rule of law. A new constitutional provision prohibiting the central bank from extending credit to the government took effect in 1995. While this is a positive step, greater commitment to monetary and price stability is needed. Adoption of a currency board approach or an inflation rate target that would increase the accountability of the central bank would be helpful in this area. The legal system often grants political officials discretionary authority. This undermines the rule of law and inevitably leads to political corruption and loss of confidence in the system. With constructive action in these areas, Guatemala could become one the world's freest economies.

HONDURAS

Economic Freedom Rating

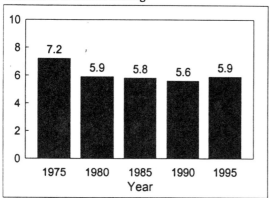

Total Government Expenditures As a Percent of GDP

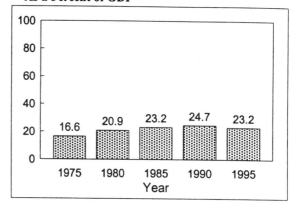

Part 1: The Economic Freedom Ratings for the Components and Various Area and Summary Indexes: 1975, 1980, 1985, 1990 and 1995.
(The numbers in parentheses indicate the actual values for the components.)

Components of Economic Freedom	1975		1980		1985		1990		1995	
I. Money and Inflation	**6.8**		**6.6**		**9.7**		**5.5**		**5.2**	
(a) Annual Money Growth (last 5 yrs.)	6	(10.6)	2	(18.0)	9	(6.6)	3	(16.6)	3	(16.3)
(b) Inflation Variablity (last 5 yrs.)	4	(5.4)	7	(3.0)	10	(1.3)	3	(6.7)	2	(8.3)
(c) Ownership of Foreign Currency	10		10		10		10		10	
(d) Maint. of Bank Account Abroad	10		10		10		10		10	
II. Government Operation	**7.0**		**6.5**		**7.2**		**5.9**		**5.7**	
(a) Gov't Consump. (% of Total Consump.)	8	(13.7)	7	(15.3)	7	(14.8)	7	(15.8)	9	(11.8)
(b) Government Enterprises	6		6		6		6		6	
(c) Price Controls	-		-		-		4		4	
(d) Entry Into Business	-		-		-		-		7.5	
(e) Legal System	-		-		-		-		2.5	
(f) Avoidance of Neg. Interest Rates	-		-		10		8		4	
III. Takings	**9.5**		**8.4**		**5.5**		**5.5**		**6.1**	
(a) Transfers and Subsidies (% of GDP)	10	(0.5)	-		8	(2.3)	8	(2.2)	7	(4.0)
(b) Marginal Tax Rates (Top Rate)	9	(27)	8	(40)	5	(46)	5	(46)	7	(40)
(c) Conscription	-		10		0		0		0	
IV. International Sector	**5.2**		**3.1**		**0.9**		**5.1**		**6.4**	
(a) Taxes on International Trade (Avg.)	6	(5.3)	4	(6.7)	-		-		-	
(b) Black Market Exchange Rates (Prem.)	10	(0)	4	(20)	1	(65)	10	(0)	8	(1)
(c) Size of Trade Sector (% of GDP)	4	(35.2)	5	(40.2)	2	(27.1)	5	(37.6)	6	(45.8)
(d) Capital Transactions with Foreigners	0		0		0		0		5	
Economic Freedom Rating	**7.2**		**5.9**		**5.8**		**5.6**		**5.9**	
Ranking of Country	**2**		**13**		**20**		**28**		**42**	

106

Part 2: Recent Economic Indicators:

Population 1996:	6.1	**Real Per Capita GDP** :	1995=	$1,884
(in millions)		(in 1995 U.S. dollars)		
Annual Rate of Change (1985-96):	3.1%	Avg. Growth Rate:	1980-90=	-0.9%
			1990-95=	-0.1%

Economic Indicators:*	1988	1989	1990	1991	1992	1993	1994	1995	1996
Change in Real GDP: Aggregate	4.6	4.3	0.1	3.3	5.6	6.2	-1.5	3.6	-
: Per Capita	1.5	1.2	-3.0	0.2	2.5	3.1	-3.6	0.5	
Inflation Rate (CPI)	4.5	9.9	23.3	34.0	8.8	10.7	21.7	29.5	-
Change in Money Supply: (M1)	11.9	20.0	23.6	11.1	22.5	11.9	36.1	21.7	-
: (M2)	14.8	14.5	21.4	17.5	22.4	10.4	30.3	29.2	-
Investment/GDP Ratio	21.0	19.1	23.0	24.7	26.0	32.4	36.0	31.5	-
Size of Trade Sector (% of GDP)	26.9	31.7	37.6	35.6	32.7	36.1	44.5	45.8	-
Total Gov't Exp./GDP Ratio	19.7	21.4	24.7	21.6	22.7	30.1	23.9	23.2	23.7
Central Government Budget Deficit (-) or Surplus (+) As a Percent of GDP	-3.0	-3.3	-3.4	+0.7	+0.9	-0.7	-0.3	+3.1	-
Unemployment Rate									

* The figures in this table are in percent form.

In the mid-1970s Honduras was one of the most economically free countries in the world. Our summary index ranked it 2nd—behind only Hong Kong—in 1975. Since that time its ranking has slid steadily downward, falling to 20th in 1985 and 42nd in 1995.

What accounts for the decline? An increase in monetary instability was clearly a contributing factor. In recent years, the growth of the money supply has been more rapid and the inflation rate more variable than was true during the early 1970s. Honduran authorities also increased the top marginal tax rates from 27% in 1975 to 46% in the 1980s. In the 1990s, the top rate was reduced to 40%, but this rate is still well above that of the mid-1970s. Conscription was instituted beginning in the 1980s. Exchange rate controls have been imposed off and on throughout the last 15 years. In the mid-1980s the controls were so rigid that the black market premium rose to 65%.

While economic freedom has fallen, government expenditures have persistently increased. As a share of the economy, they are now almost 50% greater than the levels of the mid-1970s. At the same time, the performance of the economy has declined. Per capita GDP fell by almost 10% during the 1980s and the economy continues to stagnate in the 1990s. Unless this country begins moving in the opposite direction, its economic future is bleak.

HONG KONG

Economic Freedom Rating

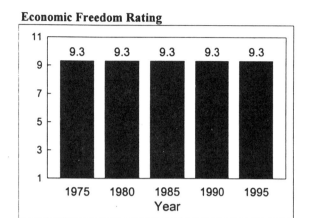

Total Government Expenditures As A Percent of GDP

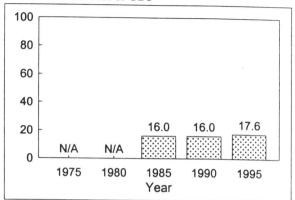

Part 1: The Economic Freedom Ratings for the Components and Various Area and Summary Indexes: 1975, 1980, 1985, 1990 and 1995.
(The numbers in parentheses indicate the actual values for the components.)

Components of Economic Freedom	1975		1980		1985		1990		1995	
I. Money and Inflation	**6.8**		**6.8**		**7.8**		**7.5**		**8.0**	
(a) Annual Money Growth (last 5 yrs.)	5	(13.1)	6	(10.4)	6	(11.8)	5	(13.1)	9	(6.4)
(b) Inflation Variablity (last 5 yrs.)	5	(3.9)	4	(5.2)	7	(2.5)	7	(2.9)	5	(4.2)
(c) Ownership of Foreign Currency	10		10		10		10		10	
(d) Maint. of Bank Account Abroad	10		10		10		10		10	
II. Government Operation	**10.0**		**10.0**		**9.6**		**9.7**		**9.1**	
(a) Gov't Consump. (% of Total Consump.)	10	(10.0)	10	(9.5)	9	(10.6)	9	(11.7)	8	(12.8)
(b) Government Enterprises	10		10		10		10		10	
(c) Price Controls	-		-		-		10		9	
(d) Entry Into Business	-		-		-		-		10.0	
(e) Legal System	-		-		-		-		7.5	
(f) Avoidance of Neg. Interest Rates	10		10		10		10		10	
III. Takings	**10.0**		**10.0**		**9.5**		**9.5**		**10.0**	
(a) Transfers and Subsidies (% of GDP)	10	(1.1)	10	(0.6)	10	(0.9)	10	(0.9)	10	(1.1)
(b) Marginal Tax Rates (Top Rate)	10	(15)	10	(15)	9	(25)	9	(25)	10	(20)
(c) Conscription	10		10		10		10		10	
IV. International Sector	**9.5**		**9.5**		**9.7**		**9.7**		**9.7**	
(a) Taxes on International Trade (Avg.)	9	(0.7)	9	(0.5)	9	(0.6)	9	(0.4)	9	(0.3)
(b) Black Market Exchange Rates (Prem.)	10	(0)	10	(0)	10	(0)	10	(0)	10	(0)
(c) Size of Trade Sector (% of GDP)	9	(81.3)	9	(90.3)	10	(104.8)	10	(131.5)	10	(148.9)
(d) Capital Transactions with Foreigners	10		10		10		10		10	
Economic Freedom Rating	**9.3**		**9.3**		**9.3**		**9.3**		**9.3**	
Ranking of Country	**1**		**1**		**1**		**1**		**1**	

Part 2: Recent Economic Indicators:

Population 1996:
(in millions)
Annual Rate of Change (1985-96):   0.9%

Real Per Capita GDP: 1996= $27,202
(in 1995 U.S. dollars)
    Avg. Growth Rate: 1980-90 =   5.4%
                    1990-96 =   3.7%

Economic Indicators:*	1988	1989	1990	1991	1992	1993	1994	1995	1996
Change in Real GDP:Aggregate	8.3	2.8	3.0	3.9	5.4	5.4	5.1	4.8	4.8
: Per Capita	7.4	1.9	2.1	3.0	4.5	4.5	4.2	3.7	3.9
Inflation Rate (CPI)	7.4	9.7	9.7	11.0	9.6	8.7	8.6	9.2	6.7
Change in Money Supply: (M1)	8.5	6.8	13.3	19.5	21.1	20.8	-0.3	2.8	14.4
: (M2)	14.2	19.9	22.3	13.3	10.8	16.0	12.8	14.0	10.6
Investment/GDP Ratio	28.6	26.7	27.4	27.2	28.5	27.7	31.8	35.0	31.0
Size of Trade Sector (% of GDP)	130.9	129.9	131.5	136.9	142.9	137.1	138.7	148.9	-
Total Gov't Exp./GDP Ratio	14.2	14.5	16.0	16.2	15.9	17.3	16.3	17.6	18.0
Central Government Budget Deficit (-) or Surplus (+) As a Percent of GDP	+4.2	+2.1	+0.7	+3.4	+2.8	+2.1	+0.8	-0.3	2.2
Unemployment Rate	1.4	1.1	1.3	1.8	2.0	2.0	1.9	3.2	2.8

* The figures in this table are in percent form.

During each of our five rating periods, Hong Kong was the freest nation in the world by a substantial margin. No doubt this has been the case for the last several decades. Hong Kong is an amazing story of what an economically free people can accomplish. In 1960 Hong Kong's per capita GDP was less than the comparable figures for Israel, Mexico, and Argentina, for example and approximately one-fourth that of the United States. Thirty-five years of sustained growth has changed this picture dramatically. In 1996 Hong Kong's per capita GDP ($27,202) was slightly greater than that of the United States. (Note: the per capita GDP figures are updates of the Summers and Heston data, which were derived by the purchasing power parity method.)

Hong Kong's rating is high for almost all of the components in our index. Its lowest rating—a five—is for the variability of inflation component. Both government consumption (as a percent of the total) and income transfers (as a percent of GDP) are low. The top marginal tax rate is 20% with a ceiling on the average tax rate set at 15% of gross income. Clearly, the citizens of Hong Kong are permitted to keep most of what they earn and allowed to decide what they want to consume.

How will Hong Kong's future be affected by its return to China later this year? This is a very difficult question to answer. Clearly, there will be changes that will affect civil liberties. With regard to economic liberty, much depends on the future of China. Even though there are substantial restraints on economic liberty, China has taken some remarkable steps toward liberalization and production for markets (rather than a central plan) since 1978. Furthermore, there is far more institutional diversity and decentralization within China than is generally perceived in the West. At this point both Hong Kong and China appear committed to the concept of "one country, two systems." If so, perhaps the Hong Kong experience will exert a positive influence on China and lead to changes that will promote their joint prosperity.

109

HUNGARY

Economic Freedom Rating

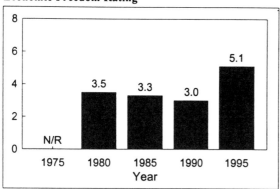

Total Government Expenditures
As a Percent of GDP

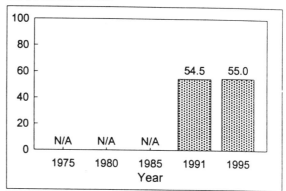

Part 1: The Economic Freedom Ratings for the Components and Various Area and Summary Indexes: 1975, 1980, 1985, 1990 and 1995.
(The numbers in parentheses indicate the actual values for the components.)

Components of Economic Freedom	1975	1980	1985	1990	1995
I. Money and Inflation	3.4	4.1	5.8	2.5	4.8
(a) Annual Money Growth (last 5 yrs.)	-	7 (8.7)	8 (6.7)	5 (13.2)	3 (15.0)
(b) Inflation Variablity (last 5 yrs.)	7 (2.9)	6 (3.8)	10 (1.0)	3 (7.8)	6 (3.3)
(c) Ownership of Foreign Currency	0	0	0	0	10
(d) Maint. of Bank Account Abroad	0	0	0	0	· 0
II. Government Operation	3.4	4.0	3.9	4.6	6.6
(a) Govern. Consumption (% of Total Consump.)	7 (15.0)	7 (14.4)	8 (13.9)	7 (14.7)	7 (14.8)
(b) Government Enterprises	0	0	0	0	2
(c) Price Controls	-	-	-	6	7
(d) Entry Into Business	-	-	-	-	10.0
(e) Legal System	-	-	-	-	7.5
(f) Avoidance of Neg. Interest Rates	-	6	-	6	6
III. Takings	0.0	0.0	0.0	1.4	1.9
(a) Transfers and Subsidies (% of GDP)	-	-	0 (33.3)	0 (28.7)	0 (25.0)
(b) Marginal Tax Rates (Top Rate)	-	-	-	3 (50)	4 (44)
(c) Conscription	0	0	0	0	0
IV. International Sector	2.3	3.3	3.4	3.7	7.4
(a) Taxes on International Trade (Avg.)	-	6 (5.0)	6 (3.7)	6 (5.0)	-
(b) Black Market Exchange Rates (Prem.)	0 (317)	0 (244)	0 (210)	4 (22)	10 (0)
(c) Size of Trade Sector (% of GDP)	10 (45.2)	9 (40.2)	10 (41.2)	5 (29.8)	7 (36.0)
(d) Capital Transactions with Foreigners	0	0	0	0	5
Economic Freedom Rating		3.5	3.3	3.0	5.1
Ranking of Country		74	80	96	63

110

Part 2: Recent Economic Indicators:

Population 1996:	10.2	**Real Per Capita GDP** :	1996 = $6,617
(in millions)		(in 1995 U.S. dollars)	
Annual Rate of Change (1985-96):	-0.4%	Avg. Growth Rate: 1980-90=	1.7%
		1990-96=	-1.6%

Economic Indicators:*	1988	1989	1990	1991	1992	1993	1994	1995	1996
Change in Real GDP: Aggregate	5.5	0.7	-3.5	-11.9	-3.0	-0.8	2.9	1.5	1.0
: Per Capita	5.9	1.1	-3.1	-11.5	-2.6	-0.4	3.3	1.9	1.2
Inflation Rate (CPI)	15.8	16.9	29.0	34.2	22.9	22.5	18.9	28.3	19.8
Change in Money Supply: (M1)	-1.5	25.8	26.4	18.2	32.4	11.4	8.0	5.8	18.0
: (M2)	2.2	16.5	29.2	29.4	27.3	16.8	13.0	18.5	20.9
Investment/GDP Ratio	25.3	26.6	25.4	19.7	18.9	18.0	19.3	18.3	-
Size of Trade Sector (% of GDP)	35.5	34.4	29.8	33.2	31.6	30.5	32.2	36.0	-
Total Gov't Exp./GDP Ratio	-	-	-	54.5	59.0	59.0	61.5	55.0	49.6
Central Government Budget Deficit (-) or Surplus (+) As a Percent of GDP	-0.2	-1.9	+0.8	-4.6	-8.3	-6.0	-9.8	-6.4	-4.0
Unemployment Rate	-	-	2.5	8.0	12.0	12.1	10.4	10.4	11.0

* The figures in this table are in percent form.

After declining during the 1980s, the economic freedom rating of Hungary jumped from 3.0 in 1990 to 5.1 in 1995. This placed it 63rd, up from 96th in 1990.

Prior to the collapse of communism, markets were utilized more extensively in Hungary than was true in the other former socialist countries. Perhaps reflecting this fact, privatization has moved forward less rapidly in Hungary than in the Czech Republic, for example. Nonetheless, important reforms have been adopted in several areas. Citizens are now free to maintain foreign currency bank accounts domestically. Exchange rate controls have been liberalized and the black market eliminated in this area. Restrictions limiting the mobility of capital have been relaxed. Marginal tax rates have been reduced slightly from 50% in 1990 to 44% in 1995.

While the foundation for a market economy has been laid, the Hungarian economy continues to be dominated by government. Total government expenditures continue to consume approximately 50% of GDP. Transfers and subsidies sum to 25% of GDP, one of the highest levels in the world. Like the big government economies of Western Europe, Hungary now confronts large budget deficits, a low rate of capital formation, and high rates of unemployment. Monetary expansion continues to fuel inflation, which is currently running at a 20% annual rate. Hungary needs to adopt reforms that will (a) encourage private saving and reduce the size of its transfer sector, (b) lead to monetary and price stability and (c) keep the budget in balance . Without such reforms, it will fail to reach its full growth potential.

ICELAND

Economic Freedom Rating

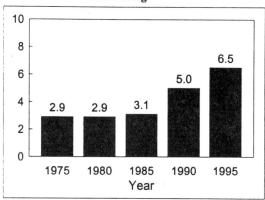

Total Goverment Expenditures
As a Percent of GDP

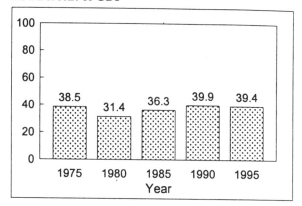

Part 1: The Economic Freedom Ratings for the Components and Various Area and Summary Indexes: 1975, 1980, 1985, 1990 and 1995.

(The numbers in parentheses indicate the actual values for the components.)

Components of Economic Freedom	1975		1980		1985		1990		1995	
I. Money and Inflation	**1.0**		**1.3**		**0.3**		**6.0**		**9.1**	
(a) Annual Money Growth (last 5 yrs.)	1	(28.6)	1	(43.0)	0	(45.8)	1	(28.2)	8	(7.8)
(b) Inflation Variablity (last 5 yrs.)	2	(11.1)	3	(7.7)	1	(17.2)	6	(3.6)	9	(1.8)
(c) Ownership of Foreign Currency	0		0		0		10		10	
(d) Maint. of Bank Account Abroad	0		0		0		10		10	
II. Government Operation	**3.6**		**3.6**		**4.0**		**4.4**		**6.4**	
(a) Gov't Consump. (% of Total Consump.)	4	(22.0)	3	(22.8)	4	(21.9)	2	(24.4)	2	(25.6)
(b) Government Enterprises	4		4		4		4		4	
(c) Price Controls	-		-		-		6		6	
(d) Entry Into Business	-		-		-		-		10.0	
(e) Legal System	-		-		-		-		10.0	
(f) Avoidance of Neg. Interest Rates	2		4		4		6		8	
III. Takings	**5.5**		**2.9**		**3.4**		**5.2**		**4.8**	
(a) Transfers and Subsidies (% of GDP)	4	(9.9)	4	(10.6)	4	(11.7)	4	(10.1)	4	(10.2)
(b) Marginal Tax Rates (Top Rate)	-		0	(63)	1	(56)	5	(40)	4	(47)
(c) Conscription	10		10		10		10		10	
IV. International Sector	**2.1**		**3.4**		**4.1**		**4.3**		**7.1**	
(a) Taxes on International Trade (Avg.)	2	(8.1)	4	(6.5)	6	(4.6)	6	(4.0)	9	(0.7)
(b) Black Market Exchange Rates (Prem.)	1	(106)	5	(9)	4	(16)	6	(3)	10	(0)
(c) Size of Trade Sector (% of GDP)	4	(39.4)	2	(36.3)	4	(40.9)	2	(34.7)	2	(35.1)
(d) Capital Transactions with Foreigners	2		2		2		2		5	
Economic Freedom Rating	**2.9**		**2.9**		**3.1**		**5.0**		**6.5**	
Ranking of Country	**85**		**92**		**87**		**41**		**21**	

Part 2: Recent Economic Indicators:

Population 1996:	0.3		**Real Per Capita GDP**	:		1996=	$19,142	
(in millions)			(in 1995 U.S. dollars)					
Annual Rate of Change (1985-96):	1.1%			Avg. Growth Rate:		1980-90=	1.6%	
						1990-96=	0.6%	

Economic Indicators:*	1988	1989	1990	1991	1992	1993	1994	1995	1996
Change in Real GDP: Aggregate	-0.1	0.2	1.2	1.3	-3.3	0.9	3.6	2.2	5.5
: Per Capita	-1.2	0.9	0.1	0.2	-4.4	-0.2	2.5	1.1	4.6
Inflation Rate (CPI)	25.8	20.8	15.5	6.8	4.0	4.1	1.6	1.7	2.3
Change in Money Supply: (M1)	16.5	32.8	24.9	19.9	1.3	5.4	10.7	11.3	10.8
: (M2)	28.8	26.3	14.2	10.5	6.6	4.4	-12.5	-2.3	2.9
Investment/GDP Ratio	15.5	17.9	20.6	18.7	15.2	14.4	14.4	15.2	18.3
Size of Trade Sector (% of GDP)	32.8	33.6	34.7	33.5	32.2	31.3	33.5	35.1	34.4
Total Gov't Exp./GDP Ratio	40.0	42.6	39.9	40.8	41.2	41.0	40.7	39.4	38.6
General Government Budget Deficit (-) or Surplus (+) As a Percent of GDP	-2.0	-4.6	-3.3	-2.9	-2.8	-4.5	-4.7	-3.1	-2.1
Unemployment Rate	0.6	1.6	1.8	1.5	3.1	4.3	4.7	4.9	3.6

* The figures in this table are in percent form.

After stagnating among the world's lowest rated countries during 1975-1985, Iceland has made significant moves toward economic freedom during the last decade. As its rating improved, so did its ranking. It jumped from 87th in 1985 to 41st in 1990 and 21st in 1995. Only New Zealand and Argentina registered larger increases in economic freedom between 1985 and 1995.

Several factors contributed to Iceland's improvement. Monetary policy was considerably more stable and legislation allowing citizens to maintain foreign currency bank accounts led to sharply higher ratings in the Money and Inflation area. Both interest rate and exchange rate controls were relaxed. Tariffs were reduced, particularly during the 1990s. The top marginal tax rate was cut from 63% in 1980 to 40% in 1990. (It was subsequently raised to 47% in 1995.) Finally, there has been some liberalization of the restrictions on the mobility of capital.

Problems remain—recent budget deficits have averaged more than 3% of GDP. Total government expenditures are still quite large, approximately 40% of GDP. If Iceland is not vigilant, it will fall into the large deficit, falling investment, rising unemployment cycle that has entrapped several European countries. Its growth rate during 1994-1996 has been strong. Continued liberalization will keep it on a healthy growth path.

113

INDIA

Economic Freedom Rating

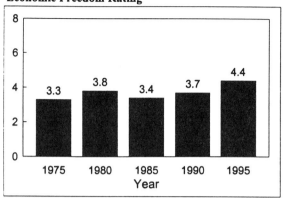

**Total Government Expenditures
As A Percent of GDP**

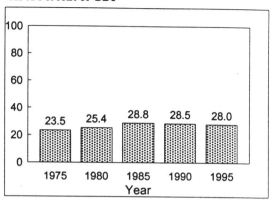

Part 1: The Economic Freedom Ratings for the Components and Various Area and Summary Indexes: 1975, 1980, 1985, 1990 and 1995.

(The numbers in parentheses indicate the actual values for the components.)

Components of Economic Freedom	1975		1980		1985		1990		1995	
I. Money and Inflation	2.8		3.5		4.6		4.8		4.8	
(a) Annual Money Growth (last 5 yrs.)	6	(10.9)	6	(10.5)	4	(14.5)	6	(12.2)	6	(12.0)
(b) Inflation Variablity (last 5 yrs.)	3	(7.2)	5	(4.8)	10	(1.1)	9	(1.4)	9	(2.1)
(c) Ownership of Foreign Currency	0		0		0		0		0	
(d) Maint. of Bank Account Abroad	0		0		0		0		0	
II. Government Operation	4.3		5.1		4.3		3.9		4.5	
(a) Gov't Consump. (% of Total Consump.)	9	(11.8)	9	(11.6)	7	(14.0)	7	(15.2)	7	(15.1)
(b) Government Enterprises	0		0		0		0		2	
(c) Price Controls	-		-		-		3		4	
(d) Entry Into Business	-		-		-		-		5.0	
(e) Legal System	-		-		-		-		2.5	
(f) Avoidance of Neg. Interest Rates	4		8		8		8		8	
III. Takings	4.1		4.2		3.3		4.3		5.7	
(a) Transfers and Subsidies (% of GDP)	7	(3.8)	6	(5.4)	5	(6.5)	5	(6.5)	5	(6.3)
(b) Marginal Tax Rates (Top Rate)	0	(77)	1	(60)	0	(62)	2	(53)	5	(40)
(c) Conscription	10		10		10		10		10	
IV. International Sector	2.1		2.5		2.0		2.1		2.6	
(a) Taxes on International Trade (Avg.)	0	(14.8)	0	(15.5)	0	(24.2)	0	(20.7)	0	(12.7)
(b) Black Market Exchange Rates (Prem.)	5	(9)	6	(5)	4	(14)	4	(10)	5	(8)
(c) Size of Trade Sector (% of GDP)	1	(6.4)	2	(8.3)	2	(7.5)	3	(9.4)	4	(11.4)
(d) Capital Transactions with Foreigners	2		2		2		2		2	
Economic Freedom Rating	3.3		3.8		3.4		3.7		4.4	
Ranking of Country	72		57		79		82		78	

Part 2: Recent Economic Indicators:

Population 1996: (in millions)	967.5			**Real Per Capita GDP** (in 1995 U.S. dollars)			1995=	$1,921	
Annual Rate of Change (1985-96):	2.2%			Avg. Growth Rate:		1980-90 =	3.5%		
						1990-96 =	2.2%		

Economic Indicators:*	1988	1989	1990	1991	1992	1993	1994	1995	1996
Change in Real GDP:Aggregate	9.9	6.6	5.7	0.5	4.6	4.5	6.3	5.0	-
: Per Capita	7.7	4.4	3.5	-1.7	2.4	2.3	4.1	2.8	-
Inflation Rate (CPI)	9.4	6.2	9.0	13.9	11.8	6.4	10.2	10.2	-
Change in Money Supply: (M1)	16.5	18.0	14.3	22.6	7.1	18.7	27.4	11.1	-
: (M2)	18.3	15.7	15.1	18.3	16.9	17.0	20.3	11.0	-
Investment/GDP Ratio	24.4	24.1	25.2	22.7	24.0	21.3	23.2	-	-
Size of Trade Sector (% of GDP)	8.2	9.0	9.4	9.6	10.6	11.4	-	-	-
Total Gov't Exp./GDP Ratio									
Central Government Budget Deficit (-) or Surplus (+) As a Percent of GDP	-8.1	-7.9	-8.2	-5.8	-5.2	-7.4	-6.7	-	-
Unemployment Rate									

* The figures in this table are in percent form.

India's 4.4 economic freedom rating of 1995 placed it 78th among the 115 countries in our study. Throughout the last two decades, it has persistently ranked in the bottom third. Along with Nepal and Bangladesh, India is the least free of the Asian economies.

Economic freedom is restricted in many areas. Legal restraints prohibit citizens from the maintenance of foreign currency bank accounts. Even though government consumption as a share of GDP is not particularly large (the most recent rating for this component was 7), the Indian economy is dominated by government. State-operated enterprises exist in almost every major sector of the economy. Price controls abound. Restrictions limit entry into various business activities. Investment by foreigners generally requires approval from the government. The legal system arms political decision-makers with a great deal of discretionary authority. The Indian tariff rates are among the highest in the world. (Note: the average tax rate on international trade was 12.7% in 1995.) All these factors serve to undermine economic freedom and the operations of markets.

In recent years, a few modest steps toward a freer economy have been taken. The top marginal tax rate has been cut from 77% in 1975 and 62% in 1985 to the current 40% rate. Exchange rate controls have been eased during the last decade. The credit market is now more fully integrated with the global market. However, much more needs to be done if this populous country is going to reach its full potential.

115

INDONESIA

Economic Freedom Rating

Total Government Expenditures
As A Percent of GDP

No Data

Part 1: The Economic Freedom Ratings for the Components and Various Area and Summary Indexes: 1975, 1980, 1985, 1990 and 1995.
(The numbers in parentheses indicate the actual values for the components.)

Components of Economic Freedom	1975		1980		1985		1990		1995	
I. Money and Inflation	**4.3**		**4.6**		**6.9**		**5.9**		**8.5**	
(a) Annual Money Growth (last 5 yrs.)	1	(37.4)	1	(31.4)	3	(14.8)	3	(15.6)	5	(13.7)
(b) Inflation Variablity (last 5 yrs.)	1	(16.3)	2	(10.2)	7	(3.0)	4	(5.1)	10	(1.1)
(c) Ownership of Foreign Currency	10		10		10		10		10	
(d) Maint. of Bank Account Abroad	10		10		10		10		10	
II. Government Operation	**5.5**		**3.5**		**4.4**		**5.7**		**3.7**	
(a) Gov't Consump. (% of Total Consump.)	9	(12.2)	6	(16.8)	7	(16.0)	7	(14.2)	8	(13.2)
(b) Government Enterprises	4		2		2		2		2	
(c) Price Controls	-		-		-		6		2	
(d) Entry Into Business	-		-		-		-		2.5	
(e) Legal System	-		-		-		-		0.0	
(f) Avoidance of Neg. Interest Rates	2		2		-		10		10	
III. Takings	**5.5**		**4.2**		**6.5**		**6.9**		**7.7**	
(a) Transfers and Subsidies (% of GDP)	9	(1.5)	7	(3.3)	8	(2.5)	9	(2.0)	10	(0.3)
(b) Marginal Tax Rates (Top Rate)	4	(48)	3	(50)	7	(35)	7	(35)	8	(30)
(c) Conscription	0		0		0		0		0	
IV. International Sector	**5.2**		**6.2**		**5.8**		**7.3**		**7.1**	
(a) Taxes on International Trade (Avg.)	6	(4.0)	7	(2.9)	8	(1.6)	8	(2.5)	8	(2.2)
(b) Black Market Exchange Rates (Prem.)	5	(7)	7	(2)	5	(7)	10	(0)	10	(0)
(c) Size of Trade Sector (% of GDP)	9	(22.1)	10	(26.6)	9	(21.3)	10	(26.3)	9	(25.6)
(d) Capital Transactions with Foreigners	2		2		2		2		2	
Economic Freedom Rating	**5.2**		**4.7**		**6.0**		**6.5**		**6.3**	
Ranking of Country	**20**		**29**		**15**		**13**		**29**	

116

Part 2: Recent Economic Indicators:

Population 1996: 196.9   **Real Per Capita GDP** : 1995 = $3,483
  (in millions)   (in 1985 U.S. dollars)
Annual Rate of Change (1985-96): 1.6%   Avg. Growth Rate: 1980-90 = 3.5%
         1990-95 = 4.7%

Economic Indicators:*	1988	1989	1990	1991	1992	1993	1994	1995	1996
Change in Real GDP:Aggregate	5.8	7.5	7.2	2.0	6.5	6.5	7.5	8.1	-
: Per Capita	4.2	5.9	5.6	0.4	4.9	4.9	5.9	6.5	-
Inflation Rate (CPI)	8.0	6.4	7.8	9.4	7.5	9.7	8.5	9.4	5.3
Change in Money Supply: (M1)	13.3	12.9	15.9	10.6	9.3	27.9	23.3	16.1	20.0
: (M2)	24.1	39.1	44.6	17.5	19.8	-	-	-	-
Investment/GDP Ratio	31.5	35.2	36.1	35.5	35.9	33.2	34.3	41.8	-
Size of Trade Sector (% of GDP)	23.2	24.3	26.3	27.4	27.9	26.5	25.0	25.6	-
Total Gov't Exp./GDP Ratio									
Central Government Budget Deficit (-) or Surplus (+) As a Percent of GDP	-3.0	-1.9	+0.4	+0.4	-0.4	-0.8	-	-	-
Unemployment Rate									

* The figures in this table are in percent form.

Indonesia's 6.3 rating in 1995 placed it 29th among our 115 countries. Neither its rating nor ranking have changed substantially during the last two decades. Among its Asian neighbors, Indonesia falls in the middle. This economy is clearly less free than those of Hong Kong, Singapore, Malaysia, Thailand, South Korea, and Taiwan, but more free than India, Bangladesh, and Nepal. There are two major areas that Indonesia must improve if it is going to achieve its full potential. These two deficiencies are:

• Legal Structure—Absence of Rule of Law. The legal structure provides public officials with too much arbitrary authority. When the discretion of government officials replaces the rule of law, the security of property rights is undermined and corruption (for example, bribes, selective enforcement of regulations, and favoritism) becomes a way of life. A legal structure of this type undermines market allocation.

• Excessive Regulation. This is a regulated economy. Price controls, limitations on entry into business and professional practice, and restrictions on the movement of capital are widespread. Government enterprises—often protected from potential market competitors—operate in many sectors of the economy.

Despite these shortcomings, Indonesia's growth record during the last two decades has been outstanding. With movement toward a freer economy, it could follow the path of Japan and become a major economic power.

IRAN

Economic Freedom Rating

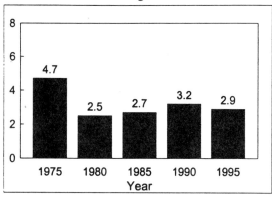

**Total Government Expenditures
As A Percent of GDP**

No Data

Part 1: The Economic Freedom Ratings for the Components and Various Area and Summary Indexes: 1975, 1980, 1985, 1990 and 1995.
(The numbers in parentheses indicate the actual values for the components.)

Components of Economic Freedom	1975		1980		1985		1990		1995	
I. Money and Inflation	**2.5**		**4.9**		**5.2**		**6.6**		**1.0**	
(a) Annual Money Growth (last 5 yrs.)	1	(26.6)	1	(37.4)	2	(20.3)	3	(15.3)	1	(26.6)
(b) Inflation Variablity (last 5 yrs.)	1	(20.4)	3	(6.1)	3	(6.8)	6	(3.6)	2	(8.9)
(c) Ownership of Foreign Currency	10		10		10		10		0	
(d) Maint. of Bank Account Abroad	0		10		10		10		0	
II. Government Operation	**2.0**		**1.5**		**3.5**		**3.6**		**2.3**	
(a) Gov't Consump. (% of Total Consump.)	0	(36.5)	1	(28.3)	5	(19.6)	7	(14.7)	6	(17.6)
(b) Government Enterprises	4		2		2		2		2	
(c) Price Controls	-		-		-		2		2	
(d) Entry Into Business	-		-		-		-		2.5	
(e) Legal System	-		-		-		-		0.0	
(f) Avoidance of Neg. Interest Rates	-		-		-		-		0	
III. Takings	**5.3**		**3.8**		**3.2**		**2.8**		**5.1**	
(a) Transfers and Subsidies (% of GDP)	4	(8.9)	5	(7.0)	8	(3.0)	7	(4.4)	8	(3.2)
(b) Marginal Tax Rates (Top Rate)	8	(40)	-		0	(90)	0	(75)	4	(54)
(c) Conscription	0		0		0		0		0	
IV. International Sector	**7.0**		**0.6**		**0.0**		**1.4**		**2.6**	
(a) Taxes on International Trade (Avg.)	7	(3.6)	0	(17.0)	0	(14.2)	3	(7.3)	6	(5.6)
(b) Black Market Exchange Rates (Prem.)	7	(2)	1	(164)	0	(533)	0	(2197)	1	(115)
(c) Size of Trade Sector (% of GDP)	10	(38.0)	2	(14.9)	0	(8.0)	3	(16.6)	3	(16.2)
(d) Capital Transactions with Foreigners	5		0		0		0		0	
Economic Freedom Rating	**4.7**		**2.5**		**2.7**		**3.2**		**2.9**	
Ranking of Country	**32**		**97**		**95**		**93**		**110**	

118

Part 2: Recent Economic Indicators:

Population 1996: (in millions)	62.4		**Real Per Capita GDP** : (in 1995 U.S. dollars)			1995=	$4,810		
Annual Rate of Change (1985-96):	3.5%		Avg. Growth Rate:			1980-90=	0.0%		
						1990-95=	2.9%		

Economic Indicators:*	1988	1989	1990	1991	1992	1993	1994	1995	1996
Change in Real GDP: Aggregate	-8.7	3.3	11.7	11.4	5.7	1.6	1.9	4.2	-
: Per Capita	-12.2	-0.2	8.2	7.9	3.2	-1.9	-1.6	1.9	-
Inflation Rate (CPI)	28.7	22.3	7.6	17.1	25.6	21.2	31.5	49.6	-
Change in Money Supply: (M1)	10.2	15.7	18.1	26.1	14.8	30.0	41.6	32.5	-
: (M2)	20.1	22.5	18.0	25.6	24.4	30.3	33.3	30.1	-
Investment/GDP Ratio	19.1	23.8	28.6	33.2	35.4	29.0	23.0	20.0	-
Size of Trade Sector (% of GDP)	7.3	11.5	16.6	17.2	15.6	23.5	21.3	16.2	-
Total Gov't Exp./GDP Ratio									
Central Government Budget Deficit (-) or Surplus (+) As a Percent of GDP	-9.2	-3.9	-1.8	-2.3	-1.4	-0.3	-0.1	-	-
Unemployment Rate									

* The figures in this table are in percent form.

In 1975, the Iranian economic freedom rating of 4.7 placed it 32nd among the countries in our study. That changed dramatically following the Iranian revolution and the overthrow of the Shah. By 1980 Iran had fallen to 97th and in 1995 it placed 110th. This means that it is one of the least free countries in the world.

Inspection of the components makes it clear why Iran received such a low rating. Monetary policy is highly expansionary—the M1 money supply grew at an annual rate of almost 30% during 1991-1995. Of course, high and variable rates of inflation have accompanied this money growth. Citizens are not allowed to have foreign currency bank accounts, so the function of money as a store of value is undermined. Government enterprises are widespread throughout the economy.

Equal protection under the law is weak; political figures have a substantial amount of discretionary authority. Taxes take 54% of the marginal earnings of productive citizens—and this is down from 90% in 1985 and 75% in 1990. Conscription takes the labor of the young. The taxes on international trade are high. Exchange rate controls have led to a more than 100% black market premium. As a share of GDP, the size of the trade sector is now *less than half* its size in 1975. Foreigners are not allowed to undertake domestic investments and neither are citizens allowed to make investments abroad without the permission of the government.

The 1995 per capita real GDP of Iran was 40% *less than* the 1975 figure. Countries that stifle economic freedom pay a price.

IRELAND

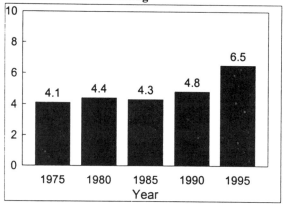

Economic Freedom Rating

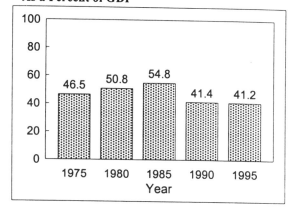

Total Government Expenditures
As a Percent of GDP

Part 1: The Economic Freedom Ratings for the Components and Various Area and Summary Indexes: 1975, 1980, 1985, 1990 and 1995.
(The numbers in parentheses indicate the actual values for the components.)

Components of Economic Freedom	1975		1980		1985		1990		1995	
I. Money and Inflation	**3.5**		**2.9**		**4.4**		**5.1**		**9.7**	
(a) Annual Money Growth (last 5 yrs.)	6	(12.0)	3	(17.2)	9	(6.0)	9	(5.6)	9	(4.9)
(b) Inflation Variablity (last 5 yrs.)	5	(4.7)	6	(3.5)	5	(4.8)	7	(2.5)	10	(0.7)
(c) Ownership of Foreign Currency	0		0		0		0		10	
(d) Maint. of Bank Account Abroad	0		0		0		0		10	
II. Government Operation	**4.0**		**4.4**		**4.9**		**5.8**		**6.4**	
(a) Gov't Consump. (% of Total Consump.)	4	(21.2)	4	(21.9)	3	(22.3)	4	(20.6)	3	(22.3)
(b) Government Enterprises	4		4		4		4		4	
(c) Price Controls	-		-		-		7		8	
(d) Entry Into Business	-		-		-		-		7.5	
(e) Legal System	-		-		-		-		7.5	
(f) Avoidance of Neg. Interest Rates	4		6		10		10		10	
III. Takings	**2.1**		**2.6**		**1.7**		**2.2**		**2.7**	
(a) Transfers and Subsidies (% of GDP)	2	(18.3)	2	(17.7)	1	(20.5)	1	(24.2)	0	(27.1)
(b) Marginal Tax Rates (Top Rate)	0	(80)	1	(60)	0	(65)	1	(58)	3	(48)
(c) Conscription	10		10		10		10		10	
IV. International Sector	**6.8**		**7.5**		**6.8**		**6.9**		**8.9**	
(a) Taxes on International Trade (Avg.)	6	(4.8)	7	(3.0)	8	(2.5)	7	(2.6)	8	(1.5)
(b) Black Market Exchange Rates (Prem.)	10	(0)	10	(0)	6	(3)	8	(1)	10	(0)
(c) Size of Trade Sector (% of GDP)	6	(43.7)	8	(53.8)	9	(56.7)	8	(56.8)	10	(71.8)
(d) Capital Transactions with Foreigners	5		5		5		5		8	
Economic Freedom Rating	**4.1**		**4.4**		**4.3**		**4.8**		**6.5**	
Ranking of Country	**50**		**40**		**51**		**43**		**21**	

Part 2: Recent Economic Indicators:

| Population 1996: | 3.6 | **Real Per Capita GDP** : | 1996= | $17,454 |

Population 1996: (in millions)   3.6

Annual Rate of Change (1985-96):   0.1%

Real Per Capita GDP : (in 1995 U.S. dollars)

1996= $17,454

Avg. Growth Rate: 1980-90=   3.3%

1990-96=   5.4%

Economic Indicators:*	1988	1989	1990	1991	1992	1993	1994	1995	1996
Change in Real GDP: Aggregate	4.3	6.1	7.8	2.2	3.9	3.1	6.7	7.0	8.0
: Per Capita	4.2	6.0	7.7	2.1	3.8	3.0	6.6	6.9	7.9
Inflation Rate (CPI)	2.2	4.1	3.3	3.2	3.1	1.4	2.3	2.5	2.0
Change in Money Supply: (M1)	7.1	10.1	7.5	1.3	-4.0	22.9	12.6	13.8	14.0
: (M2)	6.5	14.0	8.9	11.4	12.7	19.2	4.5	14.1	18.0
Investment/GDP Ratio	18.5	16.4	18.0	18.9	17.4	15.7	15.1	15.8	16.1
Size of Trade Sector (% of GDP)	56.4	60.6	56.8	57.2	58.1	62.8	67.4	71.8	72.7
Total Gov't Exp./GDP Ratio	47.2	40.6	41.1	42.6	43.2	43.1	42.9	41.2	39.7 ᴾ
General Government Budget Deficit (-) or Surplus (+) As a Percent of GDP	-4.4	-1.8	-2.3	-2.4	-2.5	-2.5	-2.0	-2.3	-1.5
Unemployment Rate	16.2	14.7	13.3	14.7	15.5	15.6	14.3	12.4	12.5

* The figures in this table are in percent form.

ᴾ Preliminary.

After earning ratings just above 4 during 1975-1985, the economic freedom rating of Ireland jumped to 4.8 in 1990 and 6.5 in 1995. Ireland ranked 21st (tied with Netherlands) in 1995, up from 51st in 1985.

Several factors contributed to this rating improvement. Monetary policy has been considerably less expansionary during recent years than was true during the 1970s and early 1980s. As a result, the inflation rate has fluctuated within a narrow band around 3% during the 1990s. The legal ban against the maintenance of foreign currency bank accounts—both domestically and abroad—was lifted in the early 1990s. The top marginal tax rate was cut from the 80% rate of the 1970s to 65% in 1985 and 48% in the 1990s. The Irish pound is now a fully convertible currency. The size of the trade sector as a share of GDP has steadily increased during the last two decades. The trade sector is now nearly twice the size of the figure during the mid-1970s. Furthermore, total government expenditures have declined slightly as a share of GDP during the last decade.

Despite these positive developments, there is reason to believe that they may paint a picture that is too rosy. Tax concessions and other indirect subsidies have often been used to attract foreign investment. As currently structured, our index fails to capture discriminatory treatment and indirect subsidies of this type. During the last two decades, GDP has grown more rapidly than GNP. Thus, the income of the "nationals" has not increased as rapidly as the growth of domestic output. Clearly, unemployment is a severe and continuing problem. Even though the Irish economy experienced a decade of strong growth, unemployment was still 12% during 1996. When a growing economy has prolonged double-digit unemployment, it invariably reflects transfer payments that reduce the cost of joblessness and/or regulations that make it expensive to hire and terminate employees. Ireland desperately needs to revise its transfer system and deregulate its labor market in order to achieve its full potential.

121

ISRAEL

Economic Freedom Rating

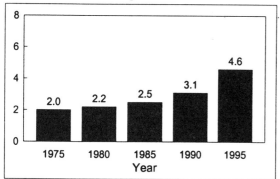

Total Government Expenditures
As A Percent of GDP

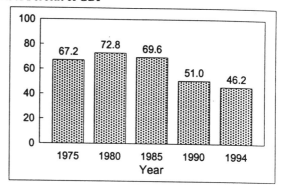

Part 1: The Economic Freedom Ratings for the Components and Various Area and Indexes: 1975, 1980, 1985, 1990 and 1995.
(The numbers in parentheses indicate the actual values for the components.)

Components of Economic Freedom	1975		1980		1985		1990		1995	
I. Money and Inflation	**2.9**		**1.9**		**1.9**		**2.9**		**5.4**	
(a) Annual Rate of Money Growth (last 5 yrs.)	1	(24.7)	0	(45.6)	0	(172.3)	1	(44.1)	5	(13.6)
(b) Inflation Variablity (last 5 yrs.)	2	(9.4)	0	(33.2)	0	(101.7)	2	(13.0)	6	(3.8)
(c) Ownership of Foreign Currency	10		10		10		10		10	
(d) Maintenance of Bank Account Abroad	0		0		0		0		0	
II. Government Operation	**1.0**		**0.8**		**0.8**		**1.4**		**4.3**	
(a) Gov't Consump. (% of Total Consump.)	0	(42.3)	0	(43.2)	0	(38.7)	0	(32.9)	0	(32.1)
(b) Government Enterprises	2		2		2		2		2	
(c) Price Controls	-		-		-		0		5	
(d) Entry Into Business	-		-		-		-		7.5	
(e) Legal System	-		-		-		-		5.0	
(f) Avoidance of Negative Interest Rates	-		0		0		6		8	
III. Takings	**0.0**		**0.9**		**1.8**		**2.7**		**2.7**	
(a) Transfers and Subsidies (% of GDP)	-		1	(20.8)	1	(19.7)	2	(16.7)	2	(18.6)
(b) Marginal Tax Rates (Top Rate)	-		1	(66)	3	(60)	4	(51)	4	(50)
(c) Conscription	0		0		0		0		0	
IV. International Sector	**2.3**		**5.2**		**4.8**		**5.4**		**6.8**	
(a) Taxes of International Trade (Avg. Rate)	2	(8.0)	6	(5.1)	7	(2.9)	9	(0.9)	10	(0.2)
(b) Black Market Exchange Rates (Premium)	2	(60)	8	(1)	5	(7)	6	(4)	10	(0)
(c) Size of Trade Sector (% of GDP)	4	(38.7)	4	(45.2)	5	(42.9)	3	(34.5)	3	(40.2)
(d) Capital Transactions with Foreigners	2		2		2		2		2	
Economic Freedom Rating	**2.0**		**2.2**		**2.5**		**3.1**		**4.6**	
Ranking of Country	**94**		**102**		**99**		**94**		**70**	

122

Part 2: Recent Economic Indicators:

Population 1996:   5.7   **Real Per Capita GDP**   :   1996 = $15,206
  (in millions)   (in 1995 U.S. dollars)
Annual Rate of Change (1985-96):   2.7%   Avg. Growth Rate: 1980-90=   1.8%
                                                           1990-96=   2.9%

Economic Indicators:*	1988	1989	1990	1991	1992	1993	1994	1995	1996
Change in Real GDP:Aggregate	3.1	1.3	5.8	6.2	6.6	3.9	6.5	6.8	3.2
: Per Capita	0.4	-1.4	3.1	3.5	3.9	1.2	3.8	4.1	0.5
Inflation Rate (CPI)	16.3	20.2	17.2	19.0	11.9	10.9	12.3	10.0	10.6
Change in Money Supply: (M1)	11.3	44.4	30.6	13.7	33.7	27.9	7.7	15.1	-
: (M2)	22.3	21.0	19.4	17.7	25.4	22.0	24.6	21.7	-
Investment/GDP Ratio	17.3	15.9	18.7	24.3	24.3	24.0	24.2	24.9	-
Size of Trade Sector (% of GDP)	34.4	35.8	34.5	32.1	32.2	35.6	40.6	40.2	-
Total Gov't Exp./GDP Ratio	47.7	47.4	48.6	47.8	48.5	46.9	46.2	-	-
Central Government Budget Deficit (-) or Surplus (+) As a Percent of GDP	-8.0	-3.9	-4.3	-8.0	-3.9	-1.8	-3.1	-	-
Unemployment Rate	6.4	8.9	9.6	10.6	11.2	10.0	7.8	6.9	-

* The figures in this table are in percent form.

Among the countries that we were able to rate in 1975, only Russia and Uganda had a lower rating than Israel. While little progress was made during the 1975-1985 period, Israel has made some modest moves toward economic freedom during the last decade. In 1995 Israel ranked 70th among the 115 nations in our study.

What factors contributed to the increase in Israel's rating? The monetary policy of the 1990s has been far less expansionary and, as the result, the inflation rate has descended from the astronomical levels of 1975-1985. While still huge, transfers and subsidies are now a little smaller as a share of the economy than was true a decade ago. Tariff rates have been reduced and both exchange and interest rate controls have been relaxed.

Despite these changes, this is still a government-dominated economy. Government accounted for one-third of the total consumption spending in 1995. Only Bahrain, Oman, Botswana, and Sweden channeled a larger share of their consumption through the government (rather than having it directed by personal choice and market prices.) There has been far more talk than action in the area of privatization. The share of resources consumed by state-operated enterprises changed very little dur-ing the last decade. While the top marginal tax rate has been reduced, it still remains at the 50% level. (Note: in 1996 Israel instituted a new payroll tax to finance health care. A plan to withhold taxes on second jobs at a 50% marginal rate has just been enacted. These efforts to squeeze still more revenue from the taxpayer reflect Israel's attempt to balance the budget. See below.) Countries that take one half of the marginal earnings of their most productive citizens are unlikely to reach their full potential.

Government expenditures as a share of the economy are now lower than was true during the 1980s. This downward trend, however should be interpreted with caution. It is primarily due to pressure—both domestic and international—to reduce the size of government debt and the budget deficit. Balancing the budget in Israel has a very unique meaning. Israel receives approximately 12% of its national income ($10 billion in 1995) in the form of "remittances" and guaranteed loans. Most of these funds are, in one form or another, transfers from abroad. No other country—certainly none with such a high per capita income level—receives transfers even close to this magnitude.

(Continued on page 203.)

123

ITALY

Economic Freedom Rating

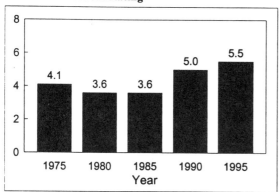

Total Government Expenditures
As A Percent of GDP

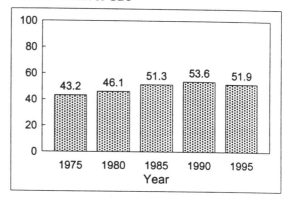

Part 1: The Economic Freedom Ratings for the Components and Various Area and Summary Indexes: 1975, 1980, 1985, 1990 and 1995.
(The numbers in parentheses indicate the actual values for the components.)

Components of Economic Freedom	1975		1980		1985		1990		1995	
I. Money and Inflation	**2.2**		**3.0**		**3.5**		**9.4**		**9.7**	
(a) Annual Money Growth (last 5 yrs.)	3	(16.9)	1	(20.7)	5	(12.5)	8	(7.7)	10	(1.9)
(b) Inflation Variablity (last 5 yrs.)	4	(5.2)	8	(2.2)	6	(3.8)	10	(0.8)	9	(1.4)
(c) Ownership of Foreign Currency	0		0		0		10		10	
(d) Maint. of Bank Account Abroad	0		0		0		10		10	
II. Government Operation	**4.0**		**3.6**		**3.6**		**4.6**		**5.6**	
(a) Gov't Consump. (% of Total Comsump.)	5	(18.5)	5	(19.4)	4	(21.1)	4	(22.1)	4	(21.6)
(b) Government Enterprises	2		2		2		2		2	
(c) Price Controls	-		-		-		5		5	
(d) Entry Into Business	-		-		-		-		7.5	
(e) Legal System	-		-		-		-		7.5	
(f) Avoidance of Neg. Interest Rates	6		4		6		10		10	
III. Takings	**3.1**		**0.4**		**0.0**		**0.5**		**0.5**	
(a) Transfers and Subsidies (% of GDP)	2	(17.5)	1	(20.9)	0	(28.5)	0	(25.8)	0	(29.3)
(b) Marginal Tax Rates (Top Rate)	5	(48)	0	(72)	0	(81)	1	(66)	1	(67)
(c) Conscription	0		0		0		0		0	
IV. International Sector	**6.5**		**7.9**		**8.0**		**7.7**		**8.7**	
(a) Taxes on International Trade (Avg.)	10	(0.3)	10	(0.0)	10	(0.0)	10	(0.0)	10	(0.0)
(b) Black Market Exchange Rates (Prem.)	5	(9)	10	(0)	10	(0)	10	(0)	10	(0)
(c) Size of Trade Sector (% of GDP)	5	(20.6)	5	(23.3)	6	(23.0)	4	(20.7)	5	(23.7)
(d) Capital Transactions with Foreigners	5		5		5		5		8	
Economic Freedom Rating	**4.1**		**3.6**		**3.6**		**5.0**		**5.5**	
Ranking of Country	**50**		**67**		**77**		**39**		**55**	

124

Part 2: Recent Economic Indicators:

Population 1996:	57.4	**Real Per Capita GDP**	:	1996=	$18,275
(in millions)		(in 1995 U.S. dollars)			
Annual Rate of Change (1984-96):	0.0%	Avg. Growth Rate:	1980-90=	2.0%	
			1990-96=	1.1%	

Economic Indicators:*	1988	1989	1990	1991	1992	1993	1994	1995	1996
Change in Real GDP: Aggregate	4.1	2.9	2.1	1.3	0.9	-1.2	2.1	3.0	0.8
: Per Capita	4.1	2.9	2.1	1.3	0.9	-1.5	1.9	2.1	0.6
Inflation Rate (CPI)	5.1	6.2	6.5	6.3	5.1	4.5	4.0	5.2	3.8
Change in Money Supply: (M1)	7.8	12.7	6.8	11.4	1.5	6.1	3.2	1.3	1.8
: (M2)	7.7	11.2	8.8	9.5	5.5	7.3	1.0	2.4	3.5
Investment/GDP Ratio	21.5	21.3	21.0	20.5	19.4	16.9	16.6	17.0	20.5
Size of Trade Sector (% of GDP)	19.2	20.4	20.7	19.5	19.9	19.8	20.9	23.7	22.5
Total Gov't Exp./GDP Ratio	50.7	51.7	53.6	53.9	54.0	57.9	54.6	52.9	53.2
General Government Budget Deficit (-) or Surplus (+) As a Percent of GDP	-10.7	-9.9	-11.0	-10.2	-9.5	-10.0	-9.5	-7.4	-7.3
Unemployment Rate	11.0	10.9	10.3	9.9	10.5	10.3	11.4	11.9	12.2

* The figures in this table are in percent form.

After declining during 1975-1985, Italy's economic freedom rating has increased during the last decade. Its ranking has followed a similar path. In 1995 the Italian economy ranked 55th, up from its ranking of 77th in 1985, but still below its 50th place position in 1975.

The bright spots of the Italian economy are monetary policy and international trade. Historically, Italy's monetary expansion and inflation rates have been the highest among the large industrial nations. This is no longer true. Monetary expansion has been moderate during the last decade and the inflation rate has hovered around 4% in the 1990s. Italy also legalized the maintenance of foreign currency bank accounts, both domestically and abroad, in the late 1980s. These factors resulted in a sharp rating increase in the monetary area. In the trade area, tariffs are low, the Italian lira is fully convertible, and restrictions limiting capital movement are liberal. Thus, Italy also rates well in this area.

The problem areas are the size of government, a huge transfer sector, and high marginal tax rates. Even through there has been some privatization, state-operated enterprises still account for almost 20% of the non-agricultural business sector. Government expenditures sum to more than 50% of GDP. In 1995, almost 30% of GDP was taxed away from its earner and transferred to another. Of course, big government means high taxes and Italy's taxes are just about the highest in the world. In fact, Italy's top marginal personal income tax rate of 67% (counting the 16% local income tax that is collected by the central government) is the highest among the 115 countries in our study. Furthermore, budget deficits are already huge—between 7% and 10% of GDP. Deficits of this size cannot be maintained over the long term. Given its high taxes, large budget deficits, and double-digit rates of unemployment, Italy is sure to confront difficult economic choices in the near future.

JAPAN

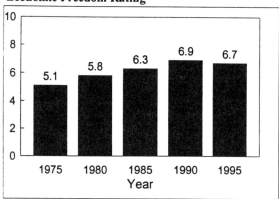

Economic Freedom Rating

Year	Rating
1975	5.1
1980	5.8
1985	6.3
1990	6.9
1995	6.7

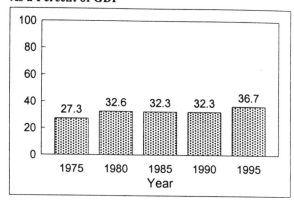

Total Government Expenditures As a Percent of GDP

Year	Percent
1975	27.3
1980	32.6
1985	32.3
1990	32.3
1995	36.7

Part 1: The Economic Freedom Ratings for the Components and Various Area and Summary Indexes: 1975, 1980, 1985, 1990 and 1995.

(The numbers in parentheses indicate the actual values for the components.)

Components of Economic Freedom	1975		1980		1985		1990		1995	
I. Money and Inflation	3.9		7.6		8.0		10.0		10.0	
(a) Annual Money Growth (last 5 yrs.)	2	(17.6)	9	(6.4)	9	(4.6)	10	(3.9)	10	(3.3)
(b) Inflation Variablity (last 5 yrs.)	4	(5.6)	9	(1.7)	10	(0.8)	10	(0.9)	10	(0.7)
(c) Ownership of Foreign Currency	10		10		10		10		10	
(d) Maint. of Bank Account Abroad	0		0		0		10		10	
II. Government Operation	6.8		8.0		8.4		7.7		7.4	
(a) Gov't Consump. (% of Total Consump.)	7	(14.9)	7	(14.3)	8	(14.0)	8	(13.7)	8	(13.9)
(b) Government Enterprises	8		8		8		8		8	
(c) Price Controls	-		-		-		6		5	
(d) Entry Into Business	-		-		-		-		7.5	
(e) Legal System	-		-		-		-		7.5	
(f) Avoidance of Neg. Interest Rates	4		10		10		10		10	
III. Takings	3.8		2.9		3.4		3.9		3.5	
(a) Transfers and Subsidies (% of GDP)	5	(6.7)	4	(9.2)	4	(10.9)	4	(11.5)	3	(12.2)
(b) Marginal Tax Rates (Top Rate)	1	(68)	0	(75)	1	(70)	2	(65)	2	(65)
(c) Conscription	10		10		10		10		10	
IV. International Sector	6.5		6.5		7.2		7.7		7.2	
(a) Taxes on International Trade (Avg.)	9	(1.3)	9	(0.9)	9	(0.8)	9	(0.9)	8	(1.6)
(b) Black Market Exchange Rates (Prem.)	10	(0)	10	(0)	10	(0)	10	(0)	10	(0)
(c) Size of Trade Sector (% of GDP)	3	(12.8)	3	(14.1)	3	(12.8)	1	(10.5)	0	(8.7)
(d) Capital Transactions with Foreigners	2		2		5		8		8	
Economic Freedom Rating	5.1		5.8		6.3		6.9		6.7	
Ranking of Country	22		16		9		8		18	

Part 2: Recent Economic Indicators:

Population 1996:	125.5	**Real Per Capita GDP** :	1996=	$22,149
(in millions)		(in 1995 U.S. dollars)		
Annual Rate of Change (1985-96):	0.4%	Avg. Growth Rate:	1980-90=	3.5%
			1990-96=	1.8%

Economic Indicators:*	1988	1989	1990	1991	1992	1993	1994	1995	1996
Change in Real GDP: Aggregate	6.2	4.8	4.8	4.3	1.4	0.1	0.5	0.9	3.2
: Per Capita	5.8	4.4	4.4	3.9	1.0	-0.3	0.1	0.5	2.8
Inflation Rate (CPI)	0.7	2.3	3.1	3.3	1.7	1.3	0.7	-0.1	0.6
Change in Money Supply: (M1)	8.6	2.4	4.5	9.5	3.9	7.0	4.2	13.1	10.3
: (M2)	9.8	11.8	8.2	2.5	-0.1	2.2	3.1	2.8	3.2
Investment/GDP Ratio	30.6	31.8	32.8	32.5	31.1	29.9	28.9	29.5	30.4
Size of Trade Sector (% of GDP)	9.0	10.0	10.5	9.5	9.0	8.3	8.4	8.7	9.0
Total/Gov't Exp./GDP Ratio	32.2	31.5	32.3	32.0	32.9	34.9	35.6	36.7	37.5 P
General Government Budget Deficit (-) or Surplus (+) As a Percent of GDP	+1.5	+2.5	+2.9	+2.9	+1.4	-1.6	-2.1	-3.3	-4.1
Unemployment Rate	2.5	2.3	2.1	2.1	2.2	2.5	2.9	3.1	3.4 a

* The figures in this table are in percent form.

a October, 1996.

P Preliminary.

Our index indicates that the economic freedom of Japan increased steadily during 1975-1990, before receding slightly during the last five years. Its 1995 rating places it 18th (out of 115), down from an 8th place ranking in 1990.

Japan's greatest strength is in the Money and Inflation area. It earned a "perfect ten" in this area in both 1990 and 1995, compared to 3.9 in 1975. For the last ten to fifteen years, Japan has been a model of monetary stability. For a high-income industrial country, Japan's government consumption expenditures are relatively small. Its rating in this area is the highest among the industrial nations. Its major weaknesses are high marginal tax rates (its top marginal rate of 65% is now one of the highest in the world) and non-tariff trade restraints (note how the size of the trade sector is much smaller than would be expected for a country of this size and location).

In contrast with the mid-1970s, Japan is no longer a small government economy. Pushed along by the growth of the transfer sector, government expenditures have steadily risen from 27% of GDP in 1975 to 36.7% in 1995. Japanese government expenditures as a share of the economy are now approximately the same size as those of the United States. The Japanese economy has struggled in the 1990s. This may well reflect that as government becomes larger, adjustments to change are increasingly difficult.

KENYA

Economic Freedom Rating

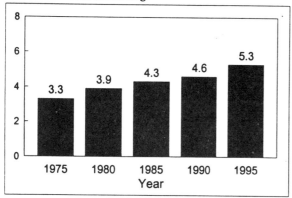

Economic Freedom Rating

Total Government Expenditures As a Percent of GDP

No Data

Part 1: The Economic Freedom Ratings for the Components and Various Area and Summary Indexes: 1975, 1980, 1985, 1990 and 1995.

(The numbers in parentheses indicate the actual values for the components.)

Components of Economic Freedom	1975		1980		1985		1990		1995	
I. Money and Inflation	**2.2**		**1.9**		**5.5**		**4.5**		**3.8**	
(a) Annual Money Growth (last 5 yrs.)	5	(12.5)	3	(15.1)	7	(8.5)	5	(13.6)	3	(16.5)
(b) Inflation Variablity (last 5 yrs.)	2	(9.3)	3	(6.1)	10	(1.2)	9	(1.4)	3	(7.9)
(c) Ownership of Foreign Currency	0		0		0		0		10	
(d) Maint. of Bank Account Abroad	0		0		0		0		0	
II. Government Operation	**4.0**		**4.1**		**4.9**		**4.0**		**4.0**	
(a) Gov't Consump. (% of Total Consump.)	4	(21.2)	2	(24.2)	3	(23.3)	3	(23.1)	6	(17.8)
(b) Government Enterprises	4		4		4		4		4	
(c) Price Controls	-		-		-		2		4	
(d) Entry Into Business	-		-		-		-		5.0	
(e) Legal System	-		-		-		-		0.0	
(f) Avoidance of Neg. Interest Rates	4		8		10		10		4	
III. Takings	**2.2**		**5.0**		**3.7**		**5.9**		**6.3**	
(a) Transfers and Subsidies (% of GDP)	-		8	(2.3)	6	(4.7)	8	(2.8)	9	(1.9)
(b) Marginal Tax Rates (Top Rate)	0	(70)	1	(65)	0	(65)	3	(50)	3	(50)
(c) Conscription	10		10		10		10		10	
IV. International Sector	**4.5**		**3.7**		**3.6**		**3.8**		**7.1**	
(a) Taxes on International Trade (Avg.)	6	(5.5)	5	(6.1)	3	(7.4)	4	(6.3)	6	(5.0)
(b) Black Market Exchange Rates (Prem.)	5	(8)	4	(10)	7	(2)	6	(6)	7	(2)
(c) Size of Trade Sector (% of GDP)	8	(32.2)	7	(33.5)	5	(25.8)	6	(28.8)	8	(36.3)
(d) Capital Transactions with Foreigners	0		0		0		0		8	
Economic Freedom Rating	**3.3**		**3.9**		**4.3**		**4.6**		**5.3**	
Ranking of Country	**72**		**52**		**51**		**56**		**61**	

Part 2: Recent Economic Indicators:

Population 1996: (in millions)	31.8	**Real Per Capita GDP** : (in 1995 U.S. dollars)	1995= $1,188
Annual Rate of Change (1985-96):	4.2%	Avg. Growth Rate: 1980-90= 1990-95=	0.4% -2.0%

Economic Indicators:*	1988	1989	1990	1991	1992	1993	1994	1995	1996
Change in Real GDP: Aggregate	6.2	4.7	4.2	1.4	-0.8	0.4	3.9	4.4	-
: Per Capita	2.0	0.5	0.0	-2.8	-5.0	-3.8	-0.3	0.2	-
Inflation Rate (CPI)	11.2	12.9	15.6	19.8	29.5	45.8	29.0	0.8	-
Change in Money Supply: (M1)	1.3	13.0	27.2	15.0	47.1	27.4	12.6	3.8	-
: (M2)	8.0	12.9	20.1	19.6	39.0	28.0	31.5	16.4	-
Investment/GDP Ratio	25.0	24.7	24.3	21.3	17.4	18.4	19.6	22.0	-
Size of Trade Sector (% of GDP)	24.5	26.8	28.8	28.0	27.0	39.5	36.1	36.3	-
Total Gov't Exp./GDP Ratio									
Central Government Budget Deficit (-) or Surplus (+) (As a Percent of GDP)	-4.4	-6.9	-4.0	-2.8	-0.4	-4.0	-3.4	-	-
Unemployment Rate									

* The figures in this table are in percent form.

While Kenya's economic freedom rating has risen during the last two decades, its ranking has declined slightly. Among the 115 of our study, it ranked 61st in 1995, down from 51st in 1980. Both its modest 5.3 rating and 1995 ranking indicate that it still has a long way to go.

Reductions in marginal tax rates (from 65% to 50%) and some deregulation of financial markets account for most of the rating improvement. Monetary and price stability continues to be a problem. There has been little privatization and inefficient government enterprises continue to exert a negative impact on the economy. The legal structure often operates in a discriminatory manner. Public officials have a great deal of discretionary authority that often reaches beyond the scope of the law. As the result, corruption is widespread and it contributes significantly to the cost of doing business.

Perhaps most significantly, the credibility of even the modest steps toward a market economy is very low—and with good reason. Responding to a recent drought, the president invoked the Emergency Powers Act in February 1997. This act provides the government with broad powers to regulate the prices of food products, control the movement of both goods and people, and determine what goods will be imported and exported. Actions of this type undermine the confidence of entrepreneurs and investors both at home and abroad. If this country is going to prosper in the future, fundamental structural reform will be required. At the moment, there is little sign that such a plan is on the horizon.

LITHUANIA

Economic Freedom Rating

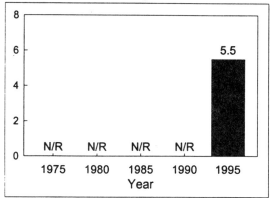

Total Government Expenditures As a Percent of GDP

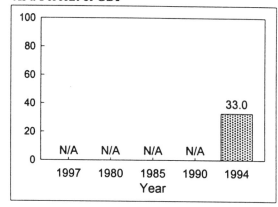

Part 1: The Economic Freedom Ratings for the Components and Various Area and Summary Indexes: 1975, 1980, 1985, 1990 and 1995.
(The numbers in parentheses indicate the actual values for the components.)

Components of Economic Freedom	1995	
I. Money and Inflation	**3.6**	
(a) Annual Money Growth (last 5 yrs.)	0	(53.0)
(b) Inflation Variablity (last 5 yrs.)	0	(357.8)
(c) Ownership of Foreign Currency	10	
(d) Maint. of Bank Account Abroad	10	
II. Government Operation	**4.5**	
(a) Gov't Consump. (% of Total Consump.)	7	(14.6)
(b) Government Enterprises	0	
(c) Price Controls	4	
(d) Entry Into Business	7.5	
(e) Legal System	7.5	
(f) Avoidance of Neg. Interest Rates	0	
III. Takings	**4.9**	
(a) Transfers and Subsidies (% of GDP)	4	(10.4)
(b) Marginal Tax Rates (Top Rate)	7	(35)
(c) Conscription	0	
IV. International Sector	**9.0**	
(a) Taxes on International Trade (Avg.)	9	(0.7)
(b) Black Market Exchange Rates (Prem.)	10	(0)
(c) Size of Trade Sector (% of GDP)	9	(63.1)
(d) Capital Transactions with Foreigners	8	
Economic Freedom Rating	**5.5**	
Ranking of Country	**55**	

130

Part 2: Recent Economic Indicators:

Population 1996:	3.7	**Real Per Capita GDP** :		1996=	$3,531
(in millions)		(in 1995 U.S. dollars)			
Annual Rate of Change (1992-96):	-0.3%	Avg. Growth Rate:	1980-90=		-
			1990-96=	-9.4%	

Economic Indicators:*	1988	1989	1990	1991	1992	1993	1994	1995	1996
Change in Real GDP: Aggregate	-	-	5.0	-13.0	-35.0	-30.3	1.0	2.6	1.5
: Per Capita	-	-	5.3	-12.7	-34.7	-30.0	1.3	2.9	1.8
Inflation Rate (CPI)	-	-	8.4	224.7	1020.3	390.2	72.2	39.7	28.0
Change in Money Supply: (M1)	-	-	-	-	-	-	-	41.7	-
: (M2)	-	-	-	-	-	-	-	29.8	-
Investment/GDP Ratio									
Size of Trade Sector (% of GDP)	-	-	-	-	68.0	63.1	-	-	-
Total Gov't Exp./GDP Ratio	-	-	-	-	32.9	30.4	33.0	-	-
Central Government Budget Deficit (-) or Surplus (+) As a Percent of GDP	-	-	-	-	-	-	-4.2	-3.3	-3.4
Unemployment Rate	-	-	-	-	1.0	1.4	3.8	6.2	6.4

* The figures in this table are in percent form.

Lithuania's 5.5 rating in 1995 placed it 55th among the 115 countries in our study. Our index indicates that Lithuania and Estonia (which had a one-tenth of a point higher rating) were the freest of the former socialist countries in 1995.

While Lithuania is not yet a free market economy, the foundation has been laid. The size of both the government consumption and the income transfer sectors are modest by European standards. Citizens are free to maintain foreign currency bank accounts and entry restraints into business are comparable to those of Western Europe. The top marginal tax rate (35% percent in 1995) is relatively low. The international trade sector is a strength of the economy. Tariffs are low, the ex-

change rate is driven by market forces, and the size of the trade sector is large, even for a country of such small size.

Monetary instability is a continuing problem. Even though the inflation rate has declined sharply from the levels of 1992-1993, it is still running in the 30% range. Like neighboring Estonia, Lithuania is off to a reasonably good start. Total government expenditures (33% of GDP in 1995) are low by European standards. If it can move toward monetary stability and control the growth of government (both spending and regulation), it can look forward to a period of expanding economic freedom and prosperity in the future.

MALAYSIA

Economic Freedom Rating

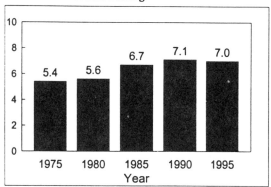

**Total Government Expenditures
As a Percent of GDP**

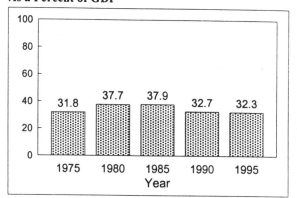

Part 1: The Economic Freedom Ratings for the Components and Various Area and Summary Indexes: 1975, 1980, 1985, 1990 and 1995.
(The numbers in parentheses indicate the actual values for the components.)

Components of Economic Freedom	1975		1980		1985		1990		1995	
I. Money and Inflation	**4.5**		**7.8**		**7.3**		**7.7**		**8.2**	
(a) Annual Money Growth (last 5 yrs.)	7	(8.6)	7	(9.6)	10	(2.5)	9	(6.0)	4	(14.4)
(b) Inflation Variablity (last 5 yrs.)	2	(8.3)	6	(3.1)	7	(2.6)	4	(5.2)	10	(1.1)
(c) Ownership of Foreign Currency	0		10		10		10		10	
(d) Maint. of Bank Account Abroad	10		10		0		10		10	
II. Government Operation	**4.5**		**3.7**		**4.9**		**5.7**		**5.4**	
(a) Gov't Consump. (% of Total Consump.)	3	(23.9)	2	(24.6)	3	(22.7)	4	(21.0)	4	(20.6)
(b) Government Enterprises	6		4		4		6		6	
(c) Price Controls	-		-		-		5		4	
(d) Entry Into Business	-		-		-		-		7.5	
(e) Legal System	-		-		-		-		2.5	
(f) Avoidance of Neg. Interest Rates	-		6		10		10		10	
III. Takings	**5.2**		**4.7**		**6.9**		**7.3**		**7.4**	
(a) Transfers and Subsidies (% of GDP)	5	(6.4)	6	(4.8)	7	(3.6)	8	(2.4)	7	(3.6)
(b) Marginal Tax Rates (Top Rate)	4	(50)	2	(60)	6	(45)	6	(45)	7	(32)
(c) Conscription	10		10		10		10		10	
IV. International Sector	**6.9**		**6.6**		**7.2**		**7.8**		**8.1**	
(a) Taxes on International Trade (Avg.)	4	(7.0)	3	(7.7)	5	(5.7)	7	(3.2)	8	(2.1)
(b) Black Market Exchange Rates (Prem.)	10	(0)	10	(0)	10	(0)	10	(0)	10	(0)
(c) Size of Trade Sector (% of GDP)	10	(43.4)	10	(56.3)	10	(52.3)	10	(75.6)	10	(90.6)
(d) Capital Transactions with Foreigners	5		5		5		5		5	
Economic Freedom Rating	**5.4**		**5.6**		**6.7**		**7.1**		**7.0**	
Ranking of Country	**18**		**19**		**6**		**5**		**10**	

132

Part 2: Recent Economic Indicators:

Population 1996:	20.9	**Real Per Capita GDP** :	1995 =	$9,644
(in millions)		(in 1995 U.S. dollars)		
Annual Rate of Change (1985-96):	2.5%	Avg. Growth Rate:	1980-90 =	3.3%
			1985-95 =	5.1%

Economic Indicators:*	1988	1989	1990	1991	1992	1993	1994	1995	1996
Change in Real GDP:Aggregate	8.9	9.2	9.7	8.7	7.8	8.3	8.7	8.3	-
: Per Capita	6.4	6.7	7.2	6.2	5.3	5.8	6.2	5.8	-
Inflation Rate (CPI)	2.6	2.8	2.6	4.4	4.8	3.5	3.7	5.3	-
Change in Money Supply: (M1)	14.4	17.3	15.6	9.9	27.3	35.3	16.8	13.2	-
: (M2)	6.7	15.2	10.6	16.9	29.2	26.6	12.7	20.0	-
Investment/GDP Ratio	26.0	28.6	31.3	35.9	33.5	35.0	38.5	-	-
Size of Trade Sector (% of GDP)	62.4	70.2	75.6	84.4	77.1	77.9	90.6	-	-
Total Gov't Exp./GDP Ratio									
Central Government Budget Deficit (-) or Surplus (+) As a Percent of GDP	-0.3	-0.5	-1.3	-0.2	+0.7	+1.6	+2.3	-	-
Unemployment Rate									

* The figures in this table are in percent form.

During the 1980s, the economic freedom of this southeast Asian nation increased substantially. As its 10th place ranking in 1995 indicates, it is now one of the freest economies in the world. As economic freedom has increased the size of government has been reduced. Total government expenditures summed to 32.3% of GDP in 1995, down from 37.7% in 1980.

Several factors contributed to the improvement. There was an increase in the stability of the price level (and inflation rate). During the last two decades, there has been a decline in both government consumption expenditures and transfers as a share of the economy. Not many countries can match that record. Marginal tax rates have been reduced. The top rate is now 32%, down from 60% in 1980.

Tariffs have been reduced and the trade sector has grown rapidly. As a share of GDP, the size of the trade sector in 1995 was twice that of 1975.

There are a few areas of concern. Malaysia shows some reluctance to give up its regulatory ways. Despite some privatization, government enterprises are still widespread throughout the economy. As the relatively low ratings for the Equality before the Law component indicates, there is ample room for improvement in this area.

Malaysia's impressive move toward economic liberalization has been rewarded. Its growth rate of per capita GDP averaged over 3% per year in the 1980's and 5% during the 1990s. Malaysia is earning the dividends of economic freedom.

133

MAURITIUS

Economic Freedom Rating

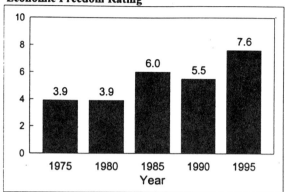

**Total Government Expenditures
As a Percent of GDP**

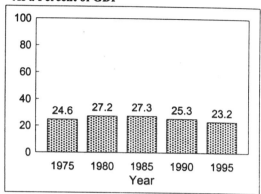

Part 1: The Economic Freedom Ratings for the Components and Various Area and Summary Indexes: 1975, 1980, 1985, 1990 and 1995.
(The numbers in parentheses indicate the actual values for the components.)

Components of Economic Freedom	1975		1980		1985		1990		1995	
I. Money and Inflation	0.6		2.8		6.0		3.6		9.4	
(a) Annual Money Growth (last 5 yrs.)	1	(32.9)	6	(11.1)	10	(2.8)	2	(18.6)	9	(5.3)
(b) Inflation Variablity (last 5 yrs.)	1	(20.1)	3	(8.0)	9	(1.4)	9	(1.3)	9	(1.3)
(c) Ownership of Foreign Currency	0		0		0		0		10	
(d) Maint. of Bank Account Abroad	0		0		0		0		10	
II. Government Operation	6.5		6.5		7.2		5.9		7.1	
(a) Gov't Consump. (% of Total Consump.)	7	(15.2)	7	(15.7)	7	(14.7)	7	(15.2)	7	(15.8)
(b) Government Enterprises	6		6		6		6		6	
(c) Price Controls	-		-		-		4		4	
(d) Entry Into Business	-		-		-		-		10.0	
(e) Legal System	-		-		-		-		7.5	
(f) Avoidance of Neg. Interest Rates	-		-		10		8		10	
III. Takings	6.2		4.7		7.0		7.4		7.9	
(a) Transfers and Subsidies (% of GDP)	5	(6.6)	5	(6.5)	6	(5.2)	7	(4.2)	7	(4.4)
(b) Marginal Tax Rates (Top Rate)	-		3	(50)	7	(35)	7	(35)	8	(30)
(c) Conscription	10		10		10		10		10	
IV. International Sector	3.1		2.2		3.8		3.9		6.9	
(a) Taxes on International Trade (Avg.)	4	(7.1)	1	(9.6)	1	(9.6)	3	(7.6)	4	(6.3)
(b) Black Market Exchange Rates (Prem.)	2	(47)	2	(40)	8	(1)	5	(8)	10	(0)
(c) Size of Trade Sector (% of GDP)	5	(56.1)	5	(56.3)	5	(54.5)	7	(71.1)	5	(61.0)
(d) Capital Transactions with Foreigners	2		2		2		2		8	
Economic Freedom Rating	3.9		3.9		6.0		5.5		7.6	
Ranking of Country	55		52		15		31		5	

134

Part 2: Recent Economic Indicators:

Population 1996: 1.2 (in millions)
Annual Rate of Change (1985-96): 1.0%

Real Per Capita GDP : 1995= $9,596
(in 1995 U.S. dollars)
Avg. Growth Rate: 1980-90 = 5.2%
1990-95 = 4.1%

Economic Indicators:*	1988	1989	1990	1991	1992	1993	1994	1995	1996
Change in Real GDP:Aggregate	6.8	4.6	7.2	4.1	6.2	5.4	4.1	4.4	-
: Per Capita	5.8	3.6	6.2	3.1	5.2	4.4	2.1	3.4	-
Inflation Rate (CPI)	9.2	12.7	13.5	7.0	4.6	10.5	7.3	6.0	-
Change in Money Supply: (M1)	15.6	18.1	23.7	19.7	8.0	3.0	19.4	8.0	-
: (M2)	28.7	15.4	21.2	21.9	15.9	17.0	12.3	18.7	-
Investment/GDP Ratio	30.6	30.7	30.4	28.0	29.4	30.8	32.2	25.4	-
Size of Trade Sector (% of GDP)	69.3	70.3	71.1	67.3	64.2	65.4	61.6	61.0	-
Total Gov't Exp./GDP Ratio	22.9	23.2	25.3	23.2	23.2	21.5	22.6	23.2	-
Central Government Budget Deficit (-) or Surplus (+) As a Percent of GDP	+0.3	-1.6	-0.5	0.0	-0.8	0.0	-0.3	-1.4	-
Unemployment Rate	10.4	6.7	4.6	3.8	-	-	-	-	-

* The figures in this table are in percent form.

This small island nation has taken substantial steps toward economic freedom since 1980. Surprisingly, our index now ranks it as the 5th freest economy in the world, behind only Hong Kong, Singapore, New Zealand, and the United States. This is certainly a dramatic improvement over its 52nd place ranking in 1980, and 31st in 1990. The figures on government expenditures also suggest increased reliance on markets. As a share of GDP, total government expenditures summed to 23% in 1995, down from 27% in 1980 and 1985.

What accounts for this relatively high ranking? In the 1990s, the growth rate of the money supply has been moderate and the inflation rate relatively stable. The government consumption and transfer sectors are both relatively small and the legal structure provides for protection of property rights and freedom of entry into business. Taxes are moderate. Unlike most other countries, Mauritius rates average or well above average for every component of our index. Its lowest rating in 1995 was a "4" for the price controls component.

The following factors have contributed to the recent jump in rating:
- A more stable monetary policy (note the rating for each of the two monetary policy components rose from 1 in 1975 to 9 in 1995;
- The recent deregulations allowing citizens to maintain foreign currency bank accounts;
- Reductions in marginal tax rates—the top marginal rate was reduced from 50% in 1980 to 35% in 1985 and 30% in 1995;
- Elimination of exchange rate controls;
- A modest reduction in tariffs;
- Removal of restrictions on both the inflow and outflow of capital as well as several regulations that were discriminatory toward foreign capital.

Like its economic freedom rating, Mauritius's growth rate has been impressive. Per capita GDP expanded at an annual rate of 5.2% during the 1980s and 4.1% thus far during the 1990s. If it continues on its current path, the economic future of this country will be bright.

MEXICO

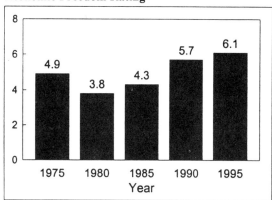

Economic Freedom Rating

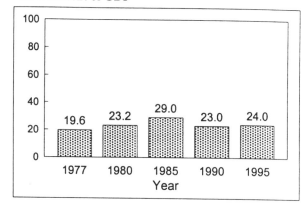

Total Government Expenditures As a Percent of GDP

Part 1: The Economic Freedom Ratings for the Components and Various Area and Summary Indexes: 1975, 1980, 1985, 1990 and 1995.
(The numbers in parentheses indicate the actual values for the components.)

Components of Economic Freedom	1975	1980	1985	1990	1995
I. Money and Inflation	**5.2**	**5.6**	**4.0**	**3.6**	**4.6**
(a) Annual Money Growth (last 5 yrs.)	2 (17.5)	1 (30.9)	0 (48.4)	0 (68.1)	1 (40.5)
(b) Inflation Variablity (last 5 yrs.)	3 (6.0)	5 (4.9)	1 (20.4)	0 (42.8)	2 (11.1)
(c) Ownership of Foreign Currency	10	10	10	10	10
(d) Maint. of Bank Account Abroad	10	10	10	10	10
II. Government Operation	**5.4**	**4.7**	**5.1**	**4.7**	**5.8**
(a) Gov't Consump. (% of Total Consump.)	9 (11.5)	8 (13.4)	9 (12.5)	9 (10.6)	8 (13.4)
(b) Government Enterprises	2	2	2	4	6
(c) Price Controls	-	-	-	0	5
(d) Entry Into Business	-	-	-	-	7.5
(e) Legal System	-	-	-	-	0.0
(f) Avoidance of Neg. Interest Rates	-	4	4	8	8
III. Takings	**5.1**	**4.7**	**4.3**	**6.5**	**6.1**
(a) Transfers and Subsidies (% of GDP)	7 (4.1)	7 (4.4)	6 (5.4)	8 (2.7)	7 (4.0)
(b) Marginal Tax Rates (Top Rate)	5 (47)	4 (55)	4 (55)	7 (40)	7 (35)
(c) Conscription	0	0	0	0	0
IV. International Sector	**4.2**	**1.0**	**3.9**	**7.1**	**7.6**
(a) Taxes on International Trade (Avg.)	3 (7.9)	0 (17.6)	7 (2.6)	8 (2.0)	8 (1.5)
(b) Black Market Exchange Rates (Prem.)	10 (0)	1 (92)	3 (25)	10 (0)	10 (0)
(c) Size of Trade Sector (% of GDP)	0 (7.4)	1 (11.8)	3 (12.9)	4 (16.4)	7 (22.6)
(d) Capital Transactions with Foreigners	2	2	2	5	5
Economic Freedom Rating	**4.9**	**3.8**	**4.3**	**5.7**	**6.1**
Ranking of Country	**27**	**57**	**51**	**27**	**36**

Part 2: Recent Economic Indicators:

Population 1996: (in millions)	96.6	**Real Per Capita GDP** : (in 1995 U.S. dollars)	1996= $8,690
Annual Rate of Change (1985-96):	1.5%	Avg. Growth Rate: 1980-90=	-0.5%
		1990-96=	0.5%

Economic Indicators:*	1988	1989	1990	1991	1992	1993	1994	1995	1996
Change in Real GDP: Aggregate	1.3	3.3	4.5	3.6	2.8	1.7	3.5	-6.9	5.1
: Per Capita	-0.2	1.8	3.0	2.1	1.3	0.2	2.0	-8.4	3.1
Inflation Rate (CPI)	114.2	20.0	26.7	22.7	15.5	9.8	7.0	35.0	27.7
Change in Money Supply: (M1)	67.8	137.3	63.1	123.9	15.1	17.7	1.1	3.5	16.1
: (M2)	-17.5	115.9	75.8	49.3	22.8	14.5	21.7	33.3	17.1
Investment/GDP Ratio	21.1	22.2	22.8	23.4	24.4	23.2	23.5	19.4	15.2
Size of Trade Sector (% of GDP)	16.0	16.1	16.4	15.5	15.4	15.8	15.2	22.6	27.6
Total Gov't Exp./GDP Ratio a	31.0	26.0	23.0	20.0	19.5	20.0	21.0	24.0	31.0
Central Government Budget Deficit (-) or Surplus (+) As a Percent of GDP	-10.3	-5.2	+0.7	-0.2	+4.5	+0.7	-0.8	-1.1	-0.9
Unemployment Rate b	3.6	3.0	2.8	2.6	2.8	3.6	3.8	6.3	4.1

* The figures in this table are in percent form.

a These figures include state and regional government expenditures, which usually account for about 3% of GDP.

b If the Mexican unemployment rate was adjusted to the concepts of unemployment used in the United States, these rates would be between 1.5% and 2% higher. See Susan Fleck and Constance Sorrentino, "Employment and Unemployment in Mexico's Labor Force," *Monthly Labor Review*, November, 1994.

After declining during 1975-1985, Mexico's economic freedom rating rose during the last decade. In 1995 Mexico ranked 36th (among the 115 countries in our study), up from 51st in 1985 and 57th in 1980.

The reduction in the economic freedom rating between 1975 and 1985 was primarily the result of unstable monetary policy, higher taxes, and imposition of exchange rate controls. Beginning in the late 1980s, Mexico undertook a number of constructive moves toward a freer economy. Exchange rate controls were eliminated. Price controls were relaxed. A number of government enterprises were privatized. The top marginal tax rate was reduced from 55% in 1985 to 40% in 1990 and 35% in 1995. These factors were responsible for the higher rating of the last decade.

If Mexico is going to reach its full economic potential, major changes are needed in two areas: monetary institutions and legal structure. As the peso crisis of 1994 illustrated, the monetary system is badly in need of reform. Even though monetary policy has been less expansionary since 1992, the credibility of the monetary authorities is still low. Some modest steps have been taken to reduce the political control over monetary policy, but more fundamental reform (for example, adoption of either a currency board or a firm price level target) are needed. The Mexican legal structure provides government officials with substantial discretion and places them in a position to hand out numerous favors (tax concessions, both direct and indirect subsidies, government contracts, etc.). A legal structure of this type undermines the operation of a market economy and breeds corruption. In 1996, the Mexican economy rebounded from the severe downturn of 1995. A more stable and transparent monetary system and a less ambiguous and politicized legal structure would help keep this economy on a healthy growth path.

NETHERLANDS

Economic Freedom Rating

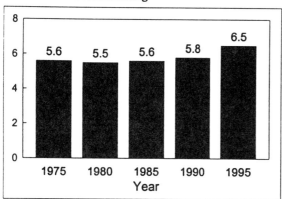

Total Government Expenditures As a Percent of GDP

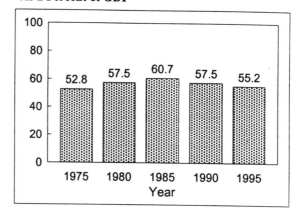

Part 1: The Economic Freedom Ratings for the Components and Various Area and Summary Indexes: 1975, 1980, 1985, 1990 and 1995.
(The numbers in parentheses indicate the actual values for the components.)

Components of Economic Freedom	1975		1980		1985		1990		1995	
I. Money and Inflation	**8.5**		**9.4**		**9.4**		**9.7**		**9.7**	
(a) Annual Money Growth (last 5 yrs.)	5	(12.8)	9	(6.5)	9	(6.5)	9	(4.9)	10	(4.5)
(b) Inflation Variablity (last 5 yrs.)	10	(0.7)	9	(1.7)	9	(1.9)	10	(1.0)	9	(1.6)
(c) Ownership of Foreign Currency	10		10		10		10		10	
(d) Maint. of Bank Account Abroad	10		10		10		10		10	
II. Government Operation	**4.8**		**5.7**		**6.1**		**6.6**		**7.3**	
(a) Gov't Consump. (% of Total Consump.)	3	(22.3)	3	(22.1)	4	(20.9)	5	(19.8)	5	(19.0)
(b) Government Enterprises	6		6		6		6		6	
(c) Price Controls	-		-		-		7		7	
(d) Entry Into Business	-		-		-		-		7.5	
(e) Legal System	-		-		-		-		10.0	
(f) Avoidance of Neg. Interest Rates	6		10		10		10		10	
III. Takings	**2.3**		**0.0**		**0.0**		**0.0**		**0.9**	
(a) Transfers and Subsidies (% of GDP)	0	(25.6)	0	(29.4)	0	(31.6)	0	(28.7)	0	(29.7)
(b) Marginal Tax Rates (Top Rate)	5	(46)	0	(72)	0	(72)	0	(72)	2	(60)
(c) Conscription	0		0		0		0		0	
IV. International Sector	**8.2**		**9.3**		**9.5**		**9.3**		**9.7**	
(a) Taxes on International Trade (Avg.)	9	(1.3)	10	(0.0)	10	(0.0)	10	(0.0)	10	(0.0)
(b) Black Market Exchange Rates (Prem.)	10	(0)	10	(0)	10	(0)	10	(0)	10	(0)
(c) Size of Trade Sector (% of GDP)	9	(46.1)	9	(50.5)	10	(58.4)	9	(51.9)	8	(50.0)
(d) Capital Transactions with Foreigners	5		8		8		8		10	
Economic Freedom Rating	**5.6**		**5.5**		**5.6**		**5.8**		**6.5**	
Ranking of Country	**15**		**21**		**22**		**25**		**21**	

Part 2: Recent Economic Indicators:

Population 1996:	15.5	**Real Per Capita GDP :**	1996=	$19,760
(in millions)		(in 1995 U.S. dollars)		
Annual Rate of Change (1985-96):	0.7%	Avg. Growth Rate:	1980-90=	1.5%
			1990-96=	1.6%

Economic Indicators:*	1988	1989	1990	1991	1992	1993	1994	1995	1996
Change in Real GDP: Aggregate	2.6	4.7	3.9	2.3	1.8	0.3	2.6	2.3	3.0
: Per Capita	1.9	4.0	3.2	1.6	1.1	-0.4	1.9	1.6	2.3
Inflation Rate (CPI)	0.7	1.1	2.5	3.1	3.2	2.6	2.8	1.9	2.5
Change in Money Supply: (M1)	7.3	6.9	4.1	4.4	4.4	10.8	1.7	13.6	12.0
: (M2)	7.4	10.2	6.9	4.7	4.9	5.7	0.3	5.9	5.8
Investment/GDP Ratio	21.4	22.6	22.2	21.4	20.6	18.9	20.0	20.3	-
Size of Trade Sector (% of GDP)	50.6	53.3	51.9	51.9	50.0	47.7	48.6	50.0	-
Total Gov't Exp./GDP Ratio	60.5	57.6	57.5	58.0	58.4	58.6	56.1	55.2	52.8 P
General Government Budget Deficit (-) or Surplus (+) As a Percent of GDP	-4.6	-4.7	-5.1	-2.9	-3.9	-3.6	-3.4	-4.0	-2.6
Unemployment Rate	9.1	8.3	7.5	7.0	5.6	6.6	7.1	7.0	6.6

* The figures in this table are in percent form.

P Preliminary.

The economic freedom rating of the Netherlands has been remarkably steady. So, too, has its ranking. In 1975, this economy ranked 15th; it slipped a little to 22nd in 1985; and it was ranked 21st (tied with Ireland and Iceland) in 1995.

Netherlands gets exceedingly high marks in both the money and international areas. The justification for these high ratings is clear. The growth rate of the money supply has been low and relatively stable. Not surprisingly, the inflation rate has followed suit. Citizens are allowed to maintain foreign currency bank accounts both domestically and abroad. Tariffs are negligible; the guilder is fully convertible; the trade sector is large; and there are virtually no restrictions on the mobility of capital.

Even in the government operations area, the rating of the Netherlands is not bad. While government consumption accounts for approximately 20% of the total, this figure has actually declined slightly during the last two decades. The legal system is supportive of competitive markets and the credit market is well integrated with the global economy. In contrast with the other areas, the rating of the Netherlands in the takings area is one of the lowest in the world. Netherlands combines a huge transfer sector (only Sweden transfers a larger share of its GDP away from those who generate it), with high taxes (the top marginal tax rate is currently 60%, down from the 72% figure of 1990), and conscription. Typically, a large transfer sector leads to two unpleasant side effects— large budget deficits and high unemployment rates. During the 1990s, budget deficits have averaged approximately 3.5% of GDP, a rate that is unsustainable in the long run. While the unemployment rate (6.6% in 1996) is moderate by European standards, it is likely to rise in the future unless there is some reduction in income transfers and the size of the budget deficits.

139

NEW ZEALAND

Economic Freedom Rating

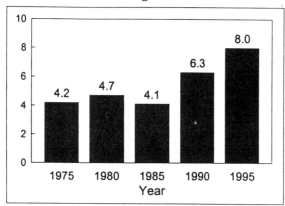

Total Government Expenditures As a Percent of GDP

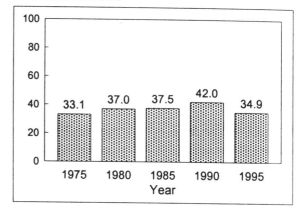

Part 1: The Economic Freedom Ratings for the Components and Various Area and Summary Indexes: 1975, 1980, 1985, 1990 and 1995.

(The numbers in parentheses indicate actual values for the components).

Components of Economic Freedom	1975	1980	1985	1990	1995
I. Money and Inflation	**3.2**	**5.4**	**4.1**	**5.3**	**9.7**
(a) Annual Money Growth (last 5 yrs.)	4 (14.3)	8 (7.3)	7 (10.0)	1 (41.6)	9 (5.3)
(b) Inflation Variablity (last 5 yrs.)	6 (3.7)	9 (2.1)	6 (3.1)	4 (5.0)	10 (1.2)
(c) Ownership of Foreign Currency	0	0	0	10	10
(d) Maint. of Bank Account Abroad	0	0	0	10	10
II. Government Operation	**4.5**	**4.0**	**4.8**	**7.0**	**8.7**
(a) Gov't Consump. (% of Total Consump.)	5 (19.7)	3 (22.3)	4 (21.1)	4 (21.6)	5 (18.8)
(b) Government Enterprises	4	4	4	6	8
(c) Price Controls	-	-	-	9	10
(d) Entry Into Business	-	-	-	-	10.0
(e) Legal System	-	-	-	-	10.0
(f) Avoidance of Neg. Interest Rates	-	6	8	10	10
III. Takings	**3.1**	**2.7**	**1.7**	**4.6**	**5.8**
(a) Transfers and Subsidies (% of GDP)	1 (20.2)	1 (21.9)	1 (20.6)	0 (27.5)	3 (12.8)
(b) Marginal Tax Rates (Top Rate)	3 (60)	2 (60)	0 (66)	7 (33)	7 (33)
(c) Conscription	10	10	10	10	10
IV. International Sector	**6.2**	**7.3**	**6.3**	**8.4**	**8.6**
(a) Taxes on International Trade (Avg.)	8 (2.4)	8 (2.5)	8 (2.0)	8 (1.7)	9 (1.4)
(b) Black Market Exchange Rates (Prem.)	6 (5)	10 (0)	6 (4)	10 (0)	10 (0)
(c) Size of Trade Sector (% of GDP)	5 (27.4)	5 (30.9)	6 (32.2)	4 (27.0)	3 (26.7)
(d) Capital Transactions with Foreigners	5	5	5	10	10
Economic Freedom Rating	**4.2**	**4.7**	**4.1**	**6.3**	**8.0**
Ranking of Country	**44**	**29**	**60**	**15**	**3**

Part 2: Recent Economic Indicators:

Population 1996: (in millions):	3.6	**Real Per Capita GDP** : (in 1995 U.S. dollars)	1996=	$17,363
Annual Rate of Change (1985-96):	0.9%	Avg. Growth Rate:	1980-90=	1.0%
			1990-95=	1.1%

Economic Indicators:[a]	1987	1988	1989	1990	1991	1992	1993	1994	1995
Change in Real GDP: Aggregate	0.6	-0.6	0.8	-0.5	-1.2	1.2	6.2	5.3	3.0
: Per Capita	-0.3	-0.8	0.2	-1.7	-2.4	0.1	5.0	3.9	1.5
Inflation Rate (CPI)	9.0	4.0	7.0	4.5	0.8	0.8	1.3	4.0	2.2
Change in Money Supply: (M1)	35.8	9.9	13.1	4.5	-1.5	2.4	5.6	8.4	0.1
: (M2)				1.8	0.8	3.6	1.3	8.8	9.8
Investment/GDP Ratio	19.7	18.7	20.1	19.2	16.0	16.5	18.1	20.1	21.1
Size of Trade Sector	27.9	27.4	26.7	27.0	27.1	26.7	27.6	27.1	26.7
Total Gov't Exp./GDP Ratio [b]	40.4	39.8	41.4	42.0	40.4	40.4	36.9	36.2	34.9
Central Government Budget Deficit (-) or Surplus (+) As a Percent of GDP	-2.1	-1.4	-1.3	-3.5	-3.4	-1.1	+0.9	+3.1	+3.6
Unemployment Rate	4.8	7.0	7.0	9.4	10.6	9.8	9.1	6.6	6.2

[a] Data are for years beginning April 1 and running through the end of March of the following year. The figures in this table are in percent form.

[b] Central government only.

In 1985, New Zealand tied for 60th among the 107 nations we were able to rate. The economy of New Zealand was characterized by high taxes, government expenditures approaching half of GDP, monetary instability, and protectionist trade policies. What a difference a decade makes. In 1995 New Zealand ranked third, behind only Hong Kong and Singapore. No country has moved more rapidly toward economic freedom during the last decade.

The following were key elements of structural change and legislative action:

- Monetary reform. Legislation requiring the central bank to achieve price stability (a pre-announced low and stable rate of inflation) and holding it accountable if it failed to do so was adopted. Foreign currency bank accounts were legalized.

- Tax reform. The progressivity of the tax structure was reduced and the top marginal tax rate sliced from 66% to 33%.
- Trade policy. Tariffs were reduced, exchange rate controls were eliminated, and the New Zealand dollar was made fully convertible.
- Price Controls. Interest rate and other price controls were abolished, the labor market was de-regulated, and agriculture subsidies phased out.

Not only has New Zealand's economic freedom rating increased, government expenditures have declined as a share of GDP. The reforms are paying off. New Zealand achieved solid growth during 1992-1995 and our analysis suggests that it can expect more of the same if it continues on its current economic course.

NICARAGUA

Economic Freedom Rating

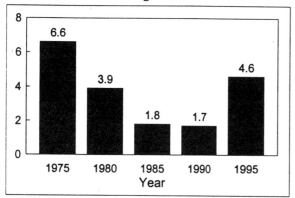

Total Government Expenditures
As a Percent of GDP

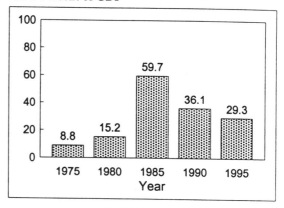

Part 1: The Economic Freedom Ratings for the Components and Various Area and Summary Indexes: 1975, 1980, 1985, 1990 and 1995.

(The numbers in parentheses indicate the actual values for the components.)

Components of Economic Freedom	1975		1980		1985		1990		1995	
I. Money and Inflation	**6.1**		**4.3**		**0.0**		**0.0**		**0.0**	
(a) Annual Money Growth (last 5 yrs.)	6	(12.3)	1	(26.6)	0	(62.0)	0	(2072.0)	0	(280.2)
(b) Inflation Variablity (last 5 yrs.)	2	(8.8)	1	(15.9)	0	(60.3)	0	(4853.2)	0	(1210.6)
(c) Ownership of Foreign Currency	10		10		0		0		0	
(d) Maint. of Bank Account Abroad	10		10		0		0		0	
II. Government Operation	**7.5**		**5.5**		**0.0**		**0.0**		**4.6**	
(a) Gov't Consump. (% of Total Consump.)	9	(10.5)	5	(19.3)	0	(42.6)	0	(32.9)	8	(13.7)
(b) Government Enterprises	6		6		0		0		2	
(c) Price Controls	-		-		-		0		2	
(d) Entry Into Business	-		-		-		-		7.5	
(e) Legal System	-		-		-		-		2.5	
(f) Avoidance of Neg. Interest Rates	-		-		-		0		6	
III. Takings	**7.9**		**5.1**		**4.3**		**3.8**		**7.1**	
(a) Transfers and Subsidies (% of GDP)	8	(2.4)	7	(4.1)	5	(6.2)	5	(6.8)	5	(6.0)
(b) Marginal Tax Rates (Top Rate)	10	(21)	5	(50)	5	(50)	-		8	(30)
(c) Conscription	0		0		0		0		10	
IV. International Sector	**4.9**		**1.4**		**1.1**		**3.4**		**5.0**	
(a) Taxes on International Trade (Avg.)	6	(4.9)	2	(8.7)	3	(7.4)	6	(4.3)	5	(5.9)
(b) Black Market Exchange Rates (Prem.)	4	(21)	1	(91)	0	(382)	4	(10)	5	(8)
(c) Size of Trade Sector (% of GDP)	4	(32.9)	3	(33.8)	1	(18.3)	3	(34.3)	5	(44.8)
(d) Capital Transactions with Foreigners	5		0		0		0		5	
Economic Freedom Rating	**6.6**		**3.9**		**1.8**		**1.7**		**4.6**	
Ranking of Country	**6**		**52**		**102**		**106**		**70**	

Part 2: Recent Economic Indicators:

Population 1996:   4.7   **Real Per Capita GDP** :   1995= $1,660
  (in millions)   (in 1995 U.S. dollars)
Annual Rate of Change (1985-96):   3.3%   Avg. Growth Rate: 1980-90=   -4.5%
                                                     1990-95=   -2.1%

Economic Indicators:*	1988	1989	1990	1991	1992	1993	1994	1995	1996
Change in Real GDP: Aggregate	-12.4	-1.7	-	-0.2	0.4	-0.4	3.3	4.2	-
: Per Capita	-15.7	-5.0	-3.5	-3.5	-2.9	-3.7	0.0	0.9	-
Inflation Rate (CPI)	10205.0	4770.4	7485.2	2945.1	23.7	20.4	7.8	10.9	-
Change in Money Supply: (M1)	11673.4	2368.3	6286.7	1336.9	11.4	-4.6	36.2	21.2	-
: (M2)	12513.1	2700.2	7677.8	1519.6	20.1	25.2	65.9	39.4	-
Investment/GDP Ratio	26.8	27.2	19.3	20.2	19.0	19.7	24.9	26.6	-
Size of Trade Sector (% of GDP)	38.1	48.9	34.3	36.1	32.6	32.9	38.1	44.8	-
Total Gov't Exp./GDP Ratio	46.8	30.7	36.1	27.4	29.9	30.0	32.0	29.3	-
Central Government Budget Deficit (-) or Surplus (+) As a Percent of GDP	-23.7	-1.9	-17.8	+5.3	-2.0	-0.1	-4.3	-	-
Unemployment Rate									

* The figures in this table are in percent form.

Since the Sandinista Revolution socialized the economy, Nicaragua's economic freedom rating plunged. The reduction in Nicaragua's rating from 6.6 in 1975 to 1.8 in 1985 was the largest in the world during that period. Its 1990 rating placed it 106th (only Russia, Somalia, and Albania had lower ratings.) With the electoral defeat of the Sandinistas, there have been some moves toward economic freedom during the 1990s. Nicaragua has rebounded to 70th among the 115 economies rated in 1995.

The Nicaraguan socialist experiment provides a vivid portrait of what happens when economic freedom is lost. In almost every area, policies that conflicted with economic freedom were adopted. By the mid-1980s, government enterprises dominated the economy and the top marginal tax rate had been pushed to 50%, up from 21% in 1975. Government consumption soared and total government expenditures rose from 8.8% of GDP in 1975 to 59.7% in 1985. As more and more of these expenditures were financed with money creation, the annual growth rate of the money supply rose from 12% during 1970-1975, to 26% in 1975-1980, to 70% in 1980-1985, and to more than 2000% during 1985-1990. Predictably, hyperinflation was the result. The government responded with price controls. Higher tariffs, rigid exchange rate controls (the black market exchange rate premium rose from 21% in 1975 to 382% in 1985), and capital market controls were also a part of this political economy experiment. The results were disastrous. Per capita real GDP fell by more than 50% between 1975 and 1993.

In the 1990s there have been some moves toward liberalization. Monetary policy is becoming more stable. Government consumption has been curtailed dramatically. Even though they have not yet been removed, exchange rate and interest rate controls have been relaxed. Much more needs to be done, however, before this troubled economy will achieved a healthy sustainable growth path.

143

NIGERIA

Total Government Expenditures
As a Percent of GDP

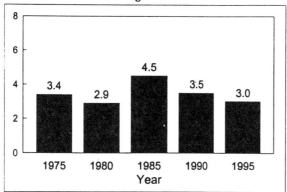

No Data

Part 1: The Economic Freedom Ratings for the Components and Various Area and Summary Indexes: 1975, 1980, 1985, 1990 and 1995.
(The numbers in parentheses indicate the actual values for the components.)

Components of Economic Freedom	1975	1980	1985	1990	1995
I. Money and Inflation	0.6	3.3	3.7	0.9	0.6
(a) Annual Money Growth (last 5 yrs.)	1 (32.5)	1 (30.7)	9 (6.6)	2 (18.9)	1 (39.8)
(b) Inflation Variablity (last 5 yrs.)	1 (15.7)	9 (1.5)	3 (6.0)	1 (19.3)	1 (20.2)
(c) Ownership of Foreign Currency	0	0	0	0	0
(d) Maint. of Bank Account Abroad	0	0	0	0	0
II. Government Operation	5.1	4.3	5.1	4.5	2.7
(a) Gov't Consump. (% of Total Consump.)	8 (13.7)	8 (13.8)	9 (12.0)	10 (7.3)	10 (4.1)
(b) Government Enterprises	4	2	2	2	2
(c) Price Controls	-	-	-	4	0
(d) Entry Into Business	-	-	-	-	2.5
(e) Legal System	-	-	-	-	0.0
(f) Avoidance of Neg. Interest Rates	2	2	4	0	0
III. Takings	4.5	2.2	6.3	3.8	7.7
(a) Transfers and Subsidies (% of GDP)	8 (2.8)	-	9 (1.3)	-	-
(b) Marginal Tax Rates (Top Rate)	0 (75)	0 (70)	3 (55)	2 (55)	7 (35)
(c) Conscription	10	10	10	10	10
IV. International Sector	2.7	2.0	2.3	4.3	1.2
(a) Taxes on International Trade (Avg.)	4 (6.6)	2 (8.5)	6 (5.1)	6 (4.0)	-
(b) Black Market Exchange Rates (Prem.)	2 (43)	1 (72)	0 (270)	3 (23)	0 (286)
(c) Size of Trade Sector (% of GDP)	6 (20.6)	7 (24.0)	3 (14.3)	10 (32.3)	5 (21.2)
(d) Capital Transactions with Foreigners	0	0	0	0	0
Economic Freedom Rating	3.4	2.9	4.5	3.5	3.0
Ranking of Country	69	92	39	87	109

Part 2: Recent Economic Indicators:

Population 1996:	115.2	**Real Per Capita GDP** :	1994= $1,349
(in millions)		(in 1995 U.S. dollars)	
Annual Rate of Change (1985-96):	1.6%	Avg. Growth Rate: 1980-90=	-0.3%
		1990-94=	2.3%

Economic Indicators:*	1988	1989	1990	1991	1992	1993	1994	1995	1996
Change in Real GDP: Aggregate	9.9	7.4	8.2	4.7	3.0	2.3	1.3	-	-
: Per Capita	8.3	5.8	6.6	3.1	1.4	0.7	-0.3	-	-
Inflation Rate (CPI)	54.5	50.5	7.4	13.0	44.6	57.2	57.0	72.8	-
Change in Money Supply: (M1)	43.9	24.3	29.5	41.0	73.2	53.4	47.3	16.9	-
: (M2)	32.9	12.9	32.7	37.4	59.1	51.5	36.5	19.9	-
Investment/GDP Ratio	6.5	8.2	11.9	11.0	10.7	11.6	9.3	6.4	-
Size of Trade Sector (% of GDP)	22.6	27.7	32.3	32.7	29.8	28.7	21.2	-	-
Total Gov't Exp./GDP Ratio									
Central Government Budget Deficit (-) or Surplus (+) As a Percent of GDP)									
Unemployment Rate									

* The figures in this table are in percent form.

The economic freedom of this resource rich country was low throughout the 1975-1995 period and it has been falling during the last decade. Nigeria's ranking of 109th in 1995 places it among the ten least free economies in the world.

Monetary instability, insecure property rights, rigid exchange rate controls, and capital market restrictions continue to undermine the Nigerian economy. Excessive monetary expansion (M1 expanded at an annual rate of more than 40% during 1991-1995) has caused high and variable rates of inflation. In 1990, the inflation rate was 7%, but it rose to 45% in 1992 and 73% in 1995. It is difficult for either businesses or households to plan for the future in this environment. In addition the economy is characterized by inefficient state enterprises and legal restrictions (and subsidies) that

retard competition from private firms. Nigeria's 1995 black market exchange rate premium (286%) was the second highest among the countries in our study. A highly politicized economy of this type almost inevitably leads to corruption that undermines the confidence of both domestics and foreigners. This is precisely what has happened to the Nigerian economy.

This country provides powerful evidence that natural resources are not the key to economic prosperity. Even though its resource endowments are among the richest in the world, incomes are low (per capita GDP was $1349 in 1994) and the economy is stagnating (real GDP per capita fell during the 1980s.) Unless the current policies that are stifling both economic freedom and growth are reversed, the poverty and stagnation will continue.

NORWAY

Economic Freedom Rating

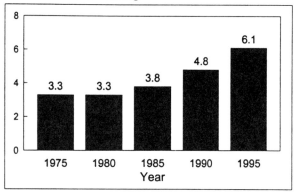

Total Government Expenditures
As A Percent of GDP

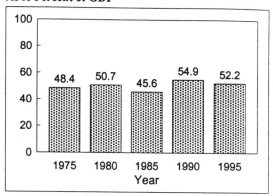

Part 1: The Economic Freedom Ratings for the Components and Various Area and Summary Indexes: 1975, 1980, 1985, 1990 and 1995.

(The numbers in parentheses indicate the actual values for the components.)

Components of Economic Freedom	1975		1980		1985		1990		1995	
I. Money and Inflation	4.5		5.1		2.9		6.3		9.4	
(a) Annual Money Growth (last 5 yrs.)	5	(13.8)	9	(5.7)	3	(16.2)	2	(18.7)	9	(6.8)
(b) Inflation Variablity (last 5 yrs.)	9	(2.1)	7	(3.0)	6	(3.3)	6	(3.5)	9	(1.6)
(c) Ownership of Foreign Currency	0		0		0		10		10	
(d) Maint. of Bank Account Abroad	0		0		0		10		10	
II. Government Operation	1.5		2.5		3.3		3.8		5.8	
(a) Govern. Consumption (% of Total Consump.)	1	(27.0)	1	(28.3)	1	(27.4)	1	(29.3)	1	(29.6)
(b) Government Enterprises	2		2		2		2		2	
(c) Price Controls	-		-		-		5		7	
(d) Entry Into Business	-		-		-		-		7.5	
(e) Legal System	-		-		-		-		10.0	
(f) Avoidance of Neg. Interest Rates	-		6		10		10		10	
III. Takings	0.4		0.4		0.9		1.4		2.7	
(a) Transfers and Subsidies (% of GDP)	1	(21.0)	1	(22.1)	1	(21.4)	0	(27.3)	1	(23.2)
(b) Marginal Tax Rates (Top Rate)	0	(74)	0	(75)	1	(64)	3	(54)	5	(42)
(c) Conscription	0		0		0		0		0	
IV. International Sector	6.9		6.0		8.4		8.8		8.4	
(a) Taxes on International Trade (Avg.)	9	(0.5)	9	(0.3)	10	(0.3)	10	(0.3)	9	(0.3)
(b) Black Market Exchange Rates (Prem.)	8	(1)	6	(3)	10	(0)	10	(0)	10	(0)
(c) Size of Trade Sector (% of GDP)	9	(45.2)	7	(44.2)	8	(43.0)	6	(40.6)	5	(40.9)
(d) Capital Transactions with Foreigners	2		2		5		8		8	
Economic Freedom Rating	3.3		3.3		3.8		4.8		6.1	
Ranking of Country	72		81		69		43		36	

Part 2: Recent Economic Indicators:

Population 1996:	4.4	**Real Per Capita GDP** :	1995=	$23,803
(in millions)		(in 1995 U.S. dollars)		
Annual Rate of Change (1985-96):	0.5%	Avg. Growth Rate:	1980-90=	1.8%
			1990-95=	2.7%

Economic Indicators:*	1988	1989	1990	1991	1992	1993	1994	1995	1996
Change in Real GDP: Aggregate	-0.5	0.9	1.9	3.1	3.3	2.8	5.0	3.3	-
: Per Capita	-1.0	0.4	1.4	2.6	2.8	2.3	4.5	2.8	-
Inflation Rate (CPI)	6.7	4.6	4.1	3.4	2.3	2.3	1.4	2.5	-
Change in Money Supply: (M1)	22.6	16.6	8.9	7.6	26.4	5.2	4.4	1.1	-
: (M2)	4.9	8.6	5.6	2.9	8.5	-0.7	5.0	3.8	-
Investment/GDP Ratio	29.2	26.3	23.3	21.4	20.7	21.6	22.7	23.9	-
Size of Trade Sector (% of GDP)	37.0	40.0	40.6	40.4	39.5	40.9	41.2	40.9	-
Total Gov't Exp./GDP Ratio	53.7	54.7	54.9	56.5	57.6	56.9	54.4	52.2	49.7 [p]
General Government Budget Deficit (-) or Surplus (+) As a Percent of GDP	+2.6	+1.8	+2.6	+0.2	-1.7	-1.5	+0.3	+3.0	+5.4
Unemployment Rate	3.2	4.9	5.2	5.5	5.9	6.1	5.5	5.0	5.0 [a]

* The figures in this table are in percent form.

[a] May, 1996.

[p] Preliminary.

Norway placed 36th (out of 115) in 1995 and there is evidence that this economy has become more free during the last decade.

The increase in Norway's rating between 1990 and 1995 is partially the result of the inclusion of the "entry into business" and "legal system" components—two areas where Norway rates high—into our index for the first time in 1995. It has, however, registered genuine improvement during the last decade in other areas—particularly those reflecting monetary policy and institutions. During the last five years, monetary expansion has been low (6.8% after adjustment for the growth of real output, down from double-digit monetary growth throughout much of the 1975-1990 period.) The recent inflation rate has been both low and relatively steady. The restrictions on the maintenance of foreign currency bank accounts were abolished in the late 1980s. As the result, Norway's rating in the Money and Inflation area rose from 2.9 in 1985 to 9.4 in 1995.

Norway's legal structure provides equal protection and restricts arbitrary authority. Its credit market is integrated with the global market and its international sector is relatively free. The major deficiencies of this economy are the huge government consumption and transfer sectors. Total government spending—mostly in these two areas—takes more than 50% of the Norwegian GDP. To date, substantial revenues from North Sea oil have made it possible for Norway to avoid the large budget deficits, increasing national debt, and rising interest costs that have entrapped several other European welfare states. However, if revenues from this source should decrease, Norway will almost surely fall into this same cycle.

147

PAKISTAN

Economic Freedom Rating

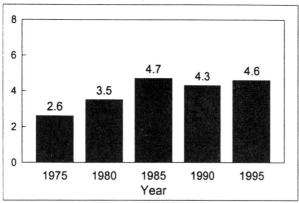

**Total Government Expenditures
As a Percent of GDP**

No Data

Part 1: The Economic Freedom Ratings for the Components and Various Area and Summary Indexes: 1975, 1980, 1985, 1990 and 1995.
(The numbers in parentheses indicate the actual values for the components.)

Components of Economic Freedom	1975	1980	1985	1990	1995
I. Money and Inflation	**2.5**	**3.3**	**4.5**	**6.1**	**6.7**
(a) Annual Money Growth (last 5 yrs.)	6 (10.8)	1 (20.6)	6 (12.3)	5 (12.8)	7 (8.7)
(b) Inflation Variablity (last 5 yrs.)	2 (8.6)	9 (1.6)	8 (2.3)	8 (2.4)	8 (2.4)
(c) Ownership of Foreign Currency	0	0	0	10	10
(d) Maint. of Bank Account Abroad	0	0	0	0	0
II. Government Operation	**5.4**	**5.5**	**5.6**	**5.2**	**4.6**
(a) Gov't Consump. (% of Total Consump.)	9 (11.2)	9 (10.8)	8 (13.0)	6 (17.5)	8 (13.2)
(b) Government Enterprises	2	2	2	4	4
(c) Price Controls	-	-	-	-	4
(d) Entry Into Business	-	-	-	-	5.0
(e) Legal System	-	-	-	-	0.0
(f) Avoidance of Neg. Interest Rates	-	6	8	6	6
III. Takings	**0.8**	**3.8**	**5.8**	**4.5**	**5.3**
(a) Transfers and Subsidies (% of GDP)	-	-	10 (0.7)	-	-
(b) Marginal Tax Rates (Top Rate)	1 (61)	2 (55)	1 (60)	3 (50)	4 (45)
(c) Conscription	0	10	10	10	10
IV. International Sector	**2.3**	**2.0**	**2.8**	**2.3**	**2.8**
(a) Taxes on International Trade (Avg.)	0 (15.3)	0 (15.3)	0 (14.7)	0 (16.5)	0 (13.6)
(b) Black Market Exchange Rates (Prem.)	4 (17)	3 (27)	6 (4)	4 (14)	6 (3)
(c) Size of Trade Sector (% of GDP)	4 (16.5)	4 (18.3)	4 (17.0)	4 (17.5)	4 (17.9)
(d) Capital Transactions with Foreigners	2	2	2	2	2
Economic Freedom Rating	**2.6**	**3.5**	**4.7**	**4.3**	**4.6**
Ranking of Country	**88**	**74**	**34**	**62**	**70**

148

Part 2: Recent Economic Indicators:

Population 1996: (in millions)	134.1	**Real Per Capita GDP** : (in 1995 U.S. dollars)		1995= $2,067
Annual Rate of Change (1985-96):	3.0%	Avg. Growth Rate:	1980-90=	3.0%
			1990-95=	2.1%

Economic Indicators:*	1988	1989	1990	1991	1992	1993	1994	1995	1996
Change in Real GDP: Aggregate	7.6	5.0	4.5	5.5	7.8	1.9	4.0	4.5	-
: Per Capita	4.6	2.0	1.5	2.5	4.8	-1.1	3.0	1.8	-
Inflation Rate (CPI)	8.8	7.8	9.1	11.8	9.5	10.0	12.4	12.3	-
Change in Money Supply: (M1)	9.7	14.3	17.3	20.2	21.5	1.7	15.1	12.8	-
: (M2)	7.7	7.4	11.6	18.9	29.3	18.1	17.4	13.8	-
Investment/GDP Ratio	18.0	18.9	18.9	19.0	20.1	20.7	19.9	18.7	-
Size of Trade Sector (% of GDP)	18.0	18.2	17.5	17.7	20.8	20.5	17.6	17.9	-
Total Gov't Exp./GDP Ratio									
Central Government Budget Deficit (-) or Surplus (+) As a Percent of GDP	-6.3	-7.4	-5.4	-7.6	-7.9	-7.4	-6.0	-4.8	-
Unemployment Rate [a]	3.1	3.1	3.1	6.3	6.3	-	-	-	-

* The figures in this table are in percent form.

[a] May, 1996.

In 1975 Pakistan's 2.6 ranking placed it 88th (out of 95). During 1975-1985 it did register some improvement, but there has been very little additional change since 1985. In 1995 Pakistan ranked 70th (out of 115).

The major deficiencies of this economy are:

- Excessive regulation—continued use of price controls, interest rate controls, and exchange rate controls, as well as regulations restricting entry into business;
- The widespread presence of government enterprises;

- A legal system that provides government officials with arbitrary authority that undermines the security of property rights and is often used in a discriminatory manner;
- Restrictive trade practices (note the high tariffs and a small trade sector); and
- Restrictions on the mobility of capital.

If Pakistan is going the follow the path of Malaysia, Thailand, and Singapore, it must improve its regulatory environment, liberalize its trade barriers, and adopt legal and monetary institutions supportive of a market economy.

PANAMA

Economic Freedom Rating

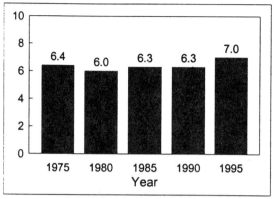

Total Government Expenditures As a Percent of GDP

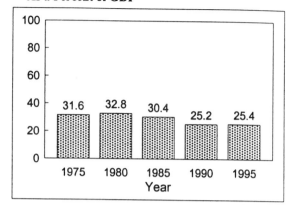

Part 1: The Economic Freedom Ratings for the Components and Various Area and Summary Indexes: 1975, 1980, 1985, 1990 and 1995.

(The numbers in parentheses indicate the actual values for the components.)

Components of Economic Freedom	1975		1980		1985		1990		1995	
I. Money and Inflation	**7.5**		**7.2**		**9.7**		**10.0**		**9.1**	
(a) Annual Money Growth (last 5 yrs.)	6	(10.5)	4	(14.2)	10	(3.6)	10	(1.8)	7	(8.7)
(b) Inflation Variablity (last 5 yrs.)	6	(3.2)	7	(2.5)	9	(1.3)	10	(0.8)	10	(0.3)
(c) Ownership of Foreign Currency	10		10		10		10		10	
(d) Maint. of Bank Account Abroad	10		10		10		10		10	
II. Government Operation	**4.0**		**4.0**		**3.0**		**4.3**		**5.1**	
(a) Gov't Consump. (% of Total Consump.)	2	(25.4)	2	(25.6)	2	(24.3)	4	(21.8)	4	(20.3)
(b) Government Enterprises	6		6		4		4		4	
(c) Price Controls	-		-		-		2		4	
(d) Entry Into Business	-		-		-		-		7.5	
(e) Legal System	-		-		-		-		2.5	
(f) Avoidance of Neg. Interest Rates	-		-		-		10		10	
III. Takings	**6.0**		**5.1**		**5.1**		**4.7**		**7.5**	
(a) Transfers and Subsidies (% of GDP)	7	(3.8)	6	(4.9)	6	(4.8)	5	(7.4)	5	(6.8)
(b) Marginal Tax Rates (Top Rate)	4	(52)	3	(56)	3	(56)	3	(56)	9	(30)
(c) Conscription	10		10		10		10		10	
IV. International Sector	**7.6**		**7.4**		**7.1**		**7.7**		**8.0**	
(a) Taxes on International Trade (Avg.)	7	(3.2)	7	(3.1)	6	(4.1)	8	(1.8)	9	(1.4)
(b) Black Market Exchange Rates (Prem.)	10	(0)	10	(0)	10	(0)	10	(0)	10	(0)
(c) Size of Trade Sector (% of GDP)	4	(37.4)	3	(38.6)	3	(34.2)	3	(37.4)	3	(38.6)
(d) Capital Transactions with Foreigners	8		8		8		8		8	
Economic Freedom Rating	**6.4**		**6.0**		**6.3**		**6.3**		**7.0**	
Ranking of Country	**8**		**10**		**9**		**15**		**10**	

Part 2: Recent Economic Indicators:

Population 1996: 2.7   **Real Per Capita GDP** :   1996= $5,063
  (in millions)   (in 1995 U.S. dollars)
Annual Rate of Change (1985-96): 1.9%   Avg. Growth Rate: 1980-90= -1.3%
                                                 1990-96= 3.1%

Economic Indicators:*	1988	1989	1990	1991	1992	1993	1994	1995	1996
Change in Real GDP: Aggregate	-13.2	-0.8	7.4	7.9	7.2	4.1	3.7	1.8	2.8
: Per Capita	-15.1	-2.7	5.5	6.0	5.3	2.2	1.8	-0.1	1.1
Inflation Rate (CPI)	0.4	0.1	0.8	1.3	1.8	0.5	1.3	1.0	0.9
Change in Money Supply: (M1)	-31.3	1.0	41.0	28.7	14.8	10.8	13.5	1.3	11.7
: (M2)	-27.6	-2.9	36.6	31.0	25.0	17.2	15.5	7.9	17.7
Investment/GDP Ratio	7.5	6.0	16.6	18.9	23.6	25.2	27.8	34.3	36.4
Size of Trade Sector (% of GDP)	30.9	32.0	37.4	37.4	37.2	37.0	37.8	38.6	-
Total Gov't Exp./GDP Ratio	26.9	25.4	25.2	25.3	27.6	27.1	26.3	25.4	25.6
Central Government Budget Deficit (-) or Surplus (+) As a Percent of GDP	-10.5	-11.3	-2.6	-1.3	+1.6	+1.5	+3.8	+3.2	+1.9
Unemployment Rate	16.3	16.3	16.2	16.1	14.7	13.3	14.0	13.7	13.9

* The figures in this table are in percent form.

Panama's 7.0 economic freedom rating placed it 10th in 1995. Both its rating and ranking have been relatively steady during the last two decades.

This high rating reflects the monetary and price stability, the freedom of citizens to maintain foreign currency bank accounts, and the relatively open finance markets. The domestic currency (it is tied to the dollar at a one-to-one rate) is fully convertible and the restrictions on the mobility of capital are quite liberal. In 1995 the top marginal tax rate was 30%, down from 56% in 1990.

The major weakness of this economy is its legal system. As is so often the case in Latin American countries, government officials are granted a great deal of discretionary power and rule of law principles are often weak. As a result, political officials are often in a position to either provide favors or impose costs on those engaging in economic activity. Structures of this type breed corruption and undermine confidence.

Panama's growth rate during the 1990s has averaged 3.1% annually. With an improvement in its legal structure and other moves toward economic freedom, it has the potential to do substantially better.

PERU

Economic Freedom Rating

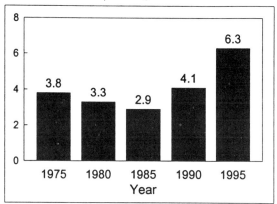

Total Government Expenditures As a Percent of GDP

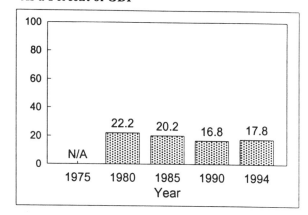

Part 1: The Economic Freedom Ratings for the Components and Various Area and Summary Indexes: 1975, 1980, 1985, 1990 and 1995.

(The numbers in parentheses indicate the actual values for the components.)

Components of Economic Freedom	1975	1980	1985	1990	1995
I. Money and Inflation	**1.6**	**0.6**	**0.0**	**1.9**	**3.6**
(a) Annual Money Growth (last 5 yrs.)	1 (24.1)	1 (42.2)	0 (99.3)	0 (690.3)	0 (64.2)
(b) Inflation Variablity (last 5 yrs.)	4 (5.9)	1 (17.5)	0 (38.1)	0 (2302.8)	0 (154.4)
(c) Ownership of Foreign Currency	0	0	0	10	10
(d) Maint. of Bank Account Abroad	0	0	0	0	10
II. Government Operation	**6.5**	**5.5**	**6.0**	**5.0**	**6.9**
(a) Gov't Consump. (% of Total Consump.)	7 (14.3)	7 (15.3)	8 (12.7)	10 (7.6)	10 (10.3)
(b) Government Enterprises	6	4	4	6	8
(c) Price Controls	-	-	-	2	6
(d) Entry Into Business	-	-	-	-	7.5
(e) Legal System	-	-	-	-	2.5
(f) Avoidance of Neg. Interest Rates	-	-	-	0	6
III. Takings	**5.5**	**4.5**	**3.6**	**5.1**	**6.5**
(a) Transfers and Subsidies (% of GDP)	9 (1.9)	9 (1.9)	9 (1.8)	8 (3.0)	7 (3.9)
(b) Marginal Tax Rates (Top Rate)	4 (51)	2 (65)	0 (65)	4 (45)	8 (30)
(c) Conscription	0	0	0	0	0
IV. International Sector	**1.9**	**2.6**	**2.3**	**3.6**	**6.8**
(a) Taxes on International Trade (Avg.)	1 (9.5)	1 (10.6)	2 (8.3)	6 (3.9)	6 (5.5)
(b) Black Market Exchange Rates (Prem.)	2 (56)	4 (18)	2 (51)	4 (16)	10 (0)
(c) Size of Trade Sector (% of GDP)	3 (16.4)	4 (20.8)	4 (19.7)	1 (13.4)	1 (14.0)
(d) Capital Transactions with Foreigners	2	2	2	2	8
Economic Freedom Rating	**3.8**	**3.3**	**2.9**	**4.1**	**6.3**
Ranking of Country	**59**	**81**	**89**	**72**	**29**

152

Part 2: Recent Economic Indicators:

Population 1996:	24.0	**Real Per Capita GDP** :	1995= $3,607
(in millions)		(in 1995 U.S. dollars)	
Annual Rate of Change (1985-96):	1.9%	Avg. Growth Rate:	1980-90= -2.9%
			1990-95= 2.1%

Economic Indicators:*	1988	1989	1990	1991	1992	1993	1994	1995	1996
Change in Real GDP: Aggregate	-8.8	-11.7	-3.8	2.9	-1.8	6.3	13.1	7.0	-
: Per Capita	-10.7	-13.6	-5.7	1.0	-3.7	4.4	11.2	5.1	-
Inflation Rate (CPI)	667.0	3398.7	7481.7	409.5	73.5	48.6	23.7	11.1	-
Change in Money Supply: (M1)	515.0	1654.9	6710.7	126.9	79.4	50.6	26.5	37.4	-
: (M2)	621.0	1917.3	6384.9	230.6	88.2	71.8	39.5	26.6	-
Investment/GDP Ratio	24.2	18.1	15.7	14.9	16.5	18.5	22.0	24.2	-
Size of Trade Sector (% of GDP)	14.9	13.5	13.4	10.7	11.2	11.0	12.9	14.0	-
Total Gov't Exp./GDP Ratio [a]	-	-	16.8	12.4	16.6	16.4	17.8	-	-
Central Government Budget Deficit (-) or Surplus (+) As a Percent of GDP	-3.6	-5.6	-3.7	-1.4	-1.8	-0.8	1.6	-2.1	-
Unemployment Rate [b]	-	7.9	-	5.8	9.4	9.9	8.9	-	-

* The figures in this table are in percent form.

[a] Includes local and regional government expenditures which generally account for approximately 2% of GDP.

[b] From the United Nations, Statistical Yearbook.

During the last decade and particularly during the last five years, Peru has made dramatic moves toward a freer economy. Its rating rose from 2.9 in 1985 to 6.3 in 1995, an increase of 3.4 units. Only New Zealand and Argentina registered more improvement during this period. In 1995 Peru's ranking was 29th, up from 72nd in 1990 and 89th in 1985.

Gains were registered in several areas. Citizens are now permitted to maintain bank accounts in alternative currencies, both domestically and abroad. There has been substantial privatization of state enterprises. The top marginal tax rate was cut from 65% in 1985 to 45% in 1990 and 30% in 1995. Exchange rate controls were relaxed and eventually eliminated. The Peruvian sole is now a fully convertible currency. Tariffs were reduced and made more uniform. Restrictions on the mobility of capital were substantially relaxed in the 1990s.

While some progress has been made—monetary expansion was reduced from the colossal fig-

ures of 1988-91 (see above)—the growth rate of the money supply is still much too rapid. Like several other Latin American countries with a history of inflation, Peru's monetary policy needs a credible anchor. There are several ways this could be accomplished, including the establishment of a currency board (as in the case of Hong Kong) or the subjection of one's monetary policy to the maintenance of a pegged exchange rate (as Argentina has done). Unless institutional change of this type is made, it will be difficult to convince decision-makers that monetary and price stability are important policy objectives. Without this credibility, the economy will fail to meet its full potential.

The changes to date are paying off. After years of decline (real per capita GDP fell by 34% between 1975 and 1992), the growth rate of real GDP averaged 8.8% during 1993-1995. If additional steps are taken to achieve monetary stability and improve the legal system, the long-term prospects for this economy are good.

153

PHILIPPINES

Economic Freedom Rating

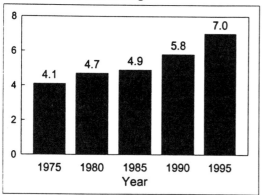

Total Government Expenditures As a Percent of GDP

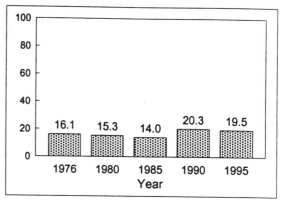

Part 1: The Economic Freedom Ratings for the Components and Various Area and Summary Indexes: 1975, 1980, 1985, 1990 and 1995.
(The numbers in parentheses indicate the actual values for the components.)

Components of Economic Freedom	1975		1980		1985		1990		1995	
I. Money and Inflation	**1.3**		**3.0**		**2.1**		**2.6**		**7.2**	
(a) Annual Money Growth (last 5 yrs.)	2	(18.2)	2	(17.7)	6	(11.0)	2	(18.1)	5	(12.6)
(b) Inflation Variablity (last 5 yrs.)	2	(9.2)	7	(2.9)	1	(16.4)	6	(3.3)	6	(3.6)
(c) Ownership of Foreign Currency	0		0		0		0		10	
(d) Maint. of Bank Account Abroad	0		0		0		0		10	
II. Government Operation	**7.6**		**6.8**		**6.3**		**5.9**		**5.7**	
(a) Gov't Consump. (% of Total Consump.)	7	(14.3)	9	(12.0)	10	(9.2)	9	(12.4)	8	(13.2)
(b) Government Enterprises	4		4		4		6		6	
(c) Price Controls	-		-		-		2		4	
(d) Entry Into Business	-		-		-		-		5.0	
(e) Legal System	-		-		-		-		2.5	
(f) Avoidance of Neg. Interest Rates	8		8		4		8		10	
III. Takings	**5.4**		**4.5**		**5.8**		**8.6**		**8.6**	
(a) Transfers and Subsidies (% of GDP)	10	(0.8)	10	(1.1)	10	(0.2)	10	(0.9)	10	(0.7)
(b) Marginal Tax Rates (Top Rate)	3	(56)	1	(70)	1	(60)	7	(35)	7	(35)
(c) Conscription	0		0		10		10		10	
IV. International Sector	**3.1**		**4.7**		**4.7**		**4.7**		**7.2**	
(a) Taxes on International Trade (Avg.)	0	(13.4)	4	(6.8)	5	(6.2)	4	(6.6)	5	(6.2)
(b) Black Market Exchange Rates (Prem.)	4	(13)	6	(3)	5	(7)	5	(7)	10	(0)
(c) Size of Trade Sector (% of GDP)	9	(24.1)	8	(26.0)	8	(22.9)	10	(30.7)	10	(40.1)
(d) Capital Transactions with Foreigners	2		2		2		2		5	
Economic Freedom Rating	**4.1**		**4.7**		**4.9**		**5.8**		**7.0**	
Ranking of Country	**50**		**29**		**30**		**25**		**10**	

Part 2: Recent Economic Indicators:

Population 1996:   69.8   **Real Per Capita GDP**   :   1996= $2,493
   (in millions)   (in 1995 U.S. dollars)
Annual Rate of Change (1985-96):   2.5%   Avg. Growth Rate: 1980-90 =   -0.8%
                                                         1990-96 =   0.3%

Economic Indicators:*	1988	1989	1990	1991	1992	1993	1994	1995	1996
Change in Real GDP:Aggregate	6.8	6.2	3.0	-0.5	0.3	2.1	4.4	4.8	5.8
: Per Capita	4.3	3.7	0.5	-3.0	-2.2	-0.4	1.9	2.3	3.1
Inflation Rate (CPI)	8.8	12.2	14.1	18.7	8.9	7.6	9.1	8.1	8.4
Change in Money Supply: (M1)	13.7	32.8	14.3	15.9	9.1	22.3	11.3	21.7	16.0
: (M2)	24.6	30.1	22.5	17.3	13.6	27.1	24.4	24.2	18.0
Investment/GDP Ratio	18.7	21.6	24.2	20.2	21.3	24.0	24.0	22.3	25.6
Size of Trade Sector (% of GDP)	27.6	29.4	30.7	30.8	31.2	35.5	37.0	40.1	-
Total Gov't Exp./GDP Ratio	16.1	18.0	19.6	19.2	19.7	18.5	18.7	19.5	18.5
Central Government Budget Deficit (-) or Surplus (+) As a Percent of GDP	-2.9	-2.1	-3.5	-2.1	-1.2	-1.5	+1.1	+1.1	+0.3
Unemployment Rate	10.8	9.2	8.3	10.6	9.8	10.2	9.4	9.4	7.6 [a]

* The figures in this table are in percent form.

[a] November, 1996.

Both the rating and ranking of this country have improved substantially during the last two decades, particularly during the 1990s. In 1995 the Philippines ranked 10th, up from 30th in 1985 and 50th in 1975. The primary factors contributing to the rating improvement were legalization of foreign currency bank accounts, reductions in marginal tax rates (the top rate was reduced from 70% in 1980 and 60% in 1985 to the current rate of 35%), relaxation of exchange rate controls, and an increase in the size of the trade sector. Privatization and deregulation of the telecommunications, shipping, civil aviation, petroleum and financial sectors have also contributed to the growth of economic freedom. The reforms are paying off handsomely. The growth of per capita GDP has accelerated significantly since 1992, and is expected to continue at a high level for the next few years.

Of course, deficiencies are still present, particularly in the institutional and legal framework. Defective bidding procedures have led to several recent cases of political and judicial interference and the reversal or suspension of several major infrastructure contracts. There is a general perception of wide-scale corruption in the awarding of public works contracts, in tax and customs collection, in the judiciary and certain other government services. The constitution also continues to prevent the entry of foreign investment in some sectors, such as mass media and certain professional services. In order to further enhance gains from economic freedom, the government needs to promote greater transparency, fairness and efficiency of public services through civil service reforms and privatization.

155

POLAND

Economic Freedom Rating

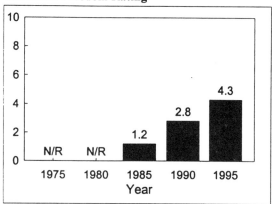

Total Government Expenditures
As a Percent of GDP

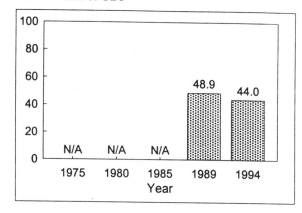

Part 1: The Economic Freedom Ratings for the Components and Various Area and Summary Indexes: 1975, 1980, 1985, 1990 and 1995.

(The numbers in parentheses indicate the actual values for the components.)

Components of Economic Freedom	1975	1980	1985	1990	1995
I. Money and Inflation	**6.6**	**7.1**	**2.5**	**3.6**	**4.6**
(a) Annual Money Growth (last 5 yrs.)	-	-	2 (20.5)	0 (110.5)	1 (31.5)
(b) Inflation Variablity (last 5 yrs.)	8 (2.4)	9 (2.0)	0 (37.4)	0 (178.3)	2 (8.5)
(c) Ownership of Foreign Currency	10	10	10	10	10
(d) Maint. of Bank Account Abroad	0	0	0	10	10
II. Government Operation	**3.4**	**4.4**	**1.0**	**0.9**	**4.9**
(a) Gov't Consump. (% of Total Consump.)	7 (15.6)	9 (12.0)	2 (25.5)	1 (28.7)	3 (22.6)
(b) Government Enterprises	0	0	0	0	2
(c) Price Controls	-	-	-	2	6
(d) Entry Into Business	-	-	-	-	7.5
(e) Legal System	-	-	-	-	5.0
(f) Avoidance of Neg. Interest Rates	-	-	-	0	6
III. Takings	**0.0**	**0.0**	**0.0**	**3.8**	**2.3**
(a) Transfers and Subsidies (% of GDP)	-	-	0 (27.4)	5 (7.2)	1 (24.4)
(b) Marginal Tax Rates (Top Rate)	-	-	-	-	4 (45)
(c) Conscription	0	0	0	0	0
IV. International Sector	**0.0**	**1.6**	**1.1**	**3.5**	**5.8**
(a) Taxes on International Trade (Avg.)	-	-	2 (8.6)	5 (6.0)	4 (6.4)
(b) Black Market Exchange Rates (Prem.)	0 (3786)	0 (298)	0 (301)	5 (9)	10 (0)
(c) Size of Trade Sector (% of GDP)	-	7 (29.6)	3 (17.5)	4 (22.9)	3 (21.0)
(d) Capital Transactions with Foreigners	0	0	0	0	5
Economic Freedom Rating			**1.2**	**2.8**	**4.3**
Ranking of Country			**106**	**98**	**81**

Part 2: Recent Economic Indicators:

Population 1996: 38.6   **Real Per Capita GDP** : 1996 = $6,570

  (in millions)   (in 1995 U.S. dollars)

Annual Rate of Change (1985-96): 0.4%   Avg. Growth Rate: 1980-90 = -0.9%

   1990-96 = 0.4%

Economic Indicators:*	1988	1989	1990	1991	1992	1993	1994	1995	1996
Change in Real GDP:Aggregate	4.0	0.2	-11.6	-7.0	2.6	3.8	5.5	7.0	5.4
: Per Capita	3.6	-0.2	-12.0	-7.4	2.2	3.4	5.1	6.6	5.0
Inflation Rate (CPI)	58.7	244.6	586.0	70.3	43.0	35.3	32.2	27.8	19.9
Change in Money Supply: (M1)	51.3	253.7	401.1	28.1	38.8	31.3	39.7	36.4	-
: (M2)	63.9	535.8	155.9	48.1	57.5	36.0	38.2	35.0	25.6
Investment/GDP Ratio	32.6	38.5	25.6	19.9	15.2	15.8	16.1	16.5	16.9
Size of Trade Sector (% of GDP)	21.4	17.0	22.9	20.1	21.8	20.4	23.8	21.0	19.9
Total Gov't Exp./GDP Ratio	-	48.9	39.8	48.0	50.7	48.4	44.0	-	-
Central Government Budget Deficit (-) or Surplus (+) As a Percent of GDP	-2.4	-7.4	+3.5	-6.2	-7.0	-4.8	-1.8	-2.6	-2.8
Unemployment Rate	-	-	6.0	9.2	12.9	15.0	16.5	14.9	14.0 [a]

* The figures in this table are in percent form.

[a] July, 1995.

The economic freedom rating of Poland jumped from 1.6 in 1985 to 4.3 in 1995. In 1995 Poland ranked 81th, up from 98th in 1990 and 105th in 1985. Thus, our index indicates that Poland has made significant moves toward economic freedom during the last decade.

During 1989-1991 the Polish economy went through a shock therapy treatment. It was a period of monetary instability and institutional change. Fueled by both monetary overhang and printing press finance, the inflation rate soared to almost 600% in 1990. But there were also significant positive developments during and immediately following this period. Price controls were eliminated on most products. Interest controls were liberalized and financial markets were allowed to develop. There was considerable privatization, although many large established enterprises continue in the hands of the state. Exchange rate controls were liberalized, increasing the convert-

ibility of the zloty. Restrictions on the mobility of capital were also relaxed.

While Poland has moved away from socialism and toward a market economy, the transition is still incomplete and many problems remain. Even though the growth rate of the money supply has fallen substantially, monetary policy is still far too expansionary for the achievement of price stability. While government expenditures have been reduced modestly (to 44% of GDP, down from 48.9 in 1989), they are still quite large. The legal structure needs reform that would reduce the ability of political officials to interfere with markets and intrude into business affairs. Overall, however, the Polish economy is now on a solid growth path. Growth of real GDP has averaged almost 5% during the last five years, the highest among the former socialist countries. With continued liberalization, Poland could well become the growth economy of Europe in the decade ahead.

157

PORTUGAL

Economic Freedom Rating

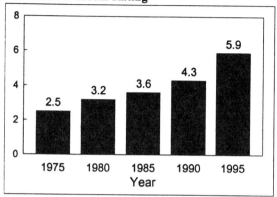

Total Government Expenditures As a Percent of GDP

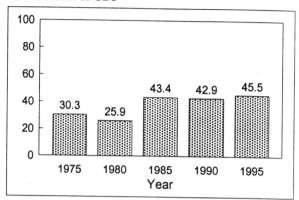

Part 1: The Economic Freedom Ratings for the Components and Various Area and Summary Indexes: 1975, 1980, 1985, 1990 and 1993-95.
(The numbers in parentheses indicate the actual values for the components.)

Components of Economic Freedom	1975		1980		1985		1990		1995	
I. Money and Inflation	**2.2**		**2.9**		**3.6**		**2.9**		**7.4**	
(a) Annual Money Growth (last 5 yrs.)	3	(17.4)	3	(17.2)	4	(14.7)	3	(17.4)	7	(9.4)
(b) Inflation Variablity (last 5 yrs.)	4	(5.2)	6	(3.4)	7	(2.5)	6	(3.4)	5	(4.3)
(c) Ownership of Foreign Currency	0		0		0		0		10	
(d) Maint. of Bank Account Abroad	0		0		0		0		10	
II. Government Operation	**3.5**		**4.0**		**4.8**		**4.0**		**5.4**	
(a) Gov't Consump. (% of Total Consump.)	5	(17.0)	6	(17.8)	5	(18.6)	4	(21.0)	3	(22.1)
(b) Government Enterprises	2		2		2		2		2	
(c) Price Controls	-		-		-		4		5	
(d) Entry Into Business	-		-		-		-		7.5	
(e) Legal System	-		-		-		-		7.5	
(f) Avoidance of Neg. Interest Rates	-		4		10		8		10	
III. Takings	**1.2**		**0.8**		**0.8**		**3.5**		**3.5**	
(a) Transfers and Subsidies (% of GDP)	3	(14.6)	2	(16.3)	2	(19.5)	3	(15.5)	3	(14.2)
(b) Marginal Tax Rates (Top Rate)	0	(82)	0	(84)	0	(69)	5	(40)	5	(40)
(c) Conscription	0		0		0		0		0	
IV. International Sector	**3.4**		**5.7**		**6.3**		**6.6**		**8.3**	
(a) Taxes on International Trade (Avg.)	6	(4.6)	8	(2.1)	9	(1.2)	9	(1.0)	10	(0.0)
(b) Black Market Exchange Rates (Prem.)	2	(42)	7	(2)	7	(2)	6	(3)	10	(0)
(c) Size of Trade Sector (% of GDP)	3	(26.6)	5	(34.7)	7	(39.4)	6	(40.9)	3	(30.5)
(d) Capital Transactions with Foreigners	2		2		2		5		8	
Economic Freedom Rating	**2.5**		**3.2**		**3.6**		**4.3**		**5.9**	
Ranking of Country	**90**		**84**		**76**		**62**		**42**	

Part 2: Recent Economic Indicators:

Population 1996: 11.8 (in millions)
Annual Rate of Change (1985-96): 0.8%

Real Per Capita GDP : 1996= $11,274
(in 1995 U.S. dollars)
Avg. Growth Rate: 1980-90 = 2.5%
1990-95 = 0.9%

Economic Indicators:*	1988	1989	1990	1991	1992	1993	1994	1995	1996
Change in Real GDP:Aggregate	5.8	5.7	4.3	2.1	1.1	-1.2	0.8	2.4	2.6
: Per Capita	5.0	4.9	3.5	1.3	0.3	-2.0	0.0	1.6	1.8
Inflation Rate (CPI)	9.6	12.6	13.4	11.4	8.9	6.8	4.9	4.1	-
Change in Money Supply: (M1)	21.6	14.2	4.7	15.6	18.1	10.2	7.0	11.0	-
: (M2)	17.7	14.4	9.4	24.3	21.1	11.0	9.6	9.8	-
Investment/GDP Ratio	30.4	28.1	28.5	26.7	25.5	24.4	25.0	-	-
Size of Trade Sector (% of GDP)	40.9	41.8	40.9	36.6	33.9	28.1	30.5	-	-
Total Gov't Exp./GDP Ratio	43.5	41.7	42.9	46.4	45.7	46.5	45.3	45.5	45.9
General Government Budget Deficit (-) or Surplus (+) As a Percent of GDP	-3.6	-2.3	-5.5	-6.4	-3.3	-6.9	-5.7	-4.9	-3.8
Unemployment Rate	5.7	5.0	4.6	4.1	4.1	5.7	7.0	7.3	7.1 [a]

* The figures in this table are in percent form.

[a] October, 1996.

In 1975, only five countries (Ghana, Egypt, Israel, Russia, and Uganda) had lower economic freedom ratings than Portugal. Since that time this country has moved steadily toward a freer economy. As its rating steadily increased, its ranking rose from 90th in 1975 to 76th in 1985 and 42nd in 1995. During the last two decades, only New Zealand, Mauritius, Chile and Iceland have registered larger increases in their economic freedom rating.

The highlights of Portugal's advancement include:
- Legalization of foreign currency accounts in the early 1990s;
- Reduction of the top marginal tax rate from 82% in 1975 to 69% in 1985 and to the current 40% in the late 1980s;
- Substantial reductions in tariffs;
- Movement to a convertible currency and therefore the elimination of the black market in foreign exchange; and
- Relaxation of restrictions limiting the mobility of capital.

Not all of the news is positive. The size of government as a share of the economy is now larger than was the case in the mid-1970s and budget deficits have been exceedingly large in recent years. This pattern—the growth of government financed with large budget deficits—generally leads to falling investment and rising unemployment. Portugal's unemployment rate (around 7% during 1994-1996) is currently one of the lowest in Europe. If Portugal is going to maintain (and lower) its unemployment rate, it must do a better job of controlling government expenditures and reducing the size of its budget deficit.

ROMANIA

Economic Freedom Ratings

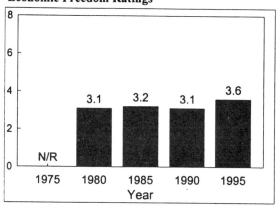

Total Government Expenditures As a Percent of GDP

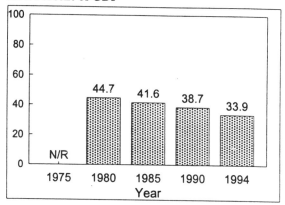

Part 1: The Economic Freedom Ratings for the Components and Various Area and Summary Indexes: 1975, 1980, 1985, 1990 and 1995.

(The numbers in parentheses indicate the actual values for the components.)

Components of Economic Freedom	1975		1980		1985		1990		1995	
I. Money and Inflation	**4.8**		**4.2**		**4.1**		**5.0**		**1.9**	
(a) Annual Money Growth (last 5 yrs.)	-		6	(11.2)	8	(7.7)	7	(8.9)	0	(100.7)
(b) Inflation Variablity (last 5 yrs.)	10	(0.4)	7	(2.8)	5	(4.8)	3	(6.0)	0	(84.7)
(c) Ownership of Foreign Currency	0		0		0		10		10	
(d) Maint. of Bank Account Abroad	0		0		0		0		0	
II. Government Operation	**0.0**		**4.9**		**4.9**		**3.1**		**4.8**	
(a) Gov't Consump. (% of Total Consump.)	-		10	(8.0)	10	(6.5)	6	(17.9)	5	(18.1)
(b) Government Enterprises	0		0		0		0		0	
(c) Price Controls	-		-		-		0		6	
(d) Entry Into Business	-		-		-		-		5.0	
(e) Legal System	-		-		-		-		5.0	
(f) Avoidance of Neg. Interest Rates	-		-		-		10		10	
III. Takings	**0.0**		**2.3**		**3.8**		**1.5**		**1.7**	
(a) Transfers and Subsidies (% of GDP)	-		3	(14.1)	5	(7.9)	2	(18.6)	3	(14.6)
(b) Marginal Tax Rates (Top Rate)	-		-		-		-		1	(60)
(c) Conscription	0		0		0		0		0	
IV. International Sector	**0.0**		**1.4**		**0.5**		**2.8**		**5.4**	
(a) Taxes on International Trade (Avg.)	-		-		-		9	(0.4)	7	(2.9)
(b) Black Market Exchange Rates (Prem.)	0	(596)	0	(628)	0	(1246)	0	(416)	6	(3)
(c) Size of Trade Sector (% of GDP)	-		6	(37.7)	2	(20.8)	1	(21.4)	2	(25.6)
(d) Capital Transactions with Foreigners	0		0		0		0		5	
Economic Freedom Rating			**3.1**		**3.2**		**3.1**		**3.6**	
Ranking of Country			**87**		**84**		**94**		**101**	

Part 2: Recent Economic Indicators:

Population 1996:	22.6	**Real Per Capita GDP** :	1995=	$3,360
(in millions)		(in 1995 U.S. dollars)		
Annual Rate of Change (1985-96):	0.0%	Avg. Growth Rate:	1980-90=	-0.8%
			1990-95=	-2.2%

Economic Indicators:*	1988	1989	1990	1991	1992	1993	1994	1995	1996
Change in Real GDP: Aggregate	-0.5	-5.8	-5.6	-12.9	-8.8	1.5	3.9	6.9	-
: Per Capita	-0.5	-5.8	-5.8	-12.8	-7.2	1.7	4.1	7.1	-
Inflation Rate (CPI)	2.8	0.7	6.1	170.2	210.4	256.1	136.7	32.3	30.0
Change in Money Supply: (M1)	16.4	2.5	15.8	193.2	51.3	126.5	103.2	56.2	-
: (M2)	10.3	5.3	22.0	101.2	79.6	143.2	138.1	71.6	-
Investment/GDP Ratio	28.4	26.8	30.2	28.0	31.4	29.0	26.9	25.7	-
Size of Trade Sector (% of GDP)	15.7	19.8	21.4	18.5	29.0	25.6	-	-	-
Total Gov't Exp./GDP Ratio	-	42.8	38.7	38.7	42.0	34.2	33.9	-	-
Central Government Budget Deficit (-) or Surplus (+) As a Percent of GDP	+5.8	+8.2	+0.9	-1.9	-4.4	-2.6	-4.2	-4.1	-3.0
Unemployment Rate	-	-	-	3.0	8.2	10.4	10.9	9.5	6.3 [a]

* The figures in this table are in percent form.

[a] December, 1996.

In 1995 Romania ranked 101th among the 115 countries rated. During the last several decades, it has been one of the least free economies in the world.

It is clear why Romania ranks so low. Like several other transitional economies, Romania used budget deficits and money creation to finance subsidies and the continued operation of inefficient state enterprises. Predictably, this policy led to inflation. Romania's inflation rate averaged nearly 200% during 1991-1994. Thus, Romania gets low marks in the monetary area. The privatization record is mixed. While there has been considerable privatization in agriculture, construction, wholesale and retail trade, and textiles; the process has been slow in other areas. Most large businesses in the heavy industry, banking, and energy sectors continue under state control. Price controls are imposed on many energy products and subsidies continue to distort the prices of several food products. While entry into business is no longer blocked, the approval of several regulatory authorities is generally required. Meeting the various regulatory criteria can be both lengthy and costly. Furthermore, this process places government offi-

cials in a position to exert considerable informal authority over economic activity. This is a major source of corruption. Transfers and subsidies continue to consume a large share of GDP and the 60% top marginal tax bracket is one of the highest in the world.

Most of the bright spots are in the financial and international sectors. Both interest rate and exchange controls have been liberalized. Citizens have been allowed to hold foreign currencies and maintain bank accounts in alternative currencies since 1990. There has also been some relaxation of restrictions on the mobility of capital.

Despite its many shortcomings, Romania has experienced modest growth during the last four years. If this growth is going to be sustained and accelerated, more needs to be done. The current government has promised to move in this direction. A systematic plan for liberalization would include the following: (1) Completion of the privatization process, (2) a significant reduction the tax and regulatory burden imposed on both businesses and individuals, (3) achieving full convertibility of the Romanian lei, and (4) providing for the free flow of capital.

161

RUSSIA (Prior to 1990, most of the data are for the former Soviet Union)

Economic Freedom Rating

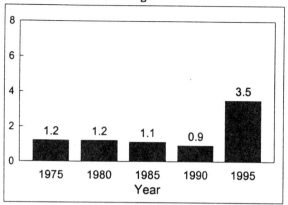

Total Government Expenditures As a Percent of GDP

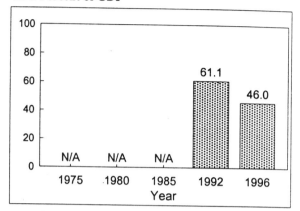

Part 1: The Economic Freedom Ratings for the Components and Various Area and Summary Indexes: 1975, 1980, 1985, 1990 and 1995.
(The numbers in parentheses indicate the actual values for the components.)

Components of Economic Freedom	1975		1980		1985		1990		1995	
I. Money and Inflation	**5.5**		**4.8**		**5.1**		**4.5**		**3.6**	
(a) Annual Money Growth (last 5 yrs.)	7	(8.3)	6	(10.6)	7	(9.6)	7	(9.7)	0	(401.4)
(b) Inflation Variablity (last 5 yrs.)	10	(1.1)	9	(1.8)	9	(1.4)	7	(2.7)	0	(228.7)
(c) Ownership of Foreign Currency	0		0		0		0		10	
(d) Maint. of Bank Account Abroad	0		0		0		0		10	
II. Government Operation	**0.0**		**0.4**		**0.0**		**0.0**		**2.5**	
(a) Gov't Consump. (% of Total Consump.)	0	(31.5)	1	(29.7)	0	(31.0)	0	(31.4)	0	(31.7)
(b) Government Enterprises	0		0		0		0		0	
(c) Price Controls	-		-		-		0		2	
(d) Entry Into Business	-		-		-		-		5.0	
(e) Legal System	-		-		-		-		2.5	
(f) Avoidance of Neg. Interest Rates	0		0		0		0		8	
III. Takings	**0.0**		**0.0**		**0.0**		**0.0**		**4.1**	
(a) Transfers and Subsidies (% of GDP)	0	(30.0)	0	(30.0)	0	(30.0)	0	(30.0)	1	(20.0)
(b) Marginal Tax Rates (Top Rate)	0	(100)	0	(100)	0	(100)	0	(80)	8	(30)
(c) Conscription	0		0		0		0		0	
IV. International Sector	**0.0**		**0.0**		**0.2**		**0.0**		**4.0**	
(a) Taxes on International Trade (Avg.)	-		-		-		-		2	(8.8)
(b) Black Market Exchange Rates (Prem.)	0	(391)	0	(359)	0	(637)	0	(6100)	7	(2)
(c) Size of Trade Sector (% of GDP)	-		-		1	(8.9)	0	(7.7)	1	(9.4)
(d) Capital Transactions with Foreigners	0		0		0		0		5	
Economic Freedom Rating	**1.2**		**1.2**		**1.1**		**0.9**		**3.5**	
Ranking of Country	**95**		**105**		**107**		**107**		**105**	

Part 2: Recent Economic Indicators:

Population 1996:	148.0	Real Per Capita GDP	:	1996 =	$4,285
(in millions)		(in 1995 U.S. dollars)			
Annual Rate of Change (1990-96)	0.0%	Avg. Growth Rate:		1980-90=	2.9%
				1990-96=	-7.7%

Economic Indicators:* ᵃ	1990	1991	1992	1993	1994	1995	1996
Change in Real GDP: Aggregate	-3.0	-5.0	-14.5	-8.7	-12.7	-4.2	-5.7
: Per Capita	-3.0	-5.0	-14.5	-8.7	-12.7	-4.2	-5.7
Inflation Rate (CPI)	5.6	168.0	2508.8	844.2	214.8	114.6	21.8
Change in Money Supply: (M1)	31.2	120.5	889.0	714.7	161.9	120.7	31.2
: (M2)	11.5	125.9	642.6	416.2	166.4	125.8	32.5
Investment/GDP Ratio	30.1	36.3	34.6	31.0	28.9	28.1	24.6
Size of Trade Sector (% of GDP)	7.7	4.8	5.3	5.9	7.7	9.4	10.1
Total Gov't Exp./GDP Ratio	-	-	61.1	49.2	50.2	44.2	46.0
Central Government Budget Deficit (-) or Surplus (+) As a Percent of GDP	-	-	-28.9	-8.3	-10.6	-8.7	-8.8
Unemployment Rate	-	0.6	2.9	5.1	7.4	8.3	9.4

* The figures in this table are in percent form.

ᵃ The data for all years are for Russia.

Rating the economic freedom of a former socialist country during a period of transition is a difficult task. Often times the quality of the data is poor and availability limited. With the assistance of our co-operating partner, the *Institute of Economic Analysis* of Moscow, we were able to include Russia (and the former Soviet Union) in our index for the first time. Our index indicates that economic freedom in the former Soviet Union was very limited. Except for the monetary and price stability components, which clearly take on less importance in an economy where the government fixes the prices of everything, the ratings for the former Soviet Union were extremely low (usually zero) for every component of our index. As a result, the former Soviet economy ranked among the bottom two or three least free economies during 1975-1990.

The 1995 rating of Russia improved a little to 3.5, but this still places it 105th (out of 115). The areas where the 1995 ratings were reasonably good were primarily institutional. Foreign currency bank accounts are now permissible. Both interest rate and exchange rate controls have been relaxed substantially. Restrictions on the mobility of capital flows have also been liberalized.

It is clear that two important elements of a market economy remain absent. Those two elements are monetary stability and a legal structure capable of providing secure property rights. Since the monetary expansion and hyperinflation of 1992, the inflation rate has persistently declined. But it is still quite high—more than 30% in 1996—and the monetary system needs an anchor. Institutional arrangements providing the central bank with a low (and stable) target inflation rate would be helpful in this regard.

The problems with the legal structure are more complex. The method of privatization left the ownership and control of most enterprises in the hands of their former managers. Even though the enterprises have been nominally privatized the struggle for favorable treatment and protected markets is likely to continue for several years. So too, is the opportunistic behavior on the part of the managers. This incentive structure will often lead to the depletion of the value of existing capital, while undermining the incentive for capital investment. Furthermore, regulations held over from the former

(Continued to page 203)

163

SINGAPORE

Economic Freedom Rating

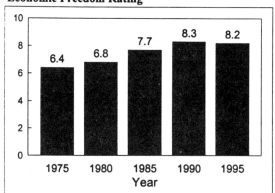

Total Government Expenditures As a Percent of GDP

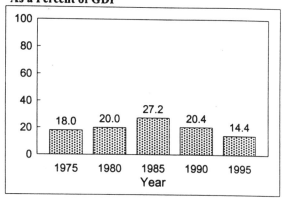

Part 1: The Economic Freedom Ratings for the Components and Various Area and Summary Indexes: 1975, 1980, 1985, 1990 and 1995.
(The numbers in parentheses indicate the actual values for the components.)

Components of Economic Freedom	1975		1980		1985		1990		1995	
I. Money and Inflation	**3.2**		**3.8**		**6.7**		**8.4**		**10.0**	
(a) Annual Money Growth (last 5 yrs.)	5	(13.9)	6	(11.3)	8	(7.6)	8	(7.8)	10	(2.8)
(b) Inflation Variablity (last 5 yrs.)	5	(4.7)	6	(3.7)	7	(2.7)	7	(2.8)	10	(0.6)
(c) Ownership of Foreign Currency	0		0		10		10		10	
(d) Maint. of Bank Account Abroad	0		0		0		10		10	
II. Government Operation	**7.5**		**8.0**		**6.5**		**7.5**		**6.7**	
(a) Gov't Consump. (% of Total Consump.)	7	(15.0)	7	(15.6)	3	(23.8)	5	(19.1)	6	(17.2)
(b) Government Enterprises	8		8		8		8		8	
(c) Price Controls	-		-		-		8		8	
(d) Entry Into Business	-		-		-		-		7.5	
(e) Legal System	-		-		-		-		0.0	
(f) Avoidance of Neg. Interest Rates	-		10		10		10		10	
III. Takings	**5.5**		**5.9**		**7.3**		**7.4**		**7.8**	
(a) Transfers and Subsidies (% of GDP)	9	(1.4)	10	(1.1)	9	(1.8)	8	(2.6)	9	(1.8)
(b) Marginal Tax Rates (Top Rate)	4	(55)	4	(55)	8	(40)	9	(33)	9	(30)
(c) Conscription	0		0		0		0		0	
IV. International Sector	**9.2**		**9.2**		**9.7**		**10.0**		**10.0**	
(a) Taxes on International Trade (Avg.)	9	(0.7)	9	(0.5)	9	(0.3)	10	(0.2)	10	(0.1)
(b) Black Market Exchange Rates (Prem.)	10	(0)	10	(0)	10	(0)	10	(0)	10	(0)
(c) Size of Trade Sector (% of GDP)	10	(144.6)	10	(211.7)	10	(159.0)	10	(176.8)	10	(166.0)
(d) Capital Transactions with Foreigners	8		8		10		10		10	
Economic Freedom Rating	**6.4**		**6.8**		**7.7**		**8.3**		**8.2**	
Ranking of Country	**8**		**3**		**2**		**2**		**2**	

164

Part 2: Recent Economic Indicators:

Population 1996:	3.1	**Real Per Capita GDP** :	1996 = $23,342
(in millions)		(in 1995 U.S. dollars)	
Annual Rate of Change (1985-96):	1.9%	Avg. Growth Rate:	1980-90 = 5.8%
			1990-96 = 6.3%

Economic Indicators:*	1988	1989	1990	1991	1992	1993	1994	1995	1996
Change in Real GDP:Aggregate	11.1	9.4	8.1	7.0	6.4	10.1	10.1	8.8	7.0
: Per Capita	9.2	7.5	6.2	5.1	4.5	8.3	8.0	6.8	5.1
Inflation Rate (CPI)	1.5	2.3	3.5	3.4	2.3	2.3	3.1	1.7	1.4
Change in Money Supply: (M1)	8.4	14.9	11.0	7.7	12.7	23.6	2.3	8.3	6.6
: (M2)	13.5	22.5	20.0	12.4	8.9	8.5	14.4	8.5	9.8
Investment/GDP Ratio	33.4	33.3	35.7	35.1	36.4	38.4	32.2	32.6	35.1
Size of Trade Sector (% of GDP)	189.4	177.8	176.8	167.1	161.3	161.3	163.3	166.0	-
Total Gov't Exp./GDP Ratio	23.0	22.3	21.0	21.2	19.7	17.7	14.5	14.4	-
Central Government Budget Deficit (-) or Surplus (+) As a Percent of GDP	+6.7	+9.9	+10.6	+8.7	+12.5	+10.9	+12.5	+11.5	+11.9
Unemployment Rate	3.3	2.2	1.7	1.9	2.7	2.7	2.0	2.0	2.0

* The figures in this table are in percent form.

Singapore's 8.2 rating in 1995 indicates that it is the 2nd freest economy in the world, behind only Hong Kong. Both its ranking and rating were persistently high throughout the last two decades.

Singapore's high ranking reflects the following:

- Its monetary policy is just about the most stable in the world and, as a result, its inflation rate has been low (1% to 3%) during the last decade;
- The Singapore dollar is fully convertible and citizens are free to maintain funds in foreign currency bank accounts;
- Government expenditures are low (less than 20% of GDP), as are taxes (the top marginal tax rate is currently 30%, down from 55% in the mid-1980s);
- International exchange is relatively free (tariffs are negligible, there are no exchange rate controls, and few restrictions on either the inflow or outflow of capital, and the trade sector is the largest in the world);
- Most of the enterprises are private (state-operated enterprises produce only a small portion of the total output) and there are few restraints limiting entry into business.

Singapore is not perfect. It uses military conscription, which is an in-kind tax that causes the taxation and expenditure figures to understate the size of government. Furthermore, three-fourths of the housing units are constructed and operated by the government.

Singapore's Central Provident Fund (CPF) provides a unique method of dealing with social welfare issues. Individuals are required to pay a large amount (approximately 20% of earnings paid by both employee and employer) into this fund. They do, however, have a property right to the funds and, as the result of recent liberalization, they may use them for several purposes other than retirement, including education, medical services, the purchasing of a home, and even certain types of real estate investments. While the payments are compulsory, saving and investment programs of this type are clearly more consistent with economy freedom than the tax and spend social security programs utilized by most countries. (Note: since the CPF payments are not included in either taxes or government expenditures, they are not registered by our index.)

All things considered, Singapore has one of the world's freest economies. Its rapid growth and now high level of per capita GDP once again illustrate the potential for growth in an economically free environment.

165

SLOVAKIA (Data prior to 1993 are for the former Czechoslovakia).

Economic Freedom Rating

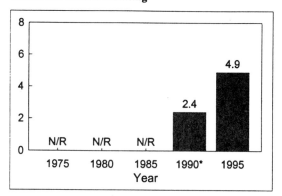

Total Government Expenditures As a Percent of GDP

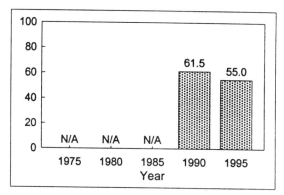

Part 1: The Economic Freedom Ratings for the Components and Various Area and Summary Indexes: 1975, 1980, 1985, 1990 and 1995.
(The numbers in parentheses indicate the actual values for the components.)

* Rating is for Czechoslovakia.

Components of Economic Freedom	1990		1995	
I. Money and Inflation	**4.7**		**5.8**	
(a) Annual Money Growth (last 5 yrs.)	10	(0.4)	5	(13.4)
(b) Inflation Variablity (last 5 yrs.)	5	(4.0)	2	(10.2)
(c) Ownership of Foreign Currency	0		10	
(d) Maint. of Bank Account Abroad	0		10	
II. Government Operation	**0.3**		**4.5**	
(a) Gov't Consumption (% of Total Consump.)	1	(29.9)	1	(27.6)
(b) Government Enterprises	0		4	
(c) Price Controls	0		4	
(d) Entry Into Business	-		7.5	
(e) Legal System	-		5.0	
(f) Avoidance of Neg. Interest Rates	-		6	
III. Takings	**1.9**		**3.1**	
(a) Transfers and Subsidies (% of GDP)	0	(37.2)	-	
(b) Marginal Tax Rates (Top Rate)	4	(55)	4	(42)
(c) Conscription	0		0	
IV. International Sector	**3.6**		**7.0**	
(a) Taxes on International Trade (Avg.)	6	(4.0)	-	
(b) Black Market Exchange Rates (Prem.)	--		10	(0)
(c) Size of Trade Sector (% of GDP)	5	(34.4)	10	(61.1)
(d) Capital Transactions with Foreigners	0		2	
Economic Freedom Rating	**2.4**		**4.9**	
Ranking of Country	**101**		**66**	

166

Part 2: Recent Economic Indicators:

Population 1996: (in millions)	5.3	**Real Per Capita GDP** : (in 1995 U.S. dollars)	1996=	$3,815
Annual Rate of Change (1990-96):	0.3%	Avg. Growth Rate:	1980-90= 1993-96=	_ 3.6%

Economic Indicators:*	1993	1994	1995	1996
Change in Real GDP: Aggregate	-3.7	4.9	6.8	6.8
: Per Capita	-4.0	4.5	7.0	6.7
Inflation Rate (CPI)	25.1	11.7	7.2	5.4
Change in Money Supply: (M1)	7.4	10.9	20.5	16.2
: (M2)	18.5	18.6	21.2	15.8
Investment/GDP Ratio	32.6	29.5	29.1	33.8
Size of Trade Sector (% of GDP)	64.0	62.0	61.1	59.0
Total Gov't Exp./GDP Ratio	68.0	57.0	55.0	-
Central Government Budget Deficit (-) or Surplus (+) As a Percent of GDP	-6.2	-5.2	-1.6	-4.6
Unemployment Rate	12.7	14.6	13.8	12.8 [a]

* The figures in this table are in percent form.

[a] December, 1996.

Slovakia's 1995 rating of 4.9 placed it 66th among our 115 countries. This rating was just a fraction lower than the ratings of the Czech Republic, Hungary and Greece, for example. This was a marked improvement on the 2.4 rating (and 101st ranking) of the former Czechoslovakia in 1990.

Several steps have been taken to provide a solid foundation for a market economy. Monetary restraint reduced the inflation rate to 7.2% in 1995 and 5.4% in 1996, the lowest rates of any former socialist country. Foreign currency bank accounts are now legal both at home and abroad. Substantial privatization, including a number of large enterprises, has occurred. The exchange rate is now primarily determined by market forces and the size of the trade sector is large for a country of this size.

Several additional steps are needed. The legal structure needs to become more transparent and less discretionary. Regulations limiting entry into business need to be reduced. The trade sector can be liberalized even more and continuation of the move toward a monetary policy consistent with a low and stable rate of inflation is vital. But the foundation has been established. Slovakia is now primarily a market economy and it is already reaping benefits. Its growth rate during the last three years (6.4%) has been impressive and the unemployment rate—while still high—fell to a post-transition low (12.8%) at year-end 1996. With continued liberalization, this economy faces a bright future.

167

SOUTH AFRICA

Economic Freedom Rating

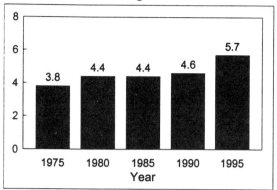

Total Government Expenditures As a Percent of GDP

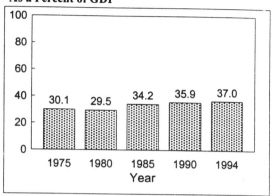

Part 1: The Economic Freedom Ratings for the Components and Various Area and Summary Indexes: 1975, 1980, 1985, 1990 and 1995.

(The numbers in parentheses indicate the actual values for the components.)

Components of Economic Freedom	1975		1980		1985		1990		1995	
I. Money and Inflation	**3.2**		**2.8**		**3.3**		**4.0**		**3.9**	
(a) Annual Money Growth (last 5 yrs.)	5	(13.4)	5	(13.9)	1	(20.6)	2	(17.7)	3	(15.0)
(b) Inflation Variablity (last 5 yrs.)	5	(4.8)	4	(5.1)	9	(1.9)	10	(0.9)	9	(1.7)
(c) Ownership of Foreign Currency	0		0		0		0		0	
(d) Maint. of Bank Account Abroad	0		0		0		0		0	
II. Government Operation	**4.5**		**3.6**		**4.1**		**3.8**		**5.8**	
(a) Gov't Consump. (% of Total Consump.)	5	(19.7)	3	(22.2)	2	(24.5)	1	(26.1)	2	(25.2)
(b) Government Enterprises	4		4		4		4		4	
(c) Price Controls	-		-		-		4		6	
(d) Entry Into Business	-		-		-		-		7.5	
(e) Legal System	-		-		-		-		7.5	
(f) Avoidance of Neg. Interest Rates	-		4		8		8		10	
III. Takings	**0.8**		**4.1**		**4.3**		**4.7**		**5.6**	
(a) Transfers and Subsidies (% of GDP)	-		8	(3.2)	6	(4.8)	6	(4.8)	6	(5.3)
(b) Marginal Tax Rates (Top Rate)	1	(66)	2	(60)	4	(40)	5	(45)	4	(43)
(c) Conscription	0		0		0		0		10	
IV. International Sector	**6.0**		**6.3**		**5.5**		**5.5**		**9.9**	
(a) Taxes on International Trade (Avg.)	8	(2.0)	9	(1.2)	9	(1.4)	8	(2.2)	9	(0.6)
(b) Black Market Exchange Rates (Prem.)	6	(6)	6	(6)	3	(25)	6	(3)	10	(0)
(c) Size of Trade Sector (% of GDP)	9	(29.3)	9	(32.4)	9	(27.7)	6	(23.6)	6	(24.5)
(d) Capital Transactions with Foreigners	2		2		2		2		2	
Economic Freedom Rating	**3.8**		**4.4**		**4.4**		**4.6**		**5.7**	
Ranking of Country	**59**		**40**		**47**		**56**		**50**	

168

Part 2: Recent Economic Indicators:

Population 1996:   42.1   **Real Per Capita GDP**   :   1996 = $4,513
   (in millions)   (in 1995 U.S. dollars)
Annual Rate of Change (1985-96):   2.2%   Avg. Growth Rate: 1980-90 =   -1.2%
                                                  1990-95 =   -1.2%

Economic Indicators:*	1988	1989	1990	1991	1992	1993	1994	1995	1996
Change in Real GDP:Aggregate	4.2	2.4	-0.3	-1.0	-2.2	1.3	2.7	3.4	3.1
: Per Capita	1.8	0.0	-2.6	-3.3	-4.4	-0.9	0.6	1.2	1.0
Inflation Rate (CPI)	12.9	14.7	14.4	15.3	13.9	9.7	9.0	8.7	7.4
Change in Money Supply: (M1)	27.6	15.3	5.3	21.6	18.6	1.8	25.7	13.5	34.7
: (M2)	34.7	28.9	12.0	20.4	11.4	2.6	19.3	11.0	18.1
Investment/GDP Ratio	19.8	20.6	19.6	17.8	16.6	15.5	16.0	16.9	17.0
Size of Trade Sector(% of GDP)	26.5	25.6	23.6	22.3	21.9	22.5	22.9	24.5	-
Total Gov't Exp./GDP Ratio	30.9	29.5	35.9	31.1	35.0	36.8	37.0	-	-
Central Government Budget Deficit (-) or Surplus (+) As a Percent of GDP	-5.3	-0.2	-4.3	-6.1	-6.2	-7.7	-5.8	-5.4	-
Unemployment Rate									

* The figures in this table are in percent form.

While South Africa's economic freedom rating has increased during the last two decades, its *ranking* continues to place it in the middle range among the countries in our study. In 1995 it ranked 50th (out of 115), compared to 47th (out of 107) in 1985.

For a country with such a low level of income (1996 per capita GDP = $4,513), government expenditures are exceedingly high. Total government expenditures consumed 37% of GDP in 1995, up from 30% in 1975. This also suggests that there has been little movement toward economic freedom during 1975-1995.

Several factors pull South Africa's economic freedom rating down. Government consumption sums to 25% of total consumption, a figure that is seldom exceeded by nations other than the high-income welfare states of Western Europe. State-operated enterprises are present in many sectors of the economy. Uncertainty about the future political stability of this racially divided country reduces the security of property rights and the incentive of both foreigners and domestics to invest. Regulations constrain the mobility of capital.

There have been some encouraging developments. Interest and exchange rate controls have been liberalized. The top marginal tax rate was reduced from 60% in 1980 to 40% in 1985 (before climbing back to a 43% rate in 1995). Conscription was abolished in 1994. Most recently, legislation permitting citizens to maintain foreign currency bank accounts both in South Africa and abroad (beginning in July of 1997) was approved.

While they do not directly enter into our index, large budget deficits are a problem. During the 1990s, budget deficits have averaged 6% of GDP. If they are not brought under control, they will depress the investment rate and lead to abnormally high rates of unemployment.

The political future of this country is both uncertain and complex. From an economic viewpoint, the best thing South Africa could do would be to move swiftly and consistently toward a freer economy. Voluntary exchange tends to bring people together, while the political process pulls them apart. South Africa needs more of the former and less of the latter.

169

SOUTH KOREA

Economic Freedom Rating

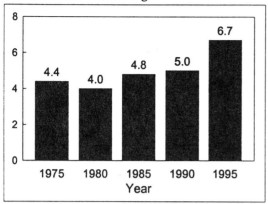

Total Government Expenditures
As a Percent of GDP

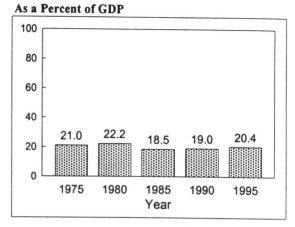

Part 1: The Economic Freedom Ratings for the Components and Various Area and Summary Indexes: 1975, 1980, 1985, 1990 and 1995.
(The numbers in parentheses indicate the actual values for the components.)

Components of Economic Freedom	1975	1980	1985	1990	1995
I. Money and Inflation	**1.3**	**2.3**	**2.9**	**2.5**	**8.5**
(a) Annual Money Growth (last 5 yrs.)	1 (28.4)	1 (25.5)	4 (14.0)	6 (11.2)	6 (10.9)
(b) Inflation Variablity (last 5 yrs.)	3 (7.1)	6 (3.3)	5 (4.9)	2 (10.2)	9 (2.0)
(c) Ownership of Foreign Currency	0	0	0	0	10
(d) Maint. of Bank Account Abroad	0	0	0	0	10
II. Government Operation	**5.9**	**6.0**	**7.2**	**5.9**	**6.3**
(a) Gov't Consump. (% of Total Consump.)	8 (13.5)	7 (15.2)	7 (14.5)	7 (15.9)	6 (16.4)
(b) Government Enterprises	6	6	6	6	6
(c) Price Controls	-	-	-	3	3
(d) Entry Into Business	-	-	-	-	7.5
(e) Legal System	-	-	-	-	7.5
(f) Avoidance of Neg. Interest Rates	2	4	10	10	10
III. Takings	**4.5**	**3.6**	**4.1**	**4.6**	**5.5**
(a) Transfers and Subsidies (% of GDP)	9 (2.0)	9 (2.0)	8 (2.2)	8 (2.9)	8 (2.9)
(b) Marginal Tax Rates (Top Rate)	2 (63)	0 (89)	2 (65)	3 (60)	5 (48)
(c) Conscription	0	0	0	0	0
IV. International Sector	**5.2**	**4.2**	**5.0**	**6.4**	**7.4**
(a) Taxes on International Trade (Avg.)	7 (3.1)	6 (4.1)	7 (3.6)	7 (3.4)	8 (2.0)
(b) Black Market Exchange Rates (Prem.)	7 (2)	4 (11)	4 (11)	8 (1)	10 (0)
(c) Size of Trade Sector (% of GDP)	7 (32.2)	8 (37.7)	8 (33.9)	5 (30.0)	6 (33.7)
(d) Capital Transactions with Foreigners	0	0	2	5	5
Economic Freedom Rating	**4.4**	**4.0**	**4.8**	**5.0**	**6.7**
Ranking of Country	**38**	**50**	**32**	**39**	**18**

Part 2: Recent Economic Indicators:

Population 1996:	45.2	**Real Per Capita GDP** :	1996 =	$13,553
(in millions)		(in 1995 U.S. dollars)		
Annual Rate of Change (1985-96):	1.0%	Avg. Growth Rate:	1980-90 =	7.9%
			1990-95 =	6.7%

Economic Indicators:*	1988	1989	1990	1991	1992	1993	1994	1995	1996
Change in Real GDP:Aggregate	11.3	6.4	9.5	9.1	5.1	5.8	8.6	8.9	7.1
: Per Capita	10.3	5.4	8.5	8.1	4.1	4.8	7.6	8.0	6.1
Inflation Rate (CPI)	7.1	5.7	8.6	9.3	6.2	4.8	6.2	4.5	5.0
Change in Money Supply: (M1)	20.2	17.9	11.0	36.8	13.0	18.1	11.9	19.6	1.5
: (M2)	21.5	19.8	17.2	21.9	14.9	16.6	18.7	15.6	15.8
Investment/GDP Ratio	31.1	33.6	36.9	38.9	36.6	35.1	36.1	37.1	-
Size of Trade Sector (% of GDP)	34.4	31.4	30.0	29.4	29.4	29.2	30.5	33.7	-
Total Gov't Exp./GDP Ratio	16.1	17.6	19.0	19.2	18.9	19.0	19.7	20.4	-
Central Government Budget Deficit (-) or Surplus (+) As a Percent of GDP	+1.5	+0.2	-0.7	-1.6	-0.5	+0.6	+0.3	+0.6	-
Unemployment Rate	2.5	2.6	2.4	2.3	2.4	2.8	2.4	2.0	2.0

* The figures in this table are in percent form.

Both the economic freedom rating and ranking of this country have improved substantially during the last two decades. In 1995, South Korea ranked 18th (among the 115 countries rated), up from 50th in 1980. This places South Korea in a tie with Japan, and well above several high-income European economies (France and Italy, for example). The relatively small size (approximately 20%) of total government expenditures as a share of GDP re-enforces the validity of this high rating.

The improvement during the 1990s was primarily the result of a more stable monetary regime and the legalization of foreign currency bank accounts both domestically and abroad. As a result, South Korea's rating in the Money and Inflation area rose from 2.5 in 1990 to 8.5 in 1995. Over the last two decades, a more competitive and stable credit market, lower marginal tax rates (the top rate is now 48%, down from 89% in 1980), and some relaxation of restrictions on capital transactions with foreigners also contributed to Korea's improved rating.

Like many other emerging economic powers in Asia, South Korea is not known for its political and civil freedoms. Nonetheless, it has achieved extraordinary growth rates. Since 1980 the annual growth rate of per capita GDP has averaged almost 7.5%. Measured in 1995 US dollars, per capita GDP in 1996 was $13,553, only slightly less than that of Spain and well above the figures for Portugal, Greece, and several other European nations.

171

SPAIN

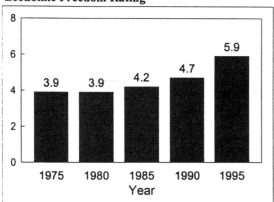

Economic Freedom Rating

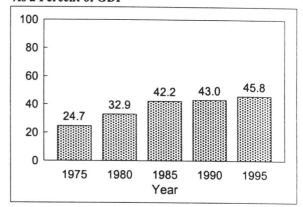

Total Government Expenditures
As a Percent of GDP

Part 1: The Economic Freedom Ratings for the Components and Various Area and Summary Indexes: 1975, 1980, 1985, 1990 and 1995.
(The numbers in parentheses indicate the actual values for the components.)

Components of Economic Freedom	1975		1980		1985		1990		1995	
I. Money and Inflation	**2.3**		**2.9**		**5.1**		**3.9**		**10.0**	
(a) Annual Money Growth (last 5 yrs.)	1	(21.1)	3	(15.7)	7	(9.7)	3	(16.7)	10	(1.2)
(b) Inflation Variablity (last 5 yrs.)	6	(3.7)	6	(3.5)	9	(2.1)	9	(2.0)	10	(1.2)
(c) Ownership of Foreign Currency	0		0		0		0		10	
(d) Maint. of Bank Account Abroad	0		0		0		0		10	
II. Government Operation	**6.0**		**5.2**		**5.7**		**5.8**		**5.6**	
(a) Gov't Consump. (% of Total Consump.)	8	(13.9)	6	(16.7)	5	(18.7)	5	(19.9)	4	(20.9)
(b) Government Enterprises	4		4		4		4		4	
(c) Price Controls	-		-		-		6		5	
(d) Entry Into Business	-		-		-		-		7.5	
(e) Legal System	-		-		-		-		5.0	
(f) Avoidance of Neg. Interest Rates	-		6		10		10		10	
III. Takings	**3.5**		**1.7**		**1.3**		**2.2**		**1.7**	
(a) Transfers and Subsidies (% of GDP)	4	(9.5)	3	(12.3)	2	(16.9)	2	(16.0)	2	(18.9)
(b) Marginal Tax Rates (Top Rate)	4	(55)	1	(66)	1	(66)	3	(56)	2	(56)
(c) Conscription	0		0		0		0		0	
IV. International Sector	**4.4**		**6.5**		**6.1**		**7.2**		**8.5**	
(a) Taxes on International Trade (Avg.)	5	(6.1)	7	(2.7)	7	(3.0)	9	(1.3)	10	(0.0)
(b) Black Market Exchange Rates (Prem.)	7	(2)	10	(0)	7	(2)	7	(2)	10	(0)
(c) Size of Trade Sector (% of GDP)	3	(15.4)	2	(16.9)	5	(21.8)	3	(18.8)	4	(23.6)
(d) Capital Transactions with Foreigners	2		5		5		8		8	
Economic Freedom Rating	**3.9**		**3.9**		**4.2**		**4.7**		**5.9**	
Ranking of Country	**55**		**52**		**55**		**51**		**42**	

Part 2: Recent Economic Indicators:

Population 1996:	39.2		**Real Per Capita GDP**	:	1996 =	$14,613	
(in millions)			(in 1995 U.S. dollars)				
Annual Rate of Change (1985-96):	0.2%		Avg. Growth Rate:		1980-90=	2.6%	
					1990-96=	1.6%	

Economic Indicators:*	1988	1989	1990	1991	1992	1993	1994	1995	1996
Change in Real GDP: Aggregate	5.2	4.7	3.7	2.3	0.7	-1.2	2.1	3.0	2.2
: Per Capita	5.0	4.5	3.5	2.1	0.5	-1.4	1.9	2.8	2.0
Inflation Rate (CPI)	4.8	6.8	6.7	5.9	5.9	4.6	4.7	4.7	3.2
Change in Money Supply: (M1)	20.4	21.3	15.8	9.5	-1.0	2.4	6.8	3.2	7.1
: (M2)	8.3	10.7	0.8	4.5	3.0	4.4	0.9	2.6	6.4
Investment/GDP Ratio	21.3	21.5	20.6	24.6	22.7	19.9	20.1	21.3	-
Size of Trade Sector (% of GDP)	19.4	19.7	18.8	18.7	19.0	19.7	22.5	23.6	-
Total Gov't Exp./GDP Ratio	40.5	41.9	43.0	44.5	45.5	48.7	46.9	45.8	44.1 [p]
General Government Budget Deficit (-) or Surplus (+) As a Percent of GDP	-3.3	-2.8	-4.1	-4.9	-3.6	-6.8	-6.3	-6.6	-4.8
Unemployment Rate	19.1	16.9	15.9	16.0	18.1	22.8	24.1	22.9	22.9 [a]

* The figures in this table are in percent form.

[a] October, 1993.

[p] Preliminary.

After struggling with an economic freedom rating of approximately 4.0 during 1975-1985, Spain's summary rating has improved in recent years. Its 5.9 rating placed it 42nd (out of 115) in 1995, up from 55th in 1985.

Spain's improvement is almost exclusively the result of steps taken in the monetary and financial areas. In the 1990s, the monetary authorities reduced the rate of money growth and the inflation rate has declined accordingly. In addition, it is now legal for the Spanish to maintain foreign currency bank accounts both domestically and abroad. As the result of the increased monetary stability and the legalization of these foreign currency accounts, Spain's rating in the monetary area jumped from 3.9 in 1990 to a "perfect 10" in 1995. In addition, exchange controls have been abolished and some restrictions limiting the mobility of capital have been eliminated.

More needs to be done. The government consumption and transfer sectors are quite large and the top marginal tax rate (56%), though down a little from the mid-1980s, is still one of the highest in the world. Total government expenditures have grown substantially since the mid-1970s and they now sum to 45% of GDP. Much of this growth has been financed with budget deficits. Recent budget deficits have averaged around 5% of GDP, a level that is unsustainable. Even though the growth has been solid and persistent (per capita GDP has risen at a 2% annual rate since 1980), the unemployment rate has hovered near or above 20% since the mid-1980s. Interestingly, the unemployment rate of Portugal, Spain's next door neighbor, has been running between 5% and 7%—less than a third the Spanish rate—during this same period. When a growing economy has prolonged double-digit unemployment, it reflects transfer payments that reduce the cost of job search and/or regulations that make it expensive to hire and terminate employees. Spain desperately needs to revise its transfer system and deregulate the labor market. It will fail to reach its full potential until these steps are taken.

173

SRI LANKA

Economic Freedom Rating

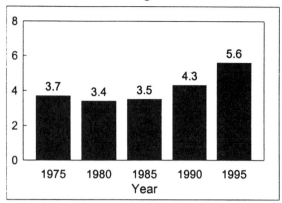

Total Government Expenditures
As a Percent of GDP

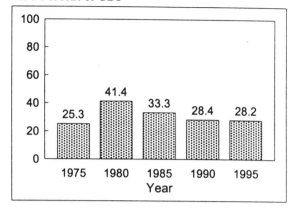

Part 1: The Economic Freedom Ratings for the Components and Various Area and Summary Indexes: 1975, 1980, 1985, 1990 and 1995.

(The numbers in parentheses indicate the actual values for the components.)

Components of Economic Freedom	1975		1980		1985		1990		1995	
I. Money and Inflation	**3.4**		**2.3**		**2.2**		**2.9**		**5.5**	
(a) Annual Money Growth (last 5 yrs.)	8	(7.7)	1	(24.5)	4	(14.4)	4	(14.6)	7	(9.7)
(b) Inflation Variablity (last 5 yrs.)	3	(8.1)	6	(3.6)	3	(6.2)	5	(4.7)	10	(1.1)
(c) Ownership of Foreign Currency	0		0		0		0		0	
(d) Maint. of Bank Account Abroad	0		0		0		0		0	
II. Government Operation	**5.9**		**5.5**		**6.0**		**5.9**		**5.1**	
(a) Gov't Consump. (% of Total Consump.)	10	(10.2)	10	(9.6)	9	(11.4)	9	(11.2)	9	(12.4)
(b) Government Enterprises	2		2		2		4		4	
(c) Price Controls	-		-		-		4		4	
(d) Entry Into Business	-		-		-		-		5.0	
(e) Legal System	-		-		-		-		0.0	
(f) Avoidance of Neg. Interest Rates	-		4		8		8		10	
III. Takings	**2.9**		**2.9**		**3.7**		**6.2**		**6.6**	
(a) Transfers and Subsidies (% of GDP)	4	(8.1)	4	(8.4)	6	(5.1)	5	(6.0)	5	(5.9)
(b) Marginal Tax Rates (Top Rate)	-		0	(60.5)	0	(60.5)	-		7	(35)
(c) Conscription	10		10		10		10		10	
IV. International Sector	**1.6**		**3.2**		**2.2**		**2.2**		**5.4**	
(a) Taxes on International Trade (Avg.)	1	(11.1)	1	(11.7)	1	(10.6)	2	(8.8)	6	(4.5)
(b) Black Market Exchange Rates (Prem.)	1	(92)	5	(9)	4	(20)	3	(24)	7	(2)
(c) Size of Trade Sector (% of GDP)	6	(31.2)	9	(43.5)	5	(31.5)	5	(33.7)	7	(40.7)
(d) Capital Transactions with Foreigners	0		0		0		0		2	
Economic Freedom Rating	**3.7**		**3.4**		**3.5**		**4.3**		**5.6**	
Ranking of Country	**63**		**78**		**78**		**62**		**52**	

174

Part 2: Recent Economic Indicators:

Population 1996:   18.3   **Real Per Capita GDP**   :   1995= $3,584
   (in millions)   (in 1995 U.S. dollars)
Annual Rate of Change (1985-96):   1.5%   Avg. Growth Rate: 1980-90=   3.0%
                                                1990-95=   3.8%

Economic Indicators:*	1988	1989	1990	1991	1992	1993	1994	1995	1996
Change in Real GDP: Aggregate	2.7	2.3	6.2	4.8	2.5	5.2	6.7	6.2	-
: Per Capita	1.2	0.8	4.7	3.3	1.0	3.7	5.2	4.7	-
Inflation Rate (CPI)	14.0	11.6	21.5	12.2	11.4	11.7	8.4	7.7	-
Change in Money Supply: (M1)	29.1	9.1	12.8	17.7	7.4	18.6	18.7	6.7	-
: (M2)	15.3	13.1	21.1	22.4	16.4	23.1	19.2	19.4	-
Investment/GDP Ratio	22.8	21.7	22.2	22.9	24.3	25.6	27.0	25.1	-
Size of Trade Sector (% of GDP)	30.8	31.5	33.7	33.4	35.8	38.1	39.7	40.7	-
Total Gov't Exp./GDP Ratio	31.1	30.8	28.4	29.3	26.9	27.0	27.2	28.2	-
Central Government Budget Deficit (-) or Surplus (+) As a Percent of GDP	-12.7	-8.6	-7.8	-9.5	-5.4	-6.4	-8.5	-7.0	-
Unemployment Rate	-	-	14.4	14.1	14.1	14.7	13.6	-	-

* The figures in this table are in percent form.

During 1975-1985, Sri Lanka's economic freedom rating fluctuated between 3.4 and 3.7. During the last decade it has increased sharply, reaching 5.6 in 1995. Between 1985 and 1995 Sri Lanka's ranking rose from 78th to 52nd.

Several factors have contributed to the improved rating. Monetary policy has been more restrained and the inflation rate less variable. The top marginal tax rate was reduced from 60.5% in 1985 to 35% in 1995. Tariff rates have been reduced and exchange rate controls liberalized. The size of the trade sector has also increased during the last decade.

The major weaknesses of this economy are excessive regulation and the absence of rule of law. Citizens are not allowed to maintain foreign currency bank accounts. Price controls continue to be imposed on many products and entry into business is often complex and costly. Furthermore, government enterprises are numerous and they are often granted monopoly status. The legal structure provides government officials with arbitrary power and places them in a position where they can either provide favors or impose costs on persons engaging in business activities. Systems of this type undermine business entrepreneurship and lead to corruption.

As Sri Lanka moved toward economic freedom during the last decade, its growth rate rose. Thus far, real GDP has increased at an annual rate of 3.8% during the 1990s, up from 3.0% during the 1980s.

SWEDEN

Economic Freedom Rating

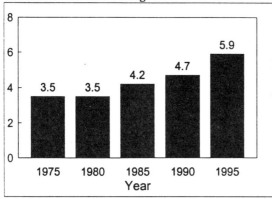

**Total Government Expenditures
As a Percent of GDP**

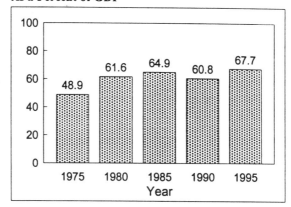

Part 1: The Economic Freedom Ratings for the Components and Various Area and Summary Indexes: 1975, 1980, 1985, 1990 and 1995.

(The numbers in parentheses indicate the actual values for the components.)

Components of Economic Freedom	1975		1980		1985		1990		1995	
I. Money and Inflation	**6.1**		**6.7**		**7.7**		**7.3**		**9.3**	
(a) Annual Money Growth (last 5 yrs.)	6	(11.4)	6	(11.6)	8	(7.2)	8	(7.0)	10	(3.1)
(b) Inflation Variablity (last 5 yrs.)	7	(2.9)	9	(1.5)	10	(1.2)	9	(1.4)	8	(2.1)
(c) Ownership of Foreign Currency	10		10		10		10		10	
(d) Maint. of Bank Account Abroad	0		0		0		0		10	
II. Government Operation	**2.5**		**3.3**		**3.7**		**4.4**		**6.7**	
(a) Gov't Consump. (% of Total Consump.)	0	(31.7)	0	(36.3)	0	(35.3)	0	(35.0)	0	(33.1)
(b) Government Enterprises	4		4		4		4		4	
(c) Price Controls	-		-		-		6		8	
(d) Entry Into Business	-		-		-		-		10	
(e) Legal System	-		-		-		-		10	
(f) Avoidance of Neg. Interest Rates	4		8		10		10		10	
III. Takings	**0.8**		**0.0**		**0.0**		**0.0**		**0.5**	
(a) Transfers and Subsidies (% of GDP)	0	(25.0)	0	(24.7)	0	(26.0)	0	(29.9)	0	(35.2)
(b) Marginal Tax Rates (Top Rate)	1	(70)	0	(87)	0	(80)	0	(72)	1	(58)
(c) Conscription	0		0		0		0		0	
IV. International Sector	**6.2**		**5.7**		**7.3**		**8.7**		**9.0**	
(a) Taxes on International Trade (Avg.)	9	(1.0)	9	(0.7)	9	(0.3)	9	(0.4)	9	(0.4)
(b) Black Market Exchange Rates (Prem.)	8	(1)	6	(5)	8	(1)	10	(0)	10	(0)
(c) Size of Trade Sector (% of GDP)	5	(27.9)	5	(30.4)	7	(34.5)	4	(29.7)	6	(37.7)
(d) Capital Transactions with Foreigners	2		2		5		10		10	
Economic Freedom Rating	**3.5**		**3.5**		**4.2**		**4.7**		**5.9**	
Ranking of Country	**68**		**74**		**55**		**51**		**42**	

Part 2: Recent Economic Indicators:

Population 1996:	8.9	Real Per Capita GDP	:	1996 =	$20,239
(in millions)		(in 1995 U.S. dollars)			
Annual Rate of Change (1985-96):	0.6%	Avg. Growth Rate:	1980-90=	1.7%	
			1990-96=	-0.1%	

Economic Indicators:*	1988	1989	1990	1991	1992	1993	1994	1995	1996
Change in Real GDP: Aggregate	2.7	2.4	1.4	-1.7	-1.4	-2.2	2.6	3.0	1.2
: Per Capita	2.1	1.8	0.8	-2.3	-2.0	-2.8	2.0	2.4	1.1
Inflation Rate (CPI)	5.8	6.4	10.5	9.3	2.3	4.6	2.2	2.5	-0.2
Change in Money Supply: (M1)	0.9	12.1	-	-	-	-	-	-	-
: (M3)	8.3	10.7	11.3	4.0	3.2	4.0	0.3	2.7	11.7
Investment/GDP Ratio	19.9	21.9	21.3	17.9	16.5	13.3	14.2	15.6	15.3
Size of Trade Sector (% of GDP)	31.5	31.7	29.7	27.2	27.0	30.9	34.4	37.7	40.4
Total Gov't Exp./GDP Ratio	59.6	60.0	60.8	62.8	68.7	72.6	70.2	67.7	67.0 [p]
Central Government Budget Deficit (-) or Surplus (+) As a Percent of GDP	+0.8	+0.6	+0.6	-1.1	-2.3	-11.9	-11.6	-9.5	-
Unemployment Rate	1.9	1.6	1.8	3.3	5.8	9.5	9.8	9.2	9.9 [a]

* The figures in this table are in percent form.

[a] October, 1996.

[p] Preliminary.

Our index ranked Sweden 42nd (among the 115 countries in our study) in 1995. The index indicates that there was an expansion in economic freedom during 1975-1995. However, there are two reasons why this increase should be interpreted with caution. First, to a large degree, it reflects the fact that the entry into business and legal system components are included only in the 1995 index. Since Sweden rates high in these two areas, their inclusion in the 1995 index pushes Sweden's rating upward. Second, unlike most countries, Sweden's rating is highly sensitive to the weight attached to (a) government consumption and (b) transfers and subsidies. It received the lowest possible rating in these two areas. If they were given a larger weight in the index, Sweden's economic freedom rating might well have declined during 1975-1995. Total government expenditures have risen from less than 50% of GDP in 1975 to 67.7% in 1995. This is not the pattern that one would expect for a country moving significantly toward a freer economy.

Sweden deservingly earns top marks in the monetary and international areas. During the last five years, inflation has been low and stable. Citizens are free to maintain foreign currency bank accounts. Tariffs are low; the kronor is fully convertible; and the trade sector is large for a country of Sweden's size. Liberalization of the financial market during the last decade removed most of the restrictions on the mobility of capital.

There is some evidence that the high level of government spending is beginning to exert an impact on the economy. Like other countries that have followed this path, Sweden is now plagued with large budget deficits, a declining investment rate, high unemployment, and sluggish economic growth. Note: per capita GDP actually declined slightly during the 1990s and the unemployment rate (OECD standardized definition) hovered near 10% during 1993-1996. If persons in training programs and protected employment categories were numbered among the unemployed, Sweden's rate would be considerably higher. Perhaps this will create an environment for economic liberalization in the near future.

SWITZERLAND

Economic Freedom Rating

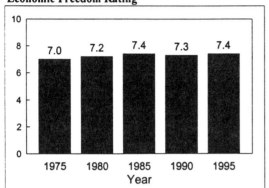

**Total Government Expenditures
As a Percent of GDP**

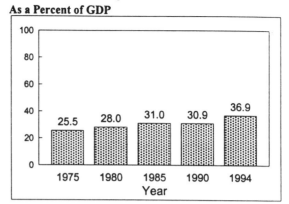

**Part 1: The Economic Freedom Ratings for the Components and Various Area and
Summary Indexes: 1975, 1980, 1985, 1990 and 1995.**
(The numbers in parentheses indicate the actual values for the components.)

Components of Economic Freedom	1975		1980		1985		1990		1995	
I. Money and Inflation	10.0		9.7		9.7		10.0		9.7	
(a) Annual Money Growth (last 5 yrs.)	10	(4.3)	9	(6.2)	10	(1.2)	10	(1.3)	10	(2.0)
(b) Inflation Variablity (last 5 yrs.)	10	(1.1)	10	(1.1)	9	(2.0)	10	(1.2)	9	(1.5)
(c) Ownership of Foreign Currency	10		10		10		10		10	
(d) Maint. of Bank Account Abroad	10		10		10		10		10	
II. Government Operation	6.8		6.8		7.7		7.2		7.9	
(a) Gov't Consump. (% of Total Consump.)	6	(17.0)	6	(16.7)	6	(17.7)	5	(19.1)	5	(19.4)
(b) Government Enterprises	8		8		8		8		8	
(c) Price Controls	-		-		-		7		6	
(d) Entry Into Business	-		-		-		-		10.0	
(e) Legal System	-		-		-		-		10.0	
(f) Avoidance of Neg. Interest Rates	6		6		10		10		10	
III. Takings	5.5		4.5		4.5		4.5		4.5	
(a) Transfers and Subsidies (% of GDP)	-		3	(13.4)	3	(13.2)	2	(16.0)	2	(18.3)
(b) Marginal Tax Rates (Top Rate)	7	(38-42)	7	(31-44)	7	(33-46)	8	(33-43)	8	(35-39)
(c) Conscription	0		0		0		0		0	
IV. International Sector	6.2		8.9		9.1		8.7		8.4	
(a) Taxes on International Trade (Avg.)	7	(3.5)	8	(2.4)	8	(2.0)	8	(1.9)	8	(2.3)
(b) Black Market Exchange Rates (Prem.)	10	(0)	10	(0)	10	(0)	10	(0)	10	(0)
(c) Size of Trade Sector (% of GDP)	5	(30.0)	7	(38.5)	8	(38.8)	6	(36.4)	4	(33.4)
(d) Capital Transactions with Foreigners	2		10		10		10		10	
Economic Freedom Rating	7		7.2		7.4		7.3		7.4	
Ranking of Country	4		2		3		4		6	

Part 2: Recent Economic Indicators:

Population 1996: 7.1
(in millions)
Annual Rate of Change (1985-96): 0.9%

Real Per Capita GDP : 1996 = $22,182
(in 1995 U.S. dollars)
Avg. Growth Rate: 1980-90= 1.5%
1990-96= -0.4%

Economic Indicators:*	1988	1989	1990	1991	1992	1993	1994	1995	1996
Change in Real GDP: Aggregate	2.9	3.9	2.3	-	-0.3	-0.8	1.2	0.7	0.7
: Per Capita	2.0	3.0	1.4	-1.3	-1.2	-1.7	0.3	-0.2	-0.2
Inflation Rate (CPI)	1.9	3.2	5.4	5.8	4.1	3.3	0.8	1.8	0.8
Change in Money Supply: (M1)	2.3	-2.7	-1.6	-1.7	4.0	5.8	4.0	6.1	9.6
: (M2)	5.4	6.3	0.8	2.3	2.6	8.9	4.2	4.6	8.4
Investment/GDP Ratio	27.9	29.7	29.3	27.0	23.4	21.2	22.2	23.4	-
Size of Trade Sector (% of GDP)	36.3	38.2	36.4	34.6	34.2	34.0	33.9	33.4	-
Total Gov't Exp./GDP Ratio	30.5	30.2	30.9	32.5	34.9	36.8	36.9	-	-
Central Government Budget Deficit (-) or Surplus (+) As a Percent of GDP	+0.5	+0.3	-0.3	-1.2	-1.4	-2.7	-1.9	-0.9	-1.2
Unemployment Rate	0.7	0.6	0.6	1.8	2.8	4.2	4.7	4.2	5.0

* The figures in this table are in percent form.

Our 1995 index ranked Switzerland as the 6th freest economy in the world. Rating one-tenth of a point higher than the United Kingdom, it is highest ranked among the European nations, Moreover, it has sustained this lofty position over a lengthy time period. Its rating was 7.0 or more during each of our rating years and it has been ranked between 2nd and 6th throughout the last two decades. No doubt, this high level of economic freedom for many years provides the explanation for its income per capita ($22,182 in 1996), one of the highest in the world.

The strengths of the Swiss economy are a very stable monetary regime buttressed with the liberty to use alternative currencies (note the near perfect rating in the monetary area), few government enterprises, freedom of entry into business, equal treatment under the law, competitive financial markets, and minimal restraints on trade and capital mobility. Like most other high income countries, both government consumption expenditures and transfers are large.

Conscription is used to obtain military personnel. Thus, the Swiss rating is low for these components. For many years, the size of government was substantially lower in Switzerland than for other OECD countries. Compared to its European neighbors, this is still true. However, the recent trend is troublesome. As a share of GDP, total government expenditures rose from 25.5% in 1975 to 31% in 1985 and 1990 to nearly 37% in 1994. Should this trend continue, it will retard both economic freedom and growth. Some negative signs may already be observable. The Swiss growth rate has been meager—per capita GDP has actually declined slightly during the 1990s—and the unemployment rate has been rising. Perhaps it is time for the Swiss to consider reforms, such as a private sector saving and investment option rather than social security taxes, designed to promote capital formation and growth.

SYRIA

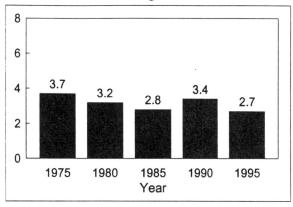

No Data

Part 1: The Economic Freedom Ratings for the Components and Various Area and Summary Indexes: 1975, 1980, 1985, 1990 and 1995.

(The numbers in parentheses indicate the actual values for the components.)

Components of Economic Freedom	1975	1980	1985	1990	1995
I. Money and Inflation	**4.6**	**6.0**	**5.6**	**4.8**	**4.8**
(a) Annual Money Growth (last 5 yrs.)	1 (23.0)	1 (26.1)	2 (19.7)	3 (16.0)	3 (16.8)
(b) Inflation Variablity (last 5 yrs.)	2 (12.2)	6 (3.8)	4 (5.3)	6 (3.2)	6 (3.2)
(c) Ownership of Foreign Currency	10	10	10	10	10
(d) Maint. of Bank Account Abroad	10	10	10	0	0
II. Government Operation	**4.0**	**3.0**	**1.5**	**4.0**	**1.9**
(a) Gov't Consump. (% of Total Consump.)	2 (24.1)	2 (25.8)	1 (26.8)	6 (17.0)	6 (17.0)
(b) Government Enterprises	6	4	2	2	2
(c) Price Controls	-	-	-	-	0
(d) Entry Into Business	-	-	-	-	2.5
(e) Legal System	-	-	-	-	0.0
(f) Avoidance of Neg. Interest Rates	-	-	-	-	0
III. Takings	**0.0**	**0.0**	**0.0**	**0.0**	**0.0**
(a) Transfers and Subsidies (% of GDP)	-	-	-	-	-
(b) Marginal Tax Rates (Top Rate)	-	-	-	-	-
(c) Conscription	0	0	0	0	0
IV. International Sector	**3.5**	**1.9**	**2.0**	**2.6**	**2.8**
(a) Taxes on International Trade (Avg.)	2 (8.5)	3 (7.1)	6 (5.6)	7 (2.9)	6 (4.0)
(b) Black Market Exchange Rates (Prem.)	8 (1)	2 (35)	0 (251)	0 (301)	0 (301)
(c) Size of Trade Sector (% of GDP)	4 (27.7)	3 (26.8)	1 (18.6)	3 (27.6)	6 (37.5)
(d) Capital Transactions with Foreigners	0	0	0	0	0
Economic Freedom Rating	**3.7**	**3.2**	**2.8**	**3.4**	**2.7**
Ranking of Country	**63**	**84**	**91**	**89**	**112**

Part 2: Recent Economic Indicators:

Population 1996:	14.8	**Real Per Capita GDP** :	1994=	$6,489
(in millions)		(in 1995 U.S. dollars)		
Annual Rate of Change (1985-96):	3.4%	Avg. Growth Rate:	1980-90=	-1.2%
			1990-94=	4.2%

Economic Indicators:*	1988	1989	1990	1991	1992	1993	1994	1995	1996
Change in Real GDP: Aggregate	13.3	-9.0	7.6	7.1	10.6	6.7	6.2	-	-
: Per Capita	9.9	-12.4	4.2	3.7	7.2	3.3	2.8	-	-
Inflation Rate (CPI)	34.6	11.4	19.4	7.7	9.5	11.8	9.2	-	-
Change in Money Supply: (M1)	17.7	19.1	24.9	23.2	24.4	14.2	-	-	-
: (M2)	22.1	20.1	26.1	30.5	23.7	14.9	-	-	-
Investment/GDP Ratio	14.0	16.5	16.5	18.0	23.2	26.0	30.3	-	-
Size of Trade Sector (% of GDP)	21.4	26.6	27.6	28.8	31.9	34.4	37.5	-	-
Total Gov't Exp./GDP Ratio									
Central Government Budget Deficit (-) or Surplus (+) As a Percent of GDP	+1.3	-0.6	+0.3	+1.4	+1.9	0.0	-	-	-
Unemployment Rate	-	5.8	-	6.8	-	-	-	-	-

* The figures in this table are in percent form.

Syria's 2.7 economic freedom rating of 1995 places it 112th among the 115 countries in our study. Its rating never rose above 4.0 during the period of our study. Clearly, this is one of the least free economies in the world.

Several factors underlie Syria's persistently low ratings. Monetary policy has generally been both erratic and highly expansionary, although there is some evidence of improvement during the last few years. Government enterprises are widespread and legal restraints limit the freedom of private firms to compete in several areas. Regulations limiting economic activity provide government officials with excessive powers that are often exercised in an arbitrary and discriminatory manner. Conscription, exchange rate controls (note that the black market premium has persistently exceeded 250% during the last decade), and restrictions on trade and capital mobility also contributed to Syria's low rating.

While there has been growth during the 1990s, Syria's 1994 per capita income was virtually unchanged from the level of 1980. Like several other countries in this region, Syria is paying a price for ignoring the laws of economics and the path to prosperity.

TAIWAN

Economic Freedom Rating

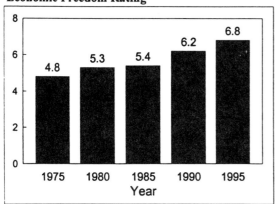

**Total Government Expenditures
As a Percent of GDP**

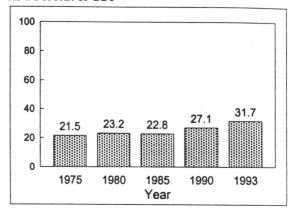

**Part 1: The Economic Freedom Ratings for the Components and Various Area and
Summary Indexes: 1975, 1980, 1985, 1990 and 1995.**
(The numbers in parentheses indicate the actual values for the components.)

Components of Economic Freedom	1975		1980		1985		1990		1995	
I. Money and Inflation	**4.9**		**6.2**		**8.0**		**7.6**		**10.0**	
(a) Annual Money Growth (last 5 yrs.)	2	(19.1)	3	(15.1)	9	(5.0)	3	(16.5)	10	(0.1)
(b) Inflation Variablity (last 5 yrs.)	2	(12.6)	5	(4.3)	5	(4.8)	9	(1.3)	10	(0.4)
(c) Ownership of Foreign Currency	10		10		10		10		10	
(d) Maint. of Bank Account Abroad	10		10		10		10		10	
II. Government Operation	**4.8**		**4.5**		**4.9**		**5.8**		**6.2**	
(a) Gov't Consump. (% of Total Consump.)	4	(21.7)	3	(23.6)	3	(24.0)	3	(23.9)	4	(20.3)
(b) Government Enterprises	4		4		4		6		6	
(c) Price Controls	-		-		-		6		6	
(d) Entry Into Business	-		-		-		-		7.5	
(e) Legal System	-		-		-		-		5.0	
(f) Avoidance of Neg. Interest Rates	8		8		10		10		10	
III. Takings	**4.6**		**4.6**		**4.2**		**4.7**		**5.3**	
(a) Transfers and Subsidies (% of GDP)	8	(2.2)	8	(2.6)	7	(3.6)	6	(4.7)	5	(5.9)
(b) Marginal Tax Rates (Top Rate)	3	(60)	3	(60)	3	(60)	5	(50)	7	(40)
(c) Conscription	0		0		0		0		0	
IV. International Sector	**4.8**		**6.0**		**5.4**		**7.3**		**7.3**	
(a) Taxes on International Trade (Avg.)	6	(4.8)	7	(3.6)	7	(2.8)	8	(2.1)	8	(2.0)
(b) Black Market Exchange Rates (Prem.)	6	(5)	8	(1)	6	(3)	10	(0)	10	(0)
(c) Size of Trade Sector (% of GDP)	5	(41.3)	7	(53.1)	7	(48.3)	5	(45.3)	5	(43.3)
(d) Capital Transactions with Foreigners	2		2		2		5		5	
Economic Freedom Rating	**4.8**		**5.3**		**5.4**		**6.2**		**6.8**	
Ranking of Country	**28**		**22**		**24**		**20**		**16**	

182

Part 2: Recent Economic Indicators:

Population 1996:
(in millions)
Annual Rate of Change (1985-96):   1.1%

Real Per Capita GDP   :   1996 = $15,059
(in 1985 U.S. dollars)
Avg. Growth Rate: 1980-90 =   6.5%
1990-96 =   5.1%

Economic Indicators:*	1988	1989	1990	1991	1992	1993	1994	1995	1996
Change in Real GDP:Aggregate	7.8	8.2	5.4	7.6	6.8	6.3	7.0	4.9	5.6
: Per Capita	6.7	7.1	4.3	6.5	5.7	5.2	5.9	3.8	4.5
Inflation Rate (CPI)	1.3	4.4	4.1	3.6	4.5	2.9	3.4	3.0	2.0
Change in Money Supply: (M1)	24.4	6.1	-6.7	12.1	12.4	15.3	-	-	-
: (M2)									
Investment/GDP Ratio	23.7	23.4	23.1	23.3	24.9	25.2	-	-	-
Size of Trade Sector (% of GDP)	49.0	45.8	45.3	45.1	42.3	43.3	43.3	-	-
Total Gov't Exp./GDP Ratio	-	-	27.1	-	-	31.7	-	-	-
Central Government Budget Deficit (-) or Surplus (+) As a Percent of GDP	+2.9	+3.6	+0.8	+0.5	+0.2	+0.6	-	-	-
Unemployment Rate	1.7	1.6	1.7	1.5	1.5	1.5	-	-	-

* The figures in this table are in percent form.

The Taiwanese economic freedom rating has continuously improved during the last two decades, rising from 4.8 in 1975 to 5.4 in 1985 and 6.8 in 1995. Our index indicates that the economy of Taiwan is the 16th freest in the world.

Improvements in the monetary and international areas account for most of the gains. In the 1970s, money growth was rapid (15% or more even after adjustment for the long-term growth of real GDP) and inflation was a persistent problem. This is no longer the case. During the last five years, the inflation rate has remained within a narrow band between 2.0% and 4.5%. (Note the perfect 10 rating in the Money and Inflation area in 1995.) In the international area, lower tariffs, elimination of exchange rate controls, and a relaxation of various restrictions on capital movements have led to a higher rating. Large government expenditures, state-operated enterprises, and conscription are the major factors pulling down the overall Taiwanese rating. As a share of the economy, government expenditures have risen from 23% in the mid-1980s to 32% in 1993. While the current figure is not particularly high for a high income economy, a status that Taiwan has now achieved, the trend is troublesome.

Rapid economic growth has accompanied the steady expansion in economic freedom. Since 1980, the per capita GDP of Taiwan has increased at an annual rate of 6%. The Taiwanese economy is now one of the fastest growing in the world.

183

TANZANIA

Economic Freedom Rating

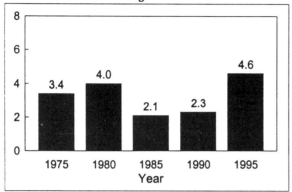

Total Government Expenditures As a Percent of GDP

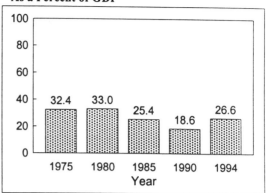

Part 1: The Economic Freedom Ratings for the Components and Various Area and Summary Indexes: 1975, 1980, 1985, 1990 and 1993-95.
(The numbers in parentheses indicate the actual values for the components.)

Components of Economic Freedom	1975		1980		1985		1990		1995	
I. Money and Inflation	**1.6**		**1.6**		**2.9**		**1.0**		**4.3**	
(a) Annual Money Growth (last 5 yrs.)	1	(20.8)	1	(25.1)	5	(13.7)	1	(30.0)	1	(27.6)
(b) Inflation Variablity (last 5 yrs.)	4	(5.8)	4	(5.7)	4	(5.9)	2	(9.5)	3	(7.4)
(c) Ownership of Foreign Currency	0		0		0		0		10	
(d) Maint. of Bank Account Abroad	0		0		0		0		0	
II. Government Operation	**3.5**		**4.3**		**2.3**		**3.0**		**4.2**	
(a) Gov't Consump. (% of Total Consump.)	5	(18.9)	7	(14.5)	6	(16.6)	9	(11.8)	10	(7.9)
(b) Government Enterprises	2		2		0		0		0	
(c) Price Controls	-		-		-		0		4	
(d) Entry Into Business	-		-		-		-		2.5	
(e) Legal System	-		-		-		-		5.0	
(f) Avoidance of Neg. Interest Rates	-		4		0		4		4	
III. Takings	**5.3**		**10.0**		**2.4**		**2.3**		**6.2**	
(a) Transfers and Subsidies (% of GDP)	10	(0.1)	10	(0.0)	6	(5.2)	-		-	
(b) Marginal Tax Rates (Top Rate)	0	(80)	-		0	(95)	3	(50)	8	(30)
(c) Conscription	10		10		0		0		0	
IV. International Sector	**2.3**		**1.4**		**1.2**		**2.7**		**5.5**	
(a) Taxes on International Trade (Avg.)	3	(7.3)	3	(7.7)	4	(6.3)	-		-	
(b) Black Market Exchange Rates (Prem.)	1	(203)	0	(224)	0	(259)	1	(78)	8	(1)
(c) Size of Trade Sector (% of GDP)	7	(26.1)	3	(19.7)	0	(10.5)	10	(38.0)	10	(40.4)
(d) Capital Transactions with Foreigners	0		0		0		0		0	
Economic Freedom Rating	**3.4**		**4.0**		**2.1**		**2.3**		**4.6**	
Ranking of Country	**69**		**50**		**101**		**103**		**70**	

184

Part 2: Recent Economic Indicators:

Population 1996:	31.9		**Real Per Capita GDP**	:	1994=	$663
(in millions)			(in 1995 U.S. dollars)			
Annual Rate of Change (1985-96):	3.4%		Avg. Growth Rate:	1980-90 =	0.4%	
				1990-94 =	0.8%	

Economic Indicators:*	1988	1989	1990	1991	1992	1993	1994	1995	1996
Change in Real GDP:Aggregate	4.1	4.0	4.5	5.7	3.5	4.2	3.0	-	-
: Per Capita	0.7	0.8	1.1	2.3	0.1	0.8	-0.4	-	-
Inflation Rate (CPI)	31.2	25.8	35.8	28.7	21.8	25.3	34.1	27.4	-
Change in Money Supply: (M1)	37.1	29.6	35.0	22.8	34.1	32.9	32.6	-	-
: (M2)	32.8	32.1	41.9	30.1	40.6	39.2	35.3	-	-
Investment/GDP Ratio	28.7	30.7	40.8	29.5	32.7	32.2	30.7	-	-
Size of Trade Sector (% of GDP)	31.5	34.9	38.0	33.2	39.5	34.6	40.4	-	-
Total Gov't Exp./GDP Ratio	-	-	18.6	-	-	-	26.6	-	-
Central Government Budget Deficit (-) or Surplus (+) As a Percent of GDP	-3.8	-2.5	-2.0	-5.1	-4.8	-8.1	-7.5	-	-
Unemployment Rate									

* The figures in this table are in percent form.

Despite recent improvements, the economic freedom rating of Tanzania is still one of the lowest in the world. In 1985, Tanzania's rating fell to 2.1. Only six countries (Nicaragua, Somalia, Uganda, Poland, Algeria, and Russia) had lower 1985 ratings. Tanzania's rating has risen significantly during the 1990s and our index now places it 70th (out of 115) in 1995.

The major factors contributing to the recent gains are lower marginal tax rates, relaxation of exchange rate controls, and a substantial increase in the size of the trade sector. Tanzania's astronomical 95% top marginal tax rate of 1985 was cut to 50% in 1990 and 30% in 1995. The black market exchange rate premium is now virtually eliminated in contrast with the 259% differential of 1985 and 78% level of 1990.

The exchange rate controls of the mid-1980s virtually stifled the ability of Tanzanians to engage in international trade. Thus, the growth of the trade sector as the controls were relaxed is not surprising. A highly unstable monetary policy (in recent years money growth has generally exceeded 30% and the inflation rate 25%), legal restraints imposed on private sector business, insecure property rights, inefficient state-operated enterprises, price controls, conscription, and restrictions on capital mobility continue to plague this extremely poor country. Major changes are needed if this nation is going to throw off the curse of both state oppression and poverty.

185

THAILAND

Economic Freedom Rating

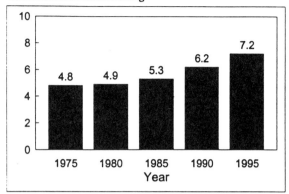

Total Government Expenditures As a Percent of GDP

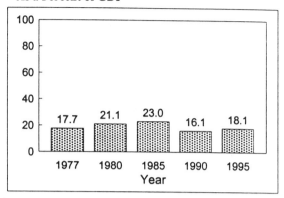

Part 1: The Economic Freedom Ratings for the Components and Various Area and Summary Indexes: 1975, 1980, 1985, 1990 and 1995.
(The numbers in parentheses indicate the actual values for the components.)

Components of Economic Freedom	1975		1980		1985		1990		1995	
I. Money and Inflation	**2.5**		**3.3**		**5.7**		**6.4**		**9.7**	
(a) Annual Money Growth (last 5 yrs.)	6	(10.8)	3	(15.0)	10	(3.3)	5	(12.8)	9	(5.5)
(b) Inflation Variablity (last 5 yrs.)	2	(8.4)	7	(2.8)	8	(2.5)	9	(1.7)	10	(0.9)
(c) Ownership of Foreign Currency	0		0		0		10		10	
(d) Maint. of Bank Account Abroad	0		0		0		0		10	
II. Government Operation	**7.0**		**6.0**		**6.5**		**5.9**		**5.5**	
(a) Gov't Consump. (% of Total Consump.)	8	(13.3)	7	(15.9)	5	(18.2)	7	(14.2)	7	(15.1)
(b) Government Enterprises	6		6		6		6		6	
(c) Price Controls	-		-		-		4		4	
(d) Entry Into Business	-		-		-		-		5.0	
(e) Legal System	-		-		-		-		2.5	
(f) Avoidance of Neg. Interest Rates	-		4		10		8		10	
III. Takings	**5.4**		**5.4**		**4.9**		**5.9**		**7.3**	
(a) Transfers and Subsidies (% of GDP)	10	(0.6)	10	(0.7)	10	(1.2)	10	(1.0)	10	(1.1)
(b) Marginal Tax Rates (Top Rate)	3	(60)	3	(60)	2	(65)	4	(55)	7	(37)
(c) Conscription	0		0		0		0		0	
IV. International Sector	**4.5**		**4.5**		**4.5**		**6.7**		**7.8**	
(a) Taxes on International Trade (Avg.)	4	(7.0)	4	(6.9)	4	(6.5)	6	(5.4)	7	(3.5)
(b) Black Market Exchange Rates (Prem.)	7	(2)	6	(5)	6	(3)	10	(0)	10	(0)
(c) Size of Trade Sector (% of GDP)	5	(20.7)	7	(27.2)	7	(24.6)	10	(37.8)	10	(45.0)
(d) Capital Transactions with Foreigners	2		2		2		2		5	
Economic Freedom Rating	**4.8**		**4.9**		**5.3**		**6.2**		**7.2**	
Ranking of Country	**28**		**27**		**26**		**20**		**8**	

186

Part 2: Recent Economic Indicators:

Population 1996:	61.0	**Real Per Capita GDP** :	1995=	$6,801
(in millions)		(in 1995 U.S. dollars)		
Annual Rate of Change (1985-96):	1.4%	Avg. Growth Rate:	1980-90 =	6.0%
			1990-95 =	7.3%

Economic Indicators:*	1988	1989	1990	1991	1992	1993	1994	1995	1996
Change in Real GDP:Aggregate	13.3	12.2	10.6	8.4	7.9	8.2	8.5	8.6	-
: Per Capita	11.9	10.8	9.2	7.0	6.5	6.8	7.1	7.2	-
Inflation Rate (CPI)	3.8	5.4	6.0	5.7	4.1	3.4	5.1	6.5	4.3
Change in Money Supply: (M1)	12.2	17.7	11.9	13.8	12.3	18.6	17.0	12.1	-
: (M2)	18.2	26.2	26.7	19.8	15.6	18.4	12.9	17.0	-
Investment/GDP Ratio	32.6	35.1	41.1	42.2	39.6	39.9	40.1	-	-
Size of Trade Sector (% of GDP)	33.7	36.2	37.8	38.9	38.6	39.4	40.9	45.0	-
Total Gov't Exp./GDP Ratio	17.6	16.4	16.1	16.5	17.2	18.2	18.8	18.1	-
Central Government Budget Deficit (-) or Surplus (+) As a Percent of GDP	0.7	3.1	4.7	4.9	2.9	2.1	1.9	3.0	-
Unemployment Rate ᵃ	4.6	3.6	2.2	3.5	3.6	-	-	-	-

* The figures in this table are in percent form.

ᵃ Data for 1987-1990 are based on an average of a few months during each year.

During the last two decades, Thailand's economic freedom rating has risen from 4.8 in 1975 to 5.3 in 1985 and 7.2 in 1995. Our index indicates that the Thai economy is now the 8th freest among the 115 countries of our study.

Thailand has improved in almost every area. Its price level is now more stable—the inflation rate has fluctuated within a narrow band around 5% in the 1990s. Beginning in the late 1980s, Thais were permitted to own foreign currency bank accounts domestically and the maintenance of bank accounts abroad was authorized in the early 1990s. These moves contributed to a jump in the Money and Inflation area rating. Deregulation of the credit market has integrated the domestic financial markets with the global economy. The negative real interest rates of the late 1970s are now a thing of the past.

The top marginal tax rate was reduced from 65% in 1985 to 55% in 1990 and 37% in 1995. Tariff rates have been reduced, the Thai baht is now fully convertible and the size of the trade sector *as a share of GDP* has more than doubled since the mid-1970s. Restrictions on the flow of capital were also relaxed in the early 1990s. All of these factors contributed to the growth of economic freedom. The low—less than 20%—and relatively steady level of government expenditures as a share of GDP also suggest reliance on markets and a high level of economic freedom.

The economy has responded. The annual growth rate of per capita GDP has averaged 7.7% during 1985-1994, up from 3.7% during 1970-1985. The central government has generally run a budget surplus in recent years and the unemployment rate is relatively low.

TURKEY

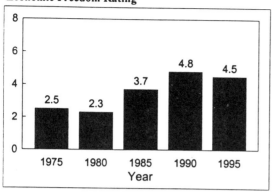

Economic Freedom Rating

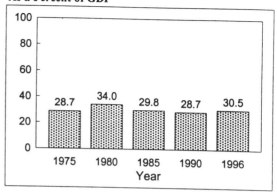

Total Government Expenditures
As a Percent of GDP

Part 1: The Economic Freedom Ratings for the Components and Various Area and Summary Indexes: 1975, 1980, 1985, 1990 and 1995.
(The numbers in parentheses indicate the actual values for the components.)

Components of Economic Freedom	1975		1980		1985		1990		1995	
I. Money and Inflation	**2.0**		**0.6**		**1.0**		**4.0**		**4.0**	
(a) Annual Money Growth (last 5 yrs.)	1	(26.0)	1	(44.3)	1	(35.0)	0	(51.3)	0	(61.7)
(b) Inflation Variablity (last 5 yrs.)	5	(4.4)	1	(31.4)	2	(8.4)	1	(13.9)	1	(19.2)
(c) Ownership of Foreign Currency	0		0		0		10		10	
(d) Maint. of Bank Account Abroad	0		0		0		10		10	
II. Government Operation	**4.7**		**4.3**		**6.8**		**5.4**		**4.5**	
(a) Govern. Consumption (% of Total Consump.)	7	(14.5)	7	(14.6)	9	(10.5)	8	(13.8)	7	(15.0)
(b) Government Enterprises	4		4		4		4		4	
(c) Price Controls	-		-		-		6		5	
(d) Entry Into Business	-		-		-		-		7.5	
(e) Legal System	-		-		-		-		0.0	
(f) Avoidance of Neg. Interest Rate	2		0		8		2		0	
III. Takings	**2.5**		**2.0**		**2.5**		**4.7**		**3.9**	
(a) Transfers and Subsidies (% of GDP)	5	(6.0)	5	(6.0)	4	(10.4)	7	(3.9)	5	(7.1)
(b) Marginal Tax Rates (Top Rate)	1	(68)	0	(75)	2	(63)	4	(50)	4	(55)
(c) Conscription	0		0		0		0		0	
IV. International Sector	**1.3**		**2.3**		**4.7**		**4.8**		**5.6**	
(a) Taxes on International Trade (Avg.)	0	(14.4)	4	(6.3)	7	(3.0)	7	(2.8)	9	(1.5)
(b) Black Market Exch. Rates (Prem.)	4	(11)	4	(16)	6	(3)	7	(2)	7.	(2)
(c) Size of Trade Sector (% of GDP)	1	(9.7)	0	(10.3)	6	(22.2)	5	(21.0)	3	(16.8)
(d) Capital Transactions with Foreigners	0		0		0		0		2	
Economic Freedom Rating	**2.5**		**2.3**		**3.7**		**4.8**		**4.5**	
Ranking of Country	**90**		**99**		**73**		**43**		**75**	

Part 2: Recent Economic Indicators:

Population 1996: 62.1
(in millions)
Annual Rate of Change (1985-96): 2.0%

Real Per Capita GDP : 1996 = $5,870
(in 1995 U.S. dollars)
Avg. Growth Rate: 1980-90= 2.9%
1990-96= 2.6%

Economic Indicators:*	1988	1989	1990	1991	1992	1993	1994	1995	1996
Change in Real GDP: Aggregate	2.3	0.3	9.2	0.8	5.0	5.8	-3.0	6.8	7.4
: Per Capita	0.3	-1.7	7.2	-1.2	2.0	3.9	-5.0	5.7	5.7
Inflation Rate (CPI)	73.7	63.3	60.3	66.0	70.1	66.1	106.3	93.6	80.2
Change in Money Supply: (M1)	30.6	73.2	58.4	46.4	72.5	64.8	81.5	68.3	66.4
: (M2)	65.3	68.9	53.2	82.7	78.7	64.4	145.3	103.6	100.0
Investment/GDP Ratio	25.8	24.2	24.6	22.4	23.2	26.1	21.3	24.6	23.5
Size of Trade Sector (% of GDP)	23.1	22.8	21.0	21.1	22.2	16.9	20.8	16.8	19.9
Total Gov't Exp./GDP Ratio	27.5	27.5	28.7	28.3	29.1	31.1	29.5	25.9	30.5
Central Government Budget Deficit (-) or Surplus (+) As a Percent of GDP	-3.8	-4.5	-4.2	-5.2	-4.3	-6.7	-3.9	-4.0	-8.9
Unemployment Rate	8.3	8.5	7.4	8.3	7.8	7.2	8.2	6.7	6.3

* The figures in this table are in percent form.

Turkey's 1995 economic freedom rating placed it 75th among the 115 countries we rated. After increasing substantially during 1975-1990, the Turkish rating declined a bit during the last five years.

During the 1980s, Turkey took several significant steps toward a freer economy. The key elements of Turkey's improvement during this period were:

- legalization of foreign currency bank accounts;
- reductions in tax rates—the top marginal rate was cut from 75% in 1980 to 50% in 1990 (it was subsequently increased to 55%);
- lower tariffs—the average tax on international trade fell from 14.4% in 1975 to 2.8% in 1990 and 1.5% in 1995;
- relaxation of exchange rate controls—the black market in this area has virtually disappeared; and
- a substantial increase in the size of the trade sector.

Two major factors continue to limit the development of this economy: monetary instability and absence of rule of law. During the last five years, the Turkish monetary authorities have expanded the money supply at a 70% annual rate. Predictably, the price level has increased by a similar magnitude. The 1996 Turkish inflation rate (86%) was one of the highest in the world. The legal structure grants political officials a great deal of discretionary regulatory authority. Not surprisingly, this authority is often used in a discriminatory manner, thereby reducing the security of property rights. Moves toward deregulation and greater transparency are badly needed in this area. After making significant progress toward economic freedom and experiencing healthy growth (per capita GDP has increased at a 2.5% annual rate since 1980), it would be tragic if policy failures in these two important areas prevented this economy from achieving its full potential.

UKRAINE

Economic Freedom Rating

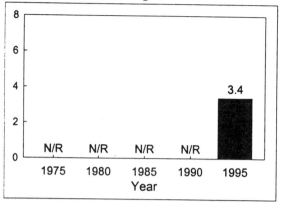

**Total Government Expenditures
As a Percent of GDP**

No Data

Part 1: The Economic Freedom Ratings for the Components and Various Area and Summary Indexes: 1975, 1980, 1985, 1990 and 1995.

(The numbers in parentheses indicate the actual values for the components.)

Components of Economic Freedom	1975	1980	1985	1990	1995
I. Money and Inflation	**0.0**	**0.0**	**0.0**	**5.3**	**1.9**
(a) Annual Money Growth (last 5 yrs.)	-	-	-	-	0 (690)
(b) Inflation Variablity (last 5 yrs.)	-	-	-	-	0 (1682.7)
(c) Ownership of Foreign Currency	0	0	0	10	10
(d) Maint. of Bank Account Abroad	0	0	0	0	0
II. Government Operation	**0.0**	**1.3**	**1.3**	**1.1**	**3.5**
(a) Gov't Consump. (% of Total Consump.)	-	2 (24.2)	2 (25.0)	3 (23.3)	8 (13.4)
(b) Government Enterprises	-	-	-	-	0
(c) Price Controls	-	-	-	0	2
(d) Entry Into Business	-	-	-	-	5.0
(e) Legal System	-	-	-	-	5.0
(f) Avoidance of Neg. Interest Rates	-	-	-	-	0
III. Takings	**0.0**	**0.0**	**0.0**	**0.0**	**0.0**
(a) Transfers and Subsidies (% of GDP)	-	-	-	-	-
(b) Marginal Tax Rates (Top Rate)	-	-	-	-	-
(c) Conscription	-	-	-	0	0
IV. International Sector	**0.0**	**0.0**	**0.0**	**0.0**	**5.4**
(a) Taxes on International Trade (Avg.)	-	-	-	-	-
(b) Black Market Exchange Rates (Prem.)	0 (391)	0 (359)	0 (637)	0 (6100)	6 (3)
(c) Size of Trade Sector (% of GDP)	-	-	-	-	10 (37.0)
(d) Capital Transactions with Foreigners	0	0	0	0	2

Economic Freedom Rating	**3.4**
Ranking of Country	**106**

Part 2: Recent Economic Indicators:

Population 1996: 52.1
(in millions)
Annual Rate of Change (1980-96): -0.3%

Real Per Capita GDP : 1996= $2,350
(in 1995 U.S. dollars)
Avg. Growth Rate: 1980-90= -
1991-96= -14.0%

Economic Indicators:*	1991	1992	1993	1994	1995	1996
Change in Real GDP: Aggregate	-14.0	-14.0	-14.2	-24.3	-11.8	-7.9
: Per Capita	-13.7	-13.7	-13.9	-24.0	-11.5	-7.6
Inflation Rate (CPI)	91.2	1210.0	4734.9	891.2	376.7	-
Change in Money Supply: (M1)	-	-	1551.0	443.6	151.5	-
: (M2)	-	-	1808.0	567.8	114.8	-
Investment/GDP Ratio	-	34.5	36.3	35.3	-	-
Size of Trade Sector (% of GDP)	30.6	23.1	26.0	37.0	-	-
Total Gov't Exp./GDP Ratio						
Central Government Budget Deficit (-) or Surplus (+) As a Percent of GDP	-	-	-	-10.5	-7.9	-6.2
Unemployment Rate	-	-	0.8	0.9	1.0	1.5

* The figures in this table are in percent form.

Ukraine's 3.4 rating placed it 106th among the 115 countries of our study. Among the former socialist countries, only Russia, Albania, Romania, and Croatia have similar ratings.

Clearly this is a troubled economy that has experienced very little constructive reform. There has been little privatization and the privatization that has occurred has been handled poorly. Large budget deficits financed with money creation continue to fuel inflation, which continues at triple-digit rates. Legal operation of a private business still involves a regulatory maze. The legal structure is highly discretionary and therefore a fertile ground for corruption.

The result is economic collapse. The region that was once referred to as "the bread basket of Europe" has experienced 7 straight years of declining income. Per capita GDP is now less than half the figure of 1990. This is a country that has potential. The labor force is reasonably well educated and the people have a reputation for both creativity and survival during difficult times. Without liberal economic reform on a major scale, however, the situation is unlikely to improve. Hopefully, the current disastrous economic situation will create an environment where meaningful reform can take place.

191

UNITED KINGDOM

Economic Freedom Rating

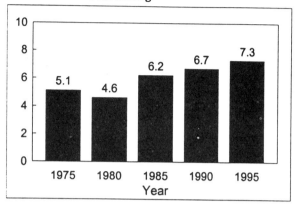

Total Government Expenditures
As a Percent of GDP

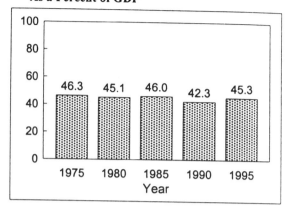

Part 1: The Economic Freedom Ratings for the Components and Various Area and Summary Indexes: 1975, 1980, 1985, 1990 and 1995.
(The numbers in parentheses indicate the actual values for the components.)

Components of Economic Freedom	1975		1980		1985		1990		1995	
I. Money and Inflation	**2.8**		**4.2**		**7.8**		**7.0**		**9.4**	
(a) Annual Money Growth (last 5 yrs.)	6	(12.2)	6	(11.9)	5	(12.5)	1	(28.9)	9	(5.4)
(b) Inflation Variability (last 5 yrs.)	3	(7.4)	7	(2.6)	8	(2.5)	9	(1.4)	9	(1.6)
(c) Ownership of Foreign Currency	0		0		10		10		10	
(d) Maint. of Bank Account Abroad	0		0		10		10		10	
II. Government Operation	**2.8**		**2.8**		**5.3**		**6.1**		**7.3**	
(a) Gov't Consump. (% of Total Consump.)	1	(27.0)	1	(26.7)	2	(25.9)	2	(24.6)	2	(25.0)
(b) Government Enterprises	4		4		6		6		6	
(c) Price Controls	-		-		-		8		9	
(d) Entry Into Business	-		-		-		-		10.0	
(e) Legal System	-		-		-		-		7.5	
(f) Avoidance of Neg. Interest Rates	4		4		10		10		10	
III. Takings	**5.8**		**2.1**		**3.1**		**4.9**		**4.5**	
(a) Transfers and Subsidies (% of GDP)	3	(15.0)	2	(15.8)	2	(17.9)	3	(14.9)	2	(17.7)
(b) Marginal Tax Rates (% of Top Rate)	7	(41)	0	(83)	2	(60)	5	(40)	5	(40)
(c) Conscription	10		10		10		10		10	
IV. International Sector	**7.4**		**9.2**		**9.5**		**9.2**		**9.2**	
(a) Taxes on International Trade (Avg.)	10	(0.0)	10	(0.0)	10	(0.0)	10	(0.0)	10	(0.0)
(b) Black Market Exchange Rates (Prem.)	10	(0)	10	(0)	10	(0)	10	(0)	10	(0)
(c) Size of Trade Sector (% of GDP)	7	(26.8)	5	(26.2)	7	(28.3)	5	(25.7)	5	(28.6)
(d) Capital Transactions with Foreigners	2		10		10		10		10	
Economic Freedom Rating	**5.1**		**4.6**		**6.2**		**6.7**		**7.3**	
Ranking of Country	**22**		**34**		**12**		**9**		**7**	

Part 2: Recent Economic Indicators:

Population 1996: (in millions)	58.8	**Real Per Capita GDP** : (in 1995 U.S. dollars)	1996 = $19,917
Annual Rate of Change (1985-96):	0.3%	Avg. Growth Rate: 1980-90= 1990-96=	2.4% 1.1%

Economic Indicators:*	1988	1989	1990	1991	1992	1993	1994	1995	1996
Change in Real GDP: Aggregate	5.0	2.2	0.4	-2.0	-0.5	2.3	3.8	2.4	3.4
: Per Capita	4.7	1.9	0.1	-2.3	-0.8	2.0	3.5	2.1	3.1
Inflation Rate (CPI)	4.9	7.8	9.5	5.9	3.7	1.6	2.5	3.4	2.5
Change in Money Supply: (M1)	10.7	14.4	10.1	6.6	4.3	9.9	0.8	16.7	7.0
: (M2)	18.3	21.6	10.6	0.5	6.9	4.8	5.8	12.9	9.6
Investment/GDP Ratio	20.3	21.0	19.2	16.1	15.4	15.0	15.4	15.6	-
Size of Trade Sector (% of GDP)	24.8	25.8	25.7	24.2	24.5	26.0	26.8	28.6	-
Total Gov't Exp./GDP Ratio	41.0	40.7	42.3	42.8	45.2	45.6	45.0	45.3	43.5 [p]
Central Government Budget Deficit (-) or Surplus (+) As a Percent of GDP	+1.6	+1.5	+0.7	-1.0	-5.0	-6.9	-5.6	-4.8	-
Unemployment Rate	8.6	7.3	6.9	8.8	10.0	10.5	9.6	8.8	6.7 [a]

* The figures in this table are in percent form.

[a] December, 1996.

[p] Preliminary.

Our analysis indicates that the United Kingdom is one of the freest economies in the world, and both its rating and ranking have been improving. Among the 115 countries in our study, the UK ranked 7th in 1995, up from 34th in 1980. The major factors underlying this improvement were greater monetary and price stability, removal of restrictions limiting the use of foreign currencies, privatization, and the sharp reduction in marginal tax rates (the top rate was sliced from 83% in 1980 to 60% in 1985 and 40% later in the decade).

During the last two decades total government expenditures have been increasing as a share of GDP in most of the high-income industrial economies of Western Europe. This has not been true in the UK. In fact, the size of government fell as a share of GDP during the 1980s, before rising a bit during the 1990s. Growth of the transfer sector has provided the engine for government growth in most European countries. This has been less true in the UK. In fact, transfers and subsidies as a share of GDP have changed little since 1985. As a share of the economy, the transfer sector is now significantly lower than that of the other large European economies. Interestingly, the British unemployment rate has also been lower than that of its neighbors.

Even though the British economy was hard hit by the 1990-1992 recession, growth since 1980 has been impressive. Between 1980 and 1996, the annual growth of *per capita* GDP averaged 2.0%, compared to, for example, 1.9% for Germany and 1.4% for France. Both these economies had grown more rapidly than the UK between 1960 and 1980. The UK economy still confronts serious problems. Its government consumption and transfer sectors are large. Employment regulations and a complex web of social benefits reduce worker mobility and labor market flexibility. A still significant "public" housing sector, rent/tenure controls in the small private rental sector and taxes on buying your own home all contribute to low labor mobility. The extent to which the size and regulatory powers of government can be reduced and labor market flexibility increased will determine the future direction of the British economy.

193

UNITED STATES

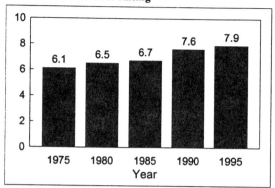

Economic Freedom Rating

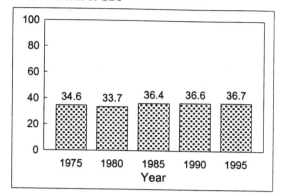

**Total Government Expenditures
As a Percent of GDP**

Part 1: The Economic Freedom Ratings for the Components and Various Area and Summary Indexes: 1975, 1980, 1985, 1990 and 1995.
(The numbers in parentheses indicate the actual values for the components).

Components of Economic Freedom	1975		1980		1985		1990		1995	
I. Money and Inflation	**9.0**		**9.4**		**8.4**		**10.0**		**10.0**	
(a) Annual Money Growth (last 5 yrs.)	9	(5.7)	9	(6.8)	7	(8.4)	10	(4.5)	10	(3.2)
(b) Inflation Variablity (last 5 yrs.)	8	(2.1)	9	(1.3)	8	(2.4)	10	(0.7)	10	(1.0)
(c) Ownership of Foreign Currency	10		10		10		10		10	
(d) Maint. of Bank Account Abroad	10		10		10		10		10	
II. Government Operation	**6.1**		**6.9**		**6.9**		**7.2**		**8.2**	
(a) Gov't Consump. (% of Total Consump.)	3	(22.6)	4	(21.3)	4	(21.1)	4	(20.3)	5	(18.8)
(b) Government Enterprises	8		8		8		8		8	
(c) Price Controls	-		-		-		8		9	
(d) Entry Into Business	-		-		-		-		10.0	
(e) Legal System	-		-		-		-		7.5	
(f) Avoidance of Neg. Interest Rates	8		10		10		10		10	
III. Takings	**2.9**		**2.9**		**4.4**		**5.8**		**5.8**	
(a) Transfers and Subsidies (% of GDP)	4	(11.1)	4	(10.9)	3	(12.5)	3	(12.7)	3	(13.9)
(b) Marginal Tax Rates (Top Rate)	0	(70-75)	0	(70-75)	4	(50-59)	7	(33-42)	7	(40-47)
(c) Conscription	10		10		10		10		10	
IV. International Sector	**8.1**		**8.6**		**8.1**		**8.6**		**8.6**	
(a) Taxes on International Trade (Avg.)	8	(1.5)	9	(1.1)	8	(1.7)	9	(1.5)	9	(1.2)
(b) Black Market Exchange Rates (Prem.)	10	(0)	10	(0)	10	(0)	10	(0)	10	(0)
(c) Size of Trade Sector (% of GDP)	2	(8.2)	3	(10.6)	2	(8.9)	3	(10.7)	3	(11.8)
(d) Capital Transactions with Foreigners	10		10		10		10		10	
Economic Freedom Rating	**6.1**		**6.5**		**6.7**		**7.6**		**7.9**	
Ranking of Country	**11**		**6**		**6**		**3**		**4**	

Part 2: Recent Economic Indicators:

Population 1996:	265.4	**Real Per Capita GDP** :		1996 =	$27,178
(in millions)		(in 1995 U.S. dollars)			
Annual Rate of Change (1985-96):	1.0%	Avg. Growth Rate:	1980-90=	1.7%	
			1990-96=	1.0%	

Economic Indicators:*	1988	1989	1990	1991	1992	1993	1994	1995	1996
Change in Real GDP: Aggregate	3.9	2.5	0.8	-1.2	3.3	3.1	4.1	2.0	2.2
: Per Capita	2.9	1.5	-0.2	-2.2	2.3	2.1	3.1	1.0	1.2
Inflation Rate (CPI)	4.0	4.8	5.4	4.2	3.0	3.0	2.6	2.8	3.3
Change in Money Supply: (M1)	4.8	1.0	5.0	8.6	11.7	9.7	0.1	-0.9	-4.3
: (M2)	6.3	5.8	4.9	3.3	1.7	1.5	0.1	5.5	4.6
Investment/GDP Ratio	18.4	18.2	16.9	15.3	15.6	16.6	17.1	17.7	-
Size of Trade Sector (% of GDP)	10.2	10.5	10.7	10.7	10.9	10.5	11.1	11.8	-
Total Gov't Exp./GDP Ratio	35.7	35.7	36.6	38.0	38.1	37.3	36.4	36.7	36.8 P
Central Government Budget Deficit (-) or Surplus (+) As a Percent of GDP	-3.2	-2.8	-4.0	-4.8	-4.9	-4.1	-3.3	-2.2	-1.6
Unemployment Rate	5.5	5.3	5.5	6.7	7.4	6.9	6.1	5.6	5.4

* The figures in this table are in percent form.

P Preliminary.

Other than Hong Kong and Switzerland, no economy has achieved more persistently high ratings throughout the last two decades than the United States. The U.S. has ranked in the top six since 1980. Its 7.9 rating in 1995 placed it 4th, behind only Hong Kong, Singapore, and New Zealand.

The U.S. received below average ratings for only two components: size of the transfer sector and international trade as a share of GDP. Increased price stability (the inflation rate has generally been between 2% and 4% for more than a decade) and a reduction in the top marginal tax rate (the combined federal and state top rate was reduced from over 70% in 1980 to the 40% range) were the primary factors contributing to the increase in the U.S. rating during the 1980s.

The size of government of the U.S. is generally smaller than that of other high income industrial countries. Total government expenditures summed to 36.7% of GDP in 1995, compared to 48% in Canada, 54% in France, 51% for Germany, and 52% for Italy. Except for Japan, no other big industrial economy has a level of government expenditures similar to that of the United States.

Even though our index does not currently do a good job of measuring differences in this area, it is widely believed that the labor market of the U.S. is more flexible than that of its European counterparts. This factor, along with the smaller size of government—particularly the transfer sector—help explain why the unemployment rate of the U.S. has persistently been lower than the rates of the European industrial economies.

The U.S. economy is neither problem free nor a bastion of economic liberalism. Most (approximately 90%) elementary and secondary students attend government-operated schools. While dissatisfaction with the poor performance of these schools is widespread, thus far the teachers' unions have managed to stifle competition, parental choice and meaningful reform. The U.S. has the highest number of lawyers per capita of any nation in the world. Perhaps because of this, the legal system—particularly liability law—has increasingly become a tool for the redistribution of income. The social security system is headed for trouble as the large baby-boom generation moves into the retirement phase of life beginning in 2010.

(Continued on page 203.)

VENEZUELA

Economic Freedom Rating

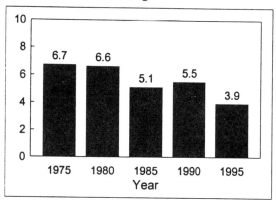

Total Government Expenditures As a Percent of GDP

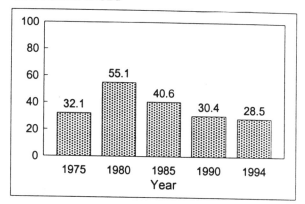

Part 1: The Economic Freedom Ratings for the Components and Various Area and Summary Indexes: 1975, 1980, 1985, 1990 and 1995.

(The numbers in parentheses indicate the actual values for the components.)

Components of Economic Freedom	1975		1980		1985		1990		1995	
I. Money and Inflation	**4.3**		**5.5**		**6.2**		**4.6**		**0.6**	
(a) Annual Money Growth (last 5 yrs.)	1	(30.0)	3	(16.2)	4	(14.0)	2	(19.4)	1	(43.1)
(b) Inflation Variablity (last 5 yrs.)	1	(15.0)	3	(7.4)	4	(5.2)	1	(30.4)	1	(15.6)
(c) Ownership of Foreign Currency	10		10		10		10		0	
(d) Maint. of Bank Account Abroad	10		10		10		10		0	
II. Government Operation	**5.5**		**5.0**		**5.2**		**4.2**		**3.6**	
(a) Gov't Consump. (% of Total Consump.)	5	(19.0)	6	(17.7)	7	(14.5)	9	(11.9)	10	(7.8)
(b) Government Enterprises	6		4		4		2		2	
(c) Price Controls	-		-		-		4		0	
(d) Entry Into Business	-		-		-		-		7.5	
(e) Legal System	-		-		-		-		0.0	
(f) Avoidance of Neg. Interest Rates	-		-		4		0		0	
III. Takings	**7.8**		**6.8**		**6.0**		**5.2**		**5.6**	
(a) Transfers and Subsidies (% of GDP)	8	(2.3)	9	(2.0)	7	(4.5)	5	(5.8)	6	(5.1)
(b) Marginal Tax Rates (Top Rate)	10	(20)	7	(45)	7	(45)	7	(45)	7	(34)
(c) Conscription	0		0		0		0		0	
IV. International Sector	**7.6**		**7.8**		**3.1**		**7.6**		**4.6**	
(a) Taxes on International Trade (Avg.)	6	(3.7)	7	(3.0)	1	(9.1)	8	(2.2)	7	(2.7)
(b) Black Market Exchange Rates (Prem.)	10	(0)	10	(0)	3	(25)	10	(0)	2	(42)
(c) Size of Trade Sector (% of GDP)	6	(25.4)	5	(25.3)	4	(20.4)	7	(29.8)	4	(22.9)
(d) Capital Transactions with Foreigners	8		8		5		5		5	
Economic Freedom Rating	**6.7**		**6.6**		**5.1**		**5.5**		**3.9**	
Ranking of Country	**5**		**6**		**28**		**31**		**92**	

Part 2: Recent Economic Indicators:

Population 1996:	21.9	**Real Per Capita GDP** :	1995=	$9,178
(in millions)		(in 1995 U.S. dollars)		
Annual Rate of Change (1985-96):	2.2%	Avg. Growth Rate:	1980-90=	-1.7%
			1990-95=	1.5%

Economic Indicators:*	1988	1989	1990	1991	1992	1993	1994	1995	1996
Change in Real GDP: Aggregate	6.2	-7.8	6.9	9.7	6.1	0.3	-2.8	2.2	-
: Per Capita	4.0	-10.0	4.7	7.5	3.9	-1.9	-5.0	0.0	-
Inflation Rate (CPI)	29.5	84.5	40.7	34.2	31.4	38.1	60.8	59.9	103.2
Change in Money Supply: (M1)	22.7	22.2	54.6	51.3	4.6	-7.1	141.7	38.1	-
: (M2)	18.4	48.0	69.0	47.6	14.5	17.6	70.7	36.7	-
Investment/GDP Ratio	27.9	12.9	10.2	18.7	23.7	18.8	13.2	15.9	-
Size of Trade Sector (% of GDP)	24.0	27.6	29.8	28.6	27.2	27.0	26.1	22.9	-
Total Gov't Exp./GDP Ratio	30.9	35.9	30.4	43.5	37.8	30.8	28.5	-	-
Central Government Budget Deficit (-) or Surplus (+) As a Percent of GDP	-7.7	-1.6	+1.1	+4.4	-3.2	-3.0	-4.1	-	-
Unemployment Rate	7.3	9.2	10.4	9.5	7.8	6.6	8.7	-	-

* The figures in this table are in percent form.

In 1975, Venezuela's 6.7 summary rating placed it as the 5th freest economy in the world. Since that time, its economic freedom rating has persistently declined. By 1995 Venezuela's rating had fallen to 3.9, 2.8 units below the 1975 level. Its ranking followed a similar path, falling from 5th in 1975 to 28th in 1985 and 92nd in 1995. No other country has experienced as sharp a decline in economic freedom during the last two decades.

Why did Venezuela's rating decline? The major contributing factors were: monetary and price instability, removal in the early 1990s of the freedom to maintain foreign currency bank accounts, and increased use of price controls. Low ratings for the widespread use of public sector enterprises, a weak and often arbitrary legal system, interest rate controls, and conscription also pull down the summary rating. As economic freedom fell, so too, did economic performance. Real GDP per capita declined during 1993-1995. The 1995 per capita real GDP was nearly 15% below the 1980 figure.

Prodded by the economic decline and a triple-digit rate of inflation, President Caldera finally took action in April 1996. Exchange rate and interest rate controls were lifted. Price controls, including those imposed on gasoline, were liberalized but they were not eliminated. Taxes were raised and plans were laid to reduce the size of the large budget deficits. While some aspects of this program are consistent with economic liberty, others are likely to enlarge the size of government and increase the fiscal burden imposed on the private sector. Clearly, the plan does not represent a systematic strategy to liberalize the economy.

If this resource-rich economy is going to reach its potential, deregulation is needed in numerous areas and the legal system needs to be made less arbitrary and more transparent. The monetary system needs to be de-politicized and the monetary authorities assigned a low inflation rate target and held accountable for its attainment. Venezuela needs to follow the lead of neighboring Chile and move systematically toward a freer economy.

ZAIRE

Economic Freedom Rating

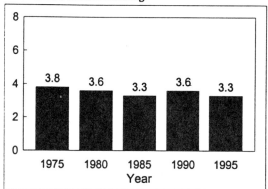

Total Government Expenditures
As a Percent of GDP

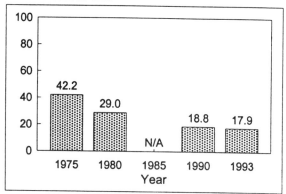

Part 1: The Economic Freedom Ratings for the Components and Various Area and Summary Indexes: 1975, 1980, 1985, 1990 and 1995.
(The numbers in parentheses indicate the actual values for the components.)

Components of Economic Freedom	1975	1980	1985	1990	1995	
I. Money and Inflation	**2.3**	**0.6**	**0.3**	**0.3**	**0.0**	
(a) Annual Money Growth (last 5 yrs.)	2 (19.5)	1 (42.1)	0 (52.7)	0 (100.)	0	(2955.0)
(b) Inflation Variablity (last 5 yrs.)	5 (4.0)	1 (25.8)	1 (25.1)	1 (28.0)	0	(8703.2)
(c) Ownership of Foreign Currency	0	0	0	0	0	
(d) Maint. of Bank Account Abroad	0	0	0	0	0	
II. Government Operation	**4.9**	**5.9**	**4.7**	**3.3**	**2.3**	
(a) Gov't Consump. (% of Total Consump.)	8 (13.3)	10 (9.3)	10 (9.0)	8 (13.9)	6	(16.2)
(b) Government Enterprises	2	2	2	2	2	
(c) Price Controls	-	-	-	2	2	
(d) Entry Into Business	-	-	-	-	2.5	
(e) Legal System	-	-	-	-	0.0	
(f) Avoidance of Neg. Interest Rates	-	-	-	0	0	
III. Takings	**6.3**	**5.8**	**3.0**	**5.8**	**5.8**	
(a) Transfers and Subsidies (% of GDP)	10 (1.0)	10 (0.6)	-	10 (0.8)	10	(0.2)
(b) Marginal Tax Rates (Top Rate)	2 (60)	1 (60)	1 (60)	1 (60)	1	(60)
(c) Conscription	10	10	10	10	10	
IV. International Sector	**1.1**	**1.6**	**4.3**	**3.6**	**3.8**	
(a) Taxes on International Trade (Avg.)	0 (19.0)	1 (10.3)	2 (8.4)	1 (9.1)	5	(6.1)
(b) Black Market Exchange Rates (Prem.)	1 (120)	1 (131)	6 (6)	4 (20)	6	(4)
(c) Size of Trade Sector (% of GDP)	2 (12.5)	3 (16.4)	9 (26.6)	10 (31.3)	1	(10.2)
(d) Capital Transactions with Foreigners	2	2	2	2	2	
Economic Freedom Rating	**3.8**	**3.6**	**3.3**	**3.6**	**3.3**	
Ranking of Country	**59**	**67**	**80**	**84**	**108**	

Part 2: Recent Economic Indicators:

Population 1994:	45.3	**Real Per Capita GDP:** [a]	1992 =	$425
(in millions)		(in 1995 U.S. dollars)		
Annual Rate of Change (1985-94):	3.6%	Avg. Growth Rate:	1980-90 =	-1.7%
			1990-92 =	-12.0%

Economic Indicators:*	1988	1989	1990	1991	1992	1993	1994	1995	1996
Change in Real GDP:Aggregate	0.6	-1.4	-2.5	-12.3	-10.5	-	-	-	-
: Per Capita	-3.0	-5.0	-6.1	-15.9	-14.1	-	-	-	-
Inflation Rate (CPI)	82.7	104.1	81.3	2154.4	4129.2	1986.9	23773.1	541.9	-
Change in Money Supply: (M1)	90.8	119.2	75.4	175.8	2386.7	4114.5	2460.6	5635.4	-
: (M2)	131.2	67.4	195.4	2388.6	3794.5	2853.1	6968.9	-	-
Investment/GDP Ratio	14.4	14.3	9.1	5.6	6.9	2.3	-	-	-
Size of Trade Sector (% of GDP)	27.5	28.2	31.3	22.1	20.3	10.2	-	-	-
Total Gov't Exp./GDP Ratio	20.1	13.6	18.8	20.5	17.3	17.9	-	-	-
Central Government Budget Deficit (-) or Surplus (+) As a Percent of GDP	-	-8.0	-	-6.5	-14.4	-12.1	-	-	-
Unemployment Rate									

* The figures in this table are in percent form.

[a] Derived by purchasing power parity method.

In 1995, this country ranked 108th among the 115 countries in our study. It is easy to see why it received such a low rating. Economic freedom is restricted in almost every area. Monetary expansion of more than 1,000% per year during the 1990s has led to hyperinflation. Citizens are prohibited from using other currencies. The legal structure is arbitrary (it is under the control of an authoritarian political regime) and corrupt. Restrictions abound. Interest and exchange rate controls, restrictions on entry into business, political control of capital movements, and high marginal tax rates

(the top rate is currently 60%) are all part of this economic tragedy. More recently, political turmoil fueled by economic restrictions and hardship has turned to civil unrest.

The results were predictable. Already one of the world's poorest nations, income has persistently declined during the last two decades. Per capita GDP is now approximately one-half the figure of the mid-1970s. Until there is a dramatic change in political and economic structure, the suffering will continue.

ZIMBABWE

Economic Freedom Rating

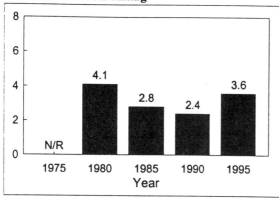

Total Government Expenditures As a Percent of GDP

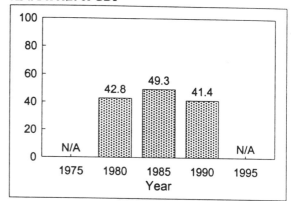

Part 1: The Economic Freedom Ratings for the Components and Various Area and Summary Indexes: 1975, 1980, 1985, 1990 and 1995.

(The numbers in parentheses indicate the actual values for the components.)

Components of Economic Freedom	1975		1980		1985		1990		1995	
I. Money and Inflation	3.4		4.2		3.7		1.9		1.3	
(a) Annual Money Growth (last 5 yrs.)	-		6	(11.5)	8	(7.4)	2	(18.0)	1	(33.6)
(b) Inflation Variablity (last 5 yrs.)	7	(2.7)	7	(2.7)	4	(5.5)	4	(5.7)	3	(7.1)
(c) Ownership of Foreign Currency	0		0		0		0		0	
(d) Maint. of Bank Account Abroad	0		0		0		0		0	
II. Government Operation	5.0		4.0		3.7		3.2		4.2	
(a) Gov't Consump. (% of Total Consump.)	6	(17.1)	3	(23.4)	1	(27.2)	1	(28.3)	3	(22.9)
(b) Government Enterprises	4		4		4		4		4	
(c) Price Controls	-		-		-		2		4	
(d) Entry Into Business	-		-		-		-		5.0	
(e) Legal System	-		-		-		-		2.5	
(f) Avoidance of Negative Interest Rates	-		6		8		8		8	
III. Takings			3.5		1.6		0.8		3.1	
(a) Transfers and Subsidies (% of GDP)	-		4	(11.4)	4	(10.0)	-		-	
(b) Marginal Tax Rates (Top Rate)	-		4	(45)	0	(63)	1	(60)	4	(45)
(c) Conscription	-		0		0		0		0	
IV. International Sector	5.8		4.3		2.8		3.1		4.6	
(a) Taxes on International Trade (Avg.)	8	(2.1)	8	(1.7)	2	(8.0)	1	(9.2)	2	(8.1)
(b) Black Market Exchange Rates (Prem)	2	(54)	1	(84)	2	(42)	4	(15)	8	(1)
(c) Size of Trade Sector (% of GDP)	8	(30.1)	7	(31.8)	7	(28.2)	7	(29.5)	8	(34.8)
(d) Capital Transactions with Foreigners	-		2		2		2		2	
Economic Freedom Rating			4.1		2.8		2.4		3.6	
Ranking of Country			48		91		101		101	

Part 2: Recent Economic Indicators:

Population 1996:	11.9	**Real Per Capita GDP** :	1993= $1,626
(in millions)		(in 1995 U.S. dollars)	
Annual Rate of Change (1985-96):	3.2%	Avg. Growth Rate:	1980-90 = 0.7%
			1990-92= -5.5%

Economic Indicators:*	1988	1989	1990	1991	1992	1993	1994	1995	1996
Change in Real GDP:Aggregate	8.8	11.6	-0.5	-2.8	-	-	-	-	-
: Per Capita	5.5	8.4	-3.7	-6.0	-6.9	-	-	-	-
Inflation Rate (CPI)	7.4	12.9	17.4	23.3	42.1	27.6	22.3	22.6	-
Change in Money Supply: (M1)	28.5	19.5	27.6	23.0	5.8	94.9	18.2	52.4	-
: (M2)	20.8	24.3	15.1	1.4	12.6	71.3	35.1	25.5	-
Investment/GDP Ratio	21.8	18.9	25.5	-	-	-	-	-	-
Size of Trade Sector (%of GDP)	27.4	29.9	29.5	33.6	37.4	34.8	-	-	-
Total Gov't Exp./GDP Ratio	42.2	41.1	41.4	-	-	-	-	-	-
Central Government Budget Deficit (-) or Surplus (+) As a Percent of GDP	-11.1	-10.0	-9.2	-8.0	-	-	-	-	-
Unemployment Rate	-	-	-	-	-	-	-	-	-

* The figures in this table are in percent form.

This country has consistently followed policies that conflict with economic freedom. Even through its 1995 summary ratings increased by approximately a point, Zimbabwe still ranked 97th among the 115 nations we were able to rate. Excessive monetary expansion (the M1 money supply has increased at an annual rate of more than 30% in recent years) has fueled inflation. Use of foreign currencies is restricted. Government enterprises operate in many sectors of the economy. The legal system is authoritarian and provides little protection for the property rights of either blacks or the few whites who remain. Price controls, foreign exchange controls, and restrictions on capital movements are also part of this economic tragedy.

Per capita GDP has declined during the last decade and there is no hope for improvement until there is a dramatic shift in policies and institutional arrangements.

(China: continued from page 75.)

Even though our index still gives China a zero rating for the state enterprise component, the size of the state enterprise sector has been shrinking (and the market sector growing). The contribution of private enterprises to China's gross industrial output increased from 3% in 1985 to 29.4% in 1995. During the same time period, output of collective enterprises rose from 32.1% to 36.6%, while the output of state-owned enterprises fell from 64.9% to 34%. In domestic wholesale and retail trade sectors, private enterprises now provide employment for 22.5 million workers, more than half of the total employment in these sectors.

The emergence of a share-holding system of business organization and the establishment of stock exchanges in Shanghai and Shenzhen have launched property rights reforms in China. State-owned enterprises are required to assign equity shares to the leading government units. Enterprises will set up their own accounts and be responsible for their own profit and loss. During 1991-1995, China issued 311 stocks denominated and traded in remenbi (A-shares), 70 stocks denominated in remenbi but traded in foreign currencies (B-shares) and 22 H-shares (listed on Hong Kong Stock Exchange) with capitalization up to 12 billion U.S. dollars, or 5% of the total fixed assets in China.

The separation of enterprise management and financial accounts from the administration of government has drastically reduced the relative size of general public expenditures. Including the extrabudgetary accounts—the activities conducted outside of the budget after the adoption of the contracting system—general government expenditures have fallen from more than 35% of GDP in the mid-1980s to 11.5% in 1995.

As the Chinese economy became more open, the trade sector has grown and foreign investment has risen. As a share of GDP, the size of the trade sector rose from 6.5% in 1980 to 20.9% in 1995. (Note the rating improvement in this area.) Foreign investment is now a central element of Chinese development. Attracted by both lower labor cost and land prices, much of the manufacturing sector of Hong Kong has moved to the Pearl River Delta. Figures indicate that foreign-owned enterprises now employ about 6 million workers in industrial processing for export trade in the Delta.

Foreign investment now accounts for 20.5% of the total. Given China's size, both international trade and foreign investment are extremely large *as a share of the economy.*

China is shifting away from granting preferential treatment to identified areas and toward the national treatment principle. The discriminatory policy has largely been replaced with nation-wide implementation of policies that reduced government intervention and provided for general tax reductions. The recent reduction in the top marginal income tax rate to 33%, down from 45% in 1995, is illustrative of this point.

Foreign investors can be the sole owners of a business in China. They are welcome to invest in industry, services, commerce, banking (in certain areas), infrastructure, resources and mineral exploration, for example. China has successfully unified the official and market exchange rates. Free convertibility for current account purposes is now present and both individuals and businesses are allowed to maintain foreign currency bank accounts domestically.

As our index indicates, China has a long way to go before it qualifies as a free economy. Progress has been made, however. (Note the increase in China's rating from 2.3 in 1980 to 4.3 in 1995.) Nonetheless, continued movement toward economic freedom is vitally important if the Chinese economy is going to maintain its growth rate and achieve a significantly higher level of per capita GDP in the future.

In 1984, China launched an urban reform plan. It caused problems with inflation and corruption, and led to social discontent and chaos in several cities. The reform program was started with the release of price controls, without building an infrastructure for the support of a market system. In the mid-1980s, collective-owned township and village enterprises (TVEs) emerged as major contributors to Chinese business activities. The TVEs are market-oriented in their operation and management. They are generally more efficient than state-owned enterprises.Due to government regulation and control, private enterprises are mainly involved in small businesses in the trading, transport, and service sectors. Hotels and luxurious restaurants are also sometimes privately owned and operated.

(This report was prepared primarily by Priscilla P. K. Lau, Associate Head of the Department of Business Studies of Hong Kong Polytechnic University, and Dr. Sung Yun-wing, Head of the Department of Economics, The Chinese University of Hong Kong.)

(Israel: continued from page 123).

Without these remittances and other monies such as loan guarantees, Israel would be running huge deficits. Most of these transfers end up in the hands of the government. Rather than a systematic move toward economic freedom, the recent reductions in the government spending/GDP ratio are designed to shore up and continue an aid-based economy dominated by government. As long as the aid, grants, and guaranteed loans are forthcoming, real reform and a permanent reduction in the size of government are unlikely to occur. Rather than aid, this economy needs liberalization—more monetary stability, deregulation of its financial and capital markets, and privatization of state enterprises. The entrepreneurial spirit and market success of the Jewish people are renown around the world. If released, these forces will also lead to prosperity and growth in the Jewish homeland.

(Russia: continued from page 163.)

socialist economy make it difficult to do business without breaking some law. Thus, entrepreneurs constantly confront the threat of harassment from both legitimate government officials and others merely seeking bribes. This increases the risks of engaging in business and reduces the competitiveness of the economy.

Russia has made some progress. There is now some hope for monetary and price stability. If the legal structure can be improved, perhaps the economic nightmare of both the prior regime and the transition will soon be over.

(United States: continued from page 195.)

Seeking to attract business, local governments often provide various tax concessions and indirect subsidies that distort the operation of markets.

Despite its deficiencies, the U.S. has been one of the two or three most persistently free economies in the world. Persistent economic freedom *over a prolonged time period* can be expected to lead to high per capita income. Along with Hong Kong, another persistently free economy, the per capita income of Americans ($27,178 in 1996) is the highest in the world. Economic freedom leads to progress.

203

Appendix I

The Ratings for Each of the Components and the Summary Ratings for 1990, 1985, 1980 and 1975

LIST OF TABLES

205

Table A1-1: Component and Summary Index Ratings: 1990

INDUSTRIAL COUNTRIES	I A	B	C	D	II A	B	C	F	III A	B	C	IV A	B	C	D	Summary Rating
United States	10	10	10	10	4	8	8	10	3	7	10	9	10	3	10	7.6
Canada	9	10	10	10	2	6	8	10	3	5	10	9	10	8	8	7.1
Australia	5	9	10	10	4	6	6	10	4	3	10	7	10	5	8	6.3
Japan	10	10	10	10	8	8	6	10	4	2	10	9	10	1	8	6.9
New Zealand	1	4	10	10	4	6	9	10	0	7	10	8	10	4	10	6.3
Austria	9	10	10	10	2	2	5	10	1	4	0	9	10	8	5	5.5
Belgium	10	10	10	10	5	6	2	10	0	2	0	10	10	10	10	5.9
Denmark	7	10	10	10	0	4	6	10	1	0	0	10	10	3	5	4.8
Finland	7	10	10	10	1	6	6	10	2	0	0	9	10	2	2	4.8
France	10	10	10	10	3	4	6	8	0	3	0	10	10	5	5	5.5
Germany	7	10	10	10	2	6	9	10	2	3	0	10	10	8	10	6.4
Iceland	1	6	10	10	2	4	6	6	4	5	10	6	6	2	2	4.9
Ireland	9	7	0	0	4	4	7	10	1	1	10	7	8	8	5	4.8
Italy	8	10	10	10	4	2	5	10	0	1	0	10	10	4	5	5.0
Netherlands	9	10	10	10	5	6	7	10	0	0	0	10	10	9	8	5.8
Norway	2	6	10	10	1	2	5	10	0	3	0	10	10	6	8	4.8
Spain	3	9	0	0	5	4	6	10	2	3	0	9	7	3	8	4.7
Sweden	8	9	10	0	0	4	6	10	0	0	0	9	10	4	10	4.7
Switzerland	10	10	10	10	5	8	7	10	2	8	0	8	10	6	10	7.3
United Kingdom	1	9	10	10	2	6	8	10	3	5	10	10	10	5	10	6.7
CENTRAL/SOUTH AMERICA																
Argentina	0	0	10	10	10	8	0	0	5	7	0	1	10	0	0	4.3
Bahamas	9	10	0	0	7	2	4	10	10	10	10	1	4	2	2	6.1
Barbados	2	3	0	0	3	4	6	10	10	4	10	7	4	1	2	4.8
Belize	7	7	0	0	5	8	0	10	10	4	10	1	3	4	5	5.1
Bolivia	1	0	10	10	7	4	6	8	8	10	0	8	6	5	2	6.1
Brazil	0	0	0	0	5	2	0	0	4	9	0	6	4	0	0	3.0
Chile	1	6	10	10	8	6	8	8	5	3	0	6	10	7	2	5.6
Colombia	1	8	0	0	8	4	6	8	7	8	0	3	4	3	0	4.8
Costa Rica	5	6	10	10	3	8	6	8	6	9	10	4	10	3	5	6.7
Dominican Rep	1	1	0	0	10	6	4	0	9	0	10	3	1	3	2	3.6
Ecuador	1	1	10	10	9	4	0	0	8	5	0	6	10	4	2	4.8
El Salvador	6	2	0	0	9	8	-	8	9	2	0	6	3	0	2	4.5
Guatemala	2	1	10	10	10	8	6	8	9	7	0	7	10	1	5	6.6
Haiti	7	3	10	10	10	6	2	-	-	9	10	4	1	0	0	5.4
Honduras	3	3	10	10	7	6	4	8	8	5	0	-	10	5	0	5.6
Jamaica	2	4	0	0	6	4	4	8	9	7	10	-	3	5	2	5.1
Mexico	0	0	10	10	9	4	0	8	8	7	0	8	10	4	5	5.7
Nicaragua	0	0	0	0	0	0	0	0	5	-	0	6	4	3	0	1.7
Panama	10	10	10	10	4	4	2	10	5	3	10	8	10	3	8	6.3
Paraguay	1	6	10	10	10	6	4	2	9	8	0	7	3	8	5	6.3
Peru	0	0	10	0	10	6	2	0	8	4	0	6	4	1	2	4.1
Trinidad/Tobago	10	4	0	0	3	2	4	6	4	7	10	7	2	1	0	4.3
Uruguay	0	2	10	10	6	6	4	8	3	10	10	6	10	1	10	6.3
Venezuela	2	1	10	10	9	2	4	0	5	7	0	8	10	7	5	5.5

206

EUROPE-MIDDLE EAST	I				II				III			IV				Summary Rating
	A	B	C	D	A	B	C	F	A	B	C	A	B	C	D	
Albania	-	-	0	0	1	0	0	0	1	-	0	-	0	5	0	0.6 *
Bahrain	10	2	10	10	0	2	4	10	10	10	10	9	10	8	2	7.1
Bulgaria	5	2	0	0	3	0	0	-	0	-	0	9	1	3	0	1.8
Croatia	-	-	10	0	-	-	0	-	-	-	0	-	1	-	0	N/R
Cyprus	9	10	0	0	3	6	0	10	4	0	0	6	6	3	0	3.6
Czechoslovakia	10	5	0	0	1	0	0	-	0	4	0	6	2	5	0	2.4
Czech Rep	-	-	-	-	-	-	-	-	-	-	-	-	-	-	-	N/R
Slovakia	-	-	-	-	-	-	-	-	-	-	-	-	-	-	-	N/R
Egypt	6	9	10	10	9	0	2	6	4	2	0	5	2	10	0	4.2
Estonia	-	-	10	0	-	-	0	-	-	-	0	9	0	-	0	N/R
Greece	2	7	10	0	6	2	0	8	1	4	0	10	6	3	2	3.9
Hungary	5	3	0	0	7	0	6	6	0	3	0	6	4	5	0	3.0
Iran	3	6	10	10	7	2	2	-	7	0	0	3	0	3	0	3.2
Israel	1	2	10	0	0	2	0	6	2	4	0	9	6	3	2	3.1
Jordan	6	2	0	0	4	6	2	4	7	5	10	6	4	10	2	4.7
Latvia	-	-	10	0	-	-	0	-	-	-	0	-	0	-	0	N/R
Lithuania	-	-	10	0	-	-	0	-	-	-	0	-	0	-	0	N/R
Malta	10	10	0	0	4	4	0	10	3	0	10	6	7	4	2	4.1
Oman	10	1	10	10	0	2	4	10	8	10	10	9	10	5	2	6.6
Poland	0	0	10	10	1	0	2	0	5	-	0	5	5	4	0	2.8
Portugal	3	6	0	0	4	2	4	8	3	5	0	9	6	6	5	4.3
Romania	7	3	10	0	6	0	0	10	2	-	0	9	0	1	0	3.1
Russia	7	7	0	0	0	0	0	0	0	0	0	-	0	0	0	0.9
Slovenia	-	-	10	0	2	-	-	-	-	-	0	-	1	-	0	N/R
Syria	3	6	10	0	6	2	-	-	-	-	0	7	0	3	0	3.4 *
Turkey	0	1	10	10	8	4	6	2	7	4	0	7	7	5	0	4.8
Ukraine	-	-	10	0	3	-	0	-	-	-	0	-	0	-	0	N/R
ASIA																
Bangladesh	9	8	0	0	7	6	0	10	-	-	10	1	1	1	0	3.9
China	5	7	10	0	-	0	2	0	-	5	0	6	1	10	5	3.9
Fiji	6	9	0	0	5	6	6	6	10	3	10	4	6	8	2	5.6
Hong Kong	5	7	10	10	9	10	10	10	10	9	10	9	10	10	10	9.3
India	6	9	0	0	7	0	3	8	5	2	10	0	4	3	2	3.7
Indonesia	3	4	10	10	7	2	6	10	9	7	0	8	10	10	2	6.5
Malaysia	9	4	10	10	4	6	5	10	8	6	10	7	10	10	5	7.1
Nepal	2	9	0	0	9	2	2	10	-	-	10	2	4	2	0	3.9
Pakistan	5	8	10	0	6	4	-	6	-	3	10	0	4	4	2	4.3
Philippines	2	6	0	0	9	6	2	8	10	7	10	4	5	10	2	5.8
Singapore	8	7	10	10	5	8	8	10	8	9	0	10	10	10	10	8.3
South Korea	6	2	0	0	7	6	3	10	8	3	0	7	8	5	5	5.0
Sri Lanka	4	5	0	0	9	4	4	8	5	-	10	2	3	5	0	4.3
Taiwan	3	9	10	10	3	6	6	10	6	5	0	8	10	5	5	6.2
Thailand	5	9	10	0	7	6	4	8	10	4	0	6	10	10	2	6.2

	I				II				III			IV				Summary Rating
	A	B	C	D	A	B	C	F	A	B	C	A	B	C	D	
AFRICA																
Algeria	9	2	0	0	3	0	2	-	-	-	0	-	1	7	0	2.1 *
Benin	10	8	0	0	8	4	-	8	-	-	0	-	6	2	0	4.6 *
Botswana	2	2	0	0	0	6	6	4	5	3	10	4	5	10	5	4.2
Burundi	10	3	0	0	5	2	2	4	-	-	10	0	6	1	0	3.3
Cameroon	10	5	0	0	7	4	2	8	8	1	10	6	6	2	0	4.6
C African Rep	10	3	0	0	10	6	2	10	-	-	0	1	6	3	0	4.1
Chad	10	3	0	0	5	4	2	8	10	-	0	6	6	7	0	4.9
Congo Peoples	10	1	0	0	1	0	0	10	-	4	10	-	6	6	0	3.4
Cote d' Ivoire	10	7	0	0	4	4	2	8	-	4	0	1	6	5	0	3.7
Gabon	10	2	0	0	1	6	-	8	10	1	10	6	6	4	0	4.7
Ghana	1	5	0	0	9	2	0	2	8	2	10	1	5	1	0	3.3
Kenya	5	9	0	0	3	4	2	10	8	3	10	4	6	6	0	4.6
Madagascar	2	5	0	0	10	6	4	-	9	-	0	0	5	4	0	4.3
Malawi	1	4	0	0	6	4	2	6	8	3	10	5	4	3	2	4.1
Mali	9	5	0	0	7	4	2	8	10	-	0	6	6	6	2	5.3
Mauritius	2	9	0	0	7	6	4	8	7	7	10	3	5	7	2	5.5
Morocco	6	7	0	0	5	2	0	8	8	0	0	2	4	6	5	3.5
Niger	10	4	0	0	7	6	2	8	-	-	0	-	6	4	0	4.2
Nigeria	2	1	0	0	10	2	4	0	-	2	10	6	3	10	0	3.5
Rwanda	10	6	0	0	7	6	-	10	7	-	10	0	3	0	0	4.7
Senegal	10	7	0	0	7	6	4	8	-	4	0	-	6	3	0	4.5
Sierra Leone	0	0	0	0	10	6	2	0	9	-	10	5	1	1	0	3.9
Somalia	0	0	0	0	-	4	0	0	-	-	0	-	1	3	0	0.8 *
South Africa	2	10	0	0	1	4	4	8	6	5	0	8	6	6	2	4.6
Tanzania	1	2	0	0	9	0	0	4	-	3	0	-	1	10	0	2.3
Togo	10	9	0	0	6	4	2	8	-	-	0	1	6	4	0	4.0
Tunisia	10	9	0	0	4	2	4	8	4	-	0	1	5	8	5	4.3
Uganda	0	0	0	0	10	2	2	0	-	3	10	-	2	1	0	2.5
Zaire	0	1	0	0	8	2	2	0	10	1	10	1	4	10	2	3.6
Zambia	0	1	0	0	3	0	0	0	7	0	10	6	0	10	2	2.5
Zimbabwe	2	4	0	0	1	4	2	8	-	1	0	1	4	7	2	2.4

* These summary ratings should be interpreted with caution because they are based on data for only 11 of the potential 15 components in the index for this year.

Table A1-2: Component and Summary Index Ratings: 1985

	I				II			III			IV				Summary Rating
INDUSTRIAL COUNTRIES	A	B	C	D	A	B	F	A	B	C	A	B	C	D	
United States	7	8	10	10	4	8	10	3	4	10	8	10	2	10	6.7
Canada	4	6	10	10	1	6	10	2	3	10	8	10	9	8	5.9
Australia	9	8	10	10	3	6	10	3	2	10	7	10	6	5	6.0
Japan	9	10	10	0	8	8	10	4	1	10	9	10	3	5	6.3
New Zealand	7	6	0	0	4	4	8	1	0	10	8	6	6	5	4.1
Austria	10	10	10	0	2	2	10	1	2	0	9	10	9	2	4.8
Belgium	10	10	10	10	4	6	10	0	0	0	10	10	10	10	5.9
Denmark	4	8	0	0	0	4	10	1	0	0	10	10	4	5	3.7
Finland	5	9	10	0	1	6	10	2	1	0	9	10	4	2	4.5
France	8	8	0	0	2	4	8	0	1	0	10	6	7	2	3.7
Germany	9	10	10	10	1	6	10	2	2	0	10	10	9	10	6.1
Iceland	0	1	0	0	4	4	4	4	1	10	6	4	4	2	3.1
Ireland	9	5	0	0	3	4	10	1	0	10	8	6	9	5	4.3
Italy	5	6	0	0	4	2	6	0	0	0	10	10	6	5	3.6
Netherlands	9	9	10	10	4	6	10	0	0	0	10	10	10	8	5.6
Norway	3	6	0	0	1	2	10	1	1	0	10	10	8	5	3.8
Spain	7	9	0	0	5	4	10	2	1	0	7	7	5	5	4.2
Sweden	8	10	10	0	0	4	10	0	0	0	9	8	7	5	4.2
Switzerland	10	9	10	10	6	8	10	3	7	0	8	10	8	10	7.4
United Kingdom	5	8	10	10	2	6	10	2	2	10	10	10	7	10	6.2
CENTRAL/SOUTH AMERICA															
Argentina	0	0	10	10	8	6	0	4	2	0	0	2	1	0	2.8
Bahamas	9	7	0	0	6	2	10	10	10	10	1	4	6	2	6.1
Barbados	1	6	0	0	3	4	10	10	1	10	7	4	2	2	4.5
Belize	8	3	0	0	3	8	8	7	4	10	1	1	3	5	4.5
Bolivia	0	0	0	0	7	4	0	9	8	0	4	5	2	2	4.2
Brazil	0	0	0	0	8	2	0	4	1	0	7	2	2	0	2.3
Chile	6	2	10	10	6	6	8	3	1	0	5	4	5	2	4.1
Colombia	2	9	10	0	8	4	-	7	5	0	3	5	1	0	4.6
Costa Rica	1	1	10	10	4	6	6	5	3	10	4	3	3	5	4.5
Dominican Rep	3	2	0	10	10	6	-	8	0	10	4	4	3	2	4.5
Ecuador	1	2	10	10	7	4	0	7	2	0	5	2	3	2	3.8
El Salvador	7	5	0	0	7	6	8	9	3	0	3	1	1	2	4.3
Guatemala	6	4	10	10	10	8	8	10	5	0	3	1	0	5	5.8
Haiti	6	6	10	10	8	6	-	5	-	10	2	2	1	0	5.0
Honduras	9	10	10	10	7	6	10	8	5	0	-	1	2	0	5.8
Jamaica	3	2	0	0	5	2	4	10	1	10	8	4	8	2	4.4
Mexico	0	1	10	10	9	2	4	6	4	0	7	3	3	2	4.3
Nicaragua	0	0	0	0	0	0	-	5	5	0	3	0	1	0	1.8
Panama	10	9	10	10	2	4	-	6	3	10	6	10	3	8	6.3
Paraguay	4	3	10	10	10	6	-	9	8	0	8	0	4	5	6.3
Peru	0	0	0	0	8	4	-	9	0	0	2	2	4	2	2.9
Trinidad/Tobago	7	1	0	0	1	4	8	3	4	10	5	2	1	0	3.3
Uruguay	1	1	10	10	6	6	8	4	10	10	5	10	1	10	6.6
Venezuela	4	4	10	10	7	4	4	7	7	0	1	3	4	5	5.1

EUROPE-MIDDLE EAST	I				II			III			IV				Summary Rating
	A	B	C	D	A	B	F	A	B	C	A	B	C	D	
Albania	-	-	0	0	-	0	-	-	-	0	-	0	-	0	N/R
Bahrain	8	2	10	10	0	2	-	10	10	10	9	10	6	2	7.0
Bulgaria	-	7	0	0	9	0	-	2	-	0	6	0	6	0	2.9
Cyprus	5	7	0	0	5	6	8	4	1	0	6	8	4	0	3.9
Czechoslovakia	10	8	0	0	1	0	-	-	-	0	-	0	7	0	N/R
Czech Rep	-	-	-	-	-	-	-	-	-	-	-	-	-	-	N/R
Slovakia	-	-	-	-	-	-	-	-	-	-	-	-	-	-	N/R
Egypt	3	6	10	10	5	0	6	3	2	0	1	1	9	0	3.2
Greece	2	8	10	0	3	2	6	2	1	0	9	3	3	2	3.3
Hungary	8	10	0	0	8	0	-	0	-	0	6	0	10	0	3.3
Iran	2	3	10	10	5	2	-	8	0	0	0	0	0	0	2.7
Israel	0	0	10	0	0	2	0	1	3	0	7	5	5	2	2.5
Jordan	8	4	10	0	3	6	-	6	-	10	5	6	9	2	5.6
Malta	10	6	0	0	5	4	10	3	0	10	6	5	4	2	4.1
Oman	3	5	10	10	0	2	10	8	10	10	9	10	6	2	6.8
Poland	2	0	10	0	2	0	-	0	-	0	2	0	3	0	1.2
Portugal	4	7	0	0	5	2	10	2	0	0	9	7	7	2	3.6
Romania	8	5	0	0	10	0	-	5	-	0	-	0	2	0	3.2
Russia	7	9	0	0	0	0	0	0	0	0	-	0	1	0	1.1
Syria	2	4	10	10	1	2	-	-	-	0	6	0	1	0	2.8
Turkey	1	2	0	0	9	4	8	4	2	0	7	6	6	0	3.7
ASIA															
Bangladesh	2	7	0	0	10	6	6	-	1	10	0	1	1	0	3.2
China	2	6	0	0	-	0	0	-	6	0	1	4	8	2	2.7
Fiji	8	5	0	0	3	6	8	7	3	10	3	5	5	5	4.9
Hong Kong	6	7	10	10	9	10	10	10	9	10	9	10	10	10	9.3
India	4	10	0	0	7	0	8	5	0	10	0	4	2	2	3.4
Indonesia	3	7	10	10	7	2	-	8	7	0	8	5	9	2	6.0
Malaysia	10	7	10	0	3	4	10	7	6	10	5	10	10	5	6.7
Nepal	5	8	0	0	9	2	6	-	-	10	3	4	2	0	4.2
Pakistan	6	8	0	0	8	2	8	10	1	10	0	6	4	2	4.7
Philippines	6	1	0	0	10	4	4	10	1	10	5	5	8	2	4.9
Singapore	8	7	10	0	3	8	10	9	8	0	9	10	10	10	7.7
South Korea	4	5	0	0	7	6	10	8	2	0	7	4	8	2	4.8
Sri Lanka	4	3	0	0	9	2	8	6	0	10	1	4	5	0	3.5
Taiwan	9	5	10	10	3	4	10	7	3	0	7	6	7	2	5.4
Thailand	10	8	0	0	5	6	10	10	2	0	4	6	7	2	5.3

210

	I				II			III			IV				Summary Rating
	A	B	C	D	A	B	F	A	B	C	A	B	C	D	
AFRICA															
Algeria	2	5	0	0	2	0	-	-	-	0	-	0	6	0	1.5 *
Benin	5	3	0	0	7	4	8	-	-	0	-	8	5	0	4.0
Botswana	3	2	0	0	0	8	8	5	2	10	3	4	10	5	4.1
Burundi	6	3	0	0	6	2	6	-	-	10	0	3	0	0	2.9
Cameroon	4	9	0	0	8	4	6	10	2	10	5	8	5	0	5.3
C African Rep	7	3	0	0	8	6	8	-	-	0	-	8	7	0	4.7
Chad	2	2	0	0	8	4	8	-	-	0	-	8	8	0	3.9
Congo Peoples	3	2	0	0	3	0	8	-	-	10	-	8	10	0	3.8
Cote d' Ivoire	9	5	0	0	5	4	10	-	5	0	1	8	8	0	4.4
Gabon	5	6	0	0	0	6	8	-	-	10	4	8	7	0	4.5
Ghana	1	0	0	0	10	0	0	9	1	10	0	1	0	0	2.7
Kenya	7	10	0	0	3	4	10	6	0	10	3	7	5	0	4.3
Madagascar	7	3	0	0	10	6	-	-	-	0	-	5	2	0	3.9 *
Malawi	6	7	0	0	4	4	8	8	3	10	2	3	3	2	4.4
Mali	5	5	0	0	9	4	6	8	-	0	6	8	9	2	5.4
Mauritius	10	9	0	0	7	6	10	6	7	10	1	8	5	2	6.0
Morocco	6	10	0	0	5	2	6	7	0	0	4	5	8	5	4.2
Niger	10	4	0	0	7	4	-	-	-	0	-	8	7	0	4.5 *
Nigeria	9	3	0	0	9	2	4	9	3	10	6	0	3	0	4.5
Rwanda	10	4	0	0	9	6	8	-	-	10	-	2	0	0	4.7
Senegal	9	9	0	0	6	4	6	-	1	0	2	8	5	0	3.8
Sierra Leone	1	1	0	0	10	6	0	10	-	10	1	1	0	0	3.9
Somalia	1	1	0	0	8	4	0	-	-	0	-	1	0	0	1.8
South Africa	1	9	0	0	2	4	8	6	4	0	9	3	9	2	4.4
Tanzania	5	4	0	0	6	0	0	6	0	0	4	0	0	0	2.1
Togo	8	4	0	0	7	4	8	-	-	0	2	8	8	0	4.3
Tunisia	3	6	0	0	4	0	6	5	2	0	0	4	6	0	2.7
Uganda	0	0	0	0	9	2	0	-	0	10	1	3	0	0	1.8
Zaire	0	1	0	0	10	2	-	-	1	10	2	6	0	2	3.3
Zambia	2	2	0	0	1	0	0	7	0	10	4	2	10	2	2.8
Zimbabwe	8	4	0	0	1	4	8	4	0	0	2	2	7	2	2.8

N/R = No rating given because data were available for less than 10 of the components of the index.

* These summary ratings should be interpreted with caution because they are based on data for only 10 of the potential 14 components in the index for this year.

Table A1-3: Component and Summary Index Ratings: 1980

	I				II			III			IV				Summary Rating
INDUSTRIAL COUNTRIES	A	B	C	D	A	B	F	A	B	C	A	B	C	D	
United States	9	9	10	10	4	8	10	4	0	10	9	10	3	10	6.5
Canada	9	9	10	10	2	6	10	3	4	10	8	10	9	8	6.7
Australia	6	9	10	10	3	6	10	4	2	10	7	8	4	2	5.6
Japan	9	9	10	0	7	8	10	4	0	10	9	10	3	2	5.8
New Zealand	8	9	0	0	3	4	6	1	2	10	8	10	5	5	4.7
Austria	10	10	10	0	2	2	8	1	2	0	9	10	8	2	4.7
Belgium	10	9	10	10	4	6	10	0	0	0	10	10	10	10	5.8
Denmark	7	10	0	0	0	4	10	1	0	0	10	7	3	5	3.8
Finland	7	9	10	0	2	6	8	3	1	0	9	8	4	2	4.6
France	5	10	0	0	3	2	8	0	3	0	10	6	5	2	3.8
Germany	8	10	10	10	1	6	10	2	3	0	10	10	7	8	6.0
Iceland	1	3	0	0	3	4	4	4	0	10	4	5	2	2	2.9
Ireland	3	6	0	0	4	4	6	2	1	10	7	10	8	5	4.4
Italy	1	8	0	0	5	2	4	1	0	0	10	10	5	5	3.6
Netherlands	9	9	10	10	3	6	10	0	0	0	10	10	9	8	5.5
Norway	9	7	0	0	1	2	6	1	0	0	9	6	7	2	3.3
Spain	3	6	0	0	6	4	6	3	1	0	7	10	2	5	3.9
Sweden	6	9	10	0	0	4	8	0	0	0	9	6	5	2	3.5
Switzerland	9	10	10	10	6	8	6	3	7	0	8	10	7	10	7.2
United Kingdom	6	7	0	0	1	4	4	2	0	10	10	10	5	10	4.6
CENTRAL/- SOUTH AMERICA															
Argentina	0	0	10	10	6	6	0	4	6	0	1	8	0	0	3.8
Bahamas	6	6	0	0	6	4	8	10	10	10	2	4	5	2	6.0
Barbados	3	2	0	0	4	4	6	10	1	10	6	4	2	2	4.1
Belize	3	6	0	0	5	8	8	8	-	10	2	3	3	5	5.1
Bolivia	1	2	10	10	6	4	6	9	3	0	3	4	3	2	4.4
Brazil	1	1	0	0	9	4	-	3	4	0	1	4	2	0	2.7
Chile	0	0	10	0	7	4	8	4	2	0	7	6	4	2	3.8
Colombia	1	5	0	0	9	4	-	8	2	0	3	4	2	0	3.6
Costa Rica	2	5	10	10	4	6	-	5	5	10	6	1	2	2	4.8
Dominican Rep	6	5	0	10	10	6	-	9	0	10	1	2	1	2	4.5
Ecuador	1	5	10	10	5	6	-	6	5	0	3	4	3	2	4.5
El Salvador	3	3	0	0	6	4	-	8	3	0	4	1	2	2	3.5
Guatemala	3	6	10	10	10	8	8	10	8	0	6	4	1	5	6.8
Haiti	2	2	10	10	9	6	-	-	-	10	1	4	1	0	4.5
Honduras	2	7	10	10	7	6	-	-	8	10	4	4	5	0	5.9
Jamaica	2	4	0	0	2	2	4	-	0	10	9	2	5	2	3.0
Mexico	1	5	10	10	8	2	4	7	4	0	0	1	1	2	3.8
Nicaragua	1	1	10	10	5	6	-	7	5	0	2	1	3	0	3.9
Panama	4	7	10	10	2	6	-	6	3	10	7	10	3	8	6.0
Paraguay	1	4	10	10	10	6	-	9	-	0	5	5	2	5	5.9
Peru	1	1	0	0	7	4	-	9	2	0	1	4	4	2	3.3
Trinidad/Tobago	1	2	0	0	4	4	-	5	-	10	7	2	2	0	3.4
Uruguay	0	2	10	10	7	6	6	4	10	10	2	10	0	10	6.3
Venezuela	3	3	10	10	6	4	-	9	7	0	7	10	5	8	6.6

Table A1-3: 1980 (con't)

EUROPE/- MIDDLE EAST	I				II			III			IV				Summary Rate
	A	B	C	D	A	B	F	A	B	C	A	B	C	D	
Albania	-	-	0	0	-	0	-	-	-	0	-	0	-	0	N/R
Bahrain	2	7	10	10	1	2	-	-	10	10	-	10	8	2	6.4
Bulgaria	-	-	0	0	10	0	-	-	-	0	-	1	3	0	N/R
Cyprus	2	8	0	0	6	6	4	5	1	0	6	6	3	0	3.6
Czechoslovakia	-	-	0	0	1	0	-	-	-	0	-	0	-	0	N/R
Czech Rep	-	-	-	-	-	-	-	-	-	-	-	-	-	-	N/R
Slovakia	-	-	-	-	-	-	-	-	-	-	-	-	-	-	N/R
Egypt	1	5	10	10	5	0	4	2	0	0	0	5	10	0	2.7
Greece	2	8	10	0	4	2	6	3	3	0	7	5	2	2	3.8
Hungary	7	6	0	0	7	0	6	-	-	0	6	0	9	0	3.5
Iran	1	3	10	10	1	2	-	5	-	0	0	1	2	0	2.5
Israel	0	0	10	0	0	2	0	1	1	0	6	8	4	2	2.2
Jordan	1	7	10	0	1	6	-	5	-	10	4	10	10	2	5.3
Malta	3	7	-	-	5	4	6	3	0	10	6	4	5	2	3.9
Oman	3	1	10	10	0	2	-	-	10	10	-	10	6	2	5.8
Poland	-	9	10	0	9	0	-	-	-	0	-	0	7	0	N/R
Portugal	3	6	0	0	6	2	4	2	0	0	8	7	5	2	3.2
Romania	6	7	0	0	10	0	-	3	-	0	-	0	6	0	3.1
Russia	6	9	0	0	1	0	0	0	0	0	-	0	-	0	1.2
Syria	1	6	10	10	2	4	-	-	-	0	3	2	3	0	3.2
Turkey	1	1	0	0	7	4	0	5	0	0	4	4	0	0	2.3
ASIA															
Bangladesh	2	1	0	0	10	6	6	-	1	10	0	1	1	0	2.8
China	2	10	0	0	-	0	0	-	-	0	5	3	1	0	2.3
Fiji	10	4	0	0	4	6	6	8	2	10	5	4	5	5	5.0
Hong Kong	6	4	10	10	10	10	10	10	10	10	9	10	9	10	9.3
India	6	5	0	0	9	0	8	6	1	10	0	6	2	2	3.8
Indonesia	1	2	10	10	6	2	2	7	3	0	7	7	10	2	4.7
Malaysia	7	6	10	10	2	4	6	6	2	10	3	10	10	5	5.6
Nepal	3	4	0	0	10	2	6	-	-	10	2	10	1	0	4.2
Pakistan	1	9	0	0	9	2	6	-	2	10	0	3	4	2	3.5
Philippines	2	7	0	0	9	4	8	10	1	0	4	6	8	2	4.7
Singapore	6	6	0	0	7	8	10	10	4	0	9	10	10	8	6.8
South Korea	1	6	0	0	7	6	4	9	0	0	6	4	8	0	4.0
Sri Lanka	1	6	0	0	10	2	4	4	0	10	1	5	9	0	3.4
Taiwan	3	5	10	10	3	4	8	8	3	0	7	8	7	2	5.3
Thailand	3	7	0	0	7	6	4	10	3	0	4	6	7	2	4.9

213

Table A1-3: 1980 (con't)

AFRICA	I A	I B	I C	I D	II A	II B	II F	III A	III B	III C	IV A	IV B	IV C	IV D	Summary Rate	
Algeria	1	4	0	0	2	0	-	-	-	0	-	0	9	0	1.5	*
Benin	7	7	0	0	10	4	6	-	-	-	1	7	3	0	4.4	
Botswana	6	2	0	0	1	8	4	6	0	10	0	4	10	5	3.7	
Burundi	1	3	0	-	6	2	2	-	-	10	0	2	0	0	2.3	
Cameroon	1	9	0	0	9	4	6	10	-	10	1	7	3	0	5.2	
C African Rep	1	3	0	0	8	6	-	-	-	0	1	7	6	0	3.3	
Chad	6	10	0	0	1	4	-	-	-	10	-	7	8	0	4.7	*
Congo Peoples Rep	4	3	0	0	1	0	6	-	-	10	6	7	9	0	3.7	
Cote d' Ivoire	2	2	0	0	4	4	8	7	5	10	0	7	7	0	4.2	
Gabon	7	2	0	0	0	6	6	-	-	10	3	7	5	0	3.8	
Ghana	1	1	0	0	9	0	0	8	1	10	0	0	0	0	2.5	
Kenya	3	3	0	0	2	4	8	8	1	10	5	4	7	0	3.9	
Madagascar	3	7	0	0	9	6	-	-	-	0	2	2	4	0	3.4	
Malawi	9	4	0	0	4	4	4	9	4	10	4	2	3	2	4.6	
Mali	5	10	0	0	10	4	4	8	-	10	6	6	5	2	5.9	
Mauritius	6	3	0	0	7	6	-	5	3	10	1	2	5	2	3.9	
Morocco	4	5	0	0	4	4	-	7	2	0	1	8	4	2	3.6	
Niger	1	6	0	0	8	4	2	8	-	0	2	7	9	0	4.3	
Nigeria	1	9	0	0	8	2	2	-	0	10	2	1	7	0	2.9	
Rwanda	2	6	0	0	8	6	6	10	-	10	0	1	1	0	4.4	
Senegal	5	7	0	0	4	4	8	-	-	0	1	7	5	0	3.6	
Sierra Leone	2	5	0	0	10	6	6	-	-	10	0	1	3	0	3.6	
Somalia	1	0	0	0	8	4	0	-	-	10	1	2	10	0	3.0	
South Africa	5	4	0	0	3	4	4	8	2	0	9	6	9	2	4.4	
Tanzania	1	4	0	0	7	2	4	10	-	10	3	0	3	0	4.0	
Togo	2	2	0	0	5	4	8	-	-	0	0	7	7	0	3.0	
Tunisia	4	6	0	0	5	0	4	6	2	0	1	4	7	0	3.0	
Uganda	1	0	0	0	-	2	0	-	-	10	7	0	4	0	2.2	
Zaire	1	1	0	0	10	2	-	10	1	10	1	1	3	2	3.6	
Zambia	7	5	0	0	0	0	4	4	0	10	8	1	10	2	3.2	
Zimbabwe	6	7	0	0	3	4	6	4	5	0	8	1	7	2	4.1	

N/R = No rating given because data were available for less than 10 of the components of the index.

* These summary ratings should be interpreted with caution because they are based on ratings for only 10 of the 14 components in the index for this year.

Table A1-4: Component and Summary Index Ratings: 1975

INDUSTRIAL COUNTRIES	I				II			III			IV				Summary Rating
	A	B	C	D	A	B	F	A	B	C	A	B	C	D	
United States	9	8	10	10	3	8	8	4	0	10	8	10	2	10	6.1
Canada	6	5	10	10	2	6	6	4	4	10	6	10	8	8	6.0
Australia	6	5	10	10	3	6	4	4	2	10	6	8	4	2	5.0
Japan	2	4	10	0	7	8	4	5	1	10	9	10	3	2	5.1
New Zealand	4	6	0	0	5	4	-	1	3	10	8	6	5	5	4.2
Austria	6	10	10	0	3	2	6	2	4	0	8	10	7	2	4.8
Belgium	6	7	10	10	4	6	6	0	2	0	10	10	10	10	5.6
Denmark	6	9	0	0	0	4	8	2	1	0	9	8	3	5	3.9
Finland	1	4	10	0	3	6	-	3	2	0	8	8	4	2	3.9
France	6	7	0	0	4	2	8	1	5	0	10	10	4	2	4.4
Germany	6	10	10	10	1	6	8	2	4	0	10	10	6	8	5.9
Iceland	1	2	0	0	4	4	2	4	-	10	2	1	4	2	2.9
Ireland	6	5	0	0	4	4	4	2	0	10	6	10	6	5	4.1
Italy	3	4	0	0	5	2	6	2	5	0	10	5	5	5	4.1
Netherlands	5	10	10	10	3	6	6	0	5	0	9	10	9	5	5.6
Norway	5	9	0	0	1	2	-	1	0	0	9	8	9	2	3.3
Spain	1	6	0	0	8	4	-	4	4	0	5	7	3	2	3.9
Sweden	6	7	10	0	0	4	4	0	1	0	9	8	5	2	3.5
Switzerland	10	10	10	10	6	8	6	-	7	0	7	10	5	2	7.0
United Kingdom	6	3	0	0	1	4	4	3	7	10	10	10	7	2	5.1

CENTRAL/SOUTH AMERICA

	A	B	C	D	A	B	F	A	B	C	A	B	C	D	
Argentina	0	0	10	10	6	6	-	5	4	0	0	1	0	0	3.1
Bahamas	10	6	0	0	6	6	8	10	10	10	2	4	6	2	6.5
Barbados	6	3	0	0	5	4	-	10	1	10	6	4	2	2	4.4
Belize	-	2	-	-	6	8	-	-	-	-	-	3	7	-	N/R
Bolivia	1	1	10	10	7	4	-	10	-	0	2	6	8	2	5.2
Brazil	1	3	0	0	8	4	-	-	5	0	5	2	2	0	3.2
Chile	0	0	0	0	5	4	-	4	0	0	6	6	5	2	2.7
Colombia	1	4	0	0	9	6	-	8	6	0	3	3	2	0	4.2
Costa Rica	1	2	10	10	6	6	-	-	5	10	5	5	3	2	5.0
Dominican Rep	3	3	0	0	10	6	-	8	0	0	0	3	3	2	3.3
Ecuador	1	1	10	10	5	6	-	-	5	0	2	6	5	2	4.2
El Salvador	2	5	0	0	8	4	-	8	4	-	4	4	4	2	4.4
Guatemala	3	3	0	10	10	8	-	10	9	0	6	4	2	5	6.4
Haiti	3	4	10	0	10	6	-	-	-	10	1	10	0	0	5.0
Honduras	6	4	10	10	8	6	-	10	9	-	6	10	4	0	7.2
Jamaica	2	2	0	0	4	2	-	5	2	10	6	4	3	2	3.3
Mexico	2	3	10	10	9	2	-	7	5	0	3	10	0	2	4.9
Nicaragua	6	2	10	10	9	6	-	8	10	0	6	4	4	5	6.6
Panama	6	6	10	10	2	6	-	7	4	10	7	10	4	8	6.4
Paraguay	2	3	10	10	10	6	-	9	-	0	2	4	1	5	5.4
Peru	1	4	0	0	7	6	-	9	4	0	1	2	3	2	3.8
Trinidad/Tobago	1	1	0	0	3	4	-	-	-	10	7	2	3	0	3.0
Uruguay	0	0	10	10	6	6	-	4	7	10	7	10	1	8	5.9
Venezuela	1	1	10	10	5	6	-	8	10	0	6	10	6	8	6.7

Table 1-4: 1975 (con't)

EUROPE/-MIDDLE EAST	I				II			III			IV				Summary Rating
	A	B	C	D	A	B	F	A	B	C	A	B	C	D	
Albania	-	-	0	0	-	0	-	-	-	0	-	0	-	0	N/R
Bahrain	7	3	10	10	-	2	-	-	10	10	-	10	9	2	7.2 *
Bulgaria	-	-	0	0	-	0	-	-	-	0	-	1	-	0	N/R
Cyprus	9	7	0	0	6	6	8	4	3	-	7	6	3	0	4.6
Czechoslovakia	-	-	0	0	1	0	-	-	-	0	-	0	-	0	N/R
Egypt	3	6	0	0	1	0	-	0	-	0	0	8	10	0	2.1
Greece	2	3	10	0	5	2	4	3	4	0	7	6	2	2	3.7
Hungary	-	7	0	0	7	0	-	-	-	0	-	0	10	0	N/R
Iran	1	1	10	0	0	4	-	4	8	0	7	7	10	5	4.7
Israel	1	2	10	0	0	2	-	-	-	0	2	2	4	2	2.0
Jordan	3	4	0	0	1	6	-	-	-	10	4	8	10	2	4.4
Malta	3	8	-	-	4	4	-	3	-	-	6	6	5	2	N/R
Oman	0	0	10	10	0	2	-	-	10	10	-	10	9	2	5.6
Poland	-	8	10	0	7	0	-	-	-	0	-	0	-	0	N/R
Portugal	3	4	0	0	6	2	-	3	0	0	6	2	3	2	2.5
Romania	-	10	0	0	-	0	-	-	-	0	-	0	-	0	N/R
Russia	7	10	0	0	0	0	0	0	0	0	-	0	-	0	1.2
Syria	1	2	10	10	2	6	-	-	-	0	2	8	4	0	3.7
Turkey	1	5	0	0	7	4	2	5	1	0	0	4	1	0	2.5
Ukraine	-	-	0	0	-	-	-	-	-	-	-	0	-	0	N/R
ASIA															
Bangladesh	6	1	0	0	10	6	-	-	-	10	3	2	0	0	3.7
China	-	-	0	0	-	0	-	-	-	0	-	3	-	0	N/R
Fiji	2	2	0	0	7	6	0	9	3	10	4	4	4	5	4.5
Hong Kong	5	5	10	10	10	10	10	10	10	10	9	10	9	10	9.3
India	6	3	0	0	9	0	4	7	0	10	0	5	1	2	3.3
Indonesia	1	1	10	10	9	4	2	9	4	0	6	5	9	2	5.2
Malaysia	7	2	0	10	3	6	-	5	4	10	4	10	10	5	5.4
Nepal	5	2	0	0	10	2	-	-	-	10	2	2	0	0	3.1
Pakistan	6	2	0	0	9	2	-	-	1	0	0	4	4	2	2.6
Philippines	2	2	0	0	7	4	8	10	3	0	0	4	9	2	4.1
Singapore	5	5	0	0	7	8	-	9	4	0	9	10	10	8	6.4
South Korea	1	3	0	0	8	6	2	9	2	0	7	7	7	0	4.4
Sri Lanka	8	3	0	0	10	2	-	4	-	10	1	1	6	0	3.7
Taiwan	2	2	10	10	4	4	8	8	3	0	6	6	5	2	4.8
Thailand	6	2	0	0	8	6	-	10	3	0	4	7	5	2	4.8

Table 1-4: 1975 (con't)

	I				II			III			IV				Summary Rating	
	A	B	C	D	A	B	F	A	B	C	A	B	C	D		
AFRICA																
Algeria	1	1	0	0	5	0	-	-	-	10	-	2	10	0	2.6	*
Benin	1	4	0	0	10	4	-	-	-	-	1	7	3	0	3.4	*
Botswana	-	3	0	0	3	8	-	6	0	10	1	2	10	-	3.6	
Burundi	7	1	-	-	7	2	-	-	-	10	1	2	0	0	N/R	
Cameroon	6	4	0	0	8	4	-	9	-	10	0	7	3	0	4.8	
C African Rep	7	3	0	0	6	6	-	-	-	-	-	7	7	0	N/R	
Chad	6	9	0	0	1	4	-	-	-	10	1	7	8	0	4.1	
Congo Peoples Rep	6	10	0	0	4	0	-	-	-	10	6	7	8	0	4.7	
Cote d' Ivoire	3	2	0	0	4	4	-	-	-	10	-	7	7	0	3.8	*
Gabon	1	1	0	0	0	6	-	-	-	10	2	7	6	0	3.0	
Ghana	1	2	0	0	7	0	-	8	0	10	0	1	2	0	2.5	
Kenya	5	2	0	0	4	4	4	-	0	10	6	5	8	0	3.3	
Madagascar	7	3	-	0	9	6	-	-	-	-	0	3	3	0	N/R	
Malawi	2	4	0	0	6	4	-	10	0	10	6	3	6	2	4.2	
Mali	2	4	0	0	10	4	-	8	-	10	0	5	4	2	4.6	
Mauritius	1	1	0	0	7	6	-	5	-	10	4	2	5	2	3.9	
Morocco	2	2	0	0	5	4	-	5	8	0	3	6	7	2	4.2	
Niger	2	1	0	0	9	4	-	-	-	10	4	7	7	0	4.2	
Nigeria	1	1	0	0	8	4	2	8	0	10	4	2	6	0	3.4	
Rwanda	3	1	-	0	6	6	-	10	-	10	0	2	0	0	4.1	
Senegal	3	4	0	0	6	4	-	9	-	-	2	7	7	0	4.5	
Sierra Leone	3	3	0	0	9	6	-	9	-	10	1	2	3	0	4.4	
Somalia	3	5	0	0	4	4	4	-	-	10	0	3	2	0	2.9	
South Africa	5	5	0	0	5	4	-	-	1	0	8	6	9	2	3.8	
Tanzania	1	4	0	0	5	2	-	10	0	10	3	1	7	0	3.4	
Togo	2	1	0	0	6	4	-	-	-	-	3	7	7	0	3.3	*
Tunisia	2	3	0	0	5	0	-	9	-	0	1	4	5	0	3.1	
Uganda	1	1	0	0	-	2	-	-	-	10	0	0	0	0	1.2	
Zaire	2	5	0	0	8	2	-	10	2	10	0	1	2	2	3.8	
Zambia	6	2	0	0	0	0	4	5	0	10	7	1	10	2	3.0	
Zimbabwe	-	7	0	0	6	4	-	-	-	-	8	2	8	-	N/R	

N/R= No rating given because data were available for less than 10 of the components of the index.

* These summary ratings should be interpreted with caution because they are based on ratings for only 10 of the 14 components in the index for this year.

217

APPENDIX II

The Underlying Data and Country Ratings for Each of the 17 Components in the Index

LIST OF TABLES

Table I-A: The Expansion in the Money Supply (M1) Minus the Annual Growth Rate of Potential Real GDP: 1971-75, 1976-80, 1981-85, 1986-90, and 1991-95

INDUSTRIAL COUNTRIES	Annual Growth Rate of the Money Supply (M1) Minus Annual Growth Rate of Potential Real GDP (The rating of each country is in parenthesis)									
	1971-75		1976-80		1981-85		1986-90		1991-95	
United States	5.7	(9)	6.8	(9)	8.4	(7)	4.5	(10)	3.2	(10)
Canada	10.4	(6)	5.4	(9)	14.2	(4)	5.5	(9)	4.7	(9)
Australia	11.8	(6)	11.4	(6)	5.9	(9)	13.5	(5)	9.4	(7)
Japan	17.6	(2)	6.4	(9)	4.6	(9)	3.9	(10)	3.3	(10)
New Zealand	14.3	(4)	7.3	(8)	10.0	(7)	41.6	(1)	5.3	(9)
Austria	12.1	(6)	4.5	(10)	4.4	(10)	4.9	(9)	7.0	(8)
Belgium	11.0	(6)	4.5	(10)	3.5	(10)	3.3	(10)	3.8	(10)
Denmark	12.2	(6)	8.8	(7)	14.7	(4)	8.6	(7)	1.8	(10)
Finland	22.4	(1)	8.6	(7)	12.8	(5)	8.2	(7)	6.8	(8)
France	12.4	(6)	13.4	(5)	8.0	(8)	3.7	(10)	-0.5	(10)
Germany	10.5	(6)	7.0	(8)	5.1	(9)	10.2	(7)	4.8	(9)
Iceland	28.6	(1)	43.0	(1)	45.8	(0)	28.2	(1)	7.8	(8)
Ireland	12.0	(6)	17.2	(3)	6.0	(9)	5.6	(9)	4.9	(9)
Italy	16.9	(3)	20.7	(1)	12.5	(5)	7.7	(8)	1.9	(10)
Netherlands	12.8	(5)	6.5	(9)	6.5	(9)	4.9	(9)	4.5	(10)
Norway	13.8	(5)	5.7	(9)	16.2	(3)	18.7	(2)	6.8	(9)
Spain	21.1	(1)	15.7	(3)	9.7	(7)	16.7	(3)	1.2	(10)
Sweden	11.4	(6)	11.6	(6)	7.2	(8)	7.0	(8)	3.1	(10)
Switzerland	4.3	(10)	6.2	(9)	1.2	(10)	1.3	(10)	2.0	(10)
United Kingdom	12.2	(6)	11.9	(6)	12.5	(5)	28.9	(1)	5.4	(9)
CENTRAL/SOUTH AMERICA										
Argentina	78.2	(0)	146.0	(0)	296.1	(0)	514.4	(0)	52.5	(0)
Bahamas	-4.0	(10)	10.6	(6)	5.9	(9)	6.0	(9)	2.8	(10)
Barbados	10.6	(6)	16.4	(3)	21.3	(1)	18.5	(2)	-5.0	(9)
Belize	-		16.2	(3)	7.0	(8)	8.1	(7)	1.0	(10)
Bolivia	26.3	(1)	25.2	(1)	570.0	(0)	37.3	(1)	28.5	(1)
Brazil	28.9	(1)	41.6	(1)	137.8	(0)	647.7	(0)	1111.6	(0)
Chile	213.3	(0)	95.6	(0)	10.6	(6)	25.2	(1)	19.9	(2)
Colombia	20.9	(1)	28.9	(1)	20.4	(2)	28.9	(1)	26.2	(1)
Costa Rica	23.1	(1)	20.5	(2)	34.8	(1)	13.2	(5)	13.4	(5)
Dominican Republic	16.6	(3)	10.6	(6)	17.4	(3)	38.2	(1)	17.3	(3)
Ecuador	24.8	(1)	23.5	(1)	23.0	(1)	40.0	(1)	34.5	(1)
El Salvador	18.4	(2)	16.9	(3)	9.8	(7)	11.5	(6)	12.3	(6)
Guatemala	16.0	(3)	16.3	(3)	12.4	(6)	17.8	(2)	15.5	(3)
Haiti	16.7	(3)	18.6	(2)	10.9	(6)	8.2	(7)	24.0	(1)
Honduras	10.6	(6)	18.0	(2)	6.6	(9)	16.6	(3)	16.3	(3)
Jamaica	20.0	(2)	17.5	(2)	16.7	(3)	19.4	(2)	49.4	(0)
Mexico	17.5	(2)	30.9	(1)	48.4	(0)	68.1	(0)	40.5	(1)

220

Table I-A: Money Supply (continued)

Annual Growth Rate of the Money Supply (M1) Minus Annual Growth Rate of Potential Real GDP

(The rating of each country is in parenthesis)

CENTRAL/- S. AMERICA	1971-75		1976-80		1981-85		1986-90		1991-95	
Nicaragua	12.3	(6)	26.6	(1)	62.0	(0)	2072.0	(0)	280.2	(0)
Panama	10.5	(6)	14.2	(4)	3.6	(10)	1.8	(10)	8.7	(7)
Paraguay	19.4	(2)	28.2	(1)	14.6	(4)	32.9	(1)	22.3	(1)
Peru	24.1	(1)	42.2	(1)	99.3	(0)	690.3	(0)	64.2	(0)
Trinidad & Tobago	22.0	(1)	29.2	(1)	9.4	(7)	3.8	(10)	16.6	(3)
Uruguay	64.0	(0)	61.4	(0)	38.2	(1)	73.9	(0)	54.6	(0)
Venezuela	30.0	(1)	16.2	(3)	14.0	(4)	19.4	(2)	43.1	(1)

EUROPE/MIDDLE EAST

	1971-75		1976-80		1981-85		1986-90		1991-95	
Albania	-		-		-		-		78.9	(0)
Bahrain	9.3	(7)	18.1	(2)	7.7	(8)	-1.7	(10)	-0.5	(10)
Bulgaria	-		-		-		13.1	(5)	67.0	(0)
Croatia	-		-		-		-		62.4	(0)
Cyprus	6.4	(9)	19.0	(2)	12.7	(5)	5.1	(9)	1.7	(10)
Czechoslovakia	-		-		3.0	(10)	0.4	(10)	-	
Czech Republic	-		-		-		-		20.0	(2)
Slovakia	-		-		-		-		13.4	(5)
Egypt	16.8	(3)	28.9	(1)	16.1	(3)	10.8	(6)	7.0	(8)
Estonia	-		-		-		-		83.3	(0) a
Greece	19.0	(2)	18.5	(2)	18.9	(2)	19.2	(2)	14.0	(4)
Hungary	-		8.7	(7)	6.7	(8)	13.2	(5)	15.0	(3)
Iran	26.6	(1)	37.4	(1)	20.3	(2)	15.3	(3)	26.6	(1)
Israel	24.7	(1)	45.6	(0)	172.3	(0)	44.1	(1)	13.6	(5)
Jordan	14.9	(3)	20.7	(1)	7.3	(8)	11.3	(6)	1.3	(10)
Latvia	-		-		-		-		49.5	(0)
Lithuania	-		-		-		-		53.0	(0) b
Malta	16.0	(3)	15.8	(3)	4.2	(10)	0.7	(10)	2.0	(10)
Oman	55.8	(0)	16.5	(3)	16.6	(3)	-3.0	(10)	-2.7	(10)
Poland	-		-		20.5	(2)	110.5	(0)	31.5	(1)
Portugal	17.4	(3)	17.2	(3)	14.7	(4)	17.4	(3)	9.4	(7)
Romania	-		11.2	(6)	7.7	(8)	8.9	(7)	100.7	(0)
Russia	8.3	(7)	10.6	(6)	9.6	(7)	9.7	(7)	401.4	(0)
Slovenia	-		-		-		-		57.5	(0) a
Syria	23.0	(1)	26.1	(1)	19.7	(2)	16.0	(3)	16.8	(3)
Turkey	26.0	(1)	44.3	(1)	35.0	(1)	51.3	(0)	61.7	(0)
Ukraine	-		-		-		-		690.0	(0) a

ASIA

	1971-75		1976-80		1981-85		1986-90		1991-95	
Bangladesh	10.9	(6)	19.0	(2)	17.5	(2)	5.4	(9)	11.4	(6)
China	-		20.0	(2)	20.3	(2)	13.8	(5)	16.2	(3)
Fiji	18.1	(2)	2.9	(10)	6.9	(8)	12.1	(6)	7.6	(8)
Hong Kong	13.1	(5)	10.4	(6)	11.8	(6)	13.1	(5)	6.4	(9)
India	10.9	(6)	10.5	(6)	14.5	(4)	12.2	(6)	12.0	(6)
Indonesia	37.4	(1)	31.4	(1)	14.8	(3)	15.6	(3)	13.7	(5)
Malaysia	8.6	(7)	9.6	(7)	2.5	(10)	6.0	(9)	14.4	(4)
Nepal	12.9	(5)	15.6	(3)	13.8	(5)	17.6	(2)	16.1	(3) c

221

Table I-A: Money Supply (continued)

Annual Growth Rate of the Money Supply (M1) Minus Annual Growth Rate of Potential Real GDP
(The rating of each country is in parenthesis)

ASIA	1971-75		1976-80		1981-85		1986-90		1991-95	
Pakistan	10.8	(6)	20.6	(1)	12.3	(6)	12.8	(5)	8.7	(7)
Philippines	18.2	(2)	17.7	(2)	11.0	(6)	18.1	(2)	12.6	(5)
Singapore	13.9	(5)	11.3	(6)	7.6	(8)	7.8	(8)	2.8	(10)
South Korea	28.4	(1)	25.5	(1)	14.0	(4)	11.2	(6)	10.9	(6)
Sri Lanka	7.7	(8)	24.5	(1)	14.4	(4)	14.6	(4)	9.7	(7)
Taiwan	19.1	(2)	15.1	(3)	5.0	(9)	16.5	(3)	0.1	(10)
Thailand	10.8	(6)	15.0	(3)	3.3	(10)	12.8	(5)	5.5	(9)
AFRICA										
Algeria	21.0	(1)	20.9	(1)	18.5	(2)	5.8	(9)	11.4	(6)
Benin	22.0	(1)	9.9	(7)	13.5	(5)	3.2	(10)	6.4	(9)
Botswana	-		11.9	(6)	15.0	(3)	20.6	(2)	-2.9	(10)
Burundi	8.5	(7)	25.5	(1)	11.9	(6)	2.9	(10)	11.2	(6)
Cameroon	12.3	(6)	22.2	(1)	14.8	(4)	0.3	(10)	-6.2	(9)
Cent African Rep	9.8	(7)	22.4	(1)	8.3	(7)	0.4	(10)	14.6	(4)
Chad	10.4	(6)	11.0	(6)	19.0	(2)	-1.9	(10)	-0.1	(10)
Congo	11.3	(6)	14.3	(4)	16.0	(3)	1.4	(10)	0.1	(10)
Cote d'Ivoire	16.5	(3)	19.8	(2)	6.7	(9)	-2.9	(10)	12.7	(5)
Gabon	35.5	(1)	9.1	(7)	13.7	(5)	0.0	(10)	3.4	(10)
Ghana	28.4	(1)	42.4	(1)	44.0	(1)	37.8	(1)	32.0	(1)
Kenya	12.5	(5)	15.1	(3)	8.5	(7)	13.6	(5)	16.5	(3)
Madagascar	9.6	(7)	16.7	(3)	9.4	(7)	17.8	(2)	25.1	(1)
Malawi	17.6	(2)	5.2	(9)	11.0	(6)	22.3	(1)	32.7	(1)
Mali	19.2	(2)	13.0	(5)	13.6	(5)	-5.3	(9)	12.2	(6)
Mauritius	32.9	(1)	11.1	(6)	2.8	(10)	18.6	(2)	5.3	(9)
Morocco	17.8	(2)	14.1	(4)	10.5	(6)	11.5	(6)	4.5	(10)
Niger	18.0	(2)	28.2	(1)	4.2	(10)	-1.7	(10)	5.9	(9)
Nigeria	32.5	(1)	30.7	(1)	6.6	(9)	18.9	(2)	39.8	(1)
Rwanda	15.9	(3)	20.4	(2)	3.8	(10)	2.2	(10)	18.2	(2)
Senegal	15.4	(3)	13.3	(5)	6.6	(9)	-0.7	(10)	6.2	(9)
Sierra Leone	15.3	(3)	20.0	(2)	43.2	(1)	72.5	(0)	27.6	(1)
Somalia	16.9	(3)	27.2	(1)	27.8	(1)	92.0	(0)	-	
South Africa	13.4	(5)	13.9	(5)	20.6	(1)	17.7	(2)	15.0	(3)
Tanzania	20.8	(1)	25.1	(1)	13.7	(5)	30.0	(1)	27.6	(1) d
Togo	17.5	(2)	20.2	(2)	7.8	(8)	-3.1	(10)	10.5	(6)
Tunisia	18.9	(2)	14.3	(4)	16.2	(3)	3.8	(10)	1.6	(10)
Uganda	22.5	(1)	34.4	(1)	74.4	(0)	410.0	(0)	25.0	(1)
Zaire	19.5	(2)	42.1	(1)	52.7	(0)	100.0	(0)	2955.0	(0)
Zambia	12.1	(6)	9.5	(7)	18.7	(2)	58.3	(0)	77.0	(0)
Zimbabwe	-		11.5	(6)	7.4	(8)	18.0	(2)	33.6	(1)

Based on 1992-95 data.

Based on 1993-95 data.

[c] Based on 1991-92 data.

[d] Based on 1991-94 data.

Source: The actual growth rate of real GDP during the last 10 years was used as the estimate for the growth rate of "potential real GDP." Thus, this variable is the annual rate of growth in the M1 money supply during the last 5 years minus the annual growth rate of real GDP during the last 10 years.

The money supply (narrow definition) and real GDP data from the International Monetary Fund, *International Financial Statistics Yearbook, 1996* (or the monthly version) were used. The base year for the rating of each country was 1985. The following conversion table divided the 1985 data into eleven intervals of equal size.

Percent Growth Rate of the Money Supply minus Percent Change in Real GDP	Rating
< −20.57	1
−20.56 — −17.45	2
−17.44 — −14.82	3
−14.81 — −13.83	4
−13.82 — −12.43	5
−12.42 — −10.34	6
−10.33 — −8.04	7
−8.03 — −6.79	8
−6.80 — −4.55	9
−4.54 — 4.53	10
4.54 — 6.79	9
6.80 — 8.02	8
8.03 — 10.32	7
10.33 — 12.41	6
12.42 13.91	5
13.92 — 14.80	4
14.81 — 17.43	3
17.44 — 20.56	2
20.57 — 44.85	1
> 44.86	0

Table I-B: The Standard Deviation of the Annual Rate of Inflation As Measured by the GDP Deflator (1971-75, 1976-80, 1981-85, 1986-90 and 1991-95)

INDUSTRIAL COUNTRIES	Standard Deviation of the Inflation Rate (percent) (The rating of each country is in parenthesis)				
	1971-75	1976-80	1981-85	1986-90	1991-95
United States	2.1 (8)	1.3 (9)	2.4 (8)	0.7 (10)	1.0 (10)
Canada	4.0 (5)	1.9 (9)	3.2 (6)	1.0 (10)	0.6 (10)
Australia	4.2 (5)	1.6 (9)	2.2 (8)	1.9 (9)	0.6 (10)
Japan	5.6 (4)	1.7 (9)	0.8 (10)	0.9 (10)	0.7 (10)
New Zealand	3.7 (6)	2.1 (9)	3.1 (6)	5.0 (4)	1.2 (10)
Austria	1.1 (10)	0.6 (10)	1.3 (10)	0.9 (10)	0.7 (10)
Belgium	3.0 (7)	1.6 (9)	0.8 (10)	1.0 (10)	0.6 (10)
Denmark	2.1 (9)	0.8 (10)	2.4 (8)	0.8 (10)	0.3 (10)
Finland	5.5 (4)	1.9 (9)	1.9 (9)	0.9 (10)	1.1 (10)
France	2.6 (7)	0.8 (10)	2.3 (8)	0.9 (10)	0.5 (10)
Germany	0.9 (10)	0.5 (10)	1.0 (10)	0.7 (10)	1.0 (10)
Iceland	11.1 (2)	7.7 (3)	17.2 (1)	3.6 (6)	1.8 (9)
Ireland	4.7 (5)	3.5 (6)	4.8 (5)	2.5 (7)	0.7 (10)
Italy	5.2 (4)	2.2 (8)	3.8 (6)	0.8 (10)	1.4 (9)
Netherlands	0.7 (10)	1.7 (9)	1.9 (9)	1.0 (10)	1.6 (9)
Norway	2.1 (9)	3.0 (7)	3.3 (6)	3.5 (6)	1.6 (9)
Spain	3.7 (6)	3.5 (6)	2.1 (9)	2.0 (9)	1.2 (10)
Sweden	2.9 (7)	1.5 (9)	1.2 (10)	1.4 (9)	2.1 (8)
Switzerland	1.1 (10)	1.1 (10)	2.0 (9)	1.2 (10)	1.5 (9)
United Kingdom	7.4 (3)	2.6 (7)	2.5 (8)	1.4 (9)	1.6 (9)
CENTRAL/S. AMERICA					
Argentina	61.8 (0)	119.8 (0)	207.6 (0)	1185.0 (0)	54.0 (0)
Bahamas	3.1 (6)	3.3 (6)	2.6 (7)	0.5 (10)	2.2 (8)
Barbados	7.7 (3)	11.0 (2)	3.2 (6)	7.0 (3)	2.6 (7)
Belize	8.3 (2)	3.6 (6)	6.5 (3)	2.8 (7)	1.2 (10)
Bolivia	21.0 (1)	11.0 (2)	4349.2 (0)	91.2 (0)	16.9 (1)
Brazil	6.9 (3)	16.6 (1)	53.1 (0)	909.8 (0)	996.6 (0)
Chile	234.0 (0)	80.6 (0)	9.6 (2)	3.2 (6)	3.6 (6)
Colombia	5.7 (4)	4.2 (5)	1.7 (9)	2.2 (8)	2.5 (7)
Costa Rica	8.9 (2)	4.5 (5)	24.2 (1)	3.3 (6)	5.8 (4)
Dominican Rep	6.8 (3)	4.7 (5)	13.1 (2)	16.7 (1)	4.1 (5)
Ecuador	14.6 (1)	4.3 (5)	10.2 (2)	16.7 (1)	10.6 (2)
El Salvador	4.5 (5)	7.5 (3)	4.7 (5)	8.2 (2)	1.8 (9)
Guatemala	7.8 (3)	3.6 (6)	5.3 (4)	15.2 (1)	9.1 (2)
Haiti	5.9 (4)	8.3 (2)	3.1 (6)	8.1 (3)	21.1 (1)
Honduras	5.4 (4)	3.0 (7)	1.3 (10)	6.7 (3)	8.3 (2)
Jamaica	9.9 (2)	5.1 (4)	10.2 (2)	5.0 (4)	14.2 (1)
Mexico	6.0 (3)	4.9 (5)	20.4 (1)	42.8 (0)	11.1 (2)
Nicaragua	8.8 (2)	15.9 (1)	60.3 (0)	4853.2 (0)	1210.6 (0)
Panama	3.2 (6)	2.5 (7)	1.3 (9)	0.8 (10)	0.3 (10)

Table I-B: Annual Rate of Inflation (continued)

CENTRAL-S. AMERICA (con't)	1971-75		1976-80		1981-85		1986-90		1991-95	
					Standard Deviation of the Inflation Rate (percent)					
					(The rating of each country is in parenthesis)					
Paraguay	7.5	(3)	5.3	(4)	8.0	(3)	3.6	(6)	4.5	(5)
Peru	5.9	(4)	17.5	(1)	38.1	(0)	2302.8	(0)	154.4	(0)
Trinidad/Tobago	18.5	(1)	9.6	(2)	13.9	(1)	5.6	(4)	4.3	(5)
Uruguay	36.4	(0)	11.9	(2)	20.4	(1)	12.6	(2)	20.6	(1)
Venezuela	15.0	(1)	7.4	(3)	5.2	(4)	30.4	(1)	15.6	(1)
EUROPE/MIDDLE EAST										
Albania	-		-		-		-		86.2	(0)
Bahrain	7.2	(3)	2.6	(7)	8.2	(2)	8.2	(2)	2.5	(8)
Bulgaria	-		-		2.5	(7)	11.3	(2)	83.9	(0)
Croatia	-		-		-		-		552.9	(0)
Cyprus	3.0	(7)	2.3	(8)	2.8	(7)	0.7	(10)	0.6	(10)
Czechoslovakia	-		-		2.2	(8)	4.0	(5)	-	
Czech Republic	-		-		-		-		13.9	(1)
Slovakia	-		-		-		-		10.2	(2)
Egypt	3.5	(6)	4.4	(5)	3.4	(6)	1.6	(9)	5.7	(4)
Estonia	-		-		-		-		395.0	(0)
Greece	7.3	(3)	2.4	(8)	2.3	(8)	2.9	(7)	2.8	(7)
Hungary	2.9	(7)	3.8	(6)	1.0	(10)	7.8	(3)	3.3	(6)
Iran	20.4	(1)	6.1	(3)	6.8	(3)	3.6	(6)	8.9	(2)
Israel	9.4	(2)	33.2	(0)	101.7	(0)	13.0	(2)	3.8	(6)
Jordan	5.8	(4)	2.6	(7)	5.1	(4)	8.3	(2)	0.5	(10)
Latvia	-		-		-		-		353.2	(0)
Lithuania	-		-		-		-		357.8	(0)
Malta	2.3	(8)	3.0	(7)	3.1	(6)	0.7	(10)	1.2	(10)
Oman	60.5	(0)	24.5	(1)	4.7	(5)	14.0	(1)	5.7	(4)
Poland	2.4	(8)	2.0	(9)	37.4	(0)	178.3	(0)	8.5	(2)
Portugal	5.2	(4)	3.4	(6)	2.5	(7)	3.4	(6)	4.3	(5)
Romania	0.4	(10)	2.8	(7)	4.8	(5)	6.0	(3)	84.7	(0)
Russia	1.1	(10)	1.8	(9)	1.4	(9)	2.7	(7)	220.7	(0)
Slovenia	-		-		-		-		58.3	(0)
Syria	12.2	(2)	3.8	(6)	5.3	(4)	3.2	(6)	3.2	(6)
Turkey	4.4	(5)	31.4	(1)	8.4	(2)	13.9	(1)	19.2	(1)
Ukraine	-		-		-		-		1682.7	(0)
ASIA										
Bangladesh	31.5	(1)	14.4	(1)	3.0	(7)	2.1	(8)	2.8	(7)
China	-		1.1	(10)	3.2	(6)	2.7	(7)	7.4	(3)
Fiji	9.0	(2)	5.7	(4)	3.9	(5)	2.0	(9)	2.9	(7)
Hong Kong	3.9	(5)	5.2	(4)	2.5	(7)	2.9	(7)	4.2	(5)
India	7.2	(3)	4.8	(5)	1.1	(10)	1.4	(9)	2.1	(9)
Indonesia	16.3	(1)	10.2	(2)	3.0	(7)	5.1	(4)	1.1	(10)
Malaysia	8.3	(2)	3.1	(6)	2.6	(7)	5.2	(4)	1.1	(10)
Nepal	11.3	(2)	5.4	(4)	2.2	(8)	1.9	(9)	4.1	(5)
Pakistan	8.6	(2)	1.6	(9)	2.3	(8)	2.4	(8)	2.4	(8)

Table I-B: Annual Rate of Inflation (continued)

Standard Deviation of the Inflation Rate (percent)

(The rating of each country is in parenthesis)

ASIA	1971-75		1976-80		1981-85		1986-90		1991-95	
Philippines	9.2	(2)	2.9	(7)	16.4	(1)	3.3	(6)	3.6	(6)
Singapore	4.7	(5)	3.7	(6)	2.7	(7)	2.8	(7)	0.6	(10)
South Korea	7.1	(3)	3.3	(6)	4.9	(5)	10.2	(2)	2.0	(9)
Sri Lanka	8.1	(3)	3.6	(6)	6.2	(3)	4.7	(5)	1.1	(10)
Taiwan	12.6	(2)	4.3	(5)	4.8	(5)	1.3	(9)	0.4	(10)
Thailand	8.4	(2)	2.8	(7)	2.5	(8)	1.7	(9)	0.9	(10)
AFRICA										
Algeria	17.3	(1)	5.7	(4)	4.2	(5)	9.5	(2)	11.5	(2)
Benin	5.7	(4)	3.0	(7)	6.8	(3)	2.4	(8)	12.9	(2)
Botswana	7.7	(3)	8.8	(2)	8.8	(2)	8.7	(2)	3.9	(5)
Burundi	16.6	(1)	6.0	(3)	7.3	(3)	6.9	(3)	6.4	(3)
Cameroon	5.3	(4)	1.9	(9)	1.5	(9)	4.2	(5)	14.5	(1)
C African Rep	6.7	(3)	6.4	(3)	6.5	(3)	6.0	(3)	10.1	(2)
Chad	2.0	(9)	0.8	(10)	9.4	(2)	8.2	(3)	16.1	(1)
Congo Peoples Rep	0.9	(10)	7.2	(3)	11.0	(2)	14.5	(1)	0.4	(10)
Cote d' Ivoire	9.6	(2)	10.1	(2)	3.9	(5)	3.0	(7)	10.6	(2)
Gabon	26.3	(1)	11.4	(2)	3.6	(6)	13.0	(2)	14.4	(1)
Ghana	8.7	(2)	16.9	(1)	38.2	(0)	4.8	(5)	21.9	(1)
Kenya	9.3	(2)	6.1	(3)	1.2	(10)	1.4	(9)	7.9	(3)
Madagascar	7.6	(3)	2.8	(7)	7.9	(3)	4.8	(5)	15.9	(1)
Malawi	5.5	(4)	5.9	(4)	2.6	(7)	5.9	(4)	9.2	(2)
Mali	5.9	(4)	1.3	(10)	4.5	(5)	3.8	(5)	9.6	(2)
Mauritius	20.1	(1)	8.0	(3)	1.4	(9)	1.3	(9)	1.3	(9)
Morocco	8.4	(2)	4.5	(5)	0.9	(10)	2.6	(7)	0.9	(10)
Niger	16.6	(1)	3.3	(6)	5.7	(4)	5.3	(4)	14.7	(1)
Nigeria	15.7	(1)	1.5	(9)	6.0	(3)	19.3	(1)	20.2	(1)
Rwanda	30.0	(1)	3.3	(6)	5.3	(4)	3.8	(6)	5.9	(4)
Senegal	5.4	(4)	2.5	(7)	1.7	(9)	2.7	(7)	11.9	(2)
Sierra Leone	7.9	(3)	4.4	(5)	28.0	(1)	38.9	(0)	33.0	(0)
Somalia	4.8	(5)	35.8	(0)	18.7	(1)	67.5	(0)	-	
South Africa	4.8	(5)	5.1	(4)	1.9	(9)	0.9	(10)	1.7	(9)
Tanzania	5.8	(4)	5.7	(4)	5.9	(4)	9.5	(2)	7.4	(3)
Togo	16.8	(1)	11.2	(2)	5.0	(4)	1.6	(9)	1.7	(9)
Tunisia	7.8	(3)	3.5	(6)	3.8	(6)	1.8	(9)	0.9	(10)
Uganda	15.5	(1)	33.8	(0)	45.7	(0)	67.7	(0)	19.0	(1)
Zaire	4.0	(5)	25.8	(1)	25.1	(1)	28.0	(1)	8703.2	(0)
Zambia	12.1	(2)	4.6	(5)	12.6	(2)	23.3	(1)	49.5	(0)
Zimbabwe	2.7	(7)	2.7	(7)	5.5	(4)	5.7	(4)	7.1	(3)

226

Source: The inflation rate for each year was obtained from the *International Financial Statistics Yearbook: 1996* (and monthly updates). In a few cases where the data for the GDP deflator were unavailable, data from the Consumer Price Index was used to derive the annual rate of inflation. The following conversion table divided the 1985 data into eleven intervals of equal size.

Standard Deviation (%) of the Inflation Rate	Rating
0.000 — 1.29	10
1.30 — 2.11	9
2.12 — 2.48	8
2.49 — 3.04	7
3.05 — 3.80	6
3.81 — 4.94	5
4.95 — 5.94	4
5.95 — 8.19	3
8.20 — 13.52	2
13.53 — 32.69	1
> 32.70	0

Table I-C: Freedom of Residents to Own Foreign Currencies Domestically
(Countries Where Citizens are Free to Own Foreign Currencies are Given a Rating of 10; Countries that Restrict This Freedom are Given a Rating of Zero.)

	Is It Legal (without restrictions) for Citizens to Own Foreign Money Domestically?									
INDUSTRIAL COUNTRIES	1975		1980		1985		1990		1995	
United States	Yes	10	Yes	10	Yes	10	Yes	10	Yes	10
Canada	Yes	10	Yes	10	Yes	10	Yes	10	Yes	10
Australia	Yes	10	Yes	10	Yes	10	Yes	10	Yes	10
Japan	Yes	10	Yes	10	Yes	10	Yes	10	Yes	10
New Zealand	No	0	No	0	No	0	Yes	10	Yes	10
Austria	Yes	10	Yes	10	Yes	10	Yes	10	Yes	10
Belgium	Yes	10	Yes	10	Yes	10	Yes	10	Yes	10
Denmark	No	0	No	0	No	0	Yes	10	Yes	10
Finland	Yes	10	Yes	10	Yes	10	Yes	10	Yes	10
France	No	0	No	0	No	0	Yes	10	Yes	10
Germany	Yes	10	Yes	10	Yes	10	Yes	10	Yes	10
Iceland	No	0	No	0	No	0	Yes	10	Yes	10
Ireland	No	0	No	0	No	0	No	0	Yes	10
Italy	No	0	No	0	No	0	Yes	10	Yes	10
Netherlands	Yes	10	Yes	10	Yes	10	Yes	10	Yes	10
Norway	No	0	No	0	No	0	Yes	10	Yes	10
Spain	No	0	No	0	No	0	No	0	Yes	10
Sweden	Yes	10	Yes	10	Yes	10	Yes	10	Yes	10
Switzerland	Yes	10	Yes	10	Yes	10	Yes	10	Yes	10
United Kingdom	No	0	No	0	Yes	10	Yes	10	Yes	10
CENTRAL/SOUTH AMERICA										
Argentina	Yes	10	Yes	10	Yes	10	Yes	10	Yes	10
Bahamas	No	0	No	0	No	0	No	0	No	0
Barbados	No	0	No	0	No	0	No	0	No	0
Belize	-		No	0	No	0	No	0	No	0
Bolivia	Yes	10	Yes	10	No	0	Yes	10	Yes	10
Brazil	No	0	No	0	No	0	No	0	No	0
Chile	No	0	Yes	10	Yes	10	Yes	10	Yes	10
Colombia	No	0	No	0	Yes	10	No	0	Yes	10
Costa Rica	Yes	10	Yes	10	Yes	10	Yes	10	Yes	10
Dominican Rep	No	0	No	0	No	0	No	0	No	0
Ecuador	Yes	10	Yes	10	Yes	10	Yes	10	Yes	10
El Salvador	No	0	No	0	No	0	No	0	Yes	10
Guatemala	No	0	Yes	10	Yes	10	Yes	10	Yes	10
Haiti	Yes	10	Yes	10	Yes	10	Yes	10	Yes	10
Honduras	Yes	10	Yes	10	Yes	10	Yes	10	Yes	10

Table I-C: Freedom to Own Foreign Money (continued)

Is It Legal (without restrictions) for Citizens to Own Foreign Money Domestically?

CENTRAL/-	1975		1980		1985		1990		1995	
S. AMERICA (con't)										
Jamaica	No	0	No	0	No	0	No	0	Yes	10
Mexico	Yes	10	Yes	10	Yes	10	Yes	10	Yes	10
Nicaragua	Yes	10	Yes	10	No	0	No	0	No	0
Panama	Yes	10	Yes	10	Yes	10	Yes	10	Yes	10
Paraguay	Yes	10	Yes	10	Yes	10	Yes	10	Yes	10
Peru	No	0	No	0	No	0	Yes	10	Yes	10
Trinidad/Tobago	No	0	No	0	No	0	No	0	Yes	10
Uruguay	Yes	10	Yes	10	Yes	10	Yes	10	Yes	10
Venezuela	Yes	10	Yes	10	Yes	10	Yes	10	No	0
EUROPE/MIDDLE EAST										
Albania	No	0	No	0	No	0	No	0	Yes	10
Bahrain	Yes	10	Yes	10	Yes	10	Yes	10	Yes	10
Bulgaria	No	0	No	0	No	0	No	0	Yes	10
Croatia	Yes	10	Yes	10	Yes	10	Yes	10	Yes	10
Cyprus	No	0	No	0	No	0	No	0	No	0
Czechoslovakia	No	0	No	0	No	0	No	0	-	
Czech Rep	-		-		-		-		Yes	10
Slovakia	-		-		-		-		Yes	10
Egypt	No	0	Yes	10	Yes	10	Yes	10	Yes	10
Estonia	No	0	No	0	No	0	Yes	10	Yes	10
Greece	Yes	10	Yes	10	Yes	10	Yes	10	Yes	10
Hungary	No	0	No	0	No	0	No	0	Yes	10
Iran	Yes	10	Yes	10	Yes	10	Yes	10	No	0
Israel	Yes	10	Yes	10	Yes	10	Yes	10	Yes	10
Jordan	No	0	Yes	10	Yes	10	No	0	No	0
Latvia	No	0	No	0	No	0	Yes	10	Yes	10
Lithuania	No	0	No	0	No	0	Yes	10	Yes	10
Malta	-		-		No	0	No	0	Yes	10
Oman	Yes	10	Yes	10	Yes	10	Yes	10	Yes	10
Poland	Yes	10	Yes	10	Yes	10	Yes	10	Yes	10
Portugal	No	0	No	0	No	0	No	0	Yes	10
Romania	No	0	No	0	No	0	Yes	10	Yes	10
Russia	No	0	No	0	No	0	No	0	Yes	10
Slovenia	Yes	10	Yes	10	Yes	10	Yes	10	Yes	10
Syria	Yes	10	Yes	10	Yes	10	Yes	10	Yes	10
Turkey	No	0	No	0	No	0	Yes	10	Yes	10
Ukraine	No	0	No	0	No	0	Yes	10	Yes	10
ASIA										
Bangladesh	No	0	No	0	No	0	No	0	No	0
China	No	0	No	0	No	0	Yes	10	Yes	10
Fiji	No	0	No	0	No	0	No	0	No	0 [a]

Table I-C: Freedom to Own Foreign Money (continued)

Is It Legal (without restrictions) for Citizens to Own Foreign Money Domestically?

	1975		1980		1985		1990		1995	
ASIA (cont.)										
Hong Kong	Yes	10	Yes	10	Yes	10	Yes	10	Yes	10
India	No	0	No	0	No	0	No	0	No	0
Indonesia	Yes	10	Yes	10	Yes	10	Yes	10	Yes	10
Malaysia	No	0	Yes	10	Yes	10	Yes	10	Yes	10
Nepal	No	0	No	0	No	0	No	0	No	0
Pakistan	No	0	No	0	No	0	Yes	10	Yes	10
Philippines	No	0	No	0	No	0	No	0	Yes	10
Singapore	No	0	No	0	Yes	10	Yes	10	Yes	10
South Korea	No	0	No	0	No	0	No	0	Yes	10
Sri Lanka	No	0	No	0	No	0	No	0	No	0
Taiwan	Yes	10	Yes	10	Yes	10	Yes	10	Yes	10
Thailand	No	0	No	0	No	0	Yes	10	Yes	10
AFRICA										
Algeria	No	0	No	0	No	0	No	0	No	0
Benin	No	0	No	0	No	0	No	0	No	0
Botswana	No	0	No	0	No	0	No	0	Yes	10
Burundi	-		No	0	No	0	No	0	No	0
Cameroon	No	0	No	0	No	0	No	0	No	0
C African Rep	No	0	No	0	No	0	No	0	No	0
Chad	No	0	No	0	No	0	No	0	No	0
Congo Peoples Rep	No	0	No	0	No	0	No	0	No	0
Cote d' Ivoire	No	0	No	0	No	0	No	0	No	0
Gabon	No	0	No	0	No	0	No	0	No	0
Ghana	No	0	No	0	No	0	No	0	No	0
Kenya	No	0	No	0	No	0	No	0	Yes	10
Madagascar	-		No	0	No	0	No	0	No	0
Malawi	No	0	No	0	No	0	No	0	No	0
Mali	No	0	No	0	No	0	No	0	No	0
Mauritius	No	0	No	0	No	0	No	0	Yes	10
Morocco	No	0	No	0	No	0	No	0	No	0
Niger	No	0	No	0	No	0	No	0	No	0
Nigeria	No	0	No	0	No	0	No	0	No	0
Rwanda	-		No	0	No	0	No	0	Yes	10
Senegal	No	0	No	0	No	0	No	0	No	0
Sierra Leone	No	0	No	0	No	0	No	0	Yes	10
Somalia	No	0	No	0	No	0	No	0	No	0
South Africa	No	0	No	0	No	0	No	0	No	0
Tanzania	No	0	No	0	No	0	No	0	Yes	10
Togo	No	0	No	0	No	0	No	0	No	0
Tunisia	No	0	No	0	No	0	No	0	No	0
Uganda	No	0	No	0	No	0	No	0	No	0
Zaire	No	0	No	0	No	0	No	0	No	0
Zambia	No	0	No	0	No	0	No	0	No	0
Zimbabwe	No	0	No	0	No	0	No	0	No	0

Source: International Currency Analysis, *World Currency Yearbook*, (various issues) and International Monetary Fund, *Exchange Arrangements and Exchange Restrictions: Annual Report 1996*.

Table I-D: Freedom of Citizens to Maintain Bank Balances Abroad
(Countries That Permit Their Citizens to Maintain Bank Balances Abroad Are Given a Rating of 10; Those That Restrict This Freedom are Given a Rating of Zero.)

Is It Legal (without restrictions) for Citizens to Maintain Bank Balances Abroad?

INDUSTRIAL COUNTRIES	1975		1980		1985		1990		1995	
United States	Yes	10	Yes	10	Yes	10	Yes	10	Yes	10
Canada	Yes	10	Yes	10	Yes	10	Yes	10	Yes	10
Australia	Yes	10	Yes	10	Yes	10	Yes	10	Yes	10
Japan	No	0	No	0	No	0	Yes	10	Yes	10
New Zealand	No	0	No	0	No	0	Yes	10	Yes	10
Austria	No	0	No	0	No	0	Yes	10	Yes	10
Belgium	Yes	10	Yes	10	Yes	10	Yes	10	Yes	10
Denmark	No	0	No	0	No	0	Yes	10	Yes	10
Finland	No	0	No	0	No	0	Yes	10	Yes	10
France	No	0	No	0	No	0	Yes	10	Yes	10
Germany	Yes	10	Yes	10	Yes	10	Yes	10	Yes	10
Iceland	No	0	No	0	No	0	Yes	10	Yes	10
Ireland	No	0	No	0	No	0	No	0	Yes	10
Italy	No	0	No	0	No	0	Yes	10	Yes	10
Netherlands	Yes	10	Yes	10	Yes	10	Yes	10	Yes	10
Norway	No	0	No	0	No	0	Yes	10	Yes	10
Spain	No	0	No	0	No	0	No	0	Yes	10
Sweden	No	0	No	0	No	0	No	0	Yes	10
Switzerland	Yes	10	Yes	10	Yes	10	Yes	10	Yes	10
United Kingdom	No	0	No	0	Yes	10	Yes	10	Yes	10

CENTRAL/SOUTH AMERICA

	1975		1980		1985		1990		1995	
Argentina	Yes	10	Yes	10	Yes	10	Yes	10	Yes	10
Bahamas	No	0	No	0	No	0	No	0	No	0
Barbados	No	0	No	0	No	0	No	0	No	0
Belize	-		No	0	No	0	No	0	No	0
Bolivia	Yes	10	Yes	10	No	0	Yes	10	Yes	10
Brazil	No	0	No	0	No	0	No	0	No	0
Chile	No	0	No	0	Yes	10	Yes	10	Yes	10
Colombia	No	0	No	0	No	0	No	0	Yes	10
Costa Rica	Yes	10	Yes	10	Yes	10	Yes	10	Yes	10
Dominican Rep	No	0	Yes	10	Yes	10	No	0	No	0
Ecuador	Yes	10	Yes	10	Yes	10	Yes	10	Yes	10
El Salvador	No	0	No	0	No	0	No	0	Yes	10
Guatemala	Yes	10	Yes	10	Yes	10	Yes	10	Yes	10
Haiti	No	0	Yes	10	Yes	10	Yes	10	Yes	10
Honduras	Yes	10	Yes	10	Yes	10	Yes	10	Yes	10

Table I-D: Freedom to Maintain Bank Balances (continued)

Is It Legal (without restrictions) for Citizens to
Maintain Bank Balances Abroad?

CENTRAL/- S. AMERICA (con't)	1975		1980		1985		1990		1995	
Jamaica	No	0	No	0	No	0	No	0	Yes	10
Mexico	Yes	10	Yes	10	Yes	10	Yes	10	Yes	10
Nicaragua	Yes	10	Yes	10	No	0	No	0	No	0
Panama	Yes	10	Yes	10	Yes	10	Yes	10	Yes	10
Paraguay	Yes	10	Yes	10	Yes	10	Yes	10	Yes	10
Peru	No	0	No	0	No	0	No	0	Yes	10
Trinidad/Tobago	No	0	No	0	No	0	No	0	Yes	10
Uruguay	Yes	10	Yes	10	Yes	10	Yes	10	Yes	10
Venezuela	Yes	10	Yes	10	Yes	10	Yes	10	No	0
EUROPE/MIDDLE EAST										
Albania	No	0	No	0	No	0	No	0	No	0
Bahrain	Yes	10	Yes	10	Yes	10	Yes	10	Yes	10
Bulgaria	No	0	No	0	No	0	No	0	Yes	10
Croatia	No	0	No	0	No	0	No	0	No	0
Cyprus	No	0	No	0	No	0	No	0	No	0
Czechoslovakia	No	0	No	0	No	0	No	0	-	
Czech Rep	-		-		-		-		Yes	10
Slovakia	-		-		-		-		Yes	10
Egypt	No	0	Yes	10	Yes	10	Yes	10	Yes	10
Estonia	No	0	No	0	No	0	No	0	Yes	10
Greece	No	0	No	0	No	0	No	0	No	0
Hungary	No	0	No	0	No	0	No	0	No	0
Iran	No	0	Yes	10	Yes	10	Yes	10	No	0
Israel	No	0	No	0	No	0	No	0	No	0
Jordan	No	0	No	0	No	0	No	0	No	0
Latvia	No	0	No	0	No	0	No	0	Yes	10
Lithuania	No	0	No	0	No	0	No	0	Yes	10
Malta	-		-		No	0	No	0	No	0
Oman	Yes	10	Yes	10	Yes	10	Yes	10	Yes	10
Poland	No	0	No	0	No	0	Yes	10	Yes	10
Portugal	No	0	No	0	No	0	No	0	Yes	10
Romania	No	0	No	0	No	0	No	0	No	0
Russia	No	0	No	0	No	0	No	0	Yes	10
Slovenia	No	0	No	0	No	0	No	0	No	0
Syria	Yes	10	Yes	10	Yes	10	No	0	No	0
Turkey	No	0	No	0	No	0	Yes	10	Yes	10
Ukraine	No	0	No	0	No	0	No	0	No	0
ASIA										
Bangladesh	No	0	No	0	No	0	No	0	No	0
China	No	0	No	0	No	0	No	0	No	0
Fiji	No	0	No	0	No	0	No	0	No	0

233

Table I-D: Freedom to Maintain Bank Balances (continued)

**Is It Legal (without restrictions) for Citizens to
Maintain Bank Balances Abroad?**

COUNTRY	1975		1980		1985		1990		1995	
ASIA (cont.)										
Hong Kong	Yes	10	Yes	10	Yes	10	Yes	10	Yes	10
India	No	0	No	0	No	0	No	0	No	0
Indonesia	Yes	10	Yes	10	Yes	10	Yes	10	Yes	10
Malaysia	Yes	10	Yes	10	No	0	Yes	10	Yes	10
Nepal	No	0	No	0	No	0	No	0	No	0
Pakistan	No	0	No	0	No	0	No	0	No	0
Philippines	No	0	No	0	No	0	No	0	Yes	10
Singapore	No	0	No	0	No	0	Yes	10	Yes	10
South Korea	No	0	No	0	No	0	No	0	Yes	10
Sri Lanka	No	0	No	0	No	0	No	0	No	0
Taiwan	Yes	10	Yes	10	Yes	10	Yes	10	Yes	10
Thailand	No	0	No	0	No	0	No	0	Yes	10
AFRICA										
Algeria	No	0	No	0	No	0	No	0	No	0
Benin	No	0	No	0	No	0	No	0	No	0
Botswana	No	0	No	0	No	0	No	0	No	0
Burundi	-		-		No	0	No	0	No	0
Cameroon	No	0	No	0	No	0	No	0	No	0
C African Rep	No	0	No	0	No	0	No	0	No	0
Chad	No	0	No	0	No	0	No	0	No	0
Congo Peoples Rep	No	0	No	0	No	0	No	0	No	0
Cote d' Ivoire	No	0	No	0	No	0	No	0	No	0
Gabon	No	0	No	0	No	0	No	0	No	0
Ghana	No	0	No	0	No	0	No	0	No	0
Kenya	No	0	No	0	No	0	No	0	No	0
Madagascar	No	0	No	0	No	0	No	0	No	0
Malawi	No	0	No	0	No	0	No	0	No	0
Mali	No	0	No	0	No	0	No	0	No	0
Mauritius	No	0	No	0	No	0	No	0	Yes	10
Morocco	No	0	No	0	No	0	No	0	No	0
Niger	No	0	No	0	No	0	No	0	No	0
Nigeria	No	0	No	0	No	0	No	0	No	0
Rwanda	No	0	No	0	No	0	No	0	No	0
Senegal	No	0	No	0	No	0	No	0	No	0
Sierra Leone	No	0	No	0	No	0	No	0	No	0
Somalia	No	0	No	0	No	0	No	0	No	0
South Africa	No	0	No	0	No	0	No	0	No	0
Tanzania	No	0	No	0	No	0	No	0	No	0
Togo	No	0	No	0	No	0	No	0	No	0
Tunisia	No	0	No	0	No	0	No	0	No	0
Uganda	No	0	No	0	No	0	No	0	No	0
Zaire	No	0	No	0	No	0	No	0	No	0
Zambia	No	0	No	0	No	0	No	0	No	0
Zimbabwe	No	0	No	0	No	0	No	0	No	0

Source: International Currency Analysis, *World Currency Yearbook*, (various issues) and International Monetary Fund, *Exchange Arrangements and Exchange Restrictions: Annual Report 1996.*

Table II-A: General Government Consumption Expenditures As A Percent of Total Consumption

	Government Consumption As A Percent of Total Consumption (The rating of each country is in parenthesis)									
INDUSTRIAL COUNTRIES	1975		1980		1985		1990		1995	
United States	22.6	(3)	21.3	(4)	21.1	(4)	20.3	(4)	18.8	(5)
Canada	25.6	(2)	25.8	(2)	26.0	(1)	25.6	(2)	24.5	(2)
Australia	23.0	(3)	23.4	(3)	23.9	(3)	22.1	(4)	21.9	(4)
Japan	14.9	(7)	14.3	(7)	14.0	(8)	13.7	(8)	13.9	(8)
New Zealand	19.7	(5)	22.3	(3)	21.1	(4)	21.6	(4)	18.8	(5)
Austria	23.5	(3)	24.4	(2)	24.7	(2)	24.3	(2)	25.5	(2)
Belgium	21.2	(4)	22.0	(4)	20.7	(4)	18.8	(5)	19.2	(5)
Denmark	30.7	(0)	32.3	(0)	31.6	(0)	32.8	(0)	31.8	(0)
Finland	23.6	(3)	25.0	(2)	26.9	(1)	28.5	(1)	28.3	(1)
France	22.0	(4)	23.6	(3)	24.1	(2)	23.1	(3)	24.6	(2)
Germany	26.5	(1)	26.3	(1)	26.1	(1)	25.2	(2)	25.5	(2)
Iceland	22.0	(4)	22.8	(3)	21.9	(4)	24.4	(2)	25.6	(2)
Ireland	21.2	(4)	21.9	(4)	22.3	(3)	20.6	(4)	22.3	(3) a
Italy	18.5	(5)	19.4	(5)	21.1	(4)	22.1	(4)	21.6	(4) a
Netherlands	22.3	(3)	22.1	(3)	20.9	(4)	19.8	(5)	19.0	(5)
Norway	27.0	(1)	28.3	(1)	27.4	(1)	29.3	(1)	29.6	(1)
Spain	13.9	(8)	16.7	(6)	18.7	(5)	19.9	(5)	20.9	(4)
Sweden	31.7	(0)	36.3	(0)	35.3	(0)	35.0	(0)	33.1	(0)
Switzerland	17.0	(6)	16.7	(6)	17.7	(6)	19.1	(5)	19.4	(5)
United Kingdom	27.0	(1)	26.7	(1)	25.9	(2)	24.6	(2)	25.0	(2)
CENTRAL/SOUTH AMERICA										
Argentina	17.8	(6)	16.5	(6)	13.0	(8)	4.7	(10)	-	
Bahamas	17.6	(6)	16.9	(6)	16.5	(6)	15.6	(7)	16.5	(6) c
Barbados	18.3	(5)	21.6	(4)	23.4	(3)	22.7	(3)	24.2	(2) a
Belize	16.4	(6)	19.3	(5)	23.1	(3)	20.2	(5)	19.7	(5)
Bolivia	15.1	(7)	17.4	(6)	14.6	(7)	15.5	(7)	15.5	(7)
Brazil	13.8	(8)	11.7	(9)	13.1	(8)	20.1	(5)	19.7	(5) a
Chile	18.4	(5)	15.7	(7)	16.7	(6)	13.3	(8)	12.4	(9)
Colombia	11.0	(9)	12.6	(9)	13.4	(8)	13.6	(8)	28.4	(1) a
Costa Rica	17.5	(6)	21.8	(4)	20.8	(4)	22.8	(3)	22.2	(3)
Dominican Republic	8.2	(10)	9.0	(10)	8.1	(10)	6.9	(10)	9.0	(10)
Ecuador	18.2	(5)	19.6	(5)	15.1	(7)	11.2	(9)	15.9	(7)
El Salvador	13.5	(8)	16.3	(6)	16.0	(7)	11.4	(9)	8.1	(10)
Guatemala	8.0	(10)	9.2	(10)	7.8	(10)	7.5	(10)	6.5	(10) a
Haiti	9.7	(10)	11.0	(9)	12.7	(8)	8.8	(10)	-	
Honduras	13.7	(8)	15.3	(7)	14.8	(7)	15.8	(7)	11.8	(9)
Jamaica	21.7	(4)	24.0	(2)	18.2	(5)	16.8	(6)	16.4	(6) a
Mexico	11.5	(9)	13.4	(8)	12.5	(9)	10.6	(9)	13.4	(8)
Nicaragua	10.5	(9)	19.3	(5)	42.6	(0)	32.9	(0)	13.7	(8)

Table II-A: (continued)

Government Consumption As A Percent of Total Consumption
(The rating of each country is in parenthesis)

CENTRAL/- SOUTH AMERICA (con't)	1975		1980		1985		1990		1995	
Panama	25.4	(2)	25.6	(2)	24.3	(2)	21.8	(4)	20.3	(4) a
Paraguay	7.7	(10)	7.4	(10)	6.9	(10)	7.7	(10)	7.7	(10)
Peru	14.3	(7)	15.3	(7)	12.7	(8)	7.6	(10)	10.3	(10)
Trinidad & Tobago	22.4	(3)	20.8	(4)	29.5	(1)	23.0	(3)	21.1	(4) a
Uruguay	16.6	(6)	14.1	(7)	17.4	(6)	16.8	(6)	14.7	(7)
Venezuela	19.0	(5)	17.7	(6)	14.5	(7)	11.9	(9)	7.8	(10)
EUROPE/MIDDLE EAST										
Albania	-		-		-		29.1	(1)	22.0	(5)
Bahrain	-		29.0	(1)	41.0	(0)	41.9	(0)	45.5	(0) a
Bulgaria	-		9.3	(10)	12.4	(9)	23.3	(3)	19.0	(5) a
Croatia	-		-		-		-		31.8	(0)
Cyprus	17.7	(6)	16.9	(6)	18.1	(5)	22.4	(3)	21.2	(4)
Czechoslovakia	26.6	(1)	27.3	(1)	30.1	(1)	29.9	(1)	-	
Czech Republic	-		-		-		-		25.9	(2)
Slovakia	-		-		-		-		27.6	(1) a
Egypt	28.4	(1)	18.5	(5)	20.2	(5)	12.3	(9)	12.6	(8)
Estonia	-		-		-		--		29.1	(1)
Greece	18.3	(5)	21.3	(4)	23.7	(3)	17.5	(6)	15.9	(7)
Hungary	15.0	(7)	14.4	(7)	13.9	(8)	14.7	(7)	14.8	(7) a
Iran	36.5	(0)	28.3	(1)	19.6	(5)	14.7	(7)	17.6	(6)
Israel	42.3	(0)	43.2	(0)	38.7	(0)	32.9	(0)	32.1	(0)
Jordan	29.6	(1)	28.5	(1)	22.8	(3)	21.6	(4)	27.2	(1)
Latvia	-		-		-		-		26.3	(1)
Lithuania	-		-		-		-		14.6	(7)
Malta	20.4	(4)	20.0	(5)	20.2	(5)	21.9	(4)	24.9	(2) b
Oman	66.6	(0)	47.5	(0)	45.4	(0)	58.8	(0)	43.0	(0)
Poland	15.6	(7)	12.0	(9)	25.5	(2)	28.7	(1)	22.6	(3) a
Portugal	17.0	(6)	17.8	(6)	18.6	(5)	21.0	(4)	22.1	(3) a
Romania	-		8.0	(10)	6.5	(10)	17.9	(6)	18.1	(5) a
Russia	31.5	(0)	29.7	(1)	31.0	(0)	31.4	(0)	31.7	(0)
Slovenia	-		-		-		25.9	(2)	27.1	(1) a
Syria	24.1	(2)	25.8	(2)	26.8	(1)	17.0	(6)	17.0	(6) a
Turkey	14.5	(7)	14.6	(7)	10.5	(9)	13.8	(8)	15.0	(7) a
Ukraine	-		24.2	(2)	25.0	(2)	23.3	(3)	13.4	(8) a
ASIA										
Bangladesh	3.5	(10)	6.5	(10)	7.5	(10)	14.4	(7)	15.0	(7)
China	-		-		-		-		23.0	(3) a
Fiji	15.0	(7)	21.8	(4)	23.6	(3)	19.6	(5)	23.3	(3) b
Hong Kong	10.0	(10)	9.5	(10)	10.6	(9)	11.7	(9)	12.8	(8)
India	11.8	(9)	11.6	(9)	14.0	(7)	15.2	(7)	15.1	(7) a
Indonesia	12.2	(9)	16.8	(6)	16.0	(7)	14.2	(7)	13.2	(8)
Malaysia	23.9	(3)	24.6	(2)	22.7	(3)	21.0	(4)	20.6	(4) a

Table II-A: (continued)

Government Consumption As A Percent of Total Consumption
(The rating of each country is in parenthesis)

	1975		1980		1985		1990		1995	
ASIA										
Nepal	8.4	(10)	7.5	(10)	11.7	(9)	12.6	(9)	10.4	(9) a
Pakistan	11.2	(9)	10.8	(9)	13.0	(8)	17.5	(6)	13.2	(8)
Philippines	14.3	(7)	12.0	(9)	9.2	(10)	12.4	(9)	13.2	(8)
Singapore	15.0	(7)	15.6	(7)	23.8	(3)	19.1	(5)	17.2	(6)
South Korea	13.5	(8)	15.2	(7)	14.5	(7)	15.9	(7)	16.4	(6)
Sri Lanka	10.2	(10)	9.6	(10)	11.4	(9)	11.2	(9)	12.4	(9) a
Taiwan	21.7	(4)	23.6	(3)	24.0	(3)	23.9	(3)	20.3	(4)
Thailand	13.3	(8)	15.9	(7)	18.2	(5)	14.2	(7)	15.1	(7)
AFRICA										
Algeria	20.2	(5)	24.2	(2)	24.7	(2)	22.7	(3)	24.2	(2) a
Benin	9.4	(10)	8.2	(10)	15.5	(7)	14.0	(8)	13.0	(8)
Botswana	24.0	(3)	26.7	(1)	36.1	(0)	30.5	(0)	41.9	(0) a
Burundi	14.7	(7)	16.4	(6)	17.2	(6)	19.0	(5)	17.8	(6)
Cameroon	13.1	(8)	10.4	(9)	14.0	(8)	14.5	(7)	15.1	(7)
Central African Rep	16.3	(6)	13.8	(8)	13.8	(8)	9.3	(10)	16.1	(6) a
Chad	27.1	(1)	26.0	(1)	14.0	(8)	18.6	(5)	15.5	(7) a
Congo Peoples Rep	20.3	(4)	27.3	(1)	23.9	(3)	26.4	(1)	29.9	(1) a
Cote d'Ivoire	22.0	(4)	21.2	(4)	18.8	(5)	22.1	(4)	15.6	(7)
Gabon	34.2	(0)	33.6	(0)	38.7	(0)	28.8	(1)	26.5	(1) a
Ghana	15.1	(7)	11.7	(9)	10.2	(10)	11.6	(9)	13.0	(8) a
Kenya	21.2	(4)	24.2	(2)	23.3	(3)	23.1	(3)	17.8	(6)
Madagascar	11.2	(9)	11.9	(9)	9.9	(10)	6.7	(10)	6.8	(10)
Malawi	17.0	(6)	21.6	(4)	20.3	(4)	16.8	(6)	21.0	(4)
Mali	9.8	(10)	10.2	(10)	11.1	(9)	14.3	(7)	14.3	(7)
Mauritius	15.2	(7)	15.7	(7)	14.7	(7)	15.2	(7)	15.8	(7)
Morocco	19.0	(5)	21.3	(4)	19.4	(5)	19.1	(5)	21.4	(4)
Niger	11.1	(9)	13.3	(8)	16.0	(7)	15.7	(7)	17.2	(6) a
Nigeria	13.7	(8)	13.8	(8)	12.0	(9)	7.3	(10)	4.1	(10)
Rwanda	17.6	(6)	13.0	(8)	12.3	(9)	16.0	(7)	18.4	(5)
Senegal	17.4	(6)	21.9	(4)	16.6	(6)	15.9	(7)	8.7	(10)
Sierra Leone	11.8	(9)	8.4	(10)	8.0	(10)	7.3	(10)	10.5	(9)
Somalia	22.1	(4)	13.8	(8)	13.9	(8)	-		-	
South Africa	19.7	(5)	22.2	(3)	24.5	(2)	26.1	(1)	25.2	(2)
Tanzania	18.9	(5)	14.5	(7)	16.6	(6)	11.8	(9)	7.9	(10) a
Togo	16.7	(6)	18.9	(5)	16.0	(7)	16.2	(6)	13.2	(8)
Tunisia	19.0	(5)	19.0	(5)	20.8	(4)	20.3	(4)	20.5	(4)
Uganda	-		-		12.5	(9)	8.8	(10)	10.2	(10) a
Zaire	13.3	(8)	9.3	(10)	9.0	(10)	13.9	(8)	16.2	(6) b
Zambia	34.0	(0)	31.6	(0)	28.2	(1)	23.1	(3)	17.7	(6)
Zimbabwe	17.1	(6)	23.4	(3)	27.2	(1)	28.3	(1)	22.9	(3) a

[a] Based on 1994 data.

[b] Based on 1993 data.

[c] Based on 1992 data.

Source: Total consumption is equal to private consumption plus government consumption. The data were derived from International Monetary Fund, *International Financial Statistics: 1996* (and monthly updates). The base year for the rating of each country was 1985. The following conversion table divided the 1985 data into eleven intervals of equal size.

General Government Consumption as a Percent of Total Consumption	Rating
< 10.330	10
10.300 — 12.597	9
12.597 — 14.035	8
14.035 — 16.000	7
16.000 — 17.904	6
17.904 — 20.220	5
20.220 — 22.109	4
22.109 — 24.009	3
24.009 — 25.929	2
25.929 — 30.228	1
> 30.228	0

Table II-B: The Role of Government Enterprises in the Economy

Size of Government Enterprises As A Share of Economy
(A higher rating indicates that government enterprises play a less significant role.)

INDUSTRIAL COUNTRIES	1975	1980	1985	1990	1995
United States	(8)	(8)	(8)	(8)	(8)
Canada	(6)	(6)	(6)	(6)	(6)
Australia	(6)	(6)	(6)	(6)	(6)
Japan	(8)	(8)	(8)	(8)	(8)
New Zealand	(4)	(4)	(4)	(6)	(8)
Austria	(2)	(2)	(2)	(2)	(2)
Belgium	(6)	(6)	(6)	(6)	(6)
Denmark	(4)	(4)	(4)	(4)	(4)
Finland	(6)	(6)	(6)	(6)	(6)
France	(2)	(2)	(4)	(4)	(6)
Germany	(6)	(6)	(6)	(6)	(6)
Iceland	(4)	(4)	(4)	(4)	(4)
Ireland	(4)	(4)	(4)	(4)	(4)
Italy	(2)	(2)	(2)	(2)	(2)
Netherlands	(6)	(6)	(6)	(6)	(6)
Norway	(2)	(2)	(2)	(2)	(2)
Spain	(4)	(4)	(4)	(4)	(4)
Sweden	(4)	(4)	(4)	(4)	(4)
Switzerland	(8)	(8)	(8)	(8)	(8)
United Kingdom	(4)	(4)	(6)	(6)	(6)

CENTRAL/SOUTH AMERICA	1975	1980	1985	1990	1995
Argentina	(6)	(6)	(6)	(8)	(8)
Bahamas	(6)	(4)	(2)	(2)	(6)
Barbados	(4)	(4)	(4)	(4)	(4)
Belize	(8)	(8)	(8)	(8)	(8)
Bolivia	(4)	(4)	(4)	(4)	(4)
Brazil	(4)	(4)	(2)	(2)	(4)
Chile	(4)	(4)	(6)	(6)	(8)
Colombia	(6)	(4)	(4)	(4)	(6)
Costa Rica	(6)	(6)	(6)	(8)	(8)
Dominican Rep	(6)	(6)	(6)	(6)	(6)
Ecuador	(6)	(6)	(4)	(4)	(4)
El Salvador	(4)	(4)	(6)	(8)	(8)
Guatemala	(8)	(8)	(8)	(8)	(8)
Haiti	(6)	(6)	(6)	(6)	(4)
Honduras	(6)	(6)	(6)	(6)	(6)
Jamaica	(2)	(2)	(2)	(4)	(4)
Mexico	(2)	(2)	(2)	(4)	(6)
Nicaragua	(6)	(6)	(0)	(0)	(2)

240

Table II-B: (continued)

Size of Government Enterprises As A Share of Economy
(A higher rating indicates that government enterprises play a less significant role.)

CENTRAL/- S. AMERICA (cont)	1975	1980	1985	1990	1995
Panama	(6)	(6)	(4)	(4)	(4)
Paraguay	(6)	(6)	(6)	(6)	(6)
Peru	(6)	(4)	(4)	(6)	(8)
Trinidad/Tobago	(4)	(4)	(4)	(2)	(2)
Uruguay	(6)	(6)	(6)	(6)	(6)
Venezuela	(6)	(4)	(4)	(2)	(2)
EUROPE/MIDDLE EAST					
Albania	(0)	(0)	(0)	(0)	(0)
Bahrain	(2)	(2)	(2)	(2)	(2)
Bulgaria	(0)	(0)	(0)	(0)	(0)
Croatia	-	-	-	-	(0)
Cyprus	(6)	(6)	(6)	(6)	(6)
Czechoslovakia	(0)	(0)	(0)	(0)	-
Czech Republic	-	-	-	-	(4)
Slovakia	-	-	-	-	(4)
Egypt	(0)	(0)	(0)	(0)	(0)
Estonia	-	-	-	-	(2)
Greece	(2)	(2)	(2)	(2)	(2)
Hungary	(0)	(0)	(0)	(0)	(2)
Iran	(4)	(2)	(2)	(2)	(2)
Israel	(2)	(2)	(2)	(2)	(2)
Jordan	(6)	(6)	(6)	(6)	(6)
Latvia	-	-	-	-	(0)
Lithuania	-	-	-	-	(0)
Malta	(4)	(4)	(4)	(4)	(4)
Oman	(2)	(2)	(2)	(2)	(2)
Poland	(0)	(0)	(0)	(0)	(2)
Portugal	(2)	(2)	(2)	(2)	(2)
Romania	(0)	(0)	(0)	(0)	(0)
Russia	(0)	(0)	(0)	(0)	(0)
Slovenia	-	-	-	-	(2)
Syria	(6)	(4)	(2)	(2)	(2)
Turkey	(4)	(4)	(4)	(4)	(4)
Ukraine	-	-	-	-	(0)
ASIA					
Bangladesh	(6)	(6)	(6)	(6)	(6)
China	(0)	(0)	(0)	(0)	(0)
Fiji	(6)	(6)	(6)	(6)	(6)
Hong Kong	(10)	(10)	(10)	(10)	(10)
India	(0)	(0)	(0)	(0)	(2)
Indonesia	(4)	(2)	(2)	(2)	(2)
Malaysia	(6)	(4)	(4)	(6)	(6)

Table II-B: (continued)

Size of Government Enterprises As A Share of Economy
(A higher rating indicates that government enterprises play a less significant role.)

	1975	1980	1985	1990	1995
ASIA					
Nepal	(2)	(2)	(2)	(2)	(2)
Pakistan	(2)	(2)	(2)	(4)	(4)
Philippines	(4)	(4)	(4)	(6)	(6)
Singapore	(8)	(8)	(8)	(8)	(8)
South Korea	(6)	(6)	(6)	(6)	(6)
Sri Lanka	(2)	(2)	(2)	(4)	(4)
Taiwan	(4)	(4)	(4)	(6)	(6)
Thailand	(6)	(6)	(6)	(6)	(6)
AFRICA					
Algeria	(0)	(0)	(0)	(0)	(0)
Benin	(4)	(4)	(4)	(4)	(4)
Botswana	(8)	(8)	(8)	(6)	(6)
Burundi	(2)	(2)	(2)	(2)	(2)
Cameroon	(4)	(4)	(4)	(4)	(4)
C African Rep	(6)	(6)	(6)	(6)	(6)
Chad	(4)	(4)	(4)	(4)	(4)
Congo Rep	(0)	(0)	(0)	(0)	(0)
Cote d' Ivoire	(4)	(4)	(4)	(4)	(4)
Gabon	(6)	(6)	(6)	(6)	(6)
Ghana	(0)	(0)	(0)	(2)	(2)
Kenya	(4)	(4)	(4)	(4)	(4)
Madagascar	(6)	(6)	(6)	(6)	(6)
Malawi	(4)	(4)	(4)	(4)	(4)
Mali	(4)	(4)	(4)	(4)	(4)
Mauritius	(6)	(6)	(6)	(6)	(6)
Morocco	(4)	(4)	(2)	(2)	(2)
Niger	(4)	(4)	(4)	(6)	(6)
Nigeria	(4)	(2)	(2)	(2)	(2)
Rwanda	(6)	(6)	(6)	(6)	(6)
Senegal	(4)	(4)	(4)	(6)	(6)
Sierra Leone	(6)	(6)	(6)	(6)	(6)
Somalia	(4)	(4)	(4)	(4)	(4)
South Africa	(4)	(4)	(4)	(4)	(4)
Tanzania	(2)	(2)	(0)	(0)	(0)
Togo	(4)	(4)	(4)	(4)	(4)
Tunisia	(0)	(0)	(0)	(2)	(2)
Uganda	(2)	(2)	(2)	(2)	(2)
Zaire	(2)	(2)	(2)	(2)	(2)
Zambia	(0)	(0)	(0)	(0)	(0)
Zimbabwe	(4)	(4)	(4)	(4)	(4)

Source and Explanation of Ratings: The rating for each country was designed to reflect the following.

Role of Government Enterprises in Country	Rating
There are very few state-operated enterprises (SOEs) and they produce less then 1 percent of the country's total output.	10
There are very few SOEs other than power-generating plants and those operating in industries where economies of scale generally reduce the effectiveness of competition.	8
SOEs are generally present in power generating, transportation (airlines, railroads, and bus lines), communications (television and radio stations, telephone companies, and post offices) and the development of energy sources, but private enterprises dominates other sectors of the economy. SOEs account for less than 10% of non-agricultural output and employment.	6
There are a substantial number of SOEs in many sectors of the economy, including the manufacturing sector. Most of the large enterprises of the economy are operated by the government; private enterprises are generally small. Employment and output in the SOEs generally comprises between 10 and 20 percent of the total non- agricultural employment and output.	4
Numerous SOEs of all sizes are present and they operate in many sectors of the economy, including manufacturing and retail sales. Employment and output in the SOEs generally comprises between 20 and 30 percent of the total non-agricultural employment and output.	2
The economy is dominated by SOEs. Employment and output in the SOEs generally exceeds 30 percent of the total non-agricultural employment and output.	0

Data on the number of government enterprises and the activities of these enterprises from the International Monetary Fund, *Government Finance Statistics Yearbook*, (various issues) and World Bank Policy Research Report, *Bureaucrats in Business* (World Bank, 1995) were used to assist with the determination of the rating for each country. In addition, the following publications were helpful in determining the proper classification for various countries: V.V. Ramanadham, ed., *Privatization in Developing Countries*, London: Routledge, 1989; Rexford A. Ahene and Bernard S. Katz, eds., *Privatization and Investment in Sub-Saharan Africa*, New York: Praeger, 1992; Manuel Sanchez and Rossana Corona, eds., *Privatization in Latin America*, Washington, D.C.: Inter-American Development Bank, 1993; Iliya Harik and Denis J. Sullivan, eds., *Privatization and Liberalization in the Middle East*, Bloomington, IN: Indiana University Press, 1992; *OECD Economic Surveys*, Italy; Organization for Economic Co-Operation and Development, January 1994; John R. Nellis, "Public Enterprises in Sub-Saharan Africa," *World Bank Discussion Paper*, no. 1 (Washington, DC: November, 1986); Bos Dieter, *Public Enterprise Economics*, New York: North Holland, 1989; and Raymond Vernon, editor, *The Promise of Privatization: A Challenge for American Foreign Policy*, New York: Council on Foreign Relations, 1988.

Table II-C: The Extent Countries Imposed Price Controls on Various Goods and Services, (1990 and 1995)

INDUSTRIAL COUNTRIES	Rating (Ten indicates little or no use of price controls)	
	1990	1995
United States	8	9
Canada	8	7
Australia	6	7
Japan	6	5
New Zealand	9	10
Austria	5	8
Belgium	2	5
Denmark	6	9
Finland	6	9
France	6	8
Germany	9	9
Iceland	6	6
Ireland	7	8
Italy	5	5
Netherlands	7	7
Norway	5	7
Spain	6	5
Sweden	6	8
Switzerland	7	6
United Kingdom	8	9
CENTRAL/S. AMERICA		
Argentina	0	8
Bahamas	4	4
Barbados	6	6
Belize	0	6
Bolivia	6	8
Brazil	0	6
Chile	8	10
Colombia	6	5
Costa Rica	6	6
Dominican Republic	4	6
Ecuador	0	0
El Salvador	-	6
Guatemala	6	6
Haiti	2	0
Honduras	4	4
Jamaica	4	4
Mexico	0	5
Nicaragua	0	2
Panama	2	4
Paraguay	4	6

CENTRAL/- S. AMERICA (con't)	Rating (Ten indicates little or no use of price controls)	
	1990	1995
Peru	2	6
Trinidad/Tobago	4	4
Uruguay	4	6
Venezuela	4	0
EUROPE/MIDDLE EAST		
Albania	0	4
Bahrain	4	4
Bulgaria	0	4
Croatia	0	2
Cyprus	0	2
Czechoslovakia	0	-
Czech Rep	-	6
Slovakia	-	4
Egypt	2	2
Estonia	0	6
Greece	0	5
Hungary	6	7
Iran	2	2
Israel	0	5
Jordan	2	2
Latvia	0	6
Lithuania	0	4
Malta	0	2
Oman	4	4
Poland	2	6
Portugal	4	5
Romania	0	6
Russia	0	2
Slovenia	-	6
Syria	-	0
Turkey	6	5
Ukraine	0	2
ASIA		
Bangladesh	0	0
China	2	3
Fiji	6	6
Hong Kong	10	9
India	3	4
Indonesia	6	2
Malaysia	5	4
Nepal	2	2

Table II-C: (continued)

	Rating (Ten indicates little or no use of price controls)				Rating (Ten indicates little or no use of price controls)	
ASIA (cont.)	1990	1995	AFRICA (cont)	1990	1995
Pakistan	-	4	Kenya	2	4
Philippines	2	4	Madagascar	4	4
Singapore	8	8	Malawi	2	2
South Korea	3	3	Mali	2	4
Sri Lanka	4	4	Mauritius	4	4
Taiwan	6	6	Morocco	0	4
Thailand	4	4	Niger	2	2
			Nigeria	4	0
AFRICA			Rwanda	-	-
Algeria	2	2	Senegal	4	4
Benin	-	2	Sierra Leone	2	2
Botswana	6	6	Somalia	0	-
Burundi	2	2	South Africa	4	6
Cameroon	2	2	Tanzania	0	4
C African Rep	2	2	Togo	2	2
Chad	2	2	Tunisia	4	6
Congo Peoples Rep	0	0	Uganda	2	4
Cote d' Ivoire	2	4	Zaire	2	2
Gabon	-	4	Zambia	0	2
Ghana	0	6	Zimbabwe	2	4

Source: The foundation for these ratings was provided by the data of the World Economic Forum, *The World Competitiveness Report*, (1990 and 1996) and Price Waterhouse, *Doing Business Series*. *The World Competitiveness Report* contains survey data indicating the "extent to which companies can set their prices freely: 0 = not at all, to 100 = very much so." In the 1996 survey, 46 countries were rated. These data were the most comprehensive quantifiable indicators of the presence or absence of price controls which we could find. The following table indicates the relationship between the World Economic Forum survey data and our 0 to 10 rating system.

Percent Indicating Companies Can Set Prices Freely	Rating
more than 90%	10
85 — 90	9
80 — 85	8
75 — 80	7
70 — 75	6
65 — 70	5
60 — 65	4
55 — 60	3
50 — 55	2
45 — 50	1
less than 40%	0

The Price Waterhouse booklet provided a verbal description on the general presence or absence of price controls which helped us classify other countries. In some instances, this information was supplemented with similar information which was available from country sources. These descriptive data were used to classify countries and place them into the following categories.

General Characteristics of Country	Rating
No price controls or marketing boards are present.	10
Except in industries (e.g., electric power generation) where economics of scale may reduce the effectiveness of competition, prices are generally determined by market forces.	8
Price controls are often applied in energy markets; marketing boards often influence prices of agricultural products; controls are also present in a few other areas, but most prices are determined by market forces.	6
Price controls are levied on energy, agricultural, and many stable products (e. g. food products, clothing and housing) that are widely purchased by households; but most other prices are set by market forces.	4
Price controls apply to a significant number of products in both agricultural and manufacturing industries.	2
There is widespread use of price controls throughout the economy.	0

Table II-D: Freedom of Businesses and Cooperatives to Compete in the Marketplace

Are Businesses and Cooperatives Free to Compete?

(1994-95 Rating--the Higher the Rating the Greater the Freedom to Compete)

INDUSTRIAL COUNTRIES		CENTRAL/- S. AMERICA (con't)	
United States	10.0	Paraguay	7.5
Canada	7.5	Peru	7.5
Australia	10.0	Trinidad/Tobago	7.5
Japan	7.5	Uruguay	7.5
New Zealand	10.0	Venezuela	7.5
Austria	7.5		
Belgium	7.5	**EUROPE/MIDDLE EAST**	
Denmark	10.0	Albania	5.0
Finland	7.5	Bahrain	5.0
France	7.5	Bulgaria	7.5
Germany	7.5	Croatia	5.0
Iceland	10.0	Cyprus	10.0
Ireland	7.5	Czech Republic	10.0
Italy	7.5	Egypt	2.5
Netherlands	7.5	Estonia	10.0
Norway	7.5	Greece	7.5
Spain	7.5	Hungary	10.0
Sweden	10.0	Iran	2.5
Switzerland	10.0	Israel	7.5
United Kingdom	10.0	Jordan	5.0
		Latvia	7.5
CENTRAL/SOUTH AMERICA		Lithuania	7.5
Argentina	10.0	Malta	7.5
Bahamas	5.0	Oman	2.5
Barbados	5.0	Poland	7.5
Belize	7.5	Portugal	7.5
Bolivia	7.5	Romania	5.0
Brazil	7.5	Russia	5.0
Chile	10.0	Slovakia	7.5
Colombia	7.5	Slovenia	5.0
Costa Rica	10.0	Syria	2.5
Dominican Rep	5.0	Turkey	7.5
Ecuador	7.5	Ukraine	5.0
El Salvador	5.0		
Guatemala	5.0	**ASIA**	
Haiti	5.0	Bangladesh	5.0
Honduras	7.5	China	5.0
Jamaica	7.5	Fiji	7.5
Mexico	7.5	Hong Kong	10.0
Nicaragua	7.5	India	5.0
Panama	7.5	Indonesia	2.5

Table II-D: (Con't)

Are Businesses and Cooperatives Free to Compete?

(1994-95 Rating--the Higher the Rating the Greater the Freedom to Compete)

ASIA (cont.)		AFRICA (cont.)	
Malaysia	7.5	Ghana	5.0
Nepal	5.0	Kenya	5.0
Pakistan	5.0	Madagascar	5.0
Philippines	5.0	Malawi	7.5
Singapore	7.5	Mali	5.0
South Korea	7.5	Mauritius	10.0
Sri Lanka	5.0	Morocco	5.0
Taiwan	7.5	Niger	5.0
Thailand	5.0	Nigeria	2.5
		Rwanda	2.5
AFRICA		Senegal	5.0
Algeria	5.0	Sierra Leone	5.0
Benin	7.5	Somalia	2.5
Botswana	7.5	South Africa	7.5
Burundi	2.5	Tanzania	2.5
Cameroon	5.0	Togo	5.0
C African Rep	5.0	Tunisia	5.0
Chad	5.0	Uganda	5.0
Congo Rep	5.0	Zaire	2.5
Cote d' Ivoire	5.0	Zambia	5.0
Gabon	7.5	Zimbabwe	5.0

Source: See Freedom House, *Freedom in the World: The Annual Survey of Political Rights and Civil Liberties, 1995-96*. The survey team of Freedom House ranked countries with regard to the economic freedom of businesses and cooperatives to compete in the marketplace (Item 9 on their checklist of 13 civil liberty categories). Each country was given a rating of 0 to 4 with a rating of 4 indicating the countries for which businesses and cooperatives were most free to compete. We transformed the 0 to 4 rating of Freedom House to our 0 to 10 scale (0 = 0, 1 = 2.5, 2 = 5, 3 = 7.5 and 4 = 10). The Freedom House ratings were quite generous. Most all countries received ratings of 5 or more. In a few cases (Bahamas, Barbados, Dominican Republic, and Benin), we reduced the rating one unit because there was substantial evidence that the Freedom House rating was overly generous.

Table II-E: Equality of Citizens Under the Law and Access to a Nondiscriminatory Judiciary

Equality of Citizens Under the Law

(1994-1995: the higher rating indicates greater equality under the law)

INDUSTRIAL COUNTRIES		CENTRAL/- S. AMERICA (con't)	
United States	7.5	Paraguay	2.5
Canada	7.5	Peru	2.5
Australia	7.5	Trinidad/Tobago	7.5
Japan	7.5	Uruguay	5.0
New Zealand	10.0	Venezuela	0.0
Austria	7.5		
Belgium	10.0	**EUROPE/MIDDLE EAST**	
Denmark	10.0	Albania	2.5
Finland	10.0	Bahrain	0.0
France	7.5	Bulgaria	5.0
Germany	7.5	Croatia	5.0
Iceland	10.0	Cyprus	7.5
Ireland	7.5	Czech Republic	5.0
Italy	7.5	Egypt	0.0
Netherlands	10.0	Estonia	7.5
Norway	10.0	Greece	5.0
Spain	5.0	Hungary	7.5
Sweden	10.0	Iran	0.0
Switzerland	10.0	Israel	5.0
United Kingdom	7.5	Jordan	2.5
		Latvia	5.0
CENTRAL/SOUTH AMERICA		Lithuania	7.5
Argentina	2.5	Malta	10.0
Bahamas	5.0	Oman	2.5
Barbados	7.5	Poland	5.0
Belize	7.5	Portugal	7.5
Bolivia	0.0	Romania	5.0
Brazil	0.0	Russia	2.5
Chile	5.0	Slovakia	5.0
Colombia	0.0	Slovenia	7.5
Costa Rica	7.5	Syria	0.0
Dominican Rep	0.0	Turkey	0.0
Ecuador	2.5	Ukraine	5.0
El Salvador	2.5		
Guatemala	0.0	**ASIA**	
Haiti	0.0	Bangladesh	5.0
Honduras	2.5	China	0.0
Jamaica	2.5	Fiji	5.0
Mexico	0.0	Hong Kong	7.5
Nicaragua	2.5	India	2.5
Panama	2.5	Indonesia	0.0

Table II-E: (continued)

Equality of Citizens Under the Law

(1994-1995: the higher rating indicates greater equality under the law)

ASIA (cont.)		AFRICA (cont.)	
Malaysia	2.5	Ghana	2.5
Nepal	0.0	Kenya	0.0
Pakistan	0.0	Madagascar	2.5
Philippines	2.5	Malawi	5.0
Singapore	0.0	Mali	2.5
South Korea	7.5	Mauritius	7.5
Sri Lanka	0.0	Morocco	0.0
Taiwan	5.0	Niger	2.5
Thailand	2.5	Nigeria	0.0
		Rwanda	0.0
AFRICA		Senegal	2.5
Algeria	0.0	Sierra Leone	0.0
Benin	5.0	Somalia	0.0
Botswana	7.5	South Africa	7.5
Burundi	0.0	Tanzania	5.0
Cameroon	0.0	Togo	0.0
C African Rep	5.0	Tunisia	0.0
Chad	0.0	Uganda	2.5
Congo Rep	2.5	Zaire	0.0
Cote d' Ivoire	0.0	Zambia	2.5
Gabon	2.5	Zimbabwe	2.5

Source: These data are from the annual survey of political and civil liberties conducted by the Freedom House. Item 5 of the 13 item civil liberties checklist is: "Are citizens equal under the law, do they have access to an independent, non-discriminatory judiciary, and are they respected by the security forces?" Countries were given ratings ranging from 0 to 4. The higher the rating, the greater the degree of equality under the law. We transformed the 0 to 4 ratings of the Freedom House to our 0 to 10 scale (0 = 0, 1 = 2.5, 2 = 5, 3 = 7.5, and 4 = 10). We are indebted to Joseph Ryan of the Freedom House for supplying the rating for each country to us. See Freedom House, *Survey of Political Rights and Civil Liberties, 1995-96.* This variable was not available for the early periods of our study.

250

Table II-F: Freedom from Government Regulations and Policies That Cause Negative Interest Rates

	Have Government Regulations, Interest Rate Controls, and Inflationary Monetary Policy Caused Negative Interest Rates and Credit Market Disruptions? (When this is the case, a country is given a low rating.)				
	1973-75	1978-80	1983-85	1988-90	1993-95
INDUSTRIAL COUNTRIES					
United States	8	10	10	10	10
Canada	6	10	10	10	10
Australia	4	10	10	10	10
Japan	4	10	10	10	10
New Zealand	-	6	8	10	10
Austria	6	8	10	10	8
Belgium	6	10	10	10	10
Denmark	8	10	10	10	10
Finland	-	8	10	10	10
France	8	8	8	8	10
Germany	8	10	10	10	10
Iceland	2	4	4	6	8
Ireland	4	6	10	10	10
Italy	6	4	6	10	10
Netherlands	6	10	10	10	10
Norway	-	6	10	10	10
Spain	-	6	10	10	10
Sweden	4	8	10	10	10
Switzerland	6	6	10	10	10
United Kingdom	4	4	10	10	10
CENTRAL/SOUTH AMERICA					
Argentina	-	0	0	0	10
Bahamas	8	8	10	10	10
Barbados	-	6	10	10	10
Belize	-	8	8	10	10
Bolivia	-	6	0	8	8
Brazil	-	-	0	0	0
Chile	-	8	8	8	10
Colombia	-	-	-	8	8
Costa Rica	-	-	6	8	8
Dominican Rep	-	-	-	0	8
Ecuador	-	-	0	0	6
El Salvador	-	-	8	8	10
Guatemala	-	8	8	8	8
Haiti	-	-	-	-	0
Honduras	-	-	10	8	4

Table II-F: (continued)

Have Government Regulations, Interest Rate
Controls, and Inflationary Monetary Policy Caused
Negative Interest Rates and Credit Market Disruptions?

(When this is the case, a country is given a low rating.)

	1973-75	1978-80	1983-85	1988-90	1993-95
CTRL/S. AMERICA (cont.)					
Jamaica	-	4	4	8	6
Mexico	-	4	4	8	8
Nicaragua	-	-	-	0	6
Panama	-	-	-	10	10
Paraguay	-	-	-	2	8
Peru	-	-	-	0	6
Trinidad/Tobago	-	-	8	6	6
Uruguay	-	6	8	8	6
Venezuela	-	-	4	0	0
EUROPE/MIDDLE EAST					
Albania	-	-	-	0	6
Bahrain	-	-	-	10	8
Bulgaria	-	-	-	-	2
Croatia	-	-	-	-	4
Cyprus	8	4	8	10	10
Czechoslovakia	-	-	-	-	-
Czech Rep	-	-	-	-	6
Slovakia	-	-	-	-	6
Egypt	-	4	6	6	10
Estonia	-	-	-	-	0
Greece	4	6	6	8	8
Hungary	-	6	-	6	6
Iran	-	-	-	-	0
Israel	-	0	0	6	8
Jordan	-	-	-	4	6
Latvia	-	-	-	-	2
Lithuania	-	-	-	-	0
Malta	-	6	10	10	10
Oman	-	-	10	10	10
Poland	-	-	-	0	6
Portugal	-	4	10	8	10
Romania	-	-	-	10	10
Russia	0	0	0	0	8
Slovenia	-	-	-	-	8
Syria	-	-	-	-	0
Turkey	2	0	8	2	0
Ukraine	-	-	-	-	0

Table II-F: (continued)

**Have Government Regulations, Interest Rate
Controls, and Inflationary Monetary Policy Caused
Negative Interest Rates and Credit Market Disruptions?**
(When this is the case, a country is given a low rating.)

	1973-75	1978-80	1983-85	1988-90	1993-95
ASIA					
Bangladesh	-	6	6	10	8
China	-	0	0	0	4
Fiji	0	6	8	6	8
Hong Kong	10	10	10	10	10
India	4	8	8	8	8
Indonesia	2	2	-	10	10
Malaysia	-	6	10	10	10
Nepal	-	6	6	10	-
Pakistan	-	6	8	6	6
Philippines	8	8	4	8	10
Singapore	-	10	10	10	10
South Korea	2	4	10	10	10
Sri Lanka	-	4	8	8	10
Taiwan	8	8	10	10	10
Thailand	-	4	10	8	10
AFRICA					
Algeria	-	-	-	-	0
Benin	-	6	8	8	2
Botswana	-	4	8	4	6
Burundi	-	2	6	4	4
Cameroon	-	6	6	8	4
C African Rep	-	-	8	10	6
Chad	-	-	8	8	4
Congo Peoples Rep	-	6	8	10	2
Cote d' Ivoire	-	8	10	8	4
Gabon	-	6	8	8	4
Ghana	-	0	0	2	4
Kenya	4	8	10	10	4
Madagascar	-	-	-	-	-
Malawi	-	4	8	6	4
Mali	-	4	6	8	6
Mauritius	-	-	10	8	10
Morocco	-	-	6	8	8
Niger	-	2	-	8	6
Nigeria	2	2	4	0	0
Rwanda	-	6	8	10	0
Senegal	-	8	6	8	4
Sierra Leone	-	6	0	0	2
Somalia	4	0	0	0	0

Table II-F: (continued)

**Have Government Regulations, Interest Rate
Controls, and Inflationary Monetary Policy Caused
Negative Interest Rates and Credit Market Disruptions?**

(When this is the case, a country is given a low rating.)

AFRICA (cont.)	1973-75	1978-80	1983-85	1988-90	1993-95
South Africa	-	4	8	8	10
Tanzania	-	4	0	4	4
Togo	-	8	8	8	8
Tunisia	-	4	6	8	8
Uganda	-	0	0	0	4
Zaire	-	-	-	0	0
Zambia	4	4	0	0	0
Zimbabwe	-	6	8	8	8

Source and Explanation of Ratings: This rating seeks to identify how credit market regulations, interest rate controls, and government operation of the banking system stifle and distort exchange in the credit market. When interest rates are determined by market forces and monetary policy is relatively stable, positive *real* borrowing and lending rates will emerge consistently in credit markets. When this is the case, the country is given a high rating. There are several ways that regulations and controls can restrict exchanges between potential borrowers and lenders. The most damaging is the combination of an inflationary monetary policy coupled with interest rate controls that lead to substantial, persistently *negative real* deposit and lending interest rates. Thus, countries with persistently large *negative real* deposit and lending interest rates are rated low. In addition, regulations and controls that drive a wedge between the deposit rate and the lending rate will stifle exchange. Thus, a country is given a lower rating if the differential between the deposit and the lending rate is abnormally large. The inflation rate, deposit rate, and lending rate data of the International Monetary Fund, *International Financial Statistics Yearbook* (or the monthly version of this publication) were used to estimate the real interest rates. The real interest rate is simply the nominal rate (either the deposit rate or the lending rate) minus the rate of inflation during the year. The following table indicates the relationship between the rating and the characteristics in the credit market.

Characteristics in Credit Market	Rating
Interest rates are determined primarily by market forces and real interest rates are consistently positive.	10
Interest rates are determined primarily by market forces, but real interest rates are sometimes slightly (less than 5%) negative and/or regulatory policies result in a persistent abnormally large differential (8% or more) between the deposit and the lending interest rate.	8
Either the deposit or lending real interest rate is persistently negative by a single-digit amount.	6
Both the deposit and lending interest rates are fixed by the government and the real rates are persistently negative by single- digit amounts.	4
Either the deposit or lending real interest rate is persistently negative by a double-digit amount.	2
Both the deposit and lending interest rates are fixed by the government and the real rates are persistently negative by double- digit amounts or hyperinflation has virtually eliminated the operation of the credit market.	0

Table III-A: Transfers and Subsides As A Percent of GDP
(1975, 1980, 1985, 1990, and 1995)

	\multicolumn{10}{c}{Transfers and Subsidies As A Percent of GDP}
	\multicolumn{10}{c}{(Rating in parenthesis)}
INDUSTRIAL COUNTRIES	\multicolumn{2}{c}{1975}	\multicolumn{2}{c}{1980}	\multicolumn{2}{c}{1985}	\multicolumn{2}{c}{1990}	\multicolumn{2}{c}{1995}
United States	11.1	(4)	10.9	(4)	12.5	(3)	12.7	(3)	13.9	(3) [a]
Canada	9.1	(4)	14.5	(3)	16.3	(2)	15.6	(3)	17.7	(2) [d]
Australia	8.5	(4)	10.1	(4)	11.9	(3)	10.7	(4)	14.2	(3)
Japan	6.7	(5)	9.2	(4)	10.9	(4)	11.5	(4)	12.2	(3)
New Zealand	20.2	(1)	21.9	(1)	20.6	(1)	27.5	(0)	12.8	(3)
Austria	19.4	(2)	22.1	(1)	23.1	(1)	22.4	(1)	24.4	(1) [a]
Belgium	28.5	(0)	26.0	(0)	27.6	(0)	25.0	(0)	26.5	(0) [a]
Denmark	17.8	(2)	20.8	(1)	20.4	(1)	22.6	(1)	26.5	(0)
Finland	14.1	(3)	14.3	(3)	15.8	(2)	16.0	(2)	22.6	(1) [a]
France	24.0	(1)	26.1	(0)	26.8	(0)	25.2	(0)	27.9	(0)
Germany	17.4	(2)	17.6	(2)	19.0	(2)	17.9	(2)	21.6	(1)
Iceland	9.9	(4)	10.6	(4)	11.7	(4)	10.1	(4)	10.2	(4) [b]
Ireland	18.3	(2)	17.7	(2)	20.5	(1)	24.2	(1)	27.1	(0) [b]
Italy	17.5	(2)	20.9	(1)	28.5	(0)	25.8	(0)	29.3	(0) [a]
Netherlands	25.6	(0)	29.4	(0)	31.6	(0)	28.7	(0)	29.7	(0)
Norway	21.0	(1)	22.1	(1)	21.4	(1)	27.3	(0)	23.2	(1) [a]
Spain	9.5	(4)	12.3	(3)	16.9	(2)	16.0	(2)	18.9	(2) [b]
Sweden	25.0	(0)	24.7	(0)	26.0	(0)	29.9	(0)	35.2	(0) [a]
Switzerland	-		13.4	(3)	13.2	(3)	16.0	(2)	18.3	(2) [b]
United Kingdom	15.0	(3)	15.8	(2)	17.9	(2)	14.9	(3)	17.7	(2)
CENTRAL/SOUTH AMERICA										
Argentina	7.9	(5)	9.7	(4)	11.7	(4)	7.2	(5)	9.4	(4) [c]
Bahamas	0.5	(10)	0.5	(10)	0.1	(10)	1.0	(10)	1.6	(9) [b]
Barbados	0.2	(10)	0.2	(10)	0.0	(10)	0.5	(10)	0.0	(10)
Belize	-		2.6	(8)	3.6	(7)	1.2	(10)	1.2	(10)
Bolivia	1.3	(10)	1.6	(9)	1.8	(9)	2.8	(8)	2.5	(8)
Brazil	-		12.4	(3)	10.0	(4)	10.7	(4)	14.9	(3) [b]
Chile	9.4	(4)	10.4	(4)	12.8	(3)	6.3	(5)	6.7	(5) [a]
Colombia	3.0	(8)	2.9	(8)	4.4	(7)	3.7	(7)	4.1	(7) [b]
Costa Rica	-		6.0	(5)	7.2	(5)	5.0	(6)	7.0	(5)
Dominican Republic	2.5	(8)	1.6	(9)	2.5	(8)	1.5	(9)	1.4	(9) [a]
Ecuador	-		4.9	(6)	4.0	(7)	2.3	(8)	1.5	(9)
El Salvador	2.5	(8)	2.7	(8)	2.0	(9)	1.4	(9)	3.2	(8) [a]
Guatemala	0.8	(10)	1.2	(10)	1.3	(10)	1.8	(9)	1.5	(9) [a]
Haiti	-		-		7.3	(5)	-		-	
Honduras	0.5	(10)	-		2.3	(8)	2.2	(8)	4.0	(7) [c]
Jamaica	7.0	(5)	-		0.5	(10)	2.0	(9)	3.9	(7) [c]
Mexico	4.1	(7)	4.4	(7)	5.4	(6)	2.7	(8)	4.0	(7) [b]
Nicaragua	2.4	(8)	4.1	(7)	6.2	(5)	6.8	(5)	6.0	(5)
Panama	3.8	(7)	4.9	(6)	4.8	(6)	7.4	(5)	6.8	(5) [a]

Table III-A: (con't)

Transfers and Subsidies As A Percent of GDP
(Rating in parenthesis)

CENTRAL/-SOUTH AMERICA	1975		1980		1985		1990		1995	
Paraguay	2.0	(9)	2.0	(9)	2.1	(9)	1.8	(9)	3.0	(8) b
Peru	1.9	(9)	1.9	(9)	1.8	(9)	3.0	(8)	3.9	(7)
Trinidad & Tobago	-		6.0	(5)	14.9	(3)	10.0	(4)	8.3	(4) c
Uruguay	11.8	(4)	9.1	(4)	10.0	(4)	12.0	(3)	17.3	(2)
Venezuela	2.3	(8)	2.0	(9)	4.5	(7)	5.8	(5)	5.1	(6) b
EUROPE/MIDDLE EAST										
Albania	-		-		-		24.3	(1)	14.9	(3) b
Bahrain	-		-		0.0	(10)	0.5	(10)	0.0	(10)
Bulgaria	-		-		17.5	(2)	27.2	(0)	15.6	(3) c
Croatia	-		-		-		-		-	
Cyprus	10.3	(4)	6.6	(5)	8.1	(4)	8.3	(4)	10.1	(4) a
Czechoslovakia	-		-		-		37.2	(0)	-	
Czech Republic	-		-		-		-		28.4	(0)
Slovakia	-		-		-		-		-	
Egypt	25.0	(0)	17.2	(2)	13.9	(3)	8.9	(4)	8.9	(4) b
Estonia	-		-		-		-		13.7	(3) d
Greece	12.5	(3)	13.8	(3)	17.7	(2)	23.8	(1)	24.6	(0) b
Hungary	-		-		33.3	(0)	28.7	(0)	25.0	(0)
Iran	8.9	(4)	7.0	(5)	3.0	(8)	4.4	(7)	3.2	(8) a
Israel	-		20.8	(1)	19.7	(1)	16.7	(2)	18.6	(2)
Jordan	-		6.3	(5)	5.1	(6)	3.7	(7)	2.9	(8) a
Latvia	-		-		-		-		18.2	(2)
Lithuania	-		-		-		-		10.4	(4)
Malta	14.7	(3)	12.2	(3)	15.7	(3)	15.6	(3)	14.0	(3) b
Oman	-		-		3.1	(8)	2.9	(8)	2.7	(8) a
Poland	-		-		27.4	(0)	7.2	(5)	24.4	(1)
Portugal	14.6	(3)	16.3	(2)	19.5	(2)	15.5	(3)	14.2	(3) a
Romania	-		14.1	(3)	7.9	(5)	18.6	(2)	14.6	(3) a
Russia	30.0	(0)	30.0	(0)	30.0	(0)	30.0	(0)	20.0	(1)
Slovenia	-		-		-		-		-	
Syria	-		-		-		-		-	
Turkey	6.0	(5)	6.0	(5)	10.4	(4)	3.9	(7)	7.1	(5) a
Ukraine	-		-		-		-		-	
ASIA										
Bangladesh	-		-		-		-		-	
China	-		-		-		-		-	
Fiji	1.9	(9)	2.5	(8)	4.5	(7)	1.0	(10)	2.7	(8) c
Hong Kong	1.1	(10)	0.6	(10)	0.9	(10)	0.9	(10)	1.1	(10)
India	3.8	(7)	5.4	(6)	6.5	(5)	6.5	(5)	6.3	(5) b
Indonesia	1.5	(9)	3.3	(7)	2.5	(8)	2.0	(9)	0.3	(10) b
Malaysia	6.4	(5)	4.8	(6)	3.6	(7)	2.4	(8)	3.6	(7) a
Nepal	-		-		-		-		-	

Table III-A: (con't)

Transfers and Subsidies As A Percent of GDP
(Rating in parenthesis)

	1975	1980	1985	1990	1995
ASIA					
Pakistan	-	-	0.7 (10)	-	-
Philippines	0.8 (10)	1.1 (10)	0.2 (10)	0.9 (10)	0.7 (10) [a]
Singapore	1.4 (9)	1.1 (10)	1.8 (9)	2.6 (8)	1.8 (9)
South Korea	2.0 (9)	2.0 (9)	2.2 (8)	2.9 (8)	2.9 (8)
Sri Lanka	8.1 (4)	8.4 (4)	5.1 (6)	6.0 (5)	5.9 (5)
Taiwan	2.2 (8)	2.6 (8)	3.6 (7)	4.7 (6)	5.9 (5)
Thailand	0.6 (10)	0.7 (10)	1.2 (10)	1.0 (10)	1.1 (10)
AFRICA					
Algeria	-	-	-	-	-
Benin	-	-	-	-	-
Botswana	5.5 (6)	4.9 (6)	7.3 (5)	6.6 (5)	7.8 (5) [b]
Burundi	-	-	-	-	-
Cameroon	1.4 (9)	0.8 (10)	0.6 (10)	2.7 (8)	1.9 (9) [b]
Central African Rep	-	-	-	-	-
Chad	-	-	-	0.9 (10)	0.8 (10) [d]
Congo	-	-	-	-	-
Cote d'Ivoire	-	4.2 (7)	-	-	-
Gabon	-	-	-	1.2 (10)	1.2 (10) [d]
Ghana	3.1 (8)	2.4 (8)	1.3 (9)	2.6 (8)	3.3 (7) [c]
Kenya	-	2.3 (8)	4.7 (6)	2.8 (8)	1.9 (9) [b]
Madagascar	-	-	-	1.4 (9)	1.1 (10)
Malawi	1.0 (10)	2.0 (9)	2.3 (8)	2.4 (8)	-
Mali	2.3 (8)	2.3 (8)	2.3 (8)	0.6 (10)	-
Mauritius	6.6 (5)	6.5 (5)	5.2 (6)	4.2 (7)	4.4 (7)
Morocco	6.0 (5)	4.1 (7)	4.6 (7)	2.3 (8)	2.8 (8) [c]
Niger		2.5 (8)	-	-	-
Nigeria	2.8 (8)	-	1.3 (9)	-	-
Rwanda	0.4 (10)	0.4 (10)	-	3.5 (7)	2.2 (8) [c]
Senegal	1.9 (9)	-	-	-	-
Sierra Leone	1.6 (9)	-	0.6 (10)	1.6 (9) [c]	4.3 (7)
Somalia	-	-	-	-	-
South Africa	-	3.2 (8)	4.8 (6)	4.8 (6)	5.3 (6) [a]
Tanzania	0.1 (10)	0.0 (10)	5.2 (6)	-	-
Togo	-	-	-	-	-
Tunisia	1.9 (9)	5.6 (6)	6.8 (5)	9.0 (4)	7.7 (5) [c]
Uganda	-	-	-	-	-
Zaire	1.0 (10)	0.6 (10)	-	0.8 (10)	0.2 (10) [b]
Zambia	7.0 (5)	8.7 (4)	4.2 (7)	4.5 (7)	2.6 (8)
Zimbabwe	-	11.4 (4)	10.0 (4)	-	-

a= 1994; b= 1993; c= 1992; d=1991 data.

257

Source: The data on transfers and subsidies are from International Monetary Fund, *Government Finance Statistics Yearbook*, (various years). In addition, supplementary data on transfers and subsides from Inter-American Development ment Bank, *Economic and Social Progress in Latin America*, 1994, were also utilized. The 1994 data were the most recent available at the time this study was completed. The base year for the rating of each country was 1985. The following conversion table divided the 1985 data into eleven intervals of equal size.

Transfers and Subsidies as a Percent of GDP	Rating
0.0% — 1.30	10
1.31 — 2.11	9
2.12 — 3.26	8
3.27 — 4.62	7
4.63 — 5.75	6
5.76 — 8.01	5
8.02 — 11.81	4
11.82 — 15.74	3
15.75 — 19.59	2
19.60 — 24.51	1
> 24.52	0

Table III-B: Top Marginal Tax Rate and Income Threshold (Measured in 1982-84 dollars) at which Top Rate Takes Affect

	1975			1980		
INDUSTRIAL COUNTRIES	Top Marginal Tax Rate	Threshold Income Level	Rating	Top Marginal Tax Rate	Threshold Income Level	Rating
United States	70-75	185,000	0	70-75	82,645	0
Canada	43-61	130,109	4	47-62	115,840	4
Australia	64	74,348	2	62	51,928	2
Japan	68	185,000	1	75	546,694	0
New Zealand	60	83,642	3	60	31,818	2
Austria	54	185,000	4	62	153,581	2
Belgium	64	185,000	2	76	187,879	0
Denmark	63	37,174	1	66	37,052	0
Finland	61-68	111,522	2	65-71	88,843	1
France	48	130,109	5	60	126,722	3
Germany	56	167,283	4	56	193,939	3
Iceland	-	-		63	17,725	0
Ireland	80	46,468	0	60	19,559	1
Italy	48	185,000	5	72	819,559	0
Netherlands	46	185,000	5	72	127,548	0
Norway	74	111,522	0	75	82,645	0
Spain	55	185,000	4	66	195,592	1
Sweden	70	74,348	1	87	53,306	0
Switzerland	38-42	111,522	7	31-44	76,171	7
United Kingdom	41	185,000	7	83	66,942	0
CENTRAL/SOUTH AMERICA						
Argentina	51	65,055	4	45	101,515	6
Bahamas	0	-	10	0	-	10
Barbados	65	45,000	1	60	15,000	1
Belize	-	-		-	-	
Bolivia	-	-		48	15,152	3
Brazil	50	65,055	5	55	105,234	4
Chile	80	185,000	0	60	42,424	2
Colombia	41	111,522	6	56	36,501	2
Costa Rica	50	83,642	5	50	56,061	5
Dominican Rep	73	185,000	0	73	125,000	0
Ecuador	50	148,696	5	50	150,000	5
El Salvador	55	185,000	4	60	137,741	3
Guatemala	34	185,000	9	40	688,700	8
Haiti	-	-		-	-	
Honduras	27	185,000	9	40	688,700	8
Jamaica	60	27,881	2	80	23,967	0
Mexico	47	83,642	5	55	90,634	4
Nicaragua	21	185,000	10	50	275,482	5
Panama	52	185,000	4	56	275,482	3
Paraguay	-	-		-	-	

Table III-B: (continued)

	1975			1980		
CENTRAL/- **S. AMERICA (con't)**	Top Marginal Tax Rate	Threshold Income Level	Rating	Top Marginal Tax Rate	Threshold Income Level	Rating
Peru	51	55,761	4	65	53,719	2
Trinidad/Tobago	-	-		-	-	
Uruguay	41	185,000	7	0	-	10
Venezuela	20	185,000	10	45	1,350,000	7
EUROPE/MIDDLE EAST						
Albania	-	-		-	-	
Bahrain	0	-	10	0	-	10
Bulgaria	-	-		-	-	
Croatia	-	-		-	-	
Cyprus	54	37,174	3	60	19,146	1
Czechoslovakia	-	-		-	-	
Czech Republic	-	-		-	-	
Slovakia	-	-		-	-	
Egypt	-	-		80	196,832	0
Estonia	-	-		-	-	
Greece	52	130,109	4	60	113,223	3
Hungary	-	-		-	-	
Iran	40	150,900	8	-	-	
Israel	-	-		66	70,000	1
Jordan	-	-		-	-	
Latvia	-	-		-	-	
Lithuania	-	-		-	-	
Malta	-	-		65	18,000	0
Oman	0	-	10	0	-	10
Poland	-	-		-	-	
Portugal	82	167,283	0	84	28,788	0
Romania	-	-		-	-	
Russia[e]	100	-	0	100	-	0
Slovenia	-	-		-	-	
Syria	-	-		-	-	
Turkey	68	n.a.	1	75	60,000	0
Ukraine	-	-		-	-	
ASIA						
Bangladesh	-	-		60	10,000	1
China	-	-		-	-	
Fiji	53	27,000	3	53	13,774	2
Hong Kong	15	27,881	10	15	28,512	10
India	77	13,940	0	60	16,529	1
Indonesia	48	37,174	4	50	21,212	3
Malaysia	50	46,468	4	60	47,383	2
Nepal	-	-		-	-	
Pakistan	61	27,881	1	55	6,887	2
Philippines	56	167,000	3	70	94,353	1

Table III-B: (continued)

	1975			1980		
	Top Marginal Tax Rate	Threshold Income Level	Rating	Top Marginal Tax Rate	Threshold Income Level	Rating
ASIA						
Singapore	55	83,642	4	55	255,096	4
South Korea	63	110,000	2	89	238,567	0
Sri Lanka	-	-		60.5	3,500	0
Taiwan	60	111,500	3	60	110,000	3
Thailand	60	100,000	3	60	68,871	3
AFRICA						
Algeria	-	-		-	-	
Benin	-	-		-	-	
Botswana	75	83,642	0	75	66,116	0
Burundi	-	-		-	-	
Cameroon	-	-		-	-	
C African Rep	-	-		-	-	
Chad	-	-		-	-	
Congo Peoples Rep	-	-		-	-	
Cote d' Ivoire	-	-		45	38,500	5
Gabon	-	-		-	-	
Ghana	70	22,000	0	60	700	1
Kenya	70	46,468	0	65	27,500	1
Madagascar	-	-		-	-	
Malawi	69	27,881	0	45	20,937	4
Mali	-	-		-	-	
Mauritius	-	-		50	20,000	3
Morocco	39	185,000	8	64	261,570	2
Niger	-	-		-	-	
Nigeria	75	74,348	0	70	62,000	0
Rwanda	-	-		-	-	
Senegal	-	-		-	-	
Sierra Leone	-	-		-	-	
Somalia	-	-		-	-	
South Africa	66	83,642	1	60	45,868	2
Tanzania	80	74,000	0			
Togo	-	-		-	-	
Tunisia	-	-		62.3	300,000	2
Uganda	-	-		-	-	
Zaire	60	37,200	2	60	8,540	1
Zambia	70	37,175	0	70	22,452	0
Zimbabwe	-	-		45	34,435	5

Table III-B: (continued)

INDUSTRIAL COUNTRIES	1985			1990			1995		
	Top Marginal Tax Rate	Threshold Income Level	Rating	Top Marginal Tax Rate	Threshold Income Level	Rating	Top Marginal Tax Rate	Threshold Income Level	Rating
United States	50-59	156,300	4	33-42	58,937	7	40-47	168,300	7
Canada	49-60	43,100	3	42-47	35,888	5	44-54	27,700	4
Australia	60	28,400	2	49	23,555	3	47	25,500	4
Japan	70	305,500	1	65	178,000	2	65	197,150	2
New Zealand	66	17,200	0	33	15,194	7	33	13,118	7
Austria	62	65,350	2	50	42,728	4	50	41,900	4
Belgium	76	60,600	0	55-65	46,379	2	58-68	49,600	1
Denmark	73	21,400	0	68	24,802	0	63.5	25,500	1
Finland	64-70	59,300	1	63-69	47,128	0	55-61	39,400	2
France	65	30,700	1	53	29,929	3	51	122,750	4
Germany	56	39,650	2	56	114,764	3	57	50,900	3
Iceland	56	9,864	1	40	10,550	5	47	39,535	4
Ireland	65	19,000	0	58	20,214	1	48	8,330	3
Italy	81	248,200	0	66	180,906	1	67	120,800	1
Netherlands	72	59,100	0	72	90,675	0	60	33,500	2
Norway	64	32,600	1	54	28,117	3	42	26,000	5
Spain	66	67,700	1	56	57,114	3	56	48,600	2
Sweden	80	38,100	0	72	24,346	0	58	18,000	1
Switzerland	33-46	145,300	7	33-43	176,000	8	35-39	500,900	8
United Kingdom	60	40,100	2	40	24,700	5	40	24,950	5

CENTRAL/SOUTH AMERICA

	1985			1990			1995		
Argentina	62	65,400	2	35	40,465	7	30	78,750	9
Bahamas	0	-	10	0	-	10	0	-	10
Barbados	60	15,000	1	50	35,700	4	40	7,900	5
Belize	50	30,000	4	45	23,980	4	45	39,370	5
Bolivia	30	45	8	10	1 a	10	13	1 a	10
Brazil	60	10,400	1	25	1,434	9	35	113,600	8
Chile	57	3,600	1	50	3,709	3	45	3,960	4
Colombia	49	55,400	5	30	32,822	8	30	25,400	8
Costa Rica	50	2,200	3	25	9,843	9	25	9,800	9
Dominican Rep	73	497,238	0	73	183,000	0	25	7,570	9
Ecuador	58	27,800	2	40	21,787	5	25	41,600	9
El Salvador	48	11,700	3	60	39,370	2	30	15,000	8
Guatemala	48	324,350	5	34	3,791	7	30	20,900	8
Haiti	-	-		30	193,000	9	-	-	
Honduras	46	476,400	5	46	393,701	5	40	70,000	7
Jamaica	58	2,400	1	33	1,489	7	27	700	8
Mexico	55	59,300	4	40	89,000	7	35	13,000	7
Nicaragua	50	67,600	5				30	16,600	8
Panama	56	192,500	3	56	157,480	3	30	131,000	9
Paraguay	30	8,200	8	30	3,822	8	0 c	-	10
Peru	65	40	0	45	12,558	4	30	32,500	8
Trinidad/Tobago	50	34,600	4	35	9,330	7	38	4,400	5
Uruguay	0	-	10	0	-	10	0	-	10
Venezuela	45	1,110,000	7	45	234,000	7	34	3,900	7

262

Table III-B: (continued)

| EUROPE/-MIDDLE EAST | 1985 | | | 1990 | | | 1995 | | |
	Top Marginal Tax Rate	Threshold Income Level	Rating	Top Marginal Tax Rate	Threshold Income Level	Rating	Top Marginal Tax Rate	Threshold Income Level	Rating
Albania	-	-		-	-		-	-	
Bahrain	0	-	10	0	-	10	0	-	10
Bulgaria	-	-		-	-		50	3,000	3
Croatia	-	-		-	-		-	-	
Cyprus	60	20,900	1	62	18,547	0	42	11000	4
Czechoslovakia	-	-		55	52,500	4	-	-	
Czech Rep.	-	-		-	-		43	25,250	5
Slovakia	-	-		-	-		42	22,700	4
Egypt	65	148,000	2	65	61,750	2	50	13,100	3
Estonia	-	-		-	-		26	200	8
Greece	63	36,500	1	50	28,594	4	45	41,000	5
Hungary	-	-		50	9,900	3	44	3,200	4
Iran	90	59,700	0	75	140,827	0	54	113,300	4
Israel	60	55,000	3	51	82,000	4	50	31,800	4
Jordan	-	-		45	49,000	5	-	-	
Latvia	-	-		-	-		35	4,300	7
Lithuania	-	-		-	-		35	20	7
Malta	65	10,000	0	65	3,030	0	35	8,900	7
Oman	0	-	10	0	-	10	0		10
Poland	-	-		-	-		45	6,700	4
Portugal	69	39,900	0	40	16,171	5	40	24	5
Romania	-	-		-	-		60	3,700	1
Russia	100	-	0	80	-	0	30	9,200	8
Slovenia	-	-		-	-		-	-	
Syria	-	-		-	-		-	-	
Turkey	63	53,800	2	50	32,800	4	55	84,500	4
Ukraine	-	-		-	-		-	-	
ASIA									
Bangladesh	60	8,200	1	-	-		-	-	
China	45	75,000	6	45	48,000	5	45	93,225	6
Fiji	50	16,650	3	50	21,872	3	35	6,900	7
Hong Kong	25 [d]	4,900	9	25 [d]	7,066	9	20 [d]	6,800	10
India	62	7,700	0	53	5,194	2	40	2,500	5
Indonesia	35	44,750	7	35	22,731	7	30	15,000	8
Malaysia	45	117,300	6	45	90,161	6	32	38,720	7
Nepal					-				
Pakistan	60	6,500	1	50	8,394	3	45	6,400	4
Philippines	60	24,350	1	35	18,031	7	35	13,500	7
Singapore	40	325,000	8	33	161,850	9	30	179,690	9
South Korea	65	69,600	2	60	110,000	3	48	53,245	5
Sri Lanka	60.5	2,220	0				35	1,200	7
Taiwan	60	100,000	3	50	97,658	5	40	84,000	7
Thailand	65	70,700	2	55	62,270	4	37	104,400	7

Table III-B: (continued)

	1985			1990			1995		
	Top Marginal Tax Rate	Threshold Income Level	Rating	Top Marginal Tax Rate	Threshold Income Level	Rating	Top Marginal Tax Rate	Threshold Income Level	Rating
AFRICA									
Algeria	-	-		-	-		-	-	
Benin	-	-		-	-		-	-	
Botswana	60	34,300	2	50	16,472	3	35	14,500	7
Burundi							-		
Cameroon	60	30,000	2	60	20,600	1	66	9,205	0
C African Rep	-	-		-	-		-	-	
Chad	-	-		-	-		-	-	
Congo	-	-		50	34,250	4	50	9,800	3
Cote d' Ivoire	45	25,050	5	45	14,500	4	49	12,400	3
Gabon	-	-		60	15,000	1	60	1,475	1
Ghana	60	400	1	55	3,700	2	35	8,800	7
Kenya	65	9,900	0	50	400	3	50	4,600	3
Madagascar	-	-		-	-		-	-	
Malawi	50	13,500	3	50	7,194	3	35	1,500	7
Mali	-	-		-	-		-	-	
Mauritius	35	10,000	7	35	2,750	7	30	2,000	8
Morocco	87	75,500	0	87	28,699	0	46	6,120	3
Niger	-	-		-	-		-	-	
Nigeria	55	40,000	3	55	4,200	2	35	3,000	7
Rwanda							-		
Senegal	65	39,000	1	48	31,000	4	64	15,500	0
Sierra Leone	-	-		-	-		-	-	
Somalia	-	-		-	-		-	-	
South Africa	50	32,250	4	45	26,456	5	43	10,500	4
Tanzania	95	19,293	0	50	1,200	3	30	400	8
Togo	-	-		-	-		-	-	
Tunisia	62.3	351,300	2	-	-		-	-	
Uganda	70	4,440	0	50	2,020	3	30	3,000	8
Zaire	60	1,350	1	60	854	1	60 b	100 b	1
Zambia	80	10,700	0	75	2,375	0	35	850	7
Zimbabwe	63	22,200	0	60	13,287	1	45	3,760	4

a Flat tax rate on all taxable income.

b Based on the 1993 data.

c Paraguay does not levy an income tax on wages and salaries. Self-employment income is taxed and the top marginal tax rate is 30 percent.

d The maximum average tax rate is 15%.

e The marginal tax rate prior to 1988 reflects the fact that it was illegal to earn income from business activities during this period.

Source: The data are from Price Waterhouse, *Individual Taxes: A Worldwide Summary,* (various issues). The exchange rate at beginning of the year was used to convert the income threshold data to U.S. dollars, and the U.S. Consumer Price Index was used to convert the threshold to real 1982-84 dollars. The following conversion table/matrix was devised to transform the marginal tax rate/income threshold data for each country into the zero to ten rating system:

Top Marginal Tax Rate	Income Threshold Level (1982-84 U.S. Dollars)			
	Less than 25,000	25,000 to 50,000	50,000 to 150,000	more than 150,000
20% or less	10	10	10	10
21 to 25	9	9	10	10
26 to 30	8	8	9	9
31 to 35	7	7	8	9
36 to 40	5	6	7	8
41 to 45	4	5	6	7
46 to 50	3	4	5	5
51 to 55	2	3	4	4
56 to 60	1	2	3	3
61 to 65	0	1	2	2
66 to 70	0	0	1	1
more than 70%	0	0	0	0

Table III-C: The Use of Conscription to Obtain Military Personnel
(Countries with Voluntary Military Service are given a Rating of
10; Countries that Use Conscription to Obtain Military Personnel
are Given a Rating of Zero.)

	Are Individuals Conscripted into the Military?									
INDUSTRIAL COUNTRIES	1974-75		1979-80		1984-85		1989-90		1994-95	
United States	No	10	No	10	No	10	No	10	No	10
Canada	No	10	No	10	No	10	No	10	No	10
Australia	No	10	No	10	No	10	No	10	No	10
Japan	No	10	No	10	No	10	No	10	No	10
New Zealand	No	10	No	10	No	10	No	10	No	10
Austria	Yes	0	Yes	0	Yes	0	Yes	0	Yes	0
Belgium	Yes	0	Yes	0	Yes	0	Yes	0	Yes	0
Denmark	Yes	0	Yes	0	Yes	0	Yes	0	Yes	0
Finland	Yes	0	Yes	0	Yes	0	Yes	0	Yes	0
France	Yes	0	Yes	0	Yes	0	Yes	0	Yes	0
Germany	Yes	0	Yes	0	Yes	0	Yes	0	Yes	0
Iceland	No	10	No	10	No	10	No	10	No	10
Ireland	No	10	No	10	No	10	No	10	No	10
Italy	Yes	0	Yes	0	Yes	0	Yes	0	Yes	0
Netherlands	Yes	0	Yes	0	Yes	0	Yes	0	Yes	0
Norway	Yes	0	Yes	0	Yes	0	Yes	0	Yes	0
Spain	Yes	0	Yes	0	Yes	0	Yes	0	Yes	0
Sweden	Yes	0	Yes	0	Yes	0	Yes	0	Yes	0
Switzerland	Yes	0	Yes	0	Yes	0	Yes	0	Yes	0
United Kingdom	No	10	No	10	No	10	No	10	No	10
CENTRAL/S. AMERICA										
Argentina	Yes	0	Yes	0	Yes	0	Yes	0	Yes	0
Bahamas	No	10	No	10	No	10	No	10	No	10
Barbados	No	10	No	10	No	10	No	10	No	10
Belize	-		No	10	No	10	No	10	No	10
Bolivia	Yes	0	Yes	0	Yes	0	Yes	0	Yes	0
Brazil	Yes	0	Yes	0	Yes	0	Yes	0	Yes	0
Chile	Yes	0	Yes	0	Yes	0	Yes	0	Yes	0
Colombia	Yes	0	Yes	0	Yes	0	Yes	0	Yes	0
Costa Rica	No	10	No	10	No	10	No	10	No	10
Dominican Rep	Yes	0	No	10	No	10	No	10	No	10
Ecuador	Yes	0	Yes	0	Yes	0	Yes	0	Yes	0
El Salvador	-		Yes	0	Yes	0	Yes	0	Yes	0
Guatemala	Yes	0	Yes	0	Yes	0	Yes	0	Yes	0
Haiti	No	10	No	10	No	10	No	10	No	10
Honduras	-		No	10	Yes	0	Yes	0	Yes	0
Jamaica	No	10	No	10	No	10	No	10	No	10
Mexico	Yes	0	Yes	0	Yes	0	Yes	0	Yes	0

Table III-C: (continued)

	Are Individuals Conscripted into the Military?									
CENTRAL/- **S. AMERICA (con't)**	1974-75		1979-80		1984-85		1989-90		1994-95	
Nicaragua	Yes	0	Yes	0	Yes	0	Yes	0	No	10
Panama	No	10	No	10	No	10	No	10	No	10
Paraguay	Yes	0	Yes	0	Yes	0	Yes	0	Yes	0
Peru	Yes	0	Yes	0	Yes	0	Yes	0	Yes	0
Trinidad/Tobago	No	10	No	10	No	10	No	10	No	10
Uruguay	No	10	No	10	No	10	No	10	No	10
Venezuela	Yes	0	Yes	0	Yes	0	Yes	0	Yes	0
EUROPE/MIDDLE EAST										
Albania	Yes	0	Yes	0	Yes	0	Yes	0	Yes	0
Bahrain	No	10	No	10	No	10	No	10	No	10
Bulgaria	Yes	0	Yes	0	Yes	0	Yes	0	Yes	0
Croatia	-		-		-		Yes	0	Yes	0
Cyprus	-		Yes	0	Yes	0	Yes	0	Yes	0
Czechoslovakia	Yes	0	Yes	0	Yes	0	Yes	0	-	
Czech Republic	-		-		-		-		Yes	0
Slovakia	-		-		-		-		Yes	0
Egypt	Yes	0	Yes	0	Yes	0	Yes	0	Yes	0
Estonia	-		-		-		Yes	0	Yes	0
Greece	Yes	0	Yes	0	Yes	0	Yes	0	Yes	0
Hungary	Yes	0	Yes	0	Yes	0	Yes	0	Yes	0
Iran	Yes	0	Yes	0	Yes	0	Yes	0	Yes	0
Israel	Yes	0	Yes	0	Yes	0	Yes	0	Yes	0
Jordan	No	10	No	10	No	10	No	10	No	10
Latvia	-		-		-		Yes	0	Yes	0
Lithuania	-		-		-		Yes	0	Yes	0
Malta	-		No	10	No	10	No	10	No	10
Oman	No	10	No	10	No	10	No	10	No	10
Poland	Yes	0	Yes	0	Yes	0	Yes	0	Yes	0
Portugal	Yes	0	Yes	0	Yes	0	Yes	0	Yes	0
Romania	Yes	0	Yes	0	Yes	0	Yes	0	Yes	0
Russia	Yes	0	Yes	0	Yes	0	Yes	0	Yes	0
Slovenia	-		-		-		Yes	0	Yes	0
Syria	Yes	0	Yes	0	Yes	0	Yes	0	Yes	0
Turkey	Yes	0	Yes	0	Yes	0	Yes	0	Yes	0
Ukraine	-		-		-		Yes	0	Yes	0
ASIA										
Bangladesh	No	10	No	10	No	10	No	10	No	10
China	Yes	0	Yes	0	Yes	0	Yes	0	Yes	0
Fiji	No	10	No	10	No	10	No	10	No	10
Hong Kong	No	10	No	10	No	10	No	10	No	10
India	No	10	No	10	No	10	No	10	No	10

267

Table III-C: (continued)

	Are Individuals Conscripted into the Military?									
	1974-75		1979-80		1984-85		1989-90		1994-95	
ASIA										
Indonesia	Yes	0	Yes	0	Yes	0	Yes	0	Yes	0
Malaysia	No	10	No	10	No	10	No	10	No	10
Nepal	No	10	No	10	No	10	No	10	No	10
Pakistan	Yes	0	No	10	No	10	No	10	No	10
Philippines	Yes	0	Yes	0	No	10	No	10	No	10
Singapore	Yes	0	Yes	0	Yes	0	Yes	0	Yes	0
South Korea	Yes	0	Yes	0	Yes	0	Yes	0	Yes	0
Sri Lanka	No	10	No	10	No	10	No	10	No	10
Taiwan	Yes	0	Yes	0	Yes	0	Yes	0	Yes	0
Thailand	Yes	0	Yes	0	Yes	0	Yes	0	Yes	0
AFRICA										
Algeria	No	10	Yes	0	Yes	0	Yes	0	Yes	0
Benin	-		-		Yes	0	Yes	0	Yes	0
Botswana	No	10	No	10	No	10	No	10	No	10
Burundi	No	10	No	10	No	10	No	10	No	10
Cameroon	No	10	No	10	No	10	No	10	No	10
C African Rep	-		Yes	0	Yes	0	Yes	0	Yes	0
Chad	No	10	No	10	Yes	0	Yes	0	Yes	0
Congo Peoples Rep	No	10	No	10	No	10	No	10	No	10
Cote d' Ivoire	No	10	No	10	Yes	0	Yes	0	Yes	0
Gabon	No	10	No	10	No	10	No	10	No	10
Ghana	No	10	No	10	No	10	No	10	No	10
Kenya	No	10	No	10	No	10	No	10	No	10
Madagascar	-		Yes	0	Yes	0	Yes	0	Yes	0
Malawi	No	10	No	10	No	10	No	10	No	10
Mali	No	10	No	10	Yes	0	Yes	0	Yes	0
Mauritius	No	10	No	10	No	10	No	10	No	10
Morocco	Yes	0	Yes	0	Yes	0	Yes	0	Yes	0
Niger	No	10	Yes	0	Yes	0	Yes	0	Yes	0
Nigeria	No	10	No	10	No	10	No	10	No	10
Rwanda	No	10	No	10	No	10	No	10	No	10
Senegal	-		Yes	0	Yes	0	Yes	0	Yes	0
Sierra Leone	No	10	No	10	No	10	No	10	No	10
Somalia	No	10	No	10	Yes	0	Yes	0	Yes	0
South Africa	Yes	0	Yes	0	Yes	0	Yes	0	No	10
Tanzania	No	10	No	10	Yes	0	Yes	0	Yes	0
Togo	-		Yes	0	Yes	0	Yes	0	Yes	0
Tunisia	Yes	0	Yes	0	Yes	0	Yes	0	Yes	0
Uganda	No	10	No	10	No	10	No	10	No	10
Zaire	No	10	No	10	No	10	No	10	No	10
Zambia	No	10	No	10	No	10	No	10	No	10
Zimbabwe	-		Yes	0	Yes	0	Yes	0	Yes	0

Source: International Institute for Strategic Studies, *The Military Balance*, (various issues).

Table IV-A: The Average Tax Rate on International Trade

	Taxes on Trade As A Percent of Exports Plus Imports (The rating of each country is in parenthesis)									
INDUSTRIAL COUNTRIES	1975		1980		1985		1990		1995	
United States	1.50	(8)	1.13	(9)	1.73	(8)	1.45	(9)	1.18	(9)
Canada	3.67	(6)	2.38	(8)	1.67	(8)	1.18	(9)	0.72	(9)
Australia	4.36	(6)	3.60	(7)	3.22	(7)	3.07	(7)	1.94	(8) [a]
Japan	1.25	(9)	0.89	(9)	0.82	(9)	0.93	(9)	1.60	(8) [a]
New Zealand	2.42	(8)	2.51	(8)	2.01	(8)	1.65	(8)	1.37	(9)
Austria	1.65	(8)	0.71	(9)	0.60	(9)	0.65	(9)	0.61	(9)
Belgium	0.01	(10)	0.00	(10)	0.00	(10)	0.01	(10)	0.00	(10)
Denmark	0.92	(9)	0.05	(10)	0.04	(10)	0.04	(10)	0.03	(10)
Finland	1.61	(8)	0.81	(9)	0.42	(9)	0.59	(9)	0.46	(9)
France	0.05	(10)	0.05	(10)	0.03	(10)	0.01	(10)	0.01	(10)
Germany	0.02	(10)	0.01	(10)	0.00	(10)	0.00	(10)	0.00	(10)
Iceland	8.06	(2)	6.54	(4)	4.57	(6)	3.96	(6)	0.67	(9)
Ireland	4.82	(6)	2.98	(7)	2.53	(8)	2.61	(7)	1.50	(8)
Italy	0.26	(10)	0.04	(10)	0.02	(10)	0.01	(10)	0.01	(10)
Netherlands	1.33	(9)	0.00	(10)	0.00	(10)	0.00	(10)	0.00	(10)
Norway	0.51	(9)	0.30	(9)	0.25	(10)	0.27	(10)	0.32	(9)
Spain	6.11	(5)	2.69	(7)	2.97	(7)	1.33	(9)	0.03	(10) [a]
Sweden	0.95	(9)	0.66	(9)	0.32	(9)	0.39	(9)	0.43	(9)
Switzerland	3.50	(7)	2.42	(8)	1.95	(8)	1.87	(8)	2.29	(8)
United Kingdom	0.00	(10)	0.04	(10)	0.00	(10)	0.04	(10)	0.04	(10)
CENTRAL/SOUTH AMERICA										
Argentina	12.90	(0)	9.50	(1)	12.72	(0)	9.85	(1)	4.80	(6)
Bahamas	8.80	(2)	8.10	(2)	9.33	(1)	9.60	(1)	10.30	(1) [a]
Barbados	4.40	(6)	3.70	(6)	3.40	(7)	3.60	(7)	3.30	(7)
Belize	-		8.70	(2)	10.86	(1)	10.76	(1)	10.85	(1)
Bolivia	8.90	(2)	7.80	(3)	7.01	(4)	2.31	(8)	2.12	(8)
Brazil	5.65	(5)	10.00	(1)	3.22	(7)	3.66	(6)	2.62	(7)
Chile	5.56	(6)	2.79	(7)	5.69	(5)	3.69	(6)	3.54	(7)
Colombia	7.39	(3)	7.77	(3)	7.46	(3)	7.09	(3)	4.00	(6)
Costa Rica	5.91	(5)	5.30	(6)	6.92	(4)	7.03	(4)	4.62	(6)
Dominican Rep	16.12	(0)	9.20	(1)	6.45	(4)	7.80	(3)	12.21	(1)
Ecuador	8.88	(2)	7.20	(3)	6.21	(5)	3.95	(6)	3.51	(7)
El Salvador	6.40	(4)	6.24	(4)	7.13	(3)	4.13	(6)	3.60	(7)
Guatemala	5.62	(6)	4.81	(6)	7.47	(3)	3.55	(7)	3.80	(6)
Haiti	9.30	(1)	9.86	(1)	8.03	(2)	6.70	(4) [d]	-	
Honduras	5.32	(6)	6.70	(4)	-		-		-	
Jamaica	3.99	(6)	0.87	(9)	1.71	(8)	-		-	
Mexico	7.87	(3)	17.56	(0)	2.57	(7)	1.95	(8)	1.52	(8)
Nicaragua	4.88	(6)	8.70	(2)	7.38	(3)	4.30	(6)	5.85	(5)

Table IV-A: (contined)

			Taxes on Trade As A Percent of Exports Plus Imports							
			(The rating of each country is in parenthesis)							
CENTRAL/-	1975		1980		1985		1990		1995	
S. AMERICA (cont)										
Panama	3.20	(7)	3.07	(7)	4.14	(6)	1.83	(8)	1.39	(9)
Paraguay	8.81	(2)	6.04	(5)	2.22	(8)	3.26	(7)	2.07	(8) [a]
Peru	9.52	(1)	10.62	(1)	8.30	(2)	3.86	(6)	5.49	(6)
Trinidad/Tobago	2.60	(7)	3.17	(7)	5.71	(5)	2.68	(7) [d]	-	
Uruguay	3.41	(7)	8.87	(2)	5.82	(5)	5.61	(6)	2.70	(7)
Venezuela	3.74	(6)	2.98	(7)	9.14	(1)	2.21	(8)	2.66	(7)
EUROPE/MIDDLE EAST										
Albania	-		-		-		-		-	
Bahrain	-		-		0.74	(9)	1.09	(9)	1.46	(9)
Bulgaria	-		-		5.40	(6)	1.30	(9)	2.22	(8) [b]
Croatia										
Cyprus	3.45	(7)	4.00	(6)	4.42	(6)	4.15	(6)	2.79	(7)
Czechoslovakia	-		-		-		3.99	(6)	-	
, Czech Republic	-		-		-		-		1.13	(9)
Slovakia	-		-		-		-		-	
Egypt	16.73	(0)	13.08	(0)	12.06	(1)	5.92	(5)	6.08	(5) [a]
Estonia							0.34	(9)	0.38	(9)
Greece	3.46	(7)	3.23	(7)	0.33	(9)	0.05	(10)	0.05	(10)
Hungary	-		4.97	(6)	3.74	(6)	4.97	(6)	-	
Iran	3.59	(7)	16.95	(0)	14.18	(0)	7.32	(3)	5.60	(6)
Israel	7.96	(2)	5.05	(6)	2.85	(7)	0.92	(9)	0.24	(10)
Jordan	6.75	(4)	7.06	(4)	6.09	(5)	4.96	(6)	6.54	(4)
Latvia	-		-		-		-		0.88	(9)
Lithuania	-		-		-		-		0.74	(9)
Malta	4.59	(6)	4.87	(6)	4.46	(6)	4.85	(6)	4.41	(6) [a]
Oman	-		-		1.37	(9)	0.97	(9)	1.07	(9)
Poland	-		-		8.59	(2)	6.00	(5)	6.38	(4)
Portugal	4.61	(6)	2.11	(8)	1.24	(9)	1.02	(9)	0.01	(10)
Romania	-				-		0.44	(9)	2.90	(7)
Russia	-		-		-		-		8.80	(2)
Slovenia	-		-		-		-		-	
Syria	8.48	(2)	7.12	(3)	5.63	(6)	2.93	(7)	3.97	(6)
Turkey	14.43	(0)	6.33	(4)	2.96	(7)	2.81	(7)	1.48	(9)
Ukraine	-		-		-		-		-	
ASIA										
Bangladesh	7.90	(3)	13.41	(0)	17.88	(0)	12.11	(1) [d]	-	
China	-		5.70	(5)	10.00	(1)	3.70	(6)	1.20	(9)
Fiji	6.58	(4)	5.78	(5)	7.87	(3)	6.43	(4)	4.75	(6)
Hong Kong	0.70	(9)	0.50	(9)	0.60	(9)	0.40	(9)	0.30	(9)
India	14.77	(0)	15.52	(0)	24.19	(0)	20.73	(0)	12.70	(0) [a]
Indonesia	4.00	(6)	2.89	(7)	1.59	(8)	2.46	(8)	2.21	(8)
Malaysia	7.04	(4)	7.71	(3)	5.65	(5)	3.20	(7)	2.08	(8)
Nepal	8.90	(2)	8.60	(2)	7.71	(3)	8.80	(2)	5.29	(6)

271

Table IV-A: (continued)

Taxes on Trade As A Percent of Exports Plus Imports
(The rating of each country is in parenthesis)

	1975		1980		1985		1990		1995	
ASIA										
Pakistan	15.32	(0)	15.29	(0)	14.74	(0)	16.45	(0)	13.62	(0)
Philippines	13.38	(0)	6.75	(4)	6.20	(5)	6.64	(4)	6.17	(5)
Singapore	0.74	(9)	0.47	(9)	0.32	(9)	0.15	(10)	0.11	(10)
South Korea	3.07	(7)	4.14	(6)	3.55	(7)	3.42	(7)	1.96	(8)
Sri Lanka	11.13	(1)	11.72	(1)	10.59	(1)	8.81	(2)	4.52	(6)
Taiwan	4.83	(6)	3.60	(7)	2.80	(7)	2.14	(8)	1.97	(8)
Thailand	7.00	(4)	6.88	(4)	6.48	(4)	5.40	(6)	3.47	(7)
AFRICA										
Algeria	-		-		-		-		-	
Benin	9.17	(1)	10.60	(1)	-		-		-	
Botswana	10.39	(1)	12.80	(0)	7.12	(3)	6.61	(4)	9.87	(1)
Burundi	12.18	(1)	18.08	(0)	17.01	(0)	22.90	(0)	-	
Cameroon	13.44	(0)	11.00	(1)	6.07	(5)	5.39	(6)	7.71	(3)
C African Rep	-		10.60	(1)	-		11.50	(1) d	-	
Chad	9.16	(1)	-		-		3.87	(6)	2.17	(8) c
Congo Peoples Rep.	5.43	(6)	3.80	(6)	-		-		-	
Cote d' Ivoire	-		12.78	(0)	11.79	(1)	10.92	(1)	-	
Gabon	8.20	(2)	7.25	(3)	6.43	(4)	4.78	(6)	6.32	(4) c
Ghana	20.58	(0)	17.27	(0)	21.67	(0)	11.59	(1)	8.05	(2) a
Kenya	5.47	(6)	6.06	(5)	7.38	(3)	6.26	(4)	4.96	(6)
Madagascar	13.80	(0)	8.50	(2)	-		14.00	(0)	8.49	(2)
Malawi	3.75	(6)	6.58	(4)	8.80	(2)	5.65	(5)	-	
Mali	14.09	(0)	3.81	(6)	4.97	(6)	4.60	(6) d	-	
Mauritius	7.06	(4)	9.55	(1)	9.64	(1)	7.61	(3)	6.26	(4)
Morocco	7.51	(3)	10.68	(1)	6.39	(4)	8.59	(2)	9.91	(1) b
Niger	6.70	(4)	8.40	(2)	-		-		-	
Nigeria	6.64	(4)	8.50	(2)	5.09	(6)	4.00	(6) d	-	
Rwanda	16.49	(0)	13.30	(0)	-		14.15	(0)	14.63	(0) b
Senegal	8.66	(2)	11.40	(1)	8.30	(2)	-		-	
Sierra Leone	10.44	(1)	13.33	(0)	11.90	(1)	5.97	(5)	7.74	(3)
Somalia	14.01	(0)	10.50	(1)	-		-		-	
South Africa	2.02	(8)	1.21	(9)	1.41	(9)	2.22	(8)	0.59	(9)
Tanzania	7.33	(3)	7.72	(3)	6.25	(4)	-		-	
Togo	7.20	(3)	12.43	(0)	8.63	(2)	9.20	(1) d	-	
Tunisia	10.70	(1)	8.99	(1)	13.30	(0)	9.49	(1)	9.54	(1) b
Uganda	20.40	(0)	3.07	(7)	11.60	(1)	-		-	
Zaire	19.02	(0)	10.28	(1)	8.39	(2)	9.10	(1)	6.05	(5) a
Zambia	2.61	(7)	2.39	(8)	6.40	(4)	4.84	(6)	3.84	(6)
Zimbabwe	2.10	(8)	1.67	(8)	8.03	(2)	9.19	(1)	8.10	(2) c

1993=a, 1992=b, 1991=c, 1989=d.

Source: The data on tax revenue are from the International Monetary Fund, *Government Finance Statistics Year-book*, (various issues), Table A, line 6 entitled, "Taxes on International Trade Transactions." The data on the volume of exports and imports are from the IMF, *International Financial Statistics* (various issues). The following conversion table divided the 1985 base year data into eleven intervals of equal size.

Average Tax Rate (%)	Rating
0.000 — 0.284	10
0.285 — 1.499	9
1.500 — 2.549	8
2.550 — 3.644	7
3.645 — 5.639	6
5.640 — 6.229	5
6.230 — 7.064	4
7.065 — 7.949	3
7.950 — 8.969	2
8.970 — 12.389	1
> 12.390	0

Table IV-B: The Black Market Exchange Rate Premium

(The premium one must pay to exchange the domestic currency for dollars in the black market relative to the official exchange rate. The data are year-end.

				Black Market Exchange Rate Premium					
				(The rating of each country is in parenthesis)					
INDUSTRIAL COUNTRIES	1975		1980		1985		1990		1995	
United States	0	(10)	0	(10)	0	(10)	0	(10)	0	(10)
Canada	0	(10)	0	(10)	0	(10)	0	(10)	0	(10)
Australia	1	(8)	1	(8)	0	(10)	0	(10)	0	(10)
Japan	0	(10)	0	(10)	0	(10)	0	(10)	0	(10)
New Zealand	5	(6)	0	(10)	4	(6)	0	(10)	0	(10)
Austria	0	(10)	0	(10)	0	(10)	0	(10)	0	(10)
Belgium	0	(10)	0	(10)	0	(10)	0	(10)	0	(10)
Denmark	1	(8)	2	(7)	0	(10)	0	(10)	0	(10)
Finland	1	(8)	1	(8)	0	(10)	0	(10)	0	(10)
France	0	(10)	3	(6)	4	(6)	0	(10)	0	(10)
Germany	0	(10)	0	(10)	0	(10)	0	(10)	0	(10)
Iceland	106	(1)	9	(5)	16	(4)	3	(6)	0	(10)
Ireland	0	(10)	0	(10)	3	(6)	1	(8)	0	(10)
Italy	9	(5)	0	(10)	0	(10)	0	(10)	0	(10)
Netherlands	0	(10)	0	(10)	0	(10)	0	(10)	0	(10)
Norway	1	(8)	3	(6)	0	(10)	0	(10)	0	(10)
Spain	2	(7)	0	(10)	2	(7)	2	(7)	0	(10)
Sweden	1	(8)	5	(6)	1	(8)	0	(10)	0	(10)
Switzerland	0	(10)	0	(10)	0	(10)	0	(10)	0	(10)
United Kingdom	0	(10)	0	(10)	0	(10)	0	(10)	0	(10)
CENTRAL/SOUTH AMERICA										
Argentina	124	(1)	1	(8)	40	(2)	0	(10)	0	(10)
Bahamas	14	(4)	20	(4)	11	(4)	13	(4)	2	(7)
Barbados	20	(4)	11	(4)	11	(4)	10	(4)	3	(6)
Belize	32	(3)	34	(3)	63	(1)	25	(3)	3	(6)
Bolivia	5	(6)	22	(4)	9	(5)	3	(6)	1	(8)
Brazil	49	(2)	18	(4)	49	(2)	10	(4)	3	(6)
Chile	5	(6)	6	(6)	22	(4)	0	(10)	2	(7)
Colombia	29	(3)	16	(4)	9	(5)	17	(4)	7	(5)
Costa Rica	8	(5)	69	(1)	24	(3)	0	(10)	0	(10)
Dominican Rep	28	(3)	37	(2)	14	(4)	66	(1)	2	(7)
Ecuador	5	(6)	13	(4)	48	(2)	0	(10)	12	(4)
El Salvador	20	(4)	100	(1)	195	(1)	24	(3)	1	(8)
Guatemala	10	(4)	10	(4)	89	(1)	0	(10)	0	(10)
Haiti	0	(10)	20	(4)	60	(2)	151	(1)	47	(2)
Honduras	0	(10)	20	(4)	65	(1)	0	(10)	1	(8)
Jamaica	22	(4)	61	(2)	19	(4)	27	(3)	7	(5)
Mexico	0	(10)	92	(1)	25	(3)	0	(10)	0	(10)
Nicaragua	21	(4)	91	(1)	382	(0)	10	(4)	8	(5)

Table IV-B: (Continued)

Black Market Exchange Rate Premium

(The rating of each country is in parenthesis)

CENTRAL/- S. AMERICA (con't)	1975		1980		1985		1990		1995	
Panama	0	(10)	0	(10)	0	(10)	0	(10)	0	(10)
Paraguay	13	(4)	7	(5)	213	(0)	26	(3)	13	(4)
Peru	56	(2)	18	(4)	51	(2)	16	(4)	0	(10)
Trinidad/Tobago	43	(2)	49	(2)	39	(2)	40	(2)	3	(6)
Uruguay	0	(10)	0	(10)	0	(10)	0	(10)	0	(10)
Venezuela	0	(10)	0	(10)	25	(3)	0	(10)	42	(2)

EUROPE/MIDDLE EAST	1975		1980		1985		1990		1995	
Albania	745	(0)	866	(0)	818	(0)	800	(0)	0	(10)
Bahrain	0	(10)	0	(10)	0	(10)	0	(10)	0	(10)
Bulgaria	175	(1)	175	(1)	435	(0)	100	(1)	5	(6)
Croatia	--		--		--		106	(1)	8	(5)
Cyprus	6	(6)	4	(6)	1	(8)	5	(6)	5	(6)
Czechoslovkia	359	(0)	387	(0)	423	(0)	61	(2)	--	
Czech Republic	--		--		--		--		0	(10)
Slovakia	--		--		--		--		0	(10)
Egypt	1	(8)	9	(5)	146	(1)	56	(2)	3	(6)
Estonia	--		--		--		6,100	(0)	0	(10)
Greece	3	(6)	7	(5)	25	(3)	3	(6)	0	(10)
Hungary	317	(0)	244	(0)	210	(0)	22	(4)	0	(10)
Iran	2	(7)	164	(1)	533	(0)	2197	(0)	115	(1)
Israel	60	(2)	1	(8)	7	(5)	4	(6)	0	(10)
Jordan	1	(8)	0	(10)	3	(6)	11	(4)	1	(8)
Latvia	--		--		--		6,100	(0)	2	(7)
Lithuania	--		--		--		6,100	(0)	0	(10)
Malta	5	(6)	12	(4)	7	(5)	2	(7)	4	(6)
Oman	0	(10)	0	(10)	0	(10)	0	(10)	0	(10)
Poland	3786	(0)	298	(0)	301	(0)	9	(5)	0	(10)
Portugal	42	(2)	2	(7)	2	(7)	3	(6)	0	(10)
Romania	596	(0)	628	(0)	1246	(0)	416	(0)	3	(6)
Russia	391	(0)	359	(0)	637	(0)	6,100	(0)	2	(7)
Slovenia	--		--		--		106	(1)	0	(10)
Syria	1	(8)	35	(2)	251	(0)	301	(0)	301	(0)
Turkey	11	(4)	16	(4)	3	(6)	2	(7)	2	(7)
Ukraine	391	(0)	359	(0)	637	(0)	6100	(0)	3	(6)

ASIA	1975		1980		1985		1990		1995	
Bangladesh	51	(2)	111	(1)	168	(1)	165	(1)	28	(3)
China	24	(3)	25	(3)	11	(4)	159	(1)	7	(5)
Fiji	17	(4)	18	(4)	8	(5)	4	(6)	1	(8)
Hong Kong	0	(10)	0	(10)	0	(10)	0	(10)	0	(10)
India	9	(5)	5	(6)	14	(4)	10	(4)	8	(5)
Indonesia	7	(5)	2	(7)	7	(5)	0	(10)	0	(10)
Malaysia	0	(10)	0	(10)	0	(10)	0	(10)	0	(10)
Nepal	40	(2)	0	(10)	11	(4)	16	(4)	19	(4)
Pakistan	17	(4)	27	(3)	4	(6)	14	(4)	3	(6)
Philippines	13	(4)	3	(6)	7	(5)	7	(5)	0	(10)

Table IV-B: (Continued)

Black Market Exchange Rate Premium
(The rating of each country is in parenthesis)

	1975		1980		1985		1990		1995	
ASIA										
Singapore	0	(10)	0	(10)	0	(10)	0	(10)	0	(10)
South Korea	2	(7)	11	(4)	11	(4)	1	(8)	0	(10)
Sri Lanka	92	(1)	9	(5)	20	(4)	24	(3)	2	(7)
Taiwan	5	(6)	1	(8)	3	(6)	0	(10)	0	(10)
Thailand	2	(7)	5	(6)	3	(6)	0	(10)	0	(10)
AFRICA										
Algeria	56	(2)	263	(0)	335	(0)	140	(1)	201	(1)
Benin	2	(7)	2	(7)	1	(8)	4	(6)	1	(8)
Botswana	44	(2)	10	(4)	22	(4)	7	(5)	2	(7)
Burundi	46	(2)	45	(2)	25	(3)	6	(6)	44	(2)
Cameroon	2	(7)	2	(7)	1	(8)	4	(6)	1	(8)
C African Rep	2	(7)	2	(7)	1	(8)	4	(6)	1	(8)
Chad	2	(7)	2	(7)	1	(8)	4	(6)	1	(8)
Congo Peoples Rep	2	(7)	2	(7)	1	(8)	4	(6)	1	(8)
Cote d' Ivoire	2	(7)	2	(7)	1	(8)	4	(6)	1	(8)
Gabon	2	(7)	2	(7)	1	(8)	4	(6)	1	(8)
Ghana	67	(1)	304	(0)	142	(1)	7	(5)	2	(7)
Kenya	8	(5)	10	(4)	2	(7)	6	(6)	2	(7)
Madagascar	23	(3)	51	(2)	9	(5)	7	(5)	2	(7)
Malawi	28	(3)	48	(2)	30	(3)	14	(4)	1	(8)
Mali	7	(5)	5	(6)	1	(8)	4	(6)	1	(8)
Mauritius	47	(2)	40	(2)	1	(8)	8	(5)	0	(10)
Morocco	3	(6)	1	(8)	7	(5)	13	(4)	1	(8)
Niger	2	(7)	2	(7)	1	(8)	4	(6)	1	(8)
Nigeria	43	(2)	72	(1)	270	(0)	23	(3)	286	(0)
Rwanda	45	(2)	67	(1)	49	(2)	28	(3)	3	(6)
Senegal	2	(7)	2	(7)	1	(8)	4	(6)	1	(8)
Sierra Leone	53	(2)	62	(1)	206	(1)	165	(1)	2	(7)
Somalia	28	(3)	41	(2)	147	(1)	200	(1)	--	
South Africa	6	(6)	6	(6)	25	(3)	3	(6)	0	(10)
Tanzania	203	(1)	224	(0)	259	(0)	78	(1)	1	(8)
Togo	2	(7)	2	(7)	1	(8)	4	(6)	1	(8)
Tunisia	11	(4)	18	(4)	12	(4)	8	(5)	1	(8)
Uganda	390	(0)	360	(0)	25	(3)	40	(2)	3	(6)
Zaire	120	(1)	131	(1)	6	(6)	20	(4)	4	(6)
Zambia	140	(1)	70	(1)	38	(2)	212	(0)	3	(6)
Zimbabwe	54	(2)	84	(1)	42	(2)	15	(4)	1	(8)

Source: International Currency Analysis, Inc., *World Currency Yearbook* (various issues of the yearbook and the monthly report supplement) and International Monetary Fund, *International Financial Statistics* (various monthly issues). The 1985 base year data were used to derive the rating intervals. The following conversion table divided the 1985 data into eleven intervals of equal size.

Black Market Exchange Rate Premium (%)	Rating
0	10
1	8
2	7
3 — 6	6
7 — 9	5
10 — 22	4
23 — 34	3
35 — 61	2
62 — 208	1
210 or more	0

Table IV-C: The Actual Size of the Trade Sector (Exports plus Imports divided by GDP) Compared to the Expected Size: 1975, 1980, 1985, 1990, and 1995

	1975				1980			
INDUSTRIAL COUNTRIES	Actual Trade	Expected Trade	Actual-Expected Expected		Actual Trade	Expected Trade	Actual-Expected Expected	
United States	8.2	11.4	-28.5%	(2)	10.6	12.8	-17.4%	(3)
Canada	23.6	17.2	37.4%	(8)	27.5	19.2	43.7%	(9)
Australia	14.4	15.3	-6.1%	(4)	17.0	17.1	-0.8%	(4)
Japan	12.8	14.9	-13.9%	(3)	14.1	16.6	-14.8%	(3)
New Zealand	27.4	26.4	4.1%	(5)	30.9	29.6	4.3%	(5)
Austria	31.5	25.7	22.7%	(7)	37.8	28.9	30.6%	(8)
Belgium	53.5	33.6	59.4%	(10)	64.2	37.8	69.9%	(10)
Denmark	30.6	36.0	-15.1%	(3)	33.3	40.5	-17.8%	(3)
Finland	27.0	30.0	-9.9%	(4)	33.6	33.7	-0.2%	(4)
France	18.5	18.5	-0.1%	(4)	22.1	20.7	6.8%	(5)
Germany	23.2	19.3	20.4%	(6)	26.7	21.8	22.6%	(7)
Iceland	39.4	43.1	-8.4%	(4)	36.3	48.2	-24.6%	(2)
Ireland	43.7	36.9	18.4%	(6)	53.8	41.1	30.8%	(8)
Italy	20.6	19.4	5.9%	(5)	23.3	21.8	6.7%	(5)
Netherlands	46.1	31.4	46.8%	(9)	50.5	35.2	43.5%	(9)
Norway	45.2	30.8	46.5%	(9)	44.2	34.6	27.9%	(7)
Spain	15.4	19.8	-22.0%	(3)	16.9	22.1	-23.5%	(2)
Sweden	27.9	26.8	4.1%	(5)	30.4	30.1	0.9%	(5)
Switzerland	30.0	28.2	6.4%	(5)	38.5	31.8	21.1%	(7)
United Kingdom	26.8	21.2	26.2%	(7)	26.2	23.9	9.5%	(5)
CENTRAL/SOUTH AMERICA								
Argentina	5.9	17.7	-66.6%	(0)	5.8	19.6	-70.6%	(0)
Bahamas	76.0	65.7	15.6%	(6)	74.8	72.9	2.7%	(5)
Barbados	63.1	87.4	-27.9%	(2)	71.1	98.4	-27.8%	(2)
Belize	80.8	66.3	21.9%	(7)	62.0	73.4	-15.6%	(3)
Bolivia	29.1	21.5	35.0%	(8)	18.8	23.8	-20.8%	(3)
Brazil	9.5	12.8	-25.7%	(2)	10.2	14.2	-28.2%	(2)
Chile	26.4	24.7	7.2%	(5)	24.9	27.4	-9.3%	(4)
Colombia	14.9	19.5	-23.4%	(2)	15.9	21.6	-26.2%	(2)
Costa Rica	34.3	40.8	-16.0%	(3)	31.7	45.0	-29.6%	(2)
Dominican Republic	28.0	35.6	-21.2%	(3)	24.1	39.3	-38.8%	(1)
Ecuador	29.5	28.7	2.8%	(5)	25.3	31.6	-19.9%	(3)
El Salvador	35.7	39.8	-10.2%	(4)	33.7	44.1	-23.5%	(2)
Guatemala	22.6	32.1	-29.5%	(2)	23.6	35.4	-33.5%	(1)
Haiti	18.8	37.6	-50.1%	(0)	26.1	41.8	-37.7%	(1)
Honduras	35.2	35.4	-0.7%	(4)	40.2	38.9	3.3%	(5)
Jamaica	40.4	47.0	-14.0%	(3)	52.7	52.5	0.4%	(5)
Mexico	7.4	16.1	-54.4%	(0)	11.8	17.8	-33.5%	(1)
Nicaragua	32.9	36.2	-9.3%	(4)	33.8	39.9	-15.4%	(3)

278

Table IV-C: (Continued)

	1975				1980			
	Actual Expected		Actual-Expected		Actual Expected		Actual-Expected	
CENTRAL/-	Trade	Trade	Expected		Trade	Trade	Expected	
S. AMERICA (cont)								
Panama	37.4	40.0	-6.5%	(4)	38.6	44.3	-12.8%	(3)
Paraguay	15.9	25.9	-38.5%	(1)	22.0	28.5	-22.7%	(2)
Peru	16.4	20.6	-20.4%	(3)	20.8	22.7	-8.6%	(4)
Trinidad & Tobago	44.1	56.2	-21.5%	(3)	44.7	62.6	-28.6%	(2)
Uruguay	18.5	34.4	-46.1%	(1)	17.8	38.5	-53.7%	(0)
Venezuela	25.4	21.9	15.9%	(6)	25.3	24.0	5.3%	(5)
EUROPE/MIDDLE EAST								
Albania	-	-	-		-	-	-	
Bahrain	120.6	83.1	45.1%	(9)	117.7	89.9	31.0%	(8)
Bulgaria	-	-	-		33.2	40.8	-18.7%	(3)
Croatia	-	-	-		0.0	-	-	
Cyprus	46.1	57.4	-19.7%	(3)	54.2	64.3	-15.8%	(3)
Czechoslovakia	-	-	-		-	-	-	
Czech Republic	-	-	-		-	-	-	
Slovakia	-	-	-		-	-	-	
Egypt	30.7	18.5	66.2%	(10)	36.7	20.4	79.5%	(10)
Estonia	-	-	-		-	-	-	
Greece	21.9	29.7	-26.3%	(2)	23.6	33.1	-28.7%	(2)
Hungary	45.2	24.2	86.8%	(10)	40.2	27.2	47.8%	(9)·
Iran	38.0	17.9	112.6%	(10)	14.9	19.6	-24.3%	(2)
Israel	38.7	40.8	-5.1%	(4)	45.2	45.1	0.2%	(4)
Jordan	64.4	39.3	64.1%	(10)	73.3	43.0	70.7%	(10)
Latvia	-	-	-		-	-	-	
Lithuania	-	-	-		-	-	-	
Malta	89.6	82.7	8.3%	(5)	93.7	91.7	2.2%	(5)
Oman	59.1	41.4	42.8%	(9)	50.9	44.7	13.9%	(6)
Poland	-	-	-		29.6	23.3	27.1%	(7)
Portugal	26.6	30.7	-13.3%	(3)	34.7	34.1	1.7%	(5)
Romania	-	-	-		37.7	33.1	13.8%	(6)
Russia	-	-	-		-	-	-	
Slovenia	-	-	-		-	-	-	
Syria	27.7	29.6	-6.4%	(4)	26.8	32.5	-17.5%	(3)
Turkey	9.7	18.6	-48.1%	(1)	10.3	20.7	-50.3%	(0)
Ukraine	-	-	-		-	-	-	
ASIA								
Bangladesh	5.5	21.3	-74.2%	(0)	12.0	23.5	-48.9%	(1)
China	-	-	-		6.5	10.2	-36.2%	(1)
Fiji	43.3	43.8	-1.2%	(4)	50.3	48.6	3.4%	(5)
Hong Kong	81.3	52.4	55.0%	(9)	90.3	57.7	56.5%	(9)
India	6.4	10.8	-40.6%	(1)	8.3	11.9	-30.3%	(2)

Table IV-C: (Continued)

	1975				1980			
	Actual Trade	Expected Trade	Actual-Expected Expected		Actual Trade	Expected Trade	Actual-Expected Expected	
ASIA								
Indonesia	22.1	14.3	54.6%	(9)	26.6	15.8	68.1%	(10)
Malaysia	43.4	26.0	67.1%	(10)	56.3	28.7	95.8%	(10)
Nepal	11.1	22.6	-50.7%	(0)	15.1	24.9	-39.3%	(1)
Pakistan	16.5	17.1	-3.1%	(4)	18.3	18.8	-2.6%	(4)
Philippines	24.1	17.5	37.4%	(9)	26.0	19.4	34.3%	(8)
Singapore	144.6	58.8	145.8%	(10)	211.7	65.1	225.2%	(10)
South Korea	32.2	24.8	29.8%	(7)	37.7	27.6	36.8%	(8)
Sri Lanka	31.2	27.7	12.6%	(6)	43.5	30.8	41.3%	(9)
Taiwan	41.3	37.0	11.6%	(5)	53.1	41.0	29.6%	(7)
Thailand	20.7	19.3	7.1%	(5)	27.2	21.3	27.7%	(7)
AFRICA								
Algeria	38.3	19.3	98.4%	(10)	32.4	21.2	52.5%	(9)
Benin	29.9	35.5	-15.7%	(3)	33.1	39.2	-15.4%	(3)
Botswana	54.6	30.3	79.9%	(10)	58.2	33.2	75.0%	(10)
Burundi	13.6	31.8	-57.1%	(0)	16.1	35.1	-54.3%	(0)
Cameroon	24.1	27.1	-10.9%	(3)	25.7	29.8	-13.8%	(3)
Central African Rep	32.6	26.0	25.7%	(7)	34.4	28.7	20.2%	(6)
Chad	28.6	21.9	30.8%	(8)	32.5	24.2	34.3%	(8)
Congo Peoples Rep	49.8	35.8	39.3%	(8)	60.1	39.4	52.4%	(9)
Cote d'Ivoire	36.7	28.5	28.6%	(7)	38.1	31.2	22.2%	(7)
Gabon	48.7	41.4	17.6%	(6)	48.2	45.1	6.8%	(5)
Ghana	18.9	27.7	-31.8%	(2)	8.8	30.8	-71.4%	(0)
Kenya	32.2	24.2	32.8%	(8)	33.5	26.5	26.4%	(7)
Madagascar	18.4	21.4	-14.0%	(3)	21.5	23.6	-8.6%	(4)
Malawi	37.5	32.5	15.3%	(6)	31.8	35.8	-11.0%	(3)
Mali	20.6	20.7	-0.3%	(4)	25.6	22.9	11.5%	(5)
Mauritius	56.1	50.5	11.2%	(5)	56.3	56.1	0.3%	(5)
Morocco	27.9	22.3	25.2%	(7)	22.6	24.7	-8.3%	(4)
Niger	25.1	19.9	26.2%	(7)	31.4	21.9	43.7%	(9)
Nigeria	20.6	17.2	19.6%	(6)	24.0	18.9	26.6%	(7)
Rwanda	13.4	31.2	-56.9%	(0)	20.4	34.2	-40.3%	(1)
Senegal	39.2	31.4	24.7%	(7)	36.1	34.6	4.3%	(5)
Sierra Leone	30.5	37.2	-17.9%	(3)	32.8	41.2	-20.4%	(3)
Somalia	19.7	28.0	-29.7%	(2)	60.8	30.8	97.3%	(10)
South Africa	29.3	19.1	53.4%	(9)	32.4	21.1	53.6%	(9)
Tanzania	26.1	21.2	23.1%	(7)	19.7	23.2	-15.1%	(3)
Togo	48.6	39.5	22.8%	(7)	53.7	43.6	23.2%	(7)
Tunisia	33.4	31.2	7.1%	(5)	42.9	34.5	24.5%	(7)
Uganda	9.2	22.0	-57.9%	(0)	22.3	24.2	-7.8%	(4)
Zaire	12.5	18.3	-31.4%	(2)	16.4	20.1	-18.3%	(3)
Zambia	46.3	22.4	107.0%	(10)	43.4	24.6	76.5%	(10)
Zimbabwe	30.1	23.0	31.0%	(8)	31.8	25.3	25.7%	(7)

Table IV-C: (Continued)

INDUSTRIAL COUNTRIES	1985 Actual Trade	1985 Expected Trade	1985 Actual-Expected Expected		1990 Actual Trade	1990 Expected Trade	1990 Actual-Expected Expected		1995 Actual Trade	1995 Expected Trade	1995 Actual-Expected Expected	
United States	8.9	11.7	-24.2%	(2)	10.7	12.6	-15.1%	(3)	11.8	13.4	-12.3%	(3)
Canada	27.2	17.6	54.5%	(9)	25.6	18.9	35.3%	(8)	36.2	20.0	81.1%	(10)
Australia	17.6	15.7	12.6%	(6)	17.2	16.8	2.7%	(5)	20.3	17.9	13.7%	(6)
Japan	12.8	15.3	-16.5%	(3)	10.5	16.5	-36.6%	(1)	8.7	17.7	-50.8%	(0)
New Zealand	32.2	27.2	18.3%	(6)	27.0	29.4	-8.2%	(4)	26.7	31.3	-14.6%	(3)
Austria	40.6	26.8	51.8%	(9)	39.6	28.9	36.9%	(8)	36.1	30.8	17.1%	(6)
Belgium	75.6	35.0	116.4%	(10)	72.5	37.8	91.8%	(10)	70.2	40.5	73.3%	(10)
Denmark	36.5	37.4	-2.5%	(4)	32.8	40.5	-19.1%	(3)	32.4	43.3	-25.1%	(2)
Finland	29.1	31.0	-6.4%	(4)	23.8	33.5	-29.0%	(2)	33.7	35.8	-6.0%	(4)
France	23.6	19.0	23.9%	(7)	22.6	20.6	9.4%	(5)	22.3	22.1	1.2%	(5)
Germany	30.8	20.2	52.7%	(9)	29.0	21.8	33.4%	(8)	22.5	21.7	3.9%	(5)
Iceland	40.9	44.2	-7.4%	(4)	34.7	47.5	-26.9%	(2)	35.1	50.5	-30.5%	(2)
Ireland	56.7	37.8	50.0%	(9)	56.8	41.0	38.3%	(8)	71.8	43.9	63.8%	(10)
Italy	23.0	20.1	14.3%	(6)	20.7	21.8	-4.9%	(4)	23.7	23.4	1.3%	(5)
Netherlands	58.4	32.4	80.2%	(10)	51.9	35.0	48.3%	(9)	50.0	37.3	34.1%	(8)
Norway	43.0	31.9	34.6%	(8)	40.6	34.5	17.5%	(6)	40.9	36.8	10.9%	(5)
Spain	21.8	20.4	6.9%	(5)	18.8	22.0	-14.8%	(3)	23.6	23.6	0.1%	(4)
Sweden	34.5	27.9	23.6%	(7)	29.7	30.1	-1.2%	(4)	37.7	32.1	17.3%	(6)
Switzerland	38.8	29.3	32.5%	(8)	36.4	31.6	15.1%	(6)	33.4	33.6	-0.6%	(4)
United Kingdom	28.3	22.1	27.9%	(7)	25.7	23.9	7.7%	(5)	28.6	25.6	11.9%	(5)
CENTRAL/SOUTH AMERICA												
Argentina	9.0	18.0	-49.9%	(1)	7.7	19.3	-60.2%	(0)	8.0	20.5	-61.2%	(0)
Bahamas	75.2	66.5	13.1%	(6)	53.5	70.8	-24.3%	(2)	51.2	75.4	-32.1%	(2)
Barbados	63.9	91.1	-29.8%	(2)	50.4	98.1	-48.6%	(1)	47.8	105.2	-54.5%	(0)
Belize	54.9	66.6	-17.6%	(3)	63.7	70.8	-10.1%	(4)	53.6	74.7	-28.3%	(2)
Bolivia	15.1	21.6	-29.9%	(2)	23.4	23.0	2.1%	(5)	24.7	24.2	2.2%	(5)
Brazil	9.7	12.9	-25.1%	(2)	6.3	13.8	-54.1%	(0)	7.3	14.6	-50.0%	(1)
Chile	26.9	25.1	7.4%	(5)	32.7	26.8	21.9%	(7)	28.3	28.5	-0.5%	(4)
Colombia	13.2	19.6	-33.0%	(1)	17.7	21.0	-15.7%	(3)	18.4	22.2	-17.1%	(3)
Costa Rica	31.6	40.7	-22.3%	(3)	37.7	43.2	-12.7%	(3)	41.5	46.0	-9.7%	(4)
Dominican Republic	28.5	35.7	-20.2%	(3)	31.2	38.2	-18.2%	(3)	27.8	40.2	-30.9%	(2)
Ecuador	23.8	28.6	-16.8%	(3)	30.1	30.4	-1.3%	(4)	27.8	32.2	-13.9%	(3)
El Salvador	26.1	40.5	-35.5%	(1)	21.5	43.3	-50.4%	(0)	29.6	45.8	-35.4%	(1)
Guatemala	12.5	32.1	-61.1%	(0)	21.7	34.0	-36.1%	(1)	22.7	35.8	-36.5%	(1)
Haiti	19.2	38.2	-49.7%	(1)	17.2	40.8	-57.7%	(0)	13.4	43.0	-68.8%	(0)
Honduras	27.1	35.0	-22.7%	(2)	37.6	37.1	1.4%	(5)	45.8	38.8	18.0%	(6)
Jamaica	66.3	48.1	37.6%	(8)	55.5	51.8	7.0%	(5)	62.1	55.4	12.1%	(5)
Mexico	12.9	16.2	-20.6%	(3)	16.4	17.3	-5.6%	(4)	22.6	18.2	24.3%	(7)
Nicaragua	18.3	36.2	-49.4%	(1)	34.3	38.4	-10.8%	(3)	44.8	39.9	12.4%	(5)
Panama	34.2	40.3	-15.1%	(3)	37.4	43.0	-13.0%	(3)	38.6	45.7	-15.5%	(3)
Paraguay	24.8	25.7	-3.6%	(4)	37.8	27.3	38.6%	(8)	43.0	28.7	49.9%	(9)
Peru	19.7	20.7	-4.7%	(4)	13.4	22.1	-39.3%	(1)	14.0	23.3	-39.9%	(1)
Trinidad & Tobago	30.5	57.3	-46.8%	(1)	36.9	61.6	-40.1%	(1)	34.9	64.2	-45.6%	(1)
Uruguay	23.9	35.5	-32.6%	(1)	23.1	38.3	-39.6%	(1)	19.5	40.9	-52.2%	(0)
Venezuela	20.4	21.8	-6.4%	(4)	29.8	23.2	28.8%	(7)	22.9	24.4	-6.2%	(4)
EUROPE/-MIDDLE EAST												
Albania	-	-	-		47.0	43.0	9.3%	(5)	38.0	46.0	-17.4%	(3)
Bahrain	95.8	80.8	18.5%	(6)	110.8	85.0	30.3%	(8)	95.5	89.6	6.6%	(5)
Bulgaria	43.0	37.8	13.9%	(6)	34.9	41.1	-15.1%	(3)	52.2	44.2	18.0%	(6)
Croatia	-	-	-		-	-	-		-	-	-	
Cyprus	53.8	59.0	-8.8%	(4)	50.9	63.4	-19.8%	(3)	49.8	67.6	-26.3%	(2)
Czechoslovakia	34.9	28.7	21.6%	(7)	34.4	30.8	11.9%	(5)	-	-	-	

281

Table IV-C: (con't)

EUROPE/-MIDDLE EAST	1985 Actual Trade	1985 Expected Trade	1985 Actual-Expected / Expected		1990 Actual Trade	1990 Expected Trade	1990 Actual-Expected / Expected		1995 Actual Trade	1995 Expected Trade	1995 Actual-Expected / Expected	
Czech Republic	-	-	-		-	-	-		61.6	29.8	106.2%	(10)
Slovakia	-	-	-		-	-	-		61.1	34.5	76.9%	(10)
Egypt	26.0	18.6	40.0%	(9)	32.5	19.8	64.7%	(10)	23.1	20.8	11.4%	(5)
Estonia	-	-	-		-	-	-		87.0	52.1	67.0%	(10)
Greece	27.0	30.5	-11.5%	(3)	27.1	32.9	-17.6%	(3)	21.8	35.1	-37.9%	(1)
Hungary	41.2	25.2	63.5%	(10)	29.8	27.3	9.2%	(5)	36.0	29.4	22.4%	(7)
Iran	8.0	17.7	-54.9%	(0)	16.6	18.7	-10.9%	(3)	16.2	19.8	-18.1%	(3)
Israel	42.9	41.2	4.1%	(5)	34.5	44.0	-21.6%	(3)	40.2	46.1	-12.8%	(3)
Jordan	56.8	38.6	47.0%	(9)	72.2	40.5	78.2%	(10)	63.8	40.5	57.5%	(9)
Latvia	-	-	-		-	-	-		60.5	46.7	29.6%	(7)
Lithuania	-	-	-		-	-	-		63.1	43.9	43.7%	(9)
Malta	80.4	85.6	-6.0%	(4)	92.1	92.4	-0.3%	(4)	101.0	98.8	2.3%	(5)
Oman	43.5	37.1	17.3%	(6)	41.7	41.1	1.5%	(5)	44.6	42.8	4.2%	(5)
Poland	17.5	21.4	-18.1%	(3)	22.9	23.1	-0.9%	(4)	21.0	24.7	-15.0%	(3)
Portugal	39.4	31.4	25.3%	(7)	40.9	34.2	19.6%	(6)	30.5	36.6	-16.8%	(3)
Romania	20.8	30.5	-31.9%	(2)	21.4	33.0	-35.1%	(1)	25.6	35.5	-27.8%	(2)
Russia	8.9	14.9	-40.3%	(1)	7.7	16.0	-51.9%	(0)	9.4	17.0	-44.7%	(1)
Slovenia	-	-	-		-	-	-		58.0	53.9	7.8%	(5)
Syria	18.6	29.3	-36.5%	(1)	27.6	31.0	-11.2%	(3)	37.5	32.6	14.9%	(6)
Turkey	22.2	18.8	18.3%	(6)	21.0	20.0	4.9%	(5)	16.8	21.2	-20.8%	(3)
Ukraine	-	-	-		-	-	-		37.0	22.2	66.2%	(10)
ASIA												
Bangladesh	12.9	21.4	-39.7%	(1)	13.5	22.8	-40.9%	(1)	18.3	24.2	-24.2%	(2)
China	13.1	9.3	39.8%	(8)	17.1	10.0	70.4%	(10)	20.9	10.7	95.3%	(10)
Fiji	44.6	44.3	0.5%	(5)	64.8	47.6	36.2%	(8)	57.3	50.8	12.9%	(6)
Hong Kong	104.8	52.8	98.5%	(10)	131.5	56.8	131.3%	(10)	148.9	60.8	145.0%	(10)
India	7.5	10.9	-30.9%	(2)	9.4	11.6	-19.1%	(3)	11.4	12.3	-7.2%	(4)
Indonesia	21.3	14.5	47.6%	(9)	26.3	15.5	70.3%	(10)	25.6	16.4	56.7%	(9)
Malaysia	52.3	26.1	100.7%	(10)	75.6	27.7	172.6%	(10)	90.6	29.3	209.3%	(10)
Nepal	15.5	22.6	-31.3%	(2)	16.9	24.1	-29.8%	(2)	29.8	25.3	17.9%	(6)
Pakistan	17.0	17.0	0.1%	(4)	17.5	18.0	-2.6%	(4)	17.9	18.9	-5.4%	(4)
Philippines	22.9	17.6	30.2%	(8)	30.7	18.7	63.5%	(10)	40.1	19.8	103.0%	(10)
Singapore	159.0	59.5	167.4%	(10)	167.1	63.6	162.6%	(10)	166.0	67.4	146.3%	(10)
South Korea	33.9	25.3	34.2%	(8)	30.0	27.2	10.5%	(5)	33.7	29.0	16.2%	(6)
Sri Lanka	31.5	28.2	11.6%	(5)	33.7	30.2	11.3%	(5)	40.7	32.2	26.6%	(7)
Taiwan	48.3	37.5	28.9%	(7)	45.3	40.3	12.4%	(5)	43.3	43.1	0.4%	(5)
Thailand	24.6	19.4	26.4%	(7)	37.8	20.8	81.5%	(10)	45.0	22.1	103.2%	(10)
AFRICA												
Algeria	21.9	19.2	14.5%	(6)	25.1	20.4	23.1%	(7)	23.2	21.6	7.6%	(5)
Benin	38.4	35.4	8.5%	(5)	26.2	37.5	-30.2%	(2)	31.8	39.2	-19.0%	(3)
Botswana	57.5	30.0	92.0%	(10)	59.1	31.6	86.7%	(10)	51.7	33.4	54.9%	(9)
Burundi	15.4	31.8	-51.6%	(0)	17.7	33.8	-47.6%	(1)	14.8	35.6	-58.5%	(0)
Cameroon	28.8	27.0	6.8%	(5)	20.8	28.6	-27.4%	(2)	20.1	30.3	-33.8%	(1)
Central African Rep	32.6	26.0	25.3%	(7)	24.5	27.6	-11.2%	(3)	18.9	29.3	-35.4%	(1)
Chad	30.7	22.0	39.4%	(8)	30.1	23.4	28.4%	(7)	23.1	24.8	-6.8%	(4)
Congo	56.4	35.7	58.1%	(10)	43.3	37.7	14.7%	(6)	47.2	40.0	18.0%	(6)
Cote d'Ivoire	39.1	28.0	39.5%	(8)	32.0	29.5	8.4%	(5)	38.0	31.2	21.7%	(7)
Gabon	50.0	40.3	24.0%	(7)	41.8	42.9	-2.5%	(4)	38.6	45.1	-14.5%	(3)
Ghana	10.6	27.8	-61.7%	(0)	19.7	29.4	-32.9%	(1)	27.7	31.0	-10.8%	(3)
Kenya	25.8	23.8	8.4%	(5)	28.8	25.2	14.0%	(6)	36.3	26.0	39.8%	(8)

Table IV-C: (Continued)

	1985				1990				1995			
	Actual Trade	Expected Trade	Actual-Expected Expected		Actual Trade	Expected Trade	Actual-Expected Expected		Actual Trade	Expected Trade	Actual-Expected Expected	
AFRICA (con't)												
Madagascar	15.3	21.4	-28.5%	(2)	22.0	22.6	-2.9%	(4)	27.4	23.5	16.3%	(6)
Malawi	27.0	32.3	-16.3%	(3)	28.9	34.2	-15.4%	(3)	32.8	35.9	-8.6%	(4)
Mali	31.1	20.9	49.3%	(9)	25.3	22.1	14.3%	(6)	30.7	23.0	33.6%	(8)
Mauritius	54.5	51.5	5.8%	(5)	71.1	55.4	28.4%	(7)	61.0	59.1	3.2%	(5)
Morocco	29.2	22.4	30.5%	(8)	27.3	23.8	14.6%	(6)	26.1	25.4	2.9%	(5)
Niger	25.6	19.7	29.6%	(7)	19.0	20.9	-8.9%	(4)	15.0	22.1	-31.9%	(2)
Nigeria	14.3	17.1	-16.6%	(3)	32.3	18.2	78.0%	(10)	21.2	19.1	10.9%	(5)
Rwanda	15.3	31.0	-50.5%	(0)	11.1	32.8	-66.1%	(0)	6.6	34.6	-81.0%	(0)
Senegal	35.3	31.4	12.6%	(5)	27.8	33.2	-16.3%	(3)	35.7	35.2	1.5%	(5)
Sierra Leone	9.8	37.5	-74.0%	(0)	22.4	39.9	-43.9%	(1)	23.7	42.4	-44.0%	(1)
Somalia	12.8	27.9	-54.0%	(0)	23.8	29.5	-19.5%	(3)	-	-	-	
South Africa	27.7	19.1	44.9%	(9)	23.6	20.4	16.0%	(6)	24.5	21.6	13.7%	(6)
Tanzania	10.5	21.0	-50.1%	(0)	38.0	22.3	70.7%	(10)	40.4	23.3	73.3%	(10)
Togo	52.8	39.4	33.8%	(8)	39.2	41.6	-5.7%	(4)	34.6	44.1	-21.6%	(3)
Tunisia	35.7	31.3	14.0%	(6)	44.7	33.4	33.8%	(8)	47.1	35.3	33.2%	(8)
Uganda	10.8	22.1	-51.0%	(0)	12.3	23.4	-47.6%	(1)	15.4	24.3	-36.5%	(1)
Zaire	26.6	18.2	46.4%	(9)	31.3	19.0	64.6%	(10)	10.2	20.3	-49.6%	(1)
Zambia	38.5	21.9	76.0%	(10)	37.1	23.5	57.7%	(10)	17.5	24.7	-29.1%	(2)
Zimbabwe	28.2	22.8	23.6%	(7)	29.5	24.2	22.1%	(7)	34.8	25.7	35.7%	(8)

Source: The data for exports, imports, and GDP used to derive the actual size of the international trade sector are from the International Monetary Fund, *Monetary International Financial Statistics: 1996* (and monthly updates). Regression analysis was used to derive the expected size of the trade sector adjusted for population, geographic size, whether the country was land locked, and percent of population living within 150 miles of a potential trading partner. The rating of each country is indicated in parenthesis. The 1985 base year data were used to derive the rating intervals. The following conversion table divided the 1985 data into eleven intervals of equal size.

Actual Relative to Expected (% Difference)	Rating
less than -50.03	0
-50.02 to -32.24	1
-32.23 to -22.52	2
-22.51 to -10.79	3
-10.78 to .29	4
.30 to 12.59	5
12.60 to 20.89	6
20.90 to 29.91	7
29.92 to 39.92	8
39.93 to 57.66	9
more than 57.67	10

Table IV-D: Freedom to Engage in Capital (Investment) Transactions with Foreigners

	Freedom to Engage in Capital Transactions with Foreigners (Countries with Fewer Restrictions on this Freedom are Rated Higher).				
INDUSTRIAL COUNTRIES	1975	1980	1985	1990	1995
United States	10	10	10	10	10
Canada	8	8	8	8	8
Australia	2	2	5	8	8
Japan	2	2	5	8	8
New Zealand	5	5	5	10	10
Austria	2	2	2	5	8
Belgium	10	10	10	10	10
Denmark	5	5	5	5	8
Finland	2	2	2	2	8
France	2	2	2	5	5
Germany	8	8	10	10	10
Iceland	2	2	2	2	5
Ireland	5	5	5	5	8
Italy	5	5	5	5	8
Netherlands	5	8	8	8	10
Norway	2	2	5	8	8
Spain	2	5	5	8	8
Sweden	2	2	5	10	10
Switzerland	2	10	10	10	10
United Kingdom	2	10	10	10	10
CENTRAL/SOUTH AMERICA					
Argentina	0	0	0	0	10
Bahamas	2	2	2	2	2
Barbados	2	2	2	2	2
Belize	-	5	5	5	5
Bolivia	2	2	2	2	5
Brazil	0	0	0	0	0
Chile	2	2	2	2	5
Colombia	0	0	0	0	5
Costa Rica	2	2	5	5	8
Dominican Rep	2	2	2	2	2
Ecuador	2	2	2	2	5
El Salvador	2	2	2	2	5
Guatemala	5	5	5	5	8
Haiti	0	0	0	0	2
Honduras	0	0	0	0	5
Jamaica	2	2	2	2	8
Mexico	2	2	2	5	5

Table IV-D: (Contined)

Freedom to Engage in Capital Transactions with Foreigners

(Countries with Fewer Restrictions on this Freedom are Rated Higher).

CENTRAL/- S. AMERICA (con't)	1975	1980	1985	1990	1995
Nicaragua	5	0	0	0	5
Panama	8	8	8	8	8
Paraguay	5	5	5	5	5
Peru	2	2	2	2	8
Trinidad/Tobago	0	0	0	0	8
Uraguay	8	10	10	10	10
Venezuela	8	8	5	5	5
EUROPE/MIDDLE EAST					
Albania	0	0	0	0	2
Bahrain	2	2	2	2	2
Bulgaria	0	0	0	0	5
Croatia	-	-	-	0	2
Cyprus	0	0	0	0	0
Czechoslovakia	0	0	0	0	-
Czech Rep	-	-	-	-	5
Slovakia	-	-	-	-	2
Egypt	0	0	0	0	0
Estonia	-	-	-	0	8
Greece	2	2	2	2	5
Hungary	0	0	0	0	5
Iran	5	0	0	0	0
Israel	2	2	2	2	2
Jordan	2	2	2	2	2
Latvia	-	-	-	0	8
Lithuania	-	-	-	0	8
Malta	2	2	2	2	2
Oman	2	2	2	2	2
Poland	0	0	0	0	5
Portugal	2	2	2	5	8
Romania	0	0	0	0	5
Russia	0	0	0	0	5
Slovenia	0	0	0	0	0
Syria	0	0	0	0	0
Turkey	0	0	0	0	2
Ukraine	0	0	0	0	2
ASIA					
Bangladesh	0	0	0	0	0
China	0	0	2	5 [a]	5 [a]
Fiji	5	5	5	2	2
Hong Kong	10	10	10	10	10
India	2	2	2	2	2
Indonesia	2	2	2	2	2
Malaysia	5	5	5	5	5

Table IV-D: (Con't)

Freedom to Engage in Capital Transactions with Foreigners
(Countries with Fewer Restrictions on this Freedom are Rated Higher).

	1975	1980	1985	1990	1995
ASIA					
Nepal	0	0	0	0	0
Pakistan	2	2	2	2	2
Philippines	2	2	2	2	5
Singapore	8	8	10	10	10
South Korea	0	0	2	5	5
Sri Lanka	0	0	0	0	2
Taiwan	2	2	2	5	5
Thailand	2	2	2	2	5
AFRICA					
Algeria	0	0	0	0	2
Benin	0	0	0	0	0
Botswana	-	5	5	5	5
Burundi	0	0	0	0	0
Cameroon	0	0	0	0	0
C African Rep	0	0	0	0	0
Chad	0	0	0	0	0
Congo Peoples Rep	0	0	0	0	0
Cote d' Ivoire	0	0	0	0	0
Gabon	0	0	0	0	0
Ghana	0	0	0	0	0
Kenya	0	0	0	0	8
Madagascar	0	0	0	0	0
Malawi	2	2	2	2	2
Mali	2	2	2	2	2
Mauritius	2	2	2	2	8
Morocco	2	2	5	5	5
Niger	0	0	0	0	0
Nigeria	0	0	0	0	0
Rwanda	0	0	0	0	0
Senegal	0	0	0	0	0
Sierra Leone	0	0	0	0	0
Somalia	0	0	0	0	0
South Africa	2	2	2	2	2
Tanzania	0	0	0	0	0
Togo	0	0	0	0	0
Tunisia	0	0	0	5	5
Uganda	0	0	0	0	0
Zaire	2	2	2	2	2
Zambia	2	2	2	2	2
Zimbabwe	-	2	2	2	2

a All foreign direct investment projects are in principle, subject to the approval of the Chinese state planning authorities. However, a number of provincial and local authorities have been granted the authority to approve foreign direct investment projects (except for those that are quite large) and in several cases they now do so with a minimal cost to the investor. This factor was taken into consideration in these ratings for China.

Source: International Monetary Fund, *Exchange Arrangements and Exchange Restrictions* (various issues) and Price-Waterhouse, *Doing Business Series* (booklets for various countries), were used to rate each country. These publications provided the descriptive characteristics of the capital market arrangements for each country. These descriptions were used to classify and rate each country as follows:

Characteristics of Capital Market	Rating
Foreigners are free to undertake domestic investments and nationals are free to undertake investments abroad.	10
With the exception of a few industries (e.g., banking, defense-related, telecommunications) and/or minor administrative procedures, foreigners are free to undertake domestic investments and nationals are free to undertake investments abroad.	8
Both domestic investments by foreigners and investments by nationals abroad are authorized, but there are regulatory restrictions (e.g., divesture after a period of time, investment must be of a specific size, limitations on the percentage share of a firm that can be owned by foreigners, or registration is required for repatriation of profits or earnings from investments) that retard the mobility of capital.	5
Either (but not both) (a) foreigners are prohibited from undertaking domestic investments or (b) nationals are prohibited from undertaking investments abroad *without the approval of governmental authorities.*	2
Regulations (including restrictions on the remittance of earnings) substantially reduce the freedom of both foreigners to undertake domestic investments and of nationals to undertake investments aboard. Generally neither are allowed *without the approval of government officials.*	0

Less Than Zero

The Case for a Falling Price Level in a Growing Economy

George Selgin

1. Most economists now accept that monetary policy should not aim at 'full employment': central banks should aim instead at limiting movements in the general price level.

2. Zero inflation is often viewed as an ideal. But there is a case for allowing the price level to vary so as to reflect changes in unit production costs.

3. Under such a 'productivity norm', monetary policy would allow 'permanent improvements in productivity...to lower prices permanently' and adverse supply shocks (such as wars and failed harvests) to bring about temporary price increases. The overall result would be '...secular deflation interrupted by occasional negative supply shocks'.

4. United States consumer prices would have halved in the 30 years after the Second World War (instead of almost tripling), had a productivity norm policy been in operation.

5. In an economy with rising productivity a constant price level cannot be relied upon to avoid '..."unnatural" fluctuations in output and employment'.

6. A productivity norm should involve lower 'menu' costs of price adjustment, minimise 'monetary misperception' effects, achieve more efficient outcomes using fixed money contracts and keep the real money stock closer to its 'optimum'.

7. The theory supporting the productivity norm runs counter to conventional macro-economic wisdom. For example, it suggests that a falling price level is not synonymous with depression. The 'Great Depression' of 1873-1896 was actually a period of '...unprecedented advances in factor productivity'.

8. In practice, implementing a productivity norm would mean choosing between a labour productivity and a total factor productivity norm. Using the latter might be preferable and would involve setting the growth rate of nominal income equal to a weighted average of labour and capital input growth rates.

9. Achieving a predetermined growth rate of nominal income would be easier under a free banking régime which tends automatically to stabilise nominal income.

10. Many countries now have inflation rates not too far from zero. But zero inflation should be recognised not as the ideal but '...as the stepping-stone towards something even better'.

The Institute of Economic Affairs

2 Lord North Street, Westminster, London SW1P 3LB
Telephone: 0171 799 3745 Facsimile: 0171 799 2137
E-mail: iea@iea.org.uk Internet: http://www.iea.org.uk

ISBN 0-255 36402-4

£8.00

Chaos, Management and Economics

The Implications of Non-Linear Thinking

David Parker & Ralph Stacey

1. Chaos theory, which is causing a revolution in the natural sciences, has important lessons for the study of how human organisations and economies function.

2. Chaos is an 'intricate mixture of order and disorder' in which behaviour patterns are irregular. Nevertheless, broad categories of behaviour can be recognised.

3. Links between causes and effects are more complex than simple linear systems can capture.

4. The behaviour of any system may well be extremely sensitive to its 'initial conditions'. Such systems cannot be controlled; they 'evolve through a process of self-organisation'.

5. Because the long-term future is unknowable, managements of both companies and economies should emphasise adaptability and creativeness.

6. Competitive markets are vital to the creative process because, unlike planned systems, they provide for 'spontaneous adaptation'.

7. Enterprise is a 'locomotive of change'. Chaos theory 'provides a new argument for the innovating entrepreneur' which complements the case made by the Austrian school. To cope with chaotic conditions, economies need to promote entrepreneurship.

8. In chaotic conditions, slight errors in demand management may lead to increased economic instability.

9. Companies and economies '...require structures and institutions which encourage self-transformation', not detailed plans for long-term futures.

10. Government economic and social policy should '...complement not conflict with economic change', avoiding policies which '...reduce the economy's ability to adapt, including regulation, monopoly and high taxation...'.

The Institute of Economic Affairs

2 Lord North Street, Westminster, London SW1P 3LB
Telephone: 0171 799 3745 Facsimile: 0171 799 2137
E-mail: iea@iea.org.uk Internet: http://www.iea.org.uk

£9.00

ISBN 0-255 36333-8

Why Schoolchildren Can't Read

Bonnie Macmillan

Learning to read is the most important task of early childhood. Success or failure in this skill has a profound effect on the future of every child. All parents, indeed all of us, should be concerned that the methods used to teach this crucial skill are the best possible.

In Why Schoolchildren Can't Read, Dr Bonnie Macmillan describes the findings of the most up-to-date experimental research on beginning reading instruction. Research points decisively to the need for direct teaching of certain key skills in order to produce maximum reading success.

However, an examination of how children are taught to read in England's primary schools reveals a large discrepancy between the methods currently used and those which research demonstrates are the most effective. The consequences of this alarming gap between reading research and teaching practice are seen in the rising number of schoolchildren who are failing to learn how to read.

This book provides answers to some of the most controversial issues in education today. What are the causes of the disturbing incidence of reading failure? Why are the best methods to teach reading not being used in our primary schools?

The Institute of Economic Affairs

2 Lord North Street, Westminster, London SW1P 3LB
Telephone: 0171 799 3745 Facsimile: 0171 799 2137
E-mail: iea@iea.org.uk Internet: http://www.iea.org.uk

£12.00

ISBN 0 255 36403-2

Zero Tolerance
Policing a Free Society

William J. Bratton, Norman Dennis (Editor)
Ray Mallon, John Orr, Charles Pollard

Few topics cause more concern than rising crime. And few remedies have been more talked about, on both sides of the Atlantic, than zero-tolerance policing.

When William Bratton was appointed Commissioner of New York Police Department in 1994 crime was perceived to be running out of control. The no-nonsense approach which he developed towards petty crime and incivility, which he believed to be indicators of potentially serious criminal behaviour, became known as 'zero-tolerance policing', and it showed spectacular results. Over the past three years the crime rate has dropped by 37 per cent and the homicide rate by 50 per cent.

In the same year that Bratton was made Commissioner of NYPD, DCI Ray Mallon became head of crime strategy in Hartlepool. His determination to restore the streets to the decent, law-abiding citizens mirrored Bratton's zero-tolerance approach, and had the same results. Reported crimes have fallen by 27 per cent, with falls of 56 per cent in vehicle thefts and 31 per cent in burglaries. Chief Constable John Orr's 'Spotlight Initiative' in Strathclyde is not described as zero tolerance, although it shares some characteristics of the Bratton/Mallon paradigm, and has seen reductions in serious crime of nearly ten per cent in its first few months.

However Charles Pollard, Chief Constable of Thames Valley Police, warns that zero-tolerance policing may have its pitfalls. The fall in crime could be more apparent than real; there may be a limit to the reductions in crime which it can achieve; and it may prove too confrontational to be of long-term benefit.

In his editor's introduction and in his detailed study (with Ray Mallon) of crime and culture in Hartlepool, Norman Dennis examines the ways in which the changing analysis of, and response to, crime can affect in fundamental ways our conception of what it is to live in a free society.

The Institute of Economic Affairs
Health and Welfare Unit
2 Lord North Street, Westminster, London SW1P 3LB
Telephone: 0171 799 3745 Facsimile: 0171 799 2137
E-mail: iea@iea.org.uk Internet: http://www.iea.org.uk

£8.00

ISBN 0-255 36395-8
ISSN 1362-9565

Alexis de Tocqueville's
Memoir on Pauperism

Translated by Seymour Drescher

With an introduction by Gertrude Himmelfarb

The 'Memoir on Pauperism' was written in 1835 immediately after Alexis de Tocqueville had completed the first volume of *Democracy in America*. It was based on his visit to England in 1833, where he found that one-sixth of the population had been reduced to reliance on poor relief at a cost approaching nearly one-fifth of total national expenditure.

Today, 17% of the population are reliant on income support – a strikingly similar proportion to Tocqueville's 1833 estimate – and if the other means-tested benefits are included the figure is 27%. In her introduction, Gertrude Himmelfarb, one of the foremost historians of the nineteenth century, shows the relevance of Tocqueville's insights for the modern debate about welfare reform in both Britain and America.

Tocqueville began the 'Memoir' with the paradox that the most impoverished countries in Europe, like Spain and Portugal, had few paupers; while England, the wealthiest country at the time, had many. It had happened, he argued, as an unforeseen consequence of good intentions. As wealth had grown, those who prospered were not prepared to tolerate hardship in their midst. But, in truth, the paradoxical result of this early experiment in compulsory state welfare was that beneficiaries were degraded by their reduction to dependency.

In contrast, Tocqueville believed, voluntary charity at its best established a 'moral tie' between giver and receiver and, instead of encouraging dishonesty and 'working the system', it sought to strengthen character and restore independence. Today, Himmelfarb writes, we can more than ever appreciate Tocqueville's criticism of 'government charity' as an 'entitlement':

"After fifty years of the welfare state in Britain and sixty years of the relief system introduced by the New Deal in the United States, the idea of such an entitlement is being called into question in both countries as they try to cope with the consequences Tocqueville foresaw."

The Institute of Economic Affairs
Health and Welfare Unit
2 Lord North Street, Westminster, London SW1P 3LB
Telephone: 0171 799 3745 Facsimile: 0171 799 2137
E-mail: iea@iea.org.uk Internet: http://www.iea.org.uk

ISBN 0-255 36394-X

£5.00

Back From the Brink: An Appeal to Fellow Europeans Over Monetary Union

Pedro Schwartz

1. European Monetary Union is an 'unprecedented experiment', a 'huge gamble' which produces mixed reactions among Europeans.

2. There are many possible pitfalls before monetary union can come into being. One particular problem is that from 1998 to 2001, national currencies will remain legal tender. The currencies of 'misbehaving countries' may therefore be '...pounced upon by speculators and marauders...'

3. A monetary zone can function effectively only if it encompasses a single market, especially a single labour market. Establishing a monetary union when there is no hope of removing some of the barriers to a single market means '...applying perpetual fetters'.

4. The labour market of the European Union is '...far from being integrated'. The entry into monetary union of countries with rigid labour markets would warp the functioning of the union: moreover, those countries would probably demand subsidies to alleviate unemployment.

5. European Monetary Union therefore faces 'a bumpy road' before and after 2002. Before 2002 there may be 'speculative storms'; after 2002 large pockets of unemployment may persist, undermining European unity.

6. If European politicians had really wanted a stable currency they would have linked their currencies to the Deutschmark and turned their Central Banks into currency boards.

7. Monetary competition among existing European currencies plus the euro would offer a better long run prospect of monetary stability than monetary union.

8. Competitive devaluation is less of a problem than industrial lobbies claim. Over-valuation is more of a danger: '...fake converts from easy virtue love the prestige of a strong currency'.

9. In practice, careful economic analysis of European Monetary Union 'counts for nothing'. The proposed union is a 'dangerous experiment...' to build a certain kind of Europe surreptitiously' and to give a '...huge boost to centralisation'.

10. If monetary union goes ahead, Britain should go it alone and '...set an example from within the European Union of what can be achieved by a competitive, deregulated, private economy with a floating and well-managed currency'.

The Institute of Economic Affairs

2 Lord North Street, Westminster, London SW1P 3LB
Telephone: 0171 799 3745 Facsimile: 0171 799 2137
E-mail: iea@iea.org.uk Internet: http://www.iea.org.uk

ISBN 0-255 36401-6

£4.00

Green Goods?
Consumers, product labels and the environment

Julian Morris

1. In the late 1980s concern over the validity of environmental claims led to demands for the creation of schemes that would provide the consumer with verified environmental information.

2. In response, governments and private sector companies developed seal of approval 'ecolabels' purporting to denote the most environment-friendly products in a particular category.

3. However, it is not possible to acquire sufficient information about the impact of a product over its life cycle to know in every case which product will be the most environment-friendly.

4. In particular, it is not possible for an expert to calculate the environmental impact of a product during its use and disposal phases – which, for most products, are the phases during which the most significant impacts take place – since these impacts will be contingent on how, where and when the product is used, factors that are only known to the consumer.

5. As a result, some consumers might purchase products that are less environment-friendly than they had been led to believe.

6. Where ecolabels are entirely voluntary, it is unlikely that they would have a significant impact (positive or negative) on the environment or the economy, since demand for labelled goods is unlikely to be high.

7. Where ecolabels are in any way compulsory (for example, where they are required by government procurement policies), they are likely to inhibit the evolution of products, slowing down economic growth and harming the environment.

8. Where national ecolabel programmes exist, governments might use procurement policies to favour indigenous companies.

9. However, if an international ecolabel was introduced, the problem of technological lock-in might be worse, since firms would have fewer markets for non-ecolabelled products.

10. Voluntary information-sharing and certification schemes are more likely than ecolabels to provide the consumer with reliable information about the likely impact of a product on the environment.

The Institute of Economic Affairs

2 Lord North Street, Westminster, London SW1P 3LB
Telephone: 0171 799 3745 Facsimile: 0171 799 2137
E-mail: iea@iea.org.uk Internet: http://www.iea.org.uk

ISBN 0-255 363441-5

£10.00

New Zealand's Remarkable Reforms

Donald T Brash

1. New Zealand's economy has revived in the last few years, following '...one of the most remarkable economic liberalisations in modern times' since 1984. There is little public enthusiasm for reversing the reforms.

2. Once one of the most regulated OECD economies, New Zealand is now one of the least regulated. Unemployment has recently fallen sharply. The estimated sustainable annual growth rate of real GDP is now 3-3½ per cent.

3. The transformation of New Zealand – from a protectionist, regulated society with 'cradle-to-grave' welfare to an open, market-based economy operating under the rule of law – has a 'Hayekian flavour'.

4. Under the guidance of Roger (now Sir Roger) Douglas, New Zealand adopted a 'big bang' approach to reform, though the pace of reform slackened for a time in the late 1980s.

5. Micro-economic reforms included removal of controls on wages, prices, and foreign exchange and floating of the New Zealand dollar. Import quotas have been removed and tariffs reduced. Agricultural and industrial subsidies have virtually disappeared.

6. '...the most remarkable liberalisation' has been that of the labour market where from 1991 contracts have been on '...almost the same basis as other commercial contracts'. By December 1995 only 17 per cent of the workforce had union-negotiated collective contracts.

7. High marginal rates of income tax have been reduced and a broad-based Value Added Tax introduced. The tax structure is now 'the least distorting of any in an OECD country'.

8. State-owned companies have been 'corporatised' and many have been privatised. Privatisation has generally not taken place until a corporation entered a contestable market: privatised companies are lightly regulated under the general powers of the Commerce Act.

9. A Fiscal Responsibility Act promotes sound fiscal policies and requires governments to explain present and projected budgetary positions.

10. Under the Reserve Bank of New Zealand Act of 1989, the government specifies an inflation target and the Bank Governor is left to implement it. The Governor can be dismissed for 'inadequate performance'. So far the monetary framework has been very successful in reducing inflation and inflationary expectations.

The Institute of Economic Affairs

2 Lord North Street, Westminster, London SW1P 3LB
Telephone: 0171 799 3745 Facsimile: 0171 799 2137
E-mail: iea@iea.org.uk Internet: http://www.iea.org.uk

£5.00

ISBN 0-255 36400-8

The IEA's Ninth Annual International State of the Economy Conference

City Conference Centre, 76 Mark Lane, London, EC3
Thursday, 30 October 1997

9.15–10.00
Economic Policy in the United States

Dr. Jerry L. Jordan, President, Federal Reserve Bank of Cleveland

10.00–11.15
The UK Economic Outlook

Professor Roger Bootle, HSBC Group
Professor Tim Congdon, Lombard Street Research Ltd.
Patrick Foley, Lloyds Bank plc.

11.15–11.45
Coffee

11.45–12.30
'Globalisation and the Waning Influence of Government'

Professor Harold James, University of Princeton

12.30–13.45
Lunch

13.45–14.45
Key Issues in the European Union:

I. Can Unemployment be Reduced?

Professor Richard Layard, London School of Economics
Professor Patrick Minford, University of Liverpool

14.45–16.15
II. The Costs and Benefits of Monetary Union

Professor Otmar Issing, Deutsche Bundesbank
Neil MacKinnon, Citibank
Professor Pedro Schwartz, Fundesco

16.15–17.00
Panel Discussion with speakers

For details contact the conference managers, Conference Profile,
Telephone 0171 236 4938, Fax 0171 236 1889